# Including . . .

- 100+ alt-rock supergroups we hope never happen.

- The set list for the Ramones' first CBGB show . . . and the number of song titles using the word Wanna.

- The ten most important hardcore bands.

- U2's first appearance . . . first demo . . . first record deal . . . first Grammy.

- Five ex-Nirvana drummers who aren't Dave Grohl.

- Eighty-five songs that R.E.M. copped from other artists—live or on record.

- Wayne Kramer's ten tips for electric guitar players.

- The industrial-rocker who threw up onstage after a smoke-bomb attack.

- The five worst rock-club rest rooms in America.

- Alt-rockers with one or more U.S. platinum albums.

- Johnny Thunders's real name . . . Captain Beefheart's real name . . . Rat Scabies's real name.

- Twenty-five U.K. hitmakers who never meant squat in the U.S.

# Alt-

ROLLING STONE'S

# Rock-
# a-Rama

# SCOTT SCHINDER

## and the Editors of
## Rolling Stone Press

Delta
Trade Paperbacks

A Delta Book
Published by
Dell Publishing
a division of
Bantam Doubleday Dell Publishing Group, Inc.
1540 Broadway
New York, New York 10036

ISBN: 0-385-31360-8

Designed by Jeffrey L. Ward
Manufactured in the United States of America
Published simultaneously in Canada

March 1996

10  9  8  7  6  5  4  3  2  1

BVG

# Contents

# Contents

## PART 6   Under the Influence

## PART 7   Advice and Anecdotes

# Contents

## PART 14   Talking Heads

## PART 15   The Critical List

# Contents

# Foreword

by Chris Mundy

It is a common misperception that all great bodies of literature must actually be about something. Well, this book isn't *about* anything at all. Not a damn thing. And it's a pretty good read. Which is fitting because this tome exists under the flag of alternative rock, a title that means absolutely nothing.

What other explanation could there be for a label broad enough to include both the silky, seventies pop of Big Star and the nineties metal-meets-construction-crew noise of Helmet. Or a book that is home to the Cramps' top ten sexploitation movies and Superchunk's list of the five worst rock-club men's rooms. Besides, the fact that subjects within this book span almost thirty years makes the stuff too old to be seriously considered alternative. Nothing that sticks around that long can lay any legitimate claim to underdog status. Just ask the kids in U2. Or R.E.M. Or any other dozen examples. It's tough to divine much definition out of a term like alternative when the bands in this category are consistently scoring the highest-selling albums in the free world.

So, what we are left with is a series of random scribblings held together by a group of musicians without an actual genre to bind them. And that's a good thing. For all the schizophrenic use of the A-word, it has always been a handle attached to groups with the common characteristic of being deemed worthy of the seal of quality and integrity that alternative music brought with it. Some came up in a common underground. Many were influenced by forefathers as diverse as the Velvet Underground and the Stooges. Others achieved the label of alternative because they just didn't seem to fit anywhere else. They might not sound anything alike, the theory went, but they don't sound like anything else either.

What makes the lists, ravings and notable pieces of worthless knowledge contained in this collection so interesting is also the most compelling component of alternative rock: its breadth and scope. From Austin, Texas, cowboys to Japanese power popsters. Rock novels to the Substance Abuse Hall of Fame. If it's out there, it's most likely in here. How else would you learn that four out of the seven songs on the Ramones' very first set list started with the words "I Don't Wanna"?

Along the way, ROLLING STONE'S *Alt-Rock-a-Rama* also serves as an informal history text. In the beginning there was punk rock and in the end there was only a list of the myriad bands who have won Grammys or scored platinum albums. In between we hear horror stories from the road, pick up a few bands' favorite recipes (for music making as well as those of a culinary nature) and try to figure out just how all this music embedded itself so deeply into the consciousness of our culture. It's entirely possible that many of the bands and categories contained within these pages will be revealing themselves to readers for the first time. That, too, is part of the educational process.

It could be argued that the information about to be ingested is apropos of nothing. This, however, is precisely the point. It is about quality music and quality musings. It is a shared interesting-ness that binds the sections of this book, just as it holds together such a diverse gathering of bands under the umbrella of alternative rock. Back in the days when the Sex Pistols set about to destroy rock & roll—never knowing that they would simultaneously reinvigorate and revive it—Johnny Rotten said: "Rock & roll is supposed to be fun. You remember fun, dontcha? You're supposed to enjoy it." Well, ROLLING STONE'S *Alt-Rock-a-Rama* is supposed to be fun. So try to take Mr. Rotten's advice.

You are holding an incredibly vast collection of nothingness, the result of tapping into the whims of a few twisted minds and thirty years of pushing the envelope on what music can mean. In the end, that might just be something after all.

# Introduction

by Scott Schinder

> "Alternative music? What's the alternative to music? Silence?"
>
> —Mike Watt

No truer words have ever been spoken. Indeed, these days it's a safe assumption that any person using the term "alternative rock" with a straight face is A), a goofball, and/or B), not to be trusted. Whatever usefulness the A-word may have once had as a genre designation flew out the window at some point—possibly the day I.R.S. released its first R.E.M. greatest-hits package, or the minute the first movie script arrived on Juliana Hatfield's manager's desk, or the first time Kurt Cobain had someone else pick up his drugs for him—and it isn't coming back.

As the term "alternative rock" has moved steadily toward utter meaninglessness, it's become increasingly prevalent in the mainstream media vocabulary, basically as a banner for any contemporary music that's not old-line corporate rock (even if it's only *pretending* not to be old-line corporate rock). In the nineties "alternative" has, absurdly enough, become a hot marketing hook, just like that urban-cowboy thing a few years back.

Which brings us to this book, whose mere existence further attests to the ongoing (and, to some, worrisome) mainstreaming of the alt-rock phenomenon. What *ROLLING STONE's Alt-Rock-a-Rama* is is a not-quite-as-random-as-it-seems compendium of facts, fantasy, profundity and ephemera that we hope will, in its own humble way, contribute to some larger understanding of alt-rock culture—which, as we've already established, does not actually exist. For the occasion, we've asked a variety of artists and others involved in the alt-rock community to add their two cents' worth to our own efforts.

Our biggest dilemma in putting this book together was the necessary matter of determining which acts we should consider fair game for inclusion—i.e., deciding what's alternative and what's just rock—and if there's a less rewarding editorial pursuit, we don't want to know about it. For our purposes, though, we've more or less designated alt-rock as music that either directly influenced, or owes its existence to the influence of, the seventies punk/new-wave explosion. Though that definition encompasses a dizzying variety of music, the distinction's still a subjective and arbitrary one—and one which we've felt free to ignore when the impulse to indulge our own personal prejudices became too strong to resist. And if any of your faves are conspicuously absent, it may well be because they never got around to delivering their entries (hi, Thurston!).

For their contributions of time, energy, patience, insight, and brain cells, I'd like to thank the following individuals: Holly George-Warren, Shawn Dahl, Greg Emmanuel, Tracie Matthews, Ira Robbins, Dave and Regina Dunton, Ken Weinstein, Jason Cohen, Michael Krugman, Ron Decker, Jill Richmond, Doug Wygal, Ted Mico, Jim Merlis, Lisa Markowitz, Vicky Wheeler, Andy Schwartz, Matthew Aberle, Nils Bernstein, Ida Langsam, Bobbie Gale, Nicole Blackman, Bettina Richards, Michelle Roche, Liz Garo, Sheri Hood, Ellen Stewart, Sally Mars, Alex DeFelice, Paula Donner, Mika El-Baz, Mary Melia, Deb Bernadini, Kenny Laguna, Seb Shelton, Mary Ellen Leahy, Hannah Bolte, Bryan Spevak, Michelle Kapustey, Rick Gershon, Leah Horwitz, Jeremy Tepper, Bill Bentley, Sue Marcus, Steve Karas, Mike Rubin, David Merline, Jill Fonaas, Jennifer Gross, Steve Martin, Laura Norden, Grant Blaisdell, Jeff Pachman, Amy Welch, Deborah Orr, Spencer Gates, Brian Long, Russell Carter, Susan Darnell, Jill Tomlinson, Christina Kelly, Joan Elliot, Steven Joerg, Spott, Stephanie Keating, David Millman, Lisa Barbaris, and Wendy Weisberg.

ROLLING STONE's Alt-Rock-a-Rama isn't meant to be all-encompassing, though it does contain much actual information that readers will find informative. Our main objective was that the book be an entertaining read, while offering some insight into the wonderful world of alternative rock (which, as we have already established, does not actually exist). So dig in—and for God's sake, please try to have fun.

# Explanations and Acknowledgments

## by Holly George-Warren

**W**eird. I can't even count how many times that word popped up in the more than 140 pieces that make up the whole of *ROLLING STONE's Alt-Rock-a-Rama*. Not only was there a consistent word that seemed to be on the minds of our contributors, though; there was an underlying theme as well: the presence of an invisible, controlling force against which one's actions were hopelessly in vain. Hmmm . . . pretty *weird*, eh?

Actually, both of those things make a lot of sense in the context of this book. Weirdness is perhaps the one characteristic that almost every bit of disparate music discussed in this book has in common. From its earliest days in garages across America in the 1960s, punk rock could be called "strikingly odd, strange" (as *Webster's* defines weird), in comparison to its slick, chart-busting pop counterpart. And as far as that invisible force goes, well, think about it. . . . Again, going back almost thirty years, there's been a strong musical force bubbling under the surface of the pop-music plain. No matter how commercially nonviable it remained for decades, no matter how many of its greatest progenitors died young or were broken by the corporate-rock system, punk rock never, ever went away. It's always managed to stay alive—often invisible to the mass culture's public eye—but still living and breathing, feeding the minds, ears, and souls of those few who stumbled upon it, sought it out or added to its canon.

Of course, like kudzu it continued to grow, and today, renamed alternative rock, it's become part of the mainstream, overtaking the top of the charts—and providing us the commercial viability of making a book like this. (Before, instead of a bound book from a big-time publishing house, this would have been hundreds of handwritten or typed pages, xeroxed and stapled together, for distribution at gigs and record stores.) Having this opportunity to gather together reams of info about punk rock, we begged for contributions from its movers and shakers and money-makers. And obviously we wanted to push our own opinions and tastes upon the unsuspecting reader.

As a whole, we tried to present every facet of the beast: its history, its sub-genres, its essential recordings, its locations, its philosophy, its lifestyle, its humor, and so on. Thus, the ten sections that make up this book. Each section is arranged somewhat chronologically or thematically—except for in some places, haphazardly. Some sections include a creative exercise by one of our musical contributors in which he or she goes a little outside the realm of his or her best-known artistic endeavors. Overall, it is truly gratifying to see how much enthusiasm and energy each and every person put into his or her contribution. I think that's just another common thread that runs through this book—as well as throughout the past thirty years of punk rock and its many chillens.

There are many, many to thank for making this book happen. First, we're grateful to all the contributors whose work you'll read in the pages to come. Also we commend Dave Marsh for his original 1981 *Book of Rock Lists*, which helped to inspire us to make a punk-rock version of our own. (Dave gave us his blessing, by the way.) Another inspiration of a kitschier nature was the 1971 out-of-print tome *Twenty Minute Fandangos and Forever Changes* (which, funnily enough, made Dave's original list of the worst rock books of all time). We also appreciate those responsible for getting this book off the ground in the first place: Sarah Lazin, Betsy Bundschuh, Scott Schinder, and the bartender and waiter at the Mexican Cantina, as well as ROLLING STONE's Jann S. Wenner, Kent Brownridge, John Lagana, Fred Woodward, and Lee Bearson. In addition, there were numerous people who contributed ideas and tidbits of cool trivia: Eric and Seija Flaum, Anthony DeCurtis, Patricia Day Cobb, David Cobb, Robert Warren, Erik Sanko, and Doug Sahm, to name a few. And there were those hearty souls who helped us pester our would-be contributors to join our merry project: Bruce Duff, Michael Hill, Jill Richmond, Jennifer Gross, and Marilyn Lipsius, among others. Thanks, also, to the folks at CMJ and In-Media. I'd also like to give a standing ovation to the hardest-workin' crew in the make-your-own-book biz: the punk-rockin' staff at Rolling Stone Press: Shawn Dahl, Greg Emmanuel, Tracie Matthews, and Catherine Wallace.

Holly George-Warren
Editor, Rolling Stone Press
January 1995

Alt-

ROLLING STONE'S

Rock-

a-Rama

# Who's Who

**PART 1**

# and What's What

# The 100 Most Influential Alternative Releases of All Time

by Neil Strauss

Neil Strauss writes for ROLLING STONE, *The New York Times, The Village Voice* and *Option,* among other publications. He owns every one of the following recordings, some of which he's been listening to since he was a wee lad.

These are not the 100 best albums of alternative music, or even the best album by each artist listed, but simply the 100 most influential. For the most part, the list consists of prepunk, punk, and postpunk albums, along with the work of a few mavericks who don't fit into any category. Absent are more mainstream artists and albums that had a big influence on alternative rock (Black Sabbath, Neil Young, the Rolling Stones' *Exile on Main Street,* the Beatles' White Album), influential artists who do not play rock music per se (Karlheinz Stockhausen, Martin Denny, AMM, Ornette Coleman) and contemporary alternative artists in whose case it is too early to feel their influence (Green Day, Pearl Jam, Stereolab, Hole). Every one of these albums (each listed with its original release date and label) has inspired at least one band to form, and most of these records continue to be plagiarized. If your collection includes every one of them, maybe it's time to start your own band.

1966: Frank Zappa and the Mothers of Invention, *Freak Out* (Verve)

1966: *13th Floor Elevators, The Psychedelic Sounds of the 13th Floor Elevators* (International Artists)

1967:  The Velvet Underground and Nico, *The Velvet Underground and Nico* (Verve)

1968:  Leonard Cohen, *Songs of Leonard Cohen* (Columbia)

1969:  The MC5, *Kick Out the Jams* (Elektra)

1969:  Captain Beefheart and the Magic Band, *Trout Mask Replica* (Straight/Reprise)

1969:  The Shaggs, *Philosophy of the World* (Third World)

1970:  The Stooges, *Fun House* (Elektra)

1970:  Syd Barrett, *The Madcap Laughs* (Harvest U.K.)

1971:  Can, *Tago Mago* (United Artists)

1971:  Funkadelic, *Maggot Brain* (Westbound)

1972:  Neu, *Neu!* (United Artists U.K.)

1972:  Roxy Music, *Roxy Music* (Atco)

1973:  Faust, *The Faust Tapes* (Virgin U.K.)

1973:  New York Dolls, *New York Dolls* (Mercury)

1974:  Big Star, *Radio City* (Ardent)

1974:  Henry Cow, *Unrest* (Virgin U.K.)

1975:  Patti Smith, *Horses* (Arista)

1975:  Tom Waits, *Nighthawks at the Diner* (Asylum)

1975:  Brian Eno, *Another Green World* (Editions EG)

1975:  Lou Reed, *Metal Machine Music* (RCA)

1976:  Ramones, *Ramones* (Sire)

1976:  Blondie, *Blondie* (Private Stock)

1976:  The Modern Lovers, *The Modern Lovers* (Beserkley)

1976:  The Runaways, *The Runaways* (Mercury)

1976:  Radio Birdman, *Burn My Eye* (Trafalgar EP Australia)

1976: The Residents, *Third Reich & Roll* (Ralph)

1977: Richard Hell and the Voidoids, *Blank Generation* (Sire)

1977: Television, *Marquee Moon* (Elektra)

1977: Talking Heads, *Talking Heads 77* (Sire)

1977: Suicide, *Suicide* (Red Star)

1977: Kraftwerk, *Trans-Europe Express* (Capitol)

1977: The Sex Pistols, *Never Mind the Bollocks, Here's the Sex Pistols* (Warner Bros.)

1977: Elvis Costello, *My Aim Is True* (Columbia)

1977: The Jam, *In the City* (Polydor)

1977: Wire, *Pink Flag* (Harvest)

1978: Throbbing Gristle, *Second Annual Report* (Industrial)

1978: Pere Ubu, *The Modern Dance* (Blank)

1978: Various Artists, *No New York* (Antilles)

1978: Devo, *Q: Are We Not Men? A: We Are Devo* (Warner Bros.)

1978: X-Ray Spex, *Germ Free Adolescents* (EMI International)

1978: Chrome, *Alien Soundtracks* (Siren)

1979: Buzzcocks, *Singles Going Steady* (I.R.S.)

1979: XTC, *Drums and Wires* (Virgin)

1979: The Heartbreakers, *Live at Max's Kansas City* (Max's Kansas City)

1979: The Specials, *The Specials* (Two Tone/Chrysalis)

1979: The Raincoats, *The Raincoats* (Rough Trade)

1979: The Slits, *Cut* (Antilles)

1979: The B-52's, *The B-52's* (Warner Bros.)

1979: Public Image Ltd., *Metal Box* (Virgin)

1979:  The Clash, *London Calling* (Epic)

1979:  Gang of Four, *Entertainment!* (Warner Bros.)

1979:  Marianne Faithfull, *Broken English* (Island)

1979:  The Sugar Hill Gang, *Rapper's Delight* (Sugarhill)

1980:  Echo and the Bunnymen, *Crocodiles* (Sire)

1980:  Joy Division, *Unknown Pleasures* (Factory U.K.)

1980:  Young Marble Giants, *Colossal Youth* (Rough Trade)

1980:  Half Japanese, *½ Gentlemen/Not Beasts* (Armageddon)

1980:  Bauhaus, *In the Flat Field* (4AD)

1980:  The Cure, *Boys Don't Cry* (Elektra)

1980:  The Soft Boys, *Underwater Moonlight* (Armageddon)

1980:  Dead Kennedys, *Fresh Fruit for Rotting Vegetables* (I.R.S.)

1980:  The Pretenders, *The Pretenders* (Sire)

1981:  Black Flag, *Damaged* (SST)

1981:  The Birthday Party, *Prayers on Fire* (Thermidor)

1981:  Mission of Burma, *Signals, Calls, and Marches* (Ace of Hearts EP)

1982:  The Fall, *Hex Enduction Hour* (Kamera U.K.)

1982:  Dream Syndicate, *The Days of Wine and Roses* (Ruby)

1983:  R.E.M., *Murmur* (I.R.S.)

1983:  Minor Threat, *Out of Step* (Dischord)

1983:  Meat Puppets, *Meat Puppets II* (SST)

1983:  Violent Femmes, *Violent Femmes* (Slash)

1984: Hüsker Dü, *Zen Arcade* (SST)

1984: The Replacements, *Let It Be* (Twin/Tone)

1984: Minutemen, *Double Nickels on the Dime* (SST)

1984: The Smiths, *The Smiths* (Rough Trade/Sire)

1984: The Red Hot Chili Peppers, *The Red Hot Chili Peppers* (EMI America)

1984: Soundtrack, *Repo Man* (San Andreas)

1985: The Jesus and Mary Chain, *Psychocandy* (Reprise)

1986: Sonic Youth, *EVOL* (SST)

1986: Big Black, *Atomizer* (Homestead)

1986: Throwing Muses, *Throwing Muses* (4AD)

1986: Bad Brains, *I Against I* (SST)

1987: Jane's Addiction, *Jane's Addiction* (Triple X)

1987: Dinosaur Jr, *You're Living All Over Me* (SST)

1987: Negativland, *Escape from Noise* (SST)

1987: The Melvins, *Gluey Porch Treatments* (Alchemy)

1987: Green River, *Dry as a Bone* (Sub Pop EP)

1988: Beat Happening, *Jamboree* (K)

1988: My Bloody Valentine, *My Bloody Valentine Isn't Anything* (Creation U.K.)

1988: The Pixies, *Surfer Rosa* (4AD)

1989: Nine Inch Nails, *Pretty Hate Machine* (TVT)

1989: Slint, *Tweez* (Jennifer Hartman)

1990: Moby, *Moby* (Instinct)

1991: The Orb, *Adventures Beyond the Ultraworld* (Big Life)

1991: Sebadoh, "Gimme Indie Rock" (Homestead seven-inch single)

1991:  Nirvana, *Nevermind* (DGC)

1992:  Pavement, *Slanted and Enchanted* (Matador)

1992:  Bikini Kill, *Bikini Kill EP* (Kill Rock Stars)

1993:  Liz Phair, *Exile in Guyville* (Matador)

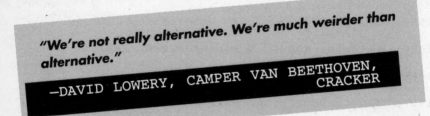

*"We're not really alternative. We're much weirder than alternative."*

—DAVID LOWERY, CAMPER VAN BEETHOVEN, CRACKER

# The Original Punks: The Greatest Garage Recordings of the Twentieth Century

## by Robot A. Hull

Robot A. Hull is an executive producer for Time-Life Music, a direct-marketing company that sells all kinds of popular music from the 1940s into the 1990s. Mr. Hull has been writing about rock since 1970; he cut his teeth on rock criticism for Creem under the tutelage of Lester Bangs. Mr. Hull's current favorite recording artists are Percy Faith, Mantovani, and Roger Williams—and he's not kidding.

Much has been made of the garage-rock bands that populated the suburban and urban communities throughout America from around 1963 and into the early seventies. The sound directly sprang from the rush of surf music with an urgency born of the economic need to throw something together—musicianship not being a precedent—to play at the local teen bash. Garage rock was, in essence, teenage desire directly translated into twanging and pounding and thump-thumping. Whereas doo-wop was begat by the harmonic convergence of a thousand street-corner vocalists, garage music (and let's just call it "punk," okay?) was shaped by the more adolescent need to make noise and to create disharmony wherever possible.

Like doo-wop in the fifties and early sixties, you could hear punk/garage music in the air, on the radio, next door, or in your mind all the time because literally hundreds of labels, most of them local, were releasing primitive recordings by kids all pumped up with a crude sense of libido that they needed to release somehow into the universe of pop harmony and Elvis wannabes. Besides, the Beatles had just arrived, and they were okay but a bit too clean-cut. So what about the Yardbirds or Them or the Rolling Stones or the fuckin' Troggs? AND WHAT ABOUT THE DAVE CLARK FIVE?

In a sense, then, the catalyst for sixties punk rock was the Beatles for one simple reason: No band was *that* good, and everyone knew it. But that didn't stop the race for the title of the Next Beatles. (? and the Mysterians, for example, were definitely *not* the Beatles, but "96 Tears" is as strange and as elusive as "Strawberry Fields Forever" and certainly far more to the point.)

What all this means is that garage rock, whether it was recorded by the Standells or the Seeds or any multitude of more obscure combos, held a certain magic that has by now had its own tradition that can be traced right up to the footprints of Kurt Cobain. Certainly, we all have our own favorite obscure nugget that Lester Bangs forgot to mention in his classic essay on Count Five published in a 1971 issue of *Creem* magazine, which probably had more to do with this whole mess than the entire recorded output of John Lydon. The British have always insisted that punk style and attitude resides with them and that it is their legacy to document so that Jon Savage can rave on and on about some third-rate Shoveling Shit single on the Puke label that nobody even heard at the time. And what makes Gang of Four or Essential Logic punk is beyond me. *Puh—leeze!*

So here we go, gang. Let's get this straight once and for all: AMERICA INVENTED PUNK. Punk rock began with James Dean and Elvis, for chrissake, so what's all this fuss about the Raincoats? In fact, garage music means just that—*garage*—as in inept, crummy, loose, primitive fun.

So here's my list of essential garage recordings, for the record.

## The Best Recordings and Popular Music Artists That Convey the Garage Sensibility to the Average Consumer

### #1A.   The Sonics: *Explosives* (BuckShot LP, 1973)

This album collects material recorded from 1964 to 1966 for the Etiquette label. The Sonics, caught somewhere between Little Richard and the early Kinks, were the band to beat in the Pacific Northwest, where the sound of rock was savage and sax-dominated. Vocalist Gary Roslie rips his larynx; he is a champion screamer—even beyond John Lennon and Mitch Ryder. It doesn't matter that guitarist Larry Parypa knows only three chords since he tangles them up in such an overwhelming and distorted manner. These raunchy recordings were all made in a makeshift studio—a vacant grocery store with egg cartons glued to the walls. Every song on this window-rattling collection perfectly captures the angst of eighteen-year-olds out of high school going nowhere but haywire.

**#1B.  The Kingsmen: "Louie, Louie"** (Jerden/Wand single, 1963)
Dave Marsh wrote an entire book on this song; see that work.

**#2.  The Memphis Goons: *The Complete Works*** (unreleased tapes,
1969–1973)
If the Sonics' recordings represent the garage equivalent to Elvis' Sun sessions, this band's prolific output is garage music's answer to the Beatles'
*Rubber Soul*. Little is known about the Memphis Goons (their name is a
tribute to the British radio comedy team, the Goons; Alice the Goon from
Popeye comics; and the MG's of Booker T. fame), except that the group
spent years recording projects in various living rooms every day after
high school. The Goons were from a suburban area of Memphis called
Whitehaven, not far from Graceland. The band practiced constantly for that
one big moment when it would perform live and conquer America. Legend
has it that the Goons did once play before an audience—a gang of neighborhood kids. The band was promptly pelted with rocks and bottle caps,
whereby its members retreated to their dens swearing never to perform live
again.

 If you ever hear these tapes, you wouldn't blame the neighborhood kids.
Nothing has ever been heard like this before or since. To describe the band's
sound, one is forced to resort to hyphenization indefinitely: "well, they sound
kinda like Captain Beefheart—Creedence Clearwater Revival—the Seeds—
the Stooges—Black Sabbath—" which may seem like gobbledegook until
you realize the Goons' brand of noise is quite distinctive.

 For one thing, the Memphis Sound is nowhere present, except in the
Southern drawls of the vocalists. Another thing is that the Memphis
Goons simply destroy all expectations. Every recorded moment contains a
curve ball; just when you think a song is so out-of-tune or chaotic that it's
about to collapse, the song comes together in an epiphany of adolescent rebellion.

 From what I can make out on the crudely labeled white boxes of reel-to-
reel tapes that I've heard, the three members of the band seem to call themselves—and I'm not making this up—Xavier Tarpit, Jackass Thompson and
Vanilla Frog. (Clearly, they were big fans of *Trout Mask Replica*.) The
Goons' projected albums (the recordings are sequenced and arranged as if
they were major "real" releases, with intricate liner notes and surrealistic
scrawlings) bear titles like *Meet the Goons, Bold Beatniks, One Mile from
Graceland, Peppo, Teenage Bar-B-Q,* and *Stuck in Whitehaven with the
Memphis Blues Again*. Here are just a few of the titles of the countless mas-
terpieces by the Goons: "All the Horny Teenagers," "Over My Dead Body,"
"You Killed My Dawg," "Tits," "Jimi's Dead," "Blow Job," "I am a Hick,"
"Tower of Babble," "Attack of the Aphids," "Toot and His Fab Gear,"

"Mongoloids for Supper," "Baby, Let's Bathe in Tang," and the lovely "I'm Gonna Beat Your Ass."

After hours of listening to these tapes, what emerges is a sense that, not only has the world gone mad, but that music is in itself madness and perhaps best experienced in a frantic state of mind. Many who have heard the Goons' tapes can no longer listen to traditional, studio-produced rock anymore: the Beatles or the Goons' hick neighbor, Elvis Presley, sound far too tame, too contrived. You just haven't lived until you've heard the Goons mangle the Archie Bell and the Drells classic (here entitled "Tighten Up Destroyed") until it's a pulp of writhing matter.

**#3.  The Shaggs: *Philosophy of the World* (Third World LP, 1969) (reissued on Rounder)**
The Shaggs were three plain sisters from New Hampshire—Betty, Helen and Dorothy Wiggin—who formed a band. Their father, Austin, upon hearing his daughters' bewildering music, piled the girls into the family truck and drove to Massachusetts for a recording session. Some have called the results of this session the tortured shrieks of sick minds sharing a lifetime of flogging and mutilation; others define it as the poetry of virgins scrawled on their underwear beneath blankets after midnight. The late-great Lester Bangs has described the Shaggs' vocal style as "three Singing Nuns who've been sniffing lighter fluid" accompanied by rhythms "sounding like a peg-leg stumbling through a field of bald Uniroyals." The spirits of both Emily Dickinson and Melanie Safka hover in the background.

The Shaggs' naivete is what makes them so endearing. They reach out for meaning, Dorothy Wiggin's lyrics groping for an astral plane—and failing. Their songs have titles like "What Should I Do?" or "Why Do I Feel?" The Shaggs are so honest about their ideals that they tend to scare away listeners, although their nerve-racking atonality may also have something to do with it.

**#4.  The Godz: *Contact High with the Godz* (ESP LP/CD, 1966)**
*Contact High,* the Godz' first album, was recorded in one day, seemingly in about the time it takes to play it, around twenty minutes. The Godz consisted of four New Yorkers who tried to play bass, violin, plastic flute, harmonica, drums, and psaltery. The liner notes state that the drummer had never played that instrument before the date of the recording. *Contact High* is a rhythmic group-therapy session, each song a mantra, a spiritual drone that the band labeled "organic body tribal music." The key to their sound is the shared vocals, hypnotic chants, moans, even yodels. Like children, the Godz were fascinated with the artless noise they could make. The band served as a precursor to all the experimentation of the No Wave, the Non-Wave, and the Numb Wave.

**#5. The Rolling Stones: *Exile on Main Street*** (Rolling Stones LP/CD, 1972)

The greatest rock recording of all time owes a huge debt to the garage tradition, even though the album's intentional garage-production values certainly disqualify it as a pure garage artifact. Nevertheless, without it, there would never have been what followed: New York punk, the Sex Pistols, English punk rock, and grunge.

**#6. Pussy Galore: *Exile on Main Street*** (Shov cassette, 1986) ***Corpse Love—The First Year*** (Caroline CD, 1992) ***1 Yr. Live*** (Shov cassette, 1986) ***Groovy Hate Fuck*** (Shov EP, 1986) ***Pussy Gold 5000*** (Buy Our Records EP, 1986) ***Sugarshit Sharp*** (Caroline EP, 1988) ***Right Now!*** (Caroline/Shov LP, 1987) ***Dial "M" for Motherfucker*** (Caroline LP, 1989)

In August 1986, in response to Sonic Youth's boasted plan to cover the Beatles' *White Album,* Pussy Galore beat them to the punch, laying down an entire version of the Stones' *Exile,* even attempting to record it in sequence. In the process, the band created a classic, a garage recording of a garage recording. If there is a band that has explored the garage sound to its full measure, it is this one. To paraphrase critic Greil Marcus, Pussy Galore's entire body of work sounds as if the band had forgotten to erase its rehearsal tapes.

**#7. The Hombres: *Let It Out*** (Verve/Forecast LP, 1967)

This is one of the great American garage albums that simply does not give a hoot. The Hombres, a Memphis combo, opted for the lighter side of punk. Originally, they had planned on being a surf band until they met up with legendary Texas producer Huey Meaux. With the Hombres, Meaux saw an opportunity to reshape the garage rebellion into a comedic sensibility. Thus, with Huey at the helm, the group's first single was "Let It All Hang Out," a parody of Bob Dylan's vocal style as well as the only pop hit to ever begin with a raspberry. The Hombres' album, with songs such as "Mau Mau Mau" and "It's a Gas," has an offhand good-heartedness about it, as if the group is perfectly aware that their own musical ineptitude is beside the point.

**#8. Hackamore Brick: *One Kiss Leads to Another*** (Kama Sutra LP, 1970)

Hackamore Brick were four kids from New York who slapped together an album long before being haphazard was fashionable. Their album sounds like they look on its cover—ragged, scruffy, and awkward. All of the songs could pass for first-takes or unreleased demos. The atmosphere suggests stoned teenagers practicing in the basement the music of their mentors—in this case, the Velvet Underground, or, judging from Tommy Moonlight's organ playing, early Grateful Dead. Vocal harmonies collide, and songs of horny innocence fall apart. This album is a significant antecedent to the rough, homegrown Manhattan punk of the seventies, exemplified by the New York Dolls and the Ramones. Reviewing this record in ROLLING STONE, rock critic Richard Meltzer wrote that it possessed the two great things required in the right rock universe: "limbo plus filler."

**#9.  Doug Clark and the Hot Nuts:** *Nuts to You, On Campus, Homecoming, Rush Week, Panty Raid, Hell Night!, Summer Session, Freak Out* (all LPs on the Gross label, recording dates unknown)
From "Baby, Let Me Bang Your Box" to the "Hot Nuts" anthem, all of the rompin', bawdy fraternity hits are here. This North Carolina–based black party-band was indeed a legend, tearing through the Dixie circuit of colleges from the late fifties right into the eighties. Every college kid in the South has a story to tell about the night he danced to Doug Clark in the animal house of his dreams. This was *the* party band. Not only is it time for a decent CD compilation of this band's work, but a movie about Doug Clark and his lifestyle wouldn't be a bad idea either.

**#10A.  Bob Dylan and the Band:** *The Genuine Basement Tapes, Volumes 1–5* (bootleg CDs, 1993)
Herein lies a piece of the monument to all garage recordings. Created in isolation in 1967, these hours of doodling and improvisation hold a mystery that is so moving you only want to hear more. And the amazing thing is that there *is* more.

**#10B.  The Velvet Underground:** *The Velvet Underground—Etc.* (Plastic Inevitable bootleg, 1979)
Until the discovery of a budget anthology called *Soundsville* on Pickwick's subsidiary label, Design, not many fans thought of the Velvet Underground as a garage band. But their garage roots are indeed apparent on the first side of this bootleg assemblage of odds and ends.

Lou Reed wrote two of these songs, "Cycle Annie" by the Beachnuts and "You're Drivin' Me Insane" by the Roughnecks, when he was a cash-and-carry songwriter for Pickwick Records in 1964. Landing this job after graduating from Syracuse University, Reed learned much from it. No doubt, it was his sojourn at Pickwick that enabled Reed to guide the Velvets through the recording of *White Light/White Heat* at breakneck speed.

No Velvets song, however, is more punk than the single "The Ostrich," recorded by the Primitives, an early incarnation of the Velvets. "I was stoned," Reed recalls in the liner notes, "and I made up this thing . . . just for laughs. I decided to make up a dance, so I said, 'You put your head on the floor and have somebody step on it'; it was years ahead of its time."

Around the time of this session, on November 11, 1965, the Velvet Underground performed live for the first time at a high school dance in Summit, New Jersey, where they opened for the Myddle Class, one of the countless garage bands of the era. No document exists to verify whether or not the Velvets performed "Louie, Louie" on this date. Let us assume that they did.

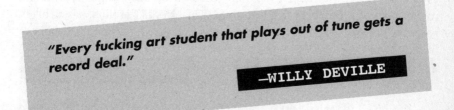

"Every fucking art student that plays out of tune gets a record deal."

—WILLY DEVILLE

# Ten Bootlegs That Illustrate the Origins of Punk

## by Clinton Heylin

Clinton Heylin is author of the biography *Dylan Behind the Shades* and the authoritative punk history *From the Velvets to the Voidoids*. Just recently, St. Martin's Press published his history of the rock bootleg industry, *Bootleg*. He also edited *The Penguin Book of Rock & Roll Writing* and has just completed his "other" Dylan book, *Dylan Behind Closed Doors: The Recordings 1960-94*, also due to bear the St. Martin's imprint.

***Metallic K.O.*, Iggy and the Stooges.**   A bootleg in all but name, this audio-vérité document of the Stooges' final onstage implosion was excavated by France's punkiest label, Skydog Records, in 1976, just in time to teach Johnny Rotten about what's real and what's not.

***Double Exposure*, Television.**   The solitary audio evidence of the Richard Hell/Tom Verlaine incarnation of TV, the originators of New York "punk" (spare me your protestations and read *From the Velvets to the Voidoids*) recorded these demos, coproduced by Eno and Richard Williams, featuring prototypes of not just Verlaine's most pop/rock dispensations ("Prove It," "Venus de Milo," "Marquee Moon") but Hell's primo anthem, "(I Belong to the) Blank Generation."

***Teenage Perversity*, Patti Smith Group.**   After making punk's first important long-playin' platter, *Horses,* the PSG took the word on the road. TAKRL's antennae was tuned to L.A.'s FM stations when the PSG unveiled their constantly evolving versions of the *Horses* material plus their ever-

16

popular covers: the Velvets' "We're Gonna Have a Real Good Time Together" and "Pale Blue Eyes" and the Who's "My Generation."

***Mechanical Man EP, Devo.***   Demos from 1974–75 of the most devolved of Akron, Ohio's, first wave, these four ditties preceded Devo's debut long-player and showed that Kraftwerk and Roxy Music had as much impact on the Blank Generation as Detroit noise.

***Spunk, Sex Pistols.***   Too edgy, too stripped-down, too damn cacophonous to be the Pistol's official debut, this was the *alternative* debut, snuck out under mysterious circumstances shortly before Virgin's *Never Mind the Bollocks*. This "Anarchy in the U.K.," in particular, says everything that needs to be said about how the Pistols sounded circa '76.

***Indecent Exposure, Sex Pistols.***   The closest a '76 Pistols live tape comes to hi-fi. This is a surprisingly clear document of the Pistols fully loaded on the River Trent lurching through their customary mixture of covers like "(Don't You Give Me) No Lip" and "(I'm Not Your) Steppin' Stone" and original anthems-to-come.

***White Riot, The Clash.***   In punk's second home, not-so-sunny Manchester, on the "White Riot" tour, the Clash rip through some decidedly unrefined workouts of "White Riot," "1977," "Capital Radio One" and that CBS debut album in toto. A garage band indeed!

***Time's Up, Buzzcocks.***   Howard Devoto and Pete Shelley's Buzzcocks found time to cut an album's worth of demos on four-track (*Time's Up*) before their single EP (*Spiral Scratch*) gave official evidence of their six-month alliance. The Troggs ("I Can't Control Myself") and Captain Beefheart ("I Love You Big Dummy") are the punk precursors given the nod this time around, plus Devoto's takes on songs like his own "Orgasm Addict" and— b'dum d'dum—"Boredom."

***Love in a Void, Siouxsie and the Banshees.***   Tuning in to John Peel's late-night "live" sessions was an integral part of the U.K. punk experience '77–'79. None was more instrumental in a band's commercial acceptance than the two sessions given by ex-Bromley babe Siouxsie Sioux and her own wailing Banshees. When some wily soul transferred the Banshees' Peel sessions to plastic in 1979 the band was not amused—primarily because the "boot" did the deed better than the group's Polygram debut.

***Warsaw, Joy Division.***   An entire album's worth of material cut pre-*Unknown Pleasures*, *Warsaw* was more rock than soundtrack-to-the-apocalypse, placing the passage from Warsaw to Herzog in a stark perspective and marking the end of the great era of punk's alternative artifacts.

# The *SoHo Weekly News* Columns: Punk's First Press

## by Danny Fields

Danny Fields has been in the music business since around the time of the Great War, as an artist's manager, writer, DJ, publicist, party giver, tour guide, and a charter member of what Lenny Kaye describes as "this industry's alternate universe." He signed the MC5 and the Stooges to Elektra, was the editor of *16 and Country Rhythms* (!) magazines, briefly managed Lou Reed, and guided the career of the Ramones from 1975-1980. Currently at work on a book about *16* magazine, he serves as a consultant for the Rock and Roll Hall of Fame and manages Elektra recording artist, Paleface.

It was fun writing this column for the *SoHo Weekly News*. Michael Goldstein, the publisher, asked me to do it about the time the second or third issue came out in 1974; the paper's distribution system at that time consisted of Michael handing out copies to people entering and leaving Max's Kansas City (a better audience I could never hope to reach), and I was promised ten dollars a column. We couldn't think of a clever name for the column, and so it was eponymous, which also suited me just fine. What was also great was that I could write the column after midnight on Monday, deliver it to the paper early Tuesday morning, and see it on the street on Wednesday—Michael was good enough to give me a later deadline than that of any other contributor, and so my piece was hot every week, with the shortest lead time any columnist at a weekly could ask for.

Please know that the following has been *extracted* from nearly one hundred columns, and that I did not only write about Patti Smith, Nico, the Modern Lovers, Television, Iggy, the Dolls, John Cale, and Lou Reed, though I'm more proud than ever to have done so, and stand by every corny superlative I used. Yes, I cringe when I read myself sounding like one of those yucky postings ("Weasels, sign this band, fools that you are!! They'll be bigger than Smashing Pumpkins!") in the AOL newsgroup for industry insiders (there's a laugh), but clearly (well, it's clear to me now in any case) I saw my role as that of a booster for the music and personalities then emerging on the CB's-Max's axis (adorable!), as well as gossip monger. If I went overboard with enthusiasm, I don't regret it. If I'm a little embarrassed by the way I expressed myself twenty years ago, well, I was so much older then, etc. (For posterity's sake, rumors that turned out to be inaccurate and name spellings that were later changed have been left as they were during original publication.)

In the way that events are guided by preposterous, unknown hands, this column led to a whole other phase of my life: the Ramones, eager to be written about, and envious of the coverage I was giving Television, hounded me to come and see them. One night, Lisa Robinson and I divided journalistic responsibilities vis-à-vis checking out new bands—she would see the Ramones and report to me, and I would see some other group and report to her. We always knew what the other would like. I don't remember what my assignment was, but Lisa knew that the Ramones and I could make a good fit (so to speak), and so I rushed to see them and fell in love.

Before you could say, "I Don't Wanna Go Down to the Basement," I was the Ramones' manager, and dubious about covering other bands—there was no way to avoid the appearance, much less the fact, of ulterior motives no matter what I said. And rightly so, as Jon Landau (a much more illustrious writer than I, I hasten to note, though it is unnecessary) warned me; Jon had faced a parallel situation when he started managing Bruce Springsteen while writing for ROLLING STONE: "You can't do both," he said, and Jon was (is) never wrong.

One thing I would revise if I could: I do not like the way I handled the Wayne County-Dick Manitoba story. Reading it now, I see I was gratuitously mean to Dick, though I was there, and that's the way it looked to me then. I was seeing it through the eyes of someone on "Wayne's side." I apologize to Dick. Oh, what the fuck. We were all so stoned.

Here goes:

*March 6, 1974:* **Lou Reed,** according to his manager Dennis Katz, is still shaken by what happened to him in Italy, and says he will never set foot in that country again. As you may or may not know, Lou's concerts in Milan and Rome, the opening shows of his current European tour, were disrupted by organized thugs. In Milan, on February 12th, a group known as the Members of the Creative Situations threw lead pipes and iron nails at the band, and bombed the amps with bags of water. The band left the stage after two songs, whereupon the Creative ones stormed the stage, raised their fists, claimed victory, and denounced Lou as a dirty decadent Jew. In Rome, three days later, it was worse, with full-scale rioting and scores of injuries. It sort of sounds like the Motherfuckers at the Fillmore in 1968, but that was little more than posturing. This was real, and it gets more astonishing the more one thinks about it. Future, here we come . . . *July 4:* **Nico** recently signed a deal with Island Records (very trendy and successful) in London. **John Cale** will produce. Last month Nico and John joined Kevin Ayers and Eno for a highly publicized and instantly sold-out concert at London's Rainbow Theater. **Nico** sang three songs: "Janitor of Lunacy," a brand new downbeat version of "Deutschland Über Alles" and the Doors' "The End." There will be a record of the concert . . . *July 25:* Continuing to keep you abreast of the international escapades of **Nico,** we give you, in its entirety, the text of a postcard just received from herself via Morocco: "Danny, my dear friend, This is the End my only friend, The End. Only because we are not together now, and when I die in the streets of Marrakesh. Love, Nico." *Isn't* that nice? . . . *August 1:* Now It Can Be Told: **Patti Smith** and **Tom Verlaine** (of **Television**) are definitely a twosome, and definitely the Downtown Couple of the Year thus far . . . *August 8:* "Everything is going to be the same. There will be no change of policy at all," says Mickey Ruskin about the future of **Max's Kansas City.** Last week rumors multiplied (It's closing? a soul disco upstairs? couples only downstairs?) and stories concerning the fate of Max's appeared in the press. New York's finest freaks waited breathlessly for some clue as to what it all meant. In fact, despite bankruptcy proceedings and a new financial management, Mickey will be actively involved in the operation of the joint for the foreseeable future. "I'll probably be there more often now than I have been before," Mickey added. Anyhow . . . whew! It lives. As Jackie Curtis said whilst the fracas was raging: "Max's is like Tiffany's—it's just nice to know it's there." . . . **Iggy Pop** went to such great lengths introducing a group called the Hollywood Stars at a recent Sunset Strip gig that he had to be forcibly removed from the stage by the Stars' road manager so that the band could go on. The audience, in a remarkable display of good taste, indicated that they much preferred Iggy to the band whose virtues he was extolling when so rudely interrupted . . . *August 15:* Ralph Bakshi, who made *Fritz the Cat* and *Heavy Traffic,* has signed the **New York Dolls** for his forthcoming part-animated/part-live film, "Hey Good Lookin'." The Dolls will appear in the live part . . . *August 22:* Ho-Hum Dept.: **Iggy Pop** slashed himself repeatedly with a knife during a performance at Rodney Bingenheimer's in L.A. last week, and had to be carried off on a stretcher, bleeding and unconscious . . . The **Modern Lovers,** led by **Jonathan Richman,** were a Boston group that had just about every biggy in the business doing flip-flops to get them under contract. We mean the likes of David Geffen, Steve Paul, Albert Grossman, Clive Davis, etc.—i.e., biggies. That's how good they were. Eventually, Warners got them, with **John Cale** producing. Warners never liked the results, the record stayed in the can, and the group broke up (this is all an amazing oversimplification, but that is what happened). Now comes word that an outfit called Bezerkely Records has purchased four of the tracks and will release two singles, including the legendary songs "Roadrunner" and "Government Center." Get them if you can—you won't be sorry . . . *August 29:* OUR HERO: **David Jo Hansen** [sic] of the **Dolls** won the hearts of everyone in Max's back room last week by systematically dumping first an ashtray, then a bowl of chick peas, and finally each of four varieties of salad dressing on the head of an obnoxious drunk. His work done, David took the hand of Cyrinda Foxx, and the couple made an elegant and graceful exit, amidst cheers and applause . . . Richard Williams and Island Records are trying to arrange a Berlin concert for **Eno, Nico,** and **John Cale.** Speaking of Nico, her amazing "Marble Index" album has been dropped from the Elektra catalogue and is now officially a rarity, with stores getting up to fifty dollars a copy for it . . . Don't forget—**Patti Smith** and **Television** are at Max's this very week! . . . *September 5:* The response to **Patti Smith** and **Television** at Max's has been so fantastic that they've been held over. They'll be there this Friday (September 7th) through Sunday. For anybody who cares about What's Happening, either act is not-to-be-missed, and the both of them together makes for the ultimate musical billing of the season, if not the year . . . **Fran Lebowitz** dropped in at the **Dictators'** recording session and was shown the lyrics of their song "Master Race," which contains many references to smelly feet, vomiting, and ass-wiping. "Mmmm," cooed Fran as she handed the lyrics back to producer Murray Krugman, "it's *much* better than Cole Porter." . . . *September 12:* The **Dictators'** song "Master Race" is very big on the jukeboxes at our town's fave S&M haunts, the Eagle's Nest and the Spike. It is unlikely, however, that any of the band members have been to either place . . . *October 3:* **Alice Cooper** was almost killed by lightning while playing golf in the Bronx on Sunday. Alice had just hit a long drive when the bolt struck a tree about ten yards behind him, blasting the tree into splinters, and throwing Alice to the ground. Shaken but intrepid, Alice resumed his game using only wooden clubs for the rest of the afternoon—however, the toll on his nerves was considerable and he shot a shameful 90 instead of his usual high 70s . . . *October 10:* **Wayne County** and **Richard Robinson** will head a music industry panel on "Glitter Rock" to be held next week. County, Robinson, et al. will speculate aloud on such issues as, "Where did it come from—where did it go?" . . . *October 17:* On the same night, **Lou Reed** sold out the Felt Forum and blew the minds of his more ancient fans by actually tying-up while singing "Heroin." Mick Jagger watched from the wings, while Andy Warhol and entourage braved the crowd from front-row seats . . . **Patti Smith** will perform at her *Third Annual Celebration of the Birth and Death of Arthur Rimbaud* at the Riverside Plaza hotel on October 27. Ticketron will handle your needs . . . *October 24:* Director Ralph Bakshi, currently shooting *Hey, Good Lookin'* with the **Dolls** in L.A. saw **David Jo Hansen's** beautiful and talented Cyrinda Foxx and announced, "I want that hair in every scene!" Cyrinda's many friends and admirers are expecting that this will be the beginning of a well-deserved movie career . . . *October 31:* **Patti Smith** had to postpone her *Rimbaud Anniversary Celebration* on Sunday because the Erotic Circus, scheduled site of the event, was shut down by the Authorities (it was deemed a neighborhood nuisance, even by Needle Park neighborhood standards). Patti and Co. did not learn of the closing until the day of the show, and tried by phone to reach as many people as they could with the news. With regrets to those who schlepped up there unaware, and renewed hope for all, Patti's manager Jane Friedman is rescheduling the concert at this very moment. It will probably be on November 10, at the Blue Hawaiian Room of the Hotel Roosevelt, but keep your ear to the ground for word on the definite venue . . . *November 7:* "Questions, questions, questions! Don't ask me questions!" shrieked **David Bowie,** in response to a casual query posed by a well-known journalist at a small party following David's opening at Radio City last week. "They're always asking me questions," Bowie went on to moan, "why can't they let me have a moment's rest?!" The party was further enhanced by a visit from **Alice Cooper,** to whom Bowie graciously said "I admire what you do. *You* are burlesque—but *I* am a performer!" And then, breaking another of the tense silences which flowed like pancake batter through the opulent hotel suite: "I never give a bad performance—the worst I can do is great!" Many who had been at the Wednesday concert disagreed, but by Friday, when we saw the show, David *was* truly in top form (at a top price of $12.50 a seat, yet) . . . *November 14:* **Television** will be at the "82" on November 20th, and at the Truck and Warehouse Theater on the 22nd. Watch for all new songs, and planeloads of record execs from England, where Bleecker Bob has been spreading the word about the mightiest of bands . . . **Patti Smith**'s show at the Roosevelt Hotel on Sunday was remarkable for many things, not the least among them the legendary **Sandy Bull,** performing in public for the first time in over a year. The next morning, Patti and her band were off to L.A. for a gig at the Whisky . . . *November 21:* **Patti Smith** got a rave review in the *L.A. Times* for her performance at the Whisky, and the crowds were so good that Patti's gig was held over. This in spite of the fact that the doorman was actually trying to keep customers away by warning them that "some New York lesbian" was singing within. That's in case anyone thought they were going to hear Crosby, Stills, Nash and Young, we suppose . . . The cover of the new **Roxy Music** album is causing some consternation at Atlantic, portraying as it does two provocatively posed women, one of whom is having an erotic daydream with her finger. You may see it in stores, but then again you may not . . . *November 28:* **Patti Smith** had the honor of introducing **Arthur Lee** from the stage of San Francisco's Winterland last week, but there was also a gloomy event to mar Ms. Smith's working visit to the toy and foggy City on the Bay— one North Beach club at which she was scheduled to perform would not let her in because she had no proof of her age . . . *December 12:* Friends of **David Bowie** are increasingly voicing concern for the health of the talented musician, now commercially at the height of his career. And David's performance on the *Dick Cavett Show* last week can't have given those who care for him cause for rejoicing, to put it gently. As are so many big stars, David has long been obsessed with the magic age of twenty-seven, at which Jimi Hendrix, Janis Joplin, Brian Jones, Duane Allman, and Jim Morrison (among, no doubt, others) shuffled off etc. Bowie will be twenty-eight in January . . . **Roxy**'s controversial album cover, which shows two girls getting off on themselves, will go out, but with an opaque shrink-wrap cover . . . *December 26:* **Patti Smith**'s unreal version of *Hey Joe* is breaking out in the Pacific Northwest . . . *January 16, 1975:* It's a shock but **Television** has apparently rejected a bid from **Eno** and Island Records for a production/recording deal. The idea of England's trendiest musician and trendiest label going to work on New York's most ultramodern band has unfortunately turned out to be too good to be true. According to an informed source, the parties concerned were not in total agreement as to the way the band should ultimately sound. But mutual admiration still abounds between them all, and the picture could change again. Meanwhile, Television is playing at CBGB's for the next three weekends— call 982-4052 for info . . . *January 23:* This week in America, Island Records is releasing new albums by **Nico, John Cale,** and **Sparks**! How fabulous can a record company get? . . . *January 30:* Lou Speaks: The ineffable **Lou Reed**—in town rehearsing with his new band—"It's everything the **Velvet Underground** was, plus" (oo-o-o-o!)—called us early in the week to tell of current plans and prospects. He and the boys (three guitars, electric viola, tenor sax, bass, drum, and keyboards) leave next week for a tour of the capitals of Europe, beginning in Rome and ending in London. Then they play America. Meanwhile, *Rock And Roll Animal* is released so that now we will have, lucky us, the whole concert at the Academy of Music available on disc and tape. Right after that comes Lou's very special solo album, *Metal Machine Music* with four sides, each exactly sixteen minutes and one second long, no vocals, no instruments, just machines and very mathematical. Then a third album is released with Lou and his new band, called *Coney Island Baby*. No grass grows under this one's feet, you can be sure. By the way, has he heard **Nico**'s new album, and/or **John Cale**'s? "Not interested," said Lou in the great tradition of ex-Velvets talking to reporters, "I heard a few minutes of each.

That was really enough." . . . **Television** was brilliant for the past three weekends at CBGB, and left few unconvinced that this is definitely the most interesting and important new American band in years . . . *February 13:* The wonderful news from London is that **Nico** has married a young(er) man named Gene Krell in a small civil ceremony attended by **John Cale** and **Lou Reed** and a few close friends. Gene is a Brooklyn boy who left for London several years ago, and there founded the very successful emporium, Granny Takes a Trip. He has very long fingernails, is a sweetie pie, and lives in the basement of Keith Richards's house on the Chelsea Embankment. We know it's her first marriage, but we're not sure if it's his. The mind boggles, but we are thrilled and wish the newlyweds all the best. Oh yes, the bride wore black . . . **Dave Alexander,** one of the original **Stooges,** died on February 10 in Detroit after a long illness. Dave was one of the sweetest people who ever lived and he will be very much missed . . . *February 27:* **The Dolls,** under new management, have sent out a release announcing an "entente cordiale with the People's Republic of China," and "the role of the People's Information Collective in direct association with the Red Guard." Shades of John Sinclair, the MC5, and Detroit in 1968, unless it's all meant to be a big giggle, which we rather hope it is. Anyhow, we'll have a chance to find out what they're up to when they play at the Little Hippodrome this weekend . . . *March 13:* Bryce Marden's great show at the Guggenheim contains a painting called *Star [for Patti Smith]* . . . **The Dolls,** doing great business at the New Hippodrome these past few weeks, admit that all their communist propaganda is supposed to be a giggle, just as we suspected. Whoever could have thought otherwise? . . . *March 20:* **David Bowie** and **Iggy Pop,** that sometime team of yesteryear, are together again. They are fooling around with Iggy's songs in a small Hollywood studio, with Claudia Linnear (said to have been the inspiration for *Brown Sugar*) a constant visitor and musical participant. We don't buy the rumor that David and Iggy got into a nasty fistfight over the subject of Claudia's favors—still there's no harm in just repeating it . . . Coming up, and of High Importance—**Patti Smith** and **Television** at CBGB this weekend; **Jonathan Richman,** the new **Modern Lovers** and **Andy Paley** at the Kitchen, 59 Wooster St., March 19–22 . . . *March 27:* The **New York Dolls** are considering relocating to England . . . It looks as if **Patti Smith** is very close to signing with Clive Davis's Arista Records. Hooray for Clive, once again. But why are the labels so slow in grabbing **Television**? Everybody today raves about how great the **Velvet Underground** was, and here is another great New York band that musically picks up where the Velvet Underground left off . . . *April 10:* **Lou Reed** is back from Europe, and wasted no time in checking out **Television** at CBGB, after he read somewhere that they had picked up where the **Velvets** left off. Lou, of course, was also anxious to hear his dear friend **Patti Smith,** and was seen grinning paternally as she performed his song, "We're Gonna Have a Real Good Time

Together." Speaking of Television, it looks as if the real big record executives are just starting to get interested, judging from who was there last weekend, and who is expected this one. It is about time . . . *April 17:* Hundreds were turned away from **Patti Smith**'s gig at CBGB last weekend. Way to go, Patti! . . . *April 24:* The **New York Dolls** have broken up. Since their debut at the Hotel Diplomat in the Spring of 1972, the Dolls have been this town's most cherished local group, and their passing gives one pause. No need to go into specifics, but obviously things were not going well with them lately, nor was help on the way, so they did the only decent thing. Anyway, **David Jo Hansen** and **Sylvain Sylvain** will remain together as a songwriting team; **Johnny Thunders** and **Jerry Nolan** are starting a group called the **Heartbreakers** with **Richard Hell,** formerly of **Television**; and **Arthur Kane** is joining an as yet unspecified band. The New York Dolls leave behind them two fantastic albums, plus countless great memories of nights when they were really hot, and that's more than enough to guarantee that I'll love them forever . . . *May 8:* On Monday night **Patti Smith** and her band returned in triumph to perform at Glassboro State College, the South Jersey institution from which Patti was expelled. Expected in the audience, said Patti, was the whole "piss factory crowd" . . . If you haven't seen the **Ramones** yet, you don't know what you're missing. Catch them at CBGB on Monday and Tuesday, May 12 & 13—they follow another worthy act, the **Unholy Modal Rounders,** who will be there from May 8–11 . . . *May 15:* Most of the audience in Central Park on Sunday had never heard—nor heard of—**Patti Smith** before, but when she finished two songs, she got a rousing ovation from the vast crowd. It was a revelation too for those of us who have only heard Patti perform in relatively tiny rooms. All great rock acts, for some reason, ultimately sound their best out-of-doors in broad daylight . . . Lisa Robinson, in London to report **John Cale's** concert, reports that **Phil Manzanera** snuck into the back of the house and sat in the last row, afraid he'd be dragged onstage if he were seen by John. Such is Phil's desirability, especially since the release of his *Diamond Head* LP. Incidentally, many New York admirers of John Cale's music were shocked by the philistinism displayed in the *V V* "review" of Cale's (and **Nico's**) recent recorded product. One hadn't realized that the *Voice* was reaching out for certified rednecks in its quest for a broader-based readership . . . **Iggy Pop** now in the studio in L.A. with Ben Edmonds producing a demo for Elton John and John Reid to hear. Among the new songs—"Killer City" [sic] and "I Got Nothin' " . . . I suppose the boys in **Sparks** thought it was really a cute idea to hold their after-concert party at the Burger King on E. 59th St., but few if any of their guests would have agreed. Sparks is an excellent group with a trendy and growing following, and many of New York's most attractive rock-followers, male and female, were there—being "served" garbage peasant food and low-rent wine poured over ice in plastic cups. And do you realize how much litter they use to wrap up all that mundungus for people who are going to eat it right there—every tabletop was buried under mounds of greasy paper that never got taken away. Boys, you want publicity for taking us someplace disgusting, you got it. Next time, though, please consider the Rainbow Room. It may be a cliché, but at least it doesn't smell bad, and I for one never do get tired of the view . . . *May 22:* I can't honestly say that this was the hottest week in the history of the world for rock gossip. Therefore, I'm using the space traditionally reserved for the "lead item" to announce that there really isn't any. I always wondered what I would do if this happened. Now I know . . . *June 12:* "One of the most exciting experiences I've had for a long, long time . . . both acts have something that rock & roll desperately needs," wrote British supercritic Charles Shaar Murray in London's prestigious *New Musical Express,* raving about—of all things—an evening at New York's own CBGB listening to **Television** and **Patti Smith**! And although he doesn't say so (he doesn't have to), I'll bet he had been expecting to hate them. Anyhow, it is interesting that Television is beginning to attract international attention without having yet signed a recording contract. Something on that front will probably happen this summer, however. Television will be back at CBGB this coming weekend, and everyone will be there to see them, so don't miss it . . . *June 19:* **Iggy Pop** has told friends he will soon end his voluntary and highly publicized confinement in an institution for the emotionally fragile. While in the hospital, Iggy had a constant stream of visitors, including **David Bowie,** who brought him a tape recorder and all the latest magazines . . . Onetime New Yorkers **Tony** and **Hunt Sales** are now in a band in Los Angeles, along with their chauffeur, known as the **Millionaires.** According to L.A. savant **Kim Fowley,** they will only perform at private functions for the very rich . . . Watch for a very tight and talented group from Park Slope called the **Shirts.** With lead singer **Annie Golden,** they went over in a big way at CBGB last weekend, where they supported the ever-cosmic **Television.** This coming weekend at CBGB, don't forget, will be the **Ramones** and **Talking Heads** . . . *June 26:* **Patti Smith**'s appearance at the Other End this Thursday (26) is likely to be her last hereabouts for several months, and it will be the first ever with a drummer in the band—he's Jay Dee Daugherty, formerly of the **Mumps.** After the gig, Patti goes into the studio to record her first LP, and after that, it's hello U.S.A., so go if you can . . . More and more record companies are checking out the **Ramones,** who headlined last weekend at CBGB, supported by the everintriguing **Talking Heads** . . . *July 10:* **Patti Smith, Bob Dylan,** and **Bobby Neuwirth** joined the ensemble onstage at the Other End Saturday night for several choruses of "Goodnight Irene," an event which will surely be carved in stone in the annals of folkie history. Neuwirth is recently returned to New York from L.A. ("They should cut it off and send it to Hawaii,") after living out there over a year, and it certainly is nice to have him back . . . **The**

**Ramones** and **Blondie** did great business at CBGB on July 4th weekend with the Ramones wrap-up set Sunday night consisting of five songs in thirteen power-packed minutes—a record even for them . . . *July 17:* **The CBGB Rock Festival,** which begins on the 16th of July and runs through the 27th, is the most important and ambitious event of its kind ever held in New York City. Hilly of CBGB is presenting "The Top 40 New York Unrecorded Rock Bands," and some of them without question will one day be among the biggest (several are already among the best) in the world. Some that we love will go under, and some that we hate will become enormously successful. And it certainly is hoped that the most deserving and professional will be ineligible for next year's festival, unable to satisfy the requirement that they be unrecorded. Record companies who do not send representatives may certainly be expected to suffer the wrath of the local music community, and then some. But do get down there—it's history in the making . . . *July 24:* **Wayne County,** performing at Pier Nine in New Jersey, was so outrageous that the club owners stopped his act mid show and had the police come and escort him to the city line. Attaboy! . . . **Television** plays its first out-of-town date this coming weekend at the famed Picadilly Inn in Cleveland, which along with Detroit is said by most musicians to be the city with the hippest rock audiences in the country. Many New York fans of the group are going there to see Television perform . . . You should have seen the **Ramones** Friday night at CBGB . . . *August 28:* A **Lou Reed** "mystery" is brewing in the English press, following Lou's cancellation of a concert in New Zealand because of (according to the local performer) "a personal problem of such magnitude that he was unable to perform." The problem appears to be related to a phone call Lou received while in New Zealand. It was so bad that he then cancelled a forthcoming European tour as well. I have no further information right now, but hope to by next week . . . **Richard Lloyd** is leaving **Television** and will be replaced by a famous musician from Cleveland, Ohio . . . **John Cale** coming here from London to discuss producing **Patti Smith**'s album . . . **David Bowie** to New York this week to record the soundtrack for his just completed film *The Man Who Fell to Earth* . . . **Beefheart** and **Zappa** will make a joint two-record LP *Bongo Fury* . . . Chris Frantz of the **Talking Heads** saw a shark off the beach at Provincetown last week, and this time I really am going to Tanglewood . . . *September 11:* **Lou Reed** and his manager Dennis Katz are severing their relationship under circumstances which can hardly be described as attractive. Lou is also plenty angry at his record company RCA for promoting his *Metal Machine Music* as a rock product, rather than as experimental classical music, which is what it is. Lou had wanted the record package to carry a printed disclaimer on the back, telling buyers, or rather warning them, that it was not an album of rock & roll songs, but a very cerebral avant-garde composition. The disclaimer was never included, and now Lou feels many kids bought the album and hate him as a result. "They made me look like an asshole," says Lou bitterly of all concerned . . . *September 18:* In his excellent *Record World* column this week, Ben Edmonds raves about an all-girl teenage power trio that's attracting all this attention in L.A., but for some reason never gives their name. Well, thanks for the lead-in, Ben—they're called the **Runaways,** and below please find a picture of them by the one-and-only Richard Creamer. "We're different because we're young and our songs are about death, sex, drugs, and violence and the things that teenagers really care about," the guitar player told me when I saw them rehearse over a drugstore in West Hollywood two weeks ago. Not since the Carrie Nations . . . And, yes, that was **Lou Reed** munching away at Vim & Vigor on 57th Street. Contrary to some rumors, he is not in Tokyo auditioning Japanese jazz musicians for a bebop combo, but is in Manhattan, in excellent spirits and hoping to be making a record soon . . . **Richard Lloyd** and **Jonathan Paley** are starting a band . . . **The Heartbreakers** are not breaking up . . . *October 9:* The **New York Dolls** at Max's Kansas City (now featuring rock on Sundays at 9) on October 19 . . . **John Cale** is wrapping up **Patti Smith**'s record any day now, so expect a pre-Xmas release . . . **Television** is quite intact, and Tom Verlaine says that their single, "Little Johnny Jewel, Parts I & II," will be available at Village Oldies in a week or so . . . *October 16:* Metropolis Video, which has been broadcasting the great CBGB bands over cable, is changing its schedule somewhat . . . The Bottom Line and Projectovision will be sending out tapes of BL shows to bars and clubs across the nation which have large Advent-type screens. Artists will receive royalties. Further announcements about this project, which is rather a major innovation, to come soon . . . Max's Kansas City is looking to change its image and go after the crowd that follows the hot new New York bands. As a first step, **Wayne County** is reprogramming the juke box, eliminating disco crap and putting in a tasty rock selection . . . *October 23:* **Lou Reed** is in the studio, and is delighted with the way work is going on his new album, *Coney Island Baby* . . . **David Bowie** comes out of the retirement he was never in and goes on tour again the beginning of the year, while the release of his film, *The Man Who Fell to Earth,* had been put off until June. His next album, *Golden Years,* is due in December . . . Is WB toying with the idea of releasing the very great **Modern Lovers** album produced over two years ago by **John Cale,** and in the can ever since? . . . Pardon me for misleading you about the **Dolls** supposed gig at Max's this past weekend. I was misinformed, and I assure you it won't be the last time . . . All the British copies of the new **Roxy** LP *Sirens* have been recalled because they were made from a tape that ran too slow, so if you see one in an import store, get it if you want a collector's item, but not if you want Roxy's music . . . **Jerry Nolan** of the **Heartbreakers** recovering nicely at St. Vincent's after being stabbed by a crazy person . . . **Patti Smith,** already at work on material for a second album, is writing a porno-reggae song

. . . **Television**'s first single, "Little Johnny Jewel," is almost sold out at Village Oldies, so get your copy while they last . . . *November 6:* I just heard **Patti Smith**'s new album, and it's amazing, and you know for a mere recording to be worth lead item status herein, it's got to be really special. It will be available by the 20th of this month . . . Everyone was at CBGB on Sunday night to see themselves and their idols in the film *Night Lunch*, made by **Amos Poe** and **Ivan Kral**. Starring **Wayne County**, the **Faces, Patti Smith, David Bowie, Blondie,** the **New York Dolls, Television, Iggy and the Stooges,** the **Ramones,** Queen, Elton John, Manhattan Transfer, Roxy Music, David Peel and others in thirty-five minutes of running time, it is some incredible document . . . *November 27:* **Patti Smith** SRO at San Francisco's Boarding House this past weekend, and the recipient of an offer from the Starship crowd to use their venerable mansion for a poetry reading . . . **Lou Reed** was at CBGB twice last weekend to hear the **Ramones** and taped the last set Sunday night on a portable Sony cassette recorder . . . *December 18:* **Television** broke the house records two nights in a row at CBGB and won such new fans as **Lou Reed** and English actor Simon Turner . . . Stephanie Hopken's colored glass and glitter image (there's no paint on it, so it's not a painting) of the **New York Dolls** is currently on display at CBGB, where the Christmas Rock Festival is now in progress. Five or six bands a night, including all the local greats. See ad nearby, and hurry on down . . . *January 1, 1976:* **Patti Smith** pulled off a major triumph at the Bottom Line last weekend taking one risk after another and coming out of the engagement way way ahead of where she was when she went in. The first risk was simply doing it at all, just at the time an awesome wave of publicity was cresting, but there was really no doubt that Patti was at least as good as her album, which is what most of the media attention had been focused on anyhow. The second was being her own opening act—telling jokes, answering questions, reading poetry, discussing her very predicament in being up there trying to entertain people without using music, reminding them that that was how she started, and wasn't it fun? Sometimes I held my breath, but in the end she handled it like an old pro. The third and possibly the riskiest risk was having a show broadcast over WNEW-FM Saturday night. One hundred minutes of **Patti Smith** was a heavy dose for a vast radio audience not very familiar with her performances, but Patti and her band kept the energy level so high that the result was absolutely electrifying. No doubt she made believers out of the curious on a grand scale. These are some of Patti's fans who came to the Bottom Line to see her: John Vaccaro, Mickey Ruskin, Peter Wolf and Faye Dunaway, David Mansfield, Lisa and Richard Robinson, John Paul Getty III, Annie Leibovitz, **Lou Reed,** James Wolcott, Bleecker Bob, **Hilly Kristal,** Scott Muni, Michael Narcisse Esteban and Speeding Lizzi Mercier, Bruce Springsteen, Tommy Ramone, **Richard Lloyd,** Gloria Stavers, David Jo Hansen and Cyrinda Foxx, Robert Mapplethorpe, Jann and

Jane Wenner, Susan Blond, Jon Landau and Richard Dreyfuss. Patti wore a Lion of Judah T-shirt, plugged *Rock Scene,* and **Television** sang "Jesse James" for the first time in years, wished Lenny Kaye a happy birthday, persuaded **John Cale** to join in on the encores, and behaved like a star. The band was amazing. Promoter Ron Delsner [sic] gave Patti a riding crop and a glass horse, and will present her in concert at Avery Fisher Hall during the last week in March—the date is not yet firm, so watch for the ads. This is not technically a review, so I've not been comprehensive—simply, it was a wonderful weekend and bodes well for everyone and everything concerned with it . . . *January 8:* The long awaited reunion of former Velvets **Lou Reed** and **John Cale** took place, portentously enough, on New Year's night at the Poetry Project's annual benefit in St. Mark's Church. First Lou was introduced, and he sang "Glory of Love," accompanying himself on guitar. Then John was announced, sat down at the piano and sang "I Keep a Close Watch," from his gorgeous new *Helen*

> "Rock & roll is trying to convince girls to pay money to be near you."
>
> —RICHARD HELL

*of Troy* album (which—astonishingly—his record company seems to have little intention of releasing in America). No one for a minute thought it was going to end there, and sure enough, with a very show-bizzy "Hey, Lou?," John persuaded his former partner to join him in one more song. A long tuning-up period provoked some signs of impatience from the audience, whereupon John pointed to the back of a long-haired person standing between him and Lou, and said angrily into the mike, "If only this fucking chick would sit down, we could get going." From all the poets seated on the stage, who could see that it was not a female that John had pointed to but a young man with a full beard, there came howls of laughter; for the ever-alert feminist fringe in the audience there came a barrage of boos, hisses, and small, old pieces of fruit. Amidst the pandemonium, Reed went over and joined Cale at the piano for a never-to-be-forgotten rendition of "Waiting for My Man." When it was over, he patted John on the head and quickly vanished. This was but one of many extraordinary highlights in an evening that I thought marked a turning point in the history of New York "underground" culture, not unrelated to **Patti Smith**'s shows at the Bottom Line the week before. For although it was an event ostensibly and actually devoted to the Spoken Word, it belonged as well to the musicians, singers, and dancers who participated, and was all the richer for encompassing such a spectrum of talent . . . Bravo to *Punk Magazine* and editor John Holmstrom for the astonishing **Lou Reed** interview in the first issue—nothing less than a new medium has been invented . . . *February 12:* **Patti Smith** is releasing "Gloria" as her first single . . . **John Cale** threw whipped cream at Lisa Robinson in Cleveland, so she dumped a banana cream pie on his head and then tossed a strawberry cheese cake at him. Robinson and Cale are said to be occasionally envious of the relationship that exists between Lester Bangs and Lou Reed . . . *March 11:* Violence erupted on the stage at CBGB Saturday night as **Wayne County,** who was performing, and "**Handsome" Dick Manitoba,** lead singer of the **Dictators**, engaged in a confrontation that left Manitoba with a fractured collarbone and a gash in his head requiring sixteen stitches. Your faithful reporter was there, so briefly here is what happened. Mr. County had finished his **Patti Smith** imitation and was in his Nearly-Naked drag when Manitoba appeared at the front of the stage, spitting at County and calling him a queer. County, infuriated, screamed at Manitoba to "get your fucking face out of my sight, you fat piece of shit." Manitoba, who is a prominent wrestler with a "tough" image, continued to taunt Wayne and moved forward. Wayne picked up the microphone stand and taking a step back into a corner, warned "Handsome Dick" to come no closer—when "Handsome" appeared to lunge, the southern transvestite underground superstar brought the bottom of the mike stand down on the macho lead singer's head. Then everybody fell down on the floor and thrashed around for a while until the combatants (there was about four at this point—it was hard to tell who was fighting and who was trying to break it up) were separated and Manitoba, all covered with blood, was rushed out of the club by his friends. Wayne went on to finish his set. The musicians in the crowd were universally shaken by the event, and though Manitoba had been heckling performers frequently at CBGB in the past few weeks, and had been "asking for it" according to some, no one likes the idea of trouble coming out of the audience with resultant bloodshed, no matter whose blood. And several of the more media-conscious musicians wondered if their reputations could ever survive being trashed by a drag queen at CBGB in front of just about everyone in town. Ominously (I haven't used that word since **Lou Reed** was stoned by fascists in Milan), ordinary members of the audience (that is, not musicians or members of bands) thought the fight was part of the act and/or seemed to enjoy it greatly. As Manitoba was being pulled from the fracas, two boys were stabbing their thumbs toward the floor shouting "Finish him off, Wayne!" while their girl friends giggled and beamed. This may be bigger than rollerball . . . *March 25:* The night after the bloody incident at CBGB, some goony looking characters came to Max's where Wayne is disquaire, saying they "want to talk to **Wayne County.**" Naturally, Wayne did not make himself available for this conversa-

·tion, and in fact cut and dyed his hair and pasted on a black mustache the very next morning. He had become "Eduardo," the new Max's disquaire, and was waiting to see what would happen next when the police telephoned him at home at five in the morning and said they had a warrant for his arrest on an assault charge, brought by the banged-up Dictator, **"Handsome" Dick Manitoba.** The police offered Wayne the choice of turning himself in, or waiting for them to come and get him. "We do it this way ever since the energy crisis," they explained. Wayne chose to surrender himself into their custody and went down to the station house, where he spent the entire day, from six-thirty in the morning to nine-thirty that night, behind bars. He says he was treated very courteously. That night, he was released without bail, and a hearing has been set for Wednesday, March 24. Next week you'll find out what happened in the hallowed halls, so do tune in . . . *April 1:* In the historic criminal proceedings against **Wayne County,** these are the latest developments: Hearings were held last Wednesday before a judge who listened to testimony from both sides and then reduced the charges from felony to misdemeanor level. Apparently, the story **"Manitoba"/Blum** told in court varied somewhat from the original account he gave to the police in an earlier affidavit. As he first related the incident, "Manitoba"/Blum was merely walking to the bathroom when Wayne attacked him. In the courtroom, however, he acknowledged putting one foot on the stage. County, on the other hand, is maintaining that "Manitoba"/Blum appeared to be on the verge of physically harming him when he (County) swung out with his mike stand and incapacitated the tubby tuffy. Mr. County is expected to plead "not guilty" as a trial by jury commences on April 26. Most observers on the CBGB scene (and one or two in the D.A.'s office as well) wonder why "Manitoba"/Blum is continuing to press charges, since the testimony of impartial witnesses tend to support County's account of what happened. County himself is appalled—"He picked a fight, lost it, then called the police. This has to be the lowest form of human behavior," says Wayne, whose legal fees are going to climb to several grand. Containing as it does so many marvelous theatrical elements—star vs. star, straight vs. screaming, audience member vs. performer, reality vs. illusion, unwelcome outsider vs. queen of the scene, music vs. show business, Saturday night at action central on the Bowery, violence, terror, blood, stitches and fractures, humiliation, disgrace, revenge, and a jury selection procedure that promises to be the stuff of which dreams are made—l'affaire County is beginning to attract the attention of the national media, from the music trades to the *Enquirer*. May all the players in the ensuing drama be true to their schools . . .

# Set List for the Ramones' First Live Performance

(At Performance Studio, New York City, March 30, 1974)

████████████████████████████

"I Don't Wanna Go Down in the Basement"

"I Don't Wanna Walk Around With You"

"Now I Wanna Sniff Some Glue"

"I Don't Wanna Be Learned, I Don't Wanna Be Tamed"

"I Don't Wanna Get Involved With You"

"I Don't Like Nobody That Don't Like Me"

"Succubus"

# Punk Then and Now

by Joey Ramone

One of punk rock's true believers, Joey Ramone has
spent two decades fronting New York punk institution
the Ramones.

When the Ramones started in the mid-seventies, we
were reacting against how bloated and serious and self-indulgent rock & roll
had become. We had grown up on Top Forty AM radio, and we fell in love
with the Beatles and the Rolling Stones and the Who and Little Richard and
Buddy Holly, and later we got into the Stooges and the MC5 and the New
York Dolls and Slade and T. Rex and Bowie and Mott the Hoople. For us,
rock & roll was magical and emotional and real. It was liberating and inspirational to us.

But by the mid-seventies, music was all about Emerson, Lake and Palmer
and corporate rock and "Disco Duck" and "Convoy" and "The Night Chicago
Died." There was no spirit left, no spark, no challenge, no fun, and so many
artists had become so full of themselves. We just weren't hearing any music
that we liked anymore, so we stripped it back down and put back the passion
and energy and emotion that were missing from the music we were hearing
at the time.

When the Ramones started, we didn't call what we were playing punk rock.
We just knew that we were playing an exciting new kind of rock & roll, and
eventually we were tagged punk rock by the press. We started playing at
CBGB's in New York, and in 1976 we went to London and were playing for
crowds of 3,000, and it seemed like everyone who came to our shows started
bands. I think we kind of turned the world on its head, but we didn't mean to.

34

We were just trying to make music that excited us. And since then, I think we've stuck to our guns and stayed true to our original ideals, and continued to make the kind of music that we found inspiring.

Over the last few years, the underground has become the mainstream, and bands like Metallica and the Red Hot Chili Peppers and Nirvana and Green Day and Offspring have taken the attitude that we started with and added their own individuality and uniqueness. It's nice when these bands come out and say that they were inspired by the Ramones.

I think that it's a healthy time for music in America now, because people are selling a lot of records with music that's creative and original. It feels like the kids are in charge again, instead of a bunch of old men dictating people's tastes, and that's good for rock & roll. To me, punk is about being an individual and going against the grain and standing up and saying "This is who I am." To me, John Lennon and Elvis Presley were punks, because they made music that evoked those emotions in people. And as long as people are making music that does that, punk rock is alive and well.

# My Introduction to Punk Rock

by Eric Ambel

After the indoctrination described below, Eric "Roscoe" Ambel returned to Wyoming and started that state's first punk-rock band, the Dirty Dogs, later known as the Accelerators, before moving to L.A. (where he became a founding member of Joan Jett's Blackhearts) and New York (where he hooked up with ex-Dictator Scott Kempner to form the Del-Lords). These days, he leads his own band, Roscoe's Gang, and produces records for the likes of the Bottle Rockets, the Blood Oranges, Blue Mountain, and the World Famous Blue Jays.

It happened in Chicago in 1976. I had been going to the University of Wyoming, but that semester my parents had sort of kicked me out of school. So I'm in Chicago working as a waiter and playing guitar in country bands on the weekends, but what I'm really trying to do is learn all these stupid Jeff Beck jazz licks. This is after *Blow by Blow,* when it felt like that was the direction music was going in, and it was really depressing me.

One day WXRT, the cool station in Chicago, was giving away tickets for these two bands I'd never heard of, the Ramones and the Dictators. I called up and won the tickets, and my friend Johan and I each ate two grams of hash, and we went to the show. We're watching the Dictators, and I'm thinking "Wow, this is pretty great, we're not in a stadium, and these guys are playin' their own songs." The Dictators were kinda cool, but the Ramones had it down to something like a beautiful one-act play.

I'm starting to get high off the hash, and the Ramones are playing, and I nudge Johan and say "Do you smell that? Is that what I think it is?" And he says "Yeah, I think it is. How could it be?" Now, how can I put this nicely? . . . It was the smell of female. I looked around, and right next to us I see a girl with a kind of hippie skirt on, with one leg up, responding to the fast and furious pace of the Ramones' jackhammer attack in the most base and beautiful way imaginable.

Eventually we realized that the smell was too strong to be from just this one woman. So I started walking around, and within twenty feet from where we were, I counted another *seven* women doing this. It was at that moment when I realized that *this* was rock & roll. *This* was real music that had real power over people, to the point that they were masturbating in public to it. When I saw how the music of the Ramones affected these women, my choice was made. As for the whole Jeff Beck thing, I was off the hook.

Years later I told this story to some people in Chicago, and it turns out that there was actually an organized group of women called the Candle Club that would go to the early punk-rock shows and participate and respond.

Anyway, that was the major turning point in my musical development. At that moment, before anyone ever explained that this was punk rock, to me this was rock & roll. Later on, when they started calling it punk rock and pigeonholing it as this whole weird thing, I always knew that it wasn't just a fringe of rock & roll. It *was* rock & roll.

# $\mathcal{J}$ust Call Me
# a Punk Rock
# Renaissance Man

## by Glenn Morrow

Glenn Morrow is currently coowner/operator of the
Hoboken, N.J.–based Bar/None label, and previously did
all the stuff mentioned below.

**W**hat lead me to dive into the indie rock underground?
Maybe it was riding in a white Cadillac convertible as a runaway teenager in
1973 and hearing Lou Reed singing "Walk on the Wild Side."

Or maybe it was hearing another amazing song on the radio in '76 and
hearing the DJ announce, "I don't know about you, but that's about the worst
garbage I've ever heard." That song was the Sex Pistols' "Anarchy in the
UK," and we knew at that moment that a huge chasm had just opened between everything we had once known and the great wide sea of possibilities
that Patti Smith had been telling us about.

Or maybe it was running down Bleecker Street in the rain on my way to
CBGB's to see a double bill of Television and Mong and thinking, "Yeah this
is it, this is where I belong."

As I write this, it's been eighteen years since that dash down Bleecker
Street and I still like being in CBGB's. I'm glad that it's survived, along with
Maxwell's in Hoboken, the Cat's Cradle in Chapel Hill, the Uptown and Sev-
enth St. Entry in Minneapolis, and all the other clubs that have kept the cross-
pollinating breeding ground of indie rock alive.

When I first started hanging at CBGB's, the music had no name. When I
first heard the term "punk rock," I didn't know the historical context that
dated back to the mid-sixties and defined American groups playing a version
of Stones-Yardbirds R&B filtered through a psychedelic scrim. Sixties punk

was music made by (mostly white) kids who couldn't play all that well but played with a passion and a desire to be a little more dangerous than their classmates. They also probably saw themselves as innovators, if only for the alternative lifestyle they wanted to be part of.

In that CBGB's scene I saw all these new aesthetic principles, or at least a new stance that flew in the face of mainstream seventies rock. Short tight songs, no extra fat or gratuitous solos. Clothing that was utilitarian, no hippie long hair and an appreciation for sixties punk style. In fact, the clothing of that period was a definite nod to the early Stones. Black jeans, Beatle boots, mod sweaters, wraparound shades, Richard Lloyd's red jacket a la James Dean. Most of the early CBGB bands covered sixties punk tunes like the Troggs "I Can't Control Myself" (Talking Heads), the Count Five's "Psychotic Reaction" (Television) and the Kinks "Tired of Waiting for You" (just about everybody else).

By 1977, the amount of dunderhead music that fell under the punk banner— and is now long forgotten—pretty much dwarfed the rest of the CBGB scene. It pissed me off that suburban kids were seizing on the safety-pin three-chord lobotomy schtick and missing all that great stuff like Talking Heads, Television, Patti Smith, etc. At least that's how it appeared to me at the time. Now seventeen years later it's clear who the most important and influential band of that period was: the Ramones. Their records sound as fresh today as the day they were cut. The Ramones seized and honed the essence of rock & roll; it was intelligent and stupid at the same time, with songs built to last.

CBGB's seemed to be the place where I had the most transcendent rock experiences: Television levitating the whole club during "Marquee Moon." Talking Heads reinventing the notion of how a band was supposed to look and act onstage while turning the pop song into a series of funky art-damaged perfect moments. . . .

Years later it would be the Replacements, whose board tapes from CBGB's circa '83 are still some of my favorite things to listen to. You can hear them surfing thru the blessed oblivion of alcohol, testosterone, youth, and Westerberg's wounded soul. Hearing "Unsatisfied" for the first time, you just knew you were in the presence of something great even if the world didn't know it yet: And Paul was just making up the lyrics as he went along. My favorites were some that he threw into the middle of the never-released "You're Getting Married" after he felt he had been rude to my wife, Elizabeth, the previous evening at Maxwell's when he turned down her request for the DeFranco Family's "Heartbeat, It's a Love Beat": "I hope he brings his wife down 'cause I didn't mean to be a jerk/I'm sorry if I was but that's my line of work."

And, oh yeah, watching the Butthole Surfers create the most ungodly throbbing jams with their two drummers (was one of them naked?). The air in the joint was so thick you could sense a kind of communal terror. Eventually people started passing chairs head over head up, and out to the back of the club, almost catching on the long line of neon beer signs hung from the ceiling.

And there was Big Black, harder, heavier and more precisely pummeling than anything I'd ever heard, but somehow redemptive and uplifting all the same.

My fandom initially lead me in two directions: rock critic and performer. The original fantasy of playing music had been simmering all through high school, but somewhere in college I got the nerve to get up and perform in front of an audience. As soon as I learned a third chord I started writing songs. As soon as I read a little Kerouac, I wanted to write the great American novel. So while I banged away on a typewriter at pumping a precious stream of unconsciousness, I was also learning to play the guitar.

After playing (mainly songs from Bob Dylan's *Blood on the Tracks*) a coffeehouse in the basement of Gorham Hall at the University of Rhode Island, I walked out behind the dorm, lay down in the grass by a small pond and, almost for the first time in my life, decided that I was feeling some kinda pure joy. I dug this feeling and would do whatever it took to get to that place again. Which meant figuring out how to get in a band.

Perhaps the next best rush I had back then was when Alan Betrock, editor of *New York Rocker,* sent me a note saying he liked the writing I'd done for a small New Jersey newspaper and inviting me to write for his magazine. That was it, I had made it. I had been accepted by the group of people I most wanted as my peers. Even though it paid nothing, it made me hold out hope that there was more to life than the legal proofreading job that a temp agency was suggesting should be my postcollege fate.

I soon found my way into the *New York Rocker* fold, initially as a freelancer writing about TV Toy, the dB's, the Feelies and Mission of Burma. Later I'd have the dual job of Advertising Director and Managing Editor, a separation of church and state I succeeded in carrying out by assuming the alternate identity of Greg McLean, a holier than thou rock critic with far more integrity than the ad director. Under the watchful editing of Andy Schwartz, Greg McLean could take on the music industry by attacking all the lame new-wave bands the majors were signing at the time (anybody remember the Elevators or Laurie and the Sighs?). McLean's article "Corporate Rock: It's Better to Churn Out Than to Pave the Way," even elicited a concerned reply from Joe Smith, then-president of Elektra/Asylum. Meanwhile ad director Glenn Morrow would bring in the dollars to hawk the aforementioned lame major-label bands and not miss a wink of sleep.

We were loving it. A cult culture was forming and we were the center of our very own universe. I remember looking out the office window one day down onto Fifth Avenue and seeing Steve Almaas of Minneapolis' Suicide

Commandos pulling up outside with a U-Haul trailer on the back of his station wagon, looking like a wagon train coming east to be part of this tribe that was going to make the new music that we knew the world needed (even if they didn't want it).

I also crashed at the *New York Rocker* office for a while, after breaking up with the woman I'd been living with for about four years. I had to fight Byron Coley for the couch, which was preferable to the La-Z-Boy recliner someone had dragged up off the street. Byron had shown up at the office one morning with a Colt 45 tallboy in his hand and never left. A larger-than-life figure, he was christened "Boy House" on the masthead. He always kept four pairs of neatly folded blue jeans in his office drawer and would stay up all night cross-referencing the early issues of *Crawdaddy*. Eventually I was rescued by Lester Bangs, who let me crash at his Fourteenth Street apartment while he recorded his *Jook Savages on the Brazos* album in Texas. But for quite a while the *Rocker* office was the center of my own personal universe. I made love there, fell in love there and ultimately married the art director.

My first real band was named "a," after the Andy Warhol book. It didn't look like much in print ads, but we thought it was cool, and we'd be the first album in every record store and automatically get our own bin card. My peak experience with that group was our first show. We'd been rehearsing in the basement forever, and suddenly I'm onstage no longer facing the other musicians in a circle. I felt funny, like I didn't quite know how to behave. So I did what felt right, which meant lurching around the stage and twitching spasmodically. It scared the shit out of my band mates, but it was a look and a feel that I would continue to develop. If the rhythmic body spasm somehow mirrored the music, and felt right, I would go for it. I didn't care how stupid I looked (fortunately, in those days video cameras were far less common than they are now, so I had and still have no idea how stupid I might have looked).

My ultimate rock & roll rush was so intense I think I was completely disconnected from it. My second band, the Individuals, was playing the Ritz in New York. When we hit the stage, I suddenly felt like I was on some weird drug. My legs were wobbling, I felt as if I was being swept away. It wasn't really pleasurable, but it felt like the music was carrying me and I was going down these rapids just trying to keep my head above water. I don't remember much else, but it must have been an exceptional show. Afterwards three women propositioned me, a number of critics came by to tell us we were great, and a young girl descended the spiral staircase from my dressing room kissing me quickly and saying, "Your music really moved me, it made me want to dance. My name is . . . Madonna." Perhaps the truly great performers get to that place on a fairly regular basis, but I never got quite that out of my head again on stage. But for that one night I was hot, I was young, and I had the city's finest movin' and groovin'.

I did meet Madonna a couple more times. We both rehearsed in the same place, the Music Building, on Eighth Avenue. She asked me to try to write songs with her. I kinda brushed her off. A year later I was working in a hot dog joint listening to the first Madonna album and kicking myself over and over again. I took that job in the hot dog stand when I had realized trying to make it on a musician's wages alone was starting to compromise my sense of art, fun, and integrity.

At the time, the Individuals were local stars with an airplay hit on Long Island's WLIR, "Dancing With My Eighty Wives." Meanwhile in D.C., our song "Walk By Your House" was breaking on WHFS. This gave us more clout on the scene; we could regularly pull in over a grand a night playing new-wave discos. The most money I ever made was playing a sweet-sixteen party for a mall developer's daughter at their mansion on Long Island. It was a pool party and we were set up right next to the pool. As soon as we started playing, these sixteen-year-olds began running in front of us and diving into the pool. It was weird; the band was making more money than ever, but the experience was totally humiliating to a sensitive young artist who expected the kids to pay attention. I decided I didn't want to go down that road while we waited for a major label to sign us and make us stars.

So every morning, with Madonna cooing in my ear, I'd make the chili. Then in the afternoon, I'd write quickie rock books under the pen name Gordon Matthews. Unlike the aforementioned holier-than-thou Greg McLean, Gordon Matthews would do anything for a buck, hence a series of tomes on the likes of Michael Jackson, Prince, and Van Halen (David Letterman once held up a copy of *Everything You Want to Know About Van Halen* while interviewing David Lee Roth and actually quoting from my text!).

With funding from Gordon Matthews—whose career timing was so sharp that he'd managed to sell over 100,000 copies of his Michael Jackson book when *Thriller* hit—I recorded an album with my third band, Rage to Live. This was the beginning of my transition to my last and most comfortable hat, that of a music-biz professional, or more specifically coowner/operator of Bar/None Records.

Rage to Live included some killer musicians and we had fun when we played. We didn't have to rehearse too much and there was no horrible tension between the players. It probably helped that I had diminished expectations of what I wanted from being in a band; I wanted to have fun, and if it was not fun I did not want to do it. But one night onstage at CBGB's, I felt an intense antibuzz. It hit me that I was up there pouring my heart out, splaying myself in front of this audience, and maybe they didn't care that much and maybe I was questioning why I felt the need to go through such humiliation. These are not the kind of questions a performer should be asking himself if he wants to be a performer. I guess that was when I knew that phase of my life was over, cause you really have to *need* to do that to yourself, and I didn't anymore.

Touring wore thin. Life on the road exists outside of time and everyone you come in contact with is there to interact with you. This is obviously ego-gratifying at first, but after a while the unreality sets in. People know you or think they know you, and yet you do not know them. Bands are magnets for loser drug-dealing types, and eventually your friends get pushed aside for the strong-arming sycophants that can quickly become your inner circle. You look up one day and all the real people are gone.

My personal theory is that one generally hits his or her peak as a per-former/artist at age twenty-five. This is when you've been honing your craft long enough to have digested your influences but aren't so jaded and road weary to have lost that initial creative spark. From twenty-five on, it's a bit of a slow road down if you haven't paced yourself. The bohemian lifestyle that's so appealing in the early twenties begins to lose its allure and one's drug and alcohol dependencies begin to catch up and take hold. For those who haven't "made it," drugs and alcohol can help create the illusion that something is re-ally happening. Many of the bands that made up the early New York scene have had to face up to some level of detoxing. Too much too soon and all that, but it was fun.

Rage to Live was the first band to be signed to Bar/None Records. The owner/operator was an old friend, Tommy Prendergast. Tom had come over from Ireland in the late seventies, got a job as a bartender at Maxwell's, saved some money and started Pier Platters (then as now one of the East Coast's finest record stores) with partners Bill Ryan and Steve Fallon. At the time, Steve was running Maxwell's, and he and Bill had their label, Coyote, which put out albums by the Feelies, the Neats, Dreams So Real, Chris Stamey, and Yo La Tengo. Tom wanted in on the indie-rock action and offered to put out the first Rage to Live album.

Meanwhile, I had been building some record-biz experience, beginning with the soon-to-be-defunct independent label Plexus, which had released the Individuals' album but had no promotion staff. I was given a desk, where I helped set up distribution, called radio stations and so on. This was in the early days of indie rock, when the underground industry network that exists today was still being built.

I knew that I dug the business, but I had managed to get my ass fired from a number of music-biz jobs. Shortly after Tom put out my album, I gently broke the news to him that it was doubtful Rage to Live was ever going to go on the road to promote the album he'd just paid to put out. I told him this just after he'd paid for us to make a video. I did, however, offer to become his fifty-fifty partner. I had just found this band called They Might Be Giants that I thought we should sign.

They Might Be Giants sold about 10,000 copies the first year we had them, but then their second video, "Don't Let's Start," miraculously broke through on MTV in 1987. It was a great way to start a label, and we thought we could do it again, but it would take a while. We signed up the Ordinaires, a nine-piece instrumental group. Bill Drummond's album, *The Man,* sold about a thousand copies—right artist, wrong record. He would go on to form the KLF and sell platinum. Shrimp Boat didn't sell too well, though they made re-markable music and their drummer went on to produce and play with Liz Phair. We also put out records by Yo La Tengo, Freedy Johnston, Tindersticks, Ben Vaughn, and Esquivel.

I think that this is the most comfortable hat I've found. I always knew the business side of things was the best place for me, mainly because I liked be-ing involved in all aspects of making records. I know my way around a stu-dio, but I hate talking about gear, and I don't have enough of an attention span to get a really good drum sound. I enjoy playing, but the road has lost its al-lure.

So I will be the puppet master, dream merchant, and provider of fantasy, and hopefully I can lead a few brave men and women into an exciting career in the pop-music field. "Rock & roll is a harsh mattress on someone's floor you barely know in some godforsaken town where only seven people showed." (I wrote that once). But where else can you make a living (maybe) getting up onstage and opening up your heart for the rest of the world to see?

At Bar/None we have a punk rock cover band called Wunderbra. We try to take one long lunch break a week and play forgotten gems like "Sex Beat" by the Gun Club, "Academy Fight Song" by Mission of Burma and "Gear Mesh Fox" by Guided by Voices—all great songs that I wish I'd written myself. I feel like the Pete Seeger of punk rock, keeping the music alive to pass down to the next generation.

We were part of a revolution. We were the scene, and that scene continues wherever four kids decide they want to make a little racket and maybe feel a little bit less alienated, and even though they probably know they're not that good they're gonna play anyway even if in their heart of hearts they know they're not gonna be big stars. Yeah, it goes like this, aww, watch me now . . .

# The Top Ten Seventies Power Pop Albums

## (in alphabetical order)

by Jordan Oakes

St. Louis—based Jordan Oakes publishes *Yellow Pills*, "the world's only power-pop 'zine" and has assembled a series of compilation albums bearing the same name.

**Artful Dodger,** *Artful Dodger*, **1975.**
With frontman Billy Paliselli's Rod Stewartesque wail and a sound that merged Brit-Invasion melodicism with AOR punch, the Cleveland (via Virginia) combo was a prime example of unpretentious seventies heartland rock.

**Badfinger,** *Wish You Were Here*, **1974.**
Containing none of their hit singles, this album is an underappreciated gem—it maintains a Beatlesque splendor from start to finish and includes "Dennis," one of the most perfect pop songs in existence.

**Big Star,** *#1 Record*, **1972.**
This seminal classic might be mistaken for a lost Byrds album if not for the undercurrent of dark aggression that keeps it from getting precious. Ill-fated coleader Chris Bell's influence is very much in evidence here, his collaborations with Alex Chilton revealing an unexpected compatibility rather than a Lennon/McCartney tension.

**Big Star,** *Radio City*, **1974.**
While their debut spotlighted straight-ahead songcraft that even a CSN fan could appreciate, the even catchier *Radio City* (recorded after Chris Bell's departure) was as quirky as a poker cheat. The accessibly crafted songs hint at under-the-surface strangeness enriching the tunes' emotional depth.

**Blue Ash,** *No More, No Less,* **1977.**
From Raspberries country came this crunchy outfit, not unlike the group's aforementioned contemporaries (minus the Eric Carmen syrup factor).

**Grin,** *1 + 1,* **1972.**
After his original liaison with Neil Young and prior to his solo career and stint as a Springsteen sideman, Nils Lofgren led this snappy combo. They offered a viable alternative to the prevailing pomposity of seventies rock with an engaging mix of British-invasion pop and rootsy folk rock, based around Lofgren's songwriting and guitar heroics. With a side of hard, raunchy pop songs and a side of dreamy ballads, *1 + 1* is a classic that's more than the sum of its parts.

**Raspberries,** *Raspberries' Best,* **1976.**
At their best, Eric Carmen and his band of Cleveland garage vets drew from the classics (Beatles, Beach Boys, et al.) to create works of surging, near-orchestral melodicism that often measured up to the work of their historical forbears. Since none of their individual albums is particularly consistent, this compilation is the best way to appreciate the group. The first four songs on side one tie for the honor of Greatest Raspberries Hit.

**Emitt Rhodes,** *Emitt Rhodes,* **1971.**
Rhodes came on like a more studious McCartney. And since he did all the voices and instruments himself, there was no need for a Linda.

**Stories,** *About Us,* **1973.**
Since they had ex-Left Banke baroque-pop mastermind Michael Brown's gorgeous tunes to work with, Stories (also featuring sandpapery vocalist Ian Lloyd) had a head start from the get-go. The irony was that the band's only major hit turned out to be the R&B-style miscegenation ballad "Brother Louie," written by Hot Chocolate leader Errol Brown (no relation).

**Dwight Twilley Band,** *Twilley Don't Mind,* **1977.**
Talented Oklahoman Dwight Twilley and his late partner, Phil Seymour, show what happens when two unreconstructed Beatleholics mix in a little Presleyesque swagger. Overflowing with poignant melodies, perfectly blended harmonies, and multiple layers of guitar jangle, the pair delivered a masterpiece of energy, mystery and heartbreak.

# . . . And the Top Ten Postpunk Power Pop Albums

![black bar]

**The Bongos,** *Drums Along the Hudson,* **1982.**
The debut LP by this Hoboken foursome went where no pop album had gone before. Away from the beach, cars, and girls, it heads tunefully into the urban abyss, where Richard Barone's catchily jittery Beatlesque folk-rock tunes hint at images of darkness and danger.

**Cheap Trick,** *In Color,* **1977.**
These cartoonishly clad idols made pop heavy and metal pretty, and their timelessly accessible approach yielded some memorable songs, many of which are featured on this consistently wonderful disc.

**Marshall Crenshaw,** *Marshall Crenshaw,* **1982.**
The New York-via-Michigan tunesmith's auspicious debut eschewed new wave's fashionable nihilism in favor of the timeless romance of vintage Top Forty radio. Mixing the subversively clean-cut tunefulness of the Beatles, the Everly Brothers, and Buddy Holly with a Spectoresque sensibility, Crenshaw traces all-American guitar pop back to its sturdiest roots.

**The dB's,** *Stands for Decibels,* **1981.**
A near-perfect pop record, its only possible flaw (if you consider it a flaw) being a personalized quirkiness that probably put off pop purists. Mainmen Peter Holsapple and Chris Stamey came on like a nerdy Lennon and McCartney, wallowing in romantic frustrations with a vintage whine.

**The Loud Family,** *Plants and Birds and Rocks and Things,* **1993.**
Former Game Theory leader Scott Miller's off-center genius didn't skip a beat as he transferred his unique perspective to his new group, whose muscular musicality gave his hook-intensive tunes the sonic clout to make them knockouts.

**Material Issue,** *Freak City Soundtrack,* **1994.**

Jim Ellison's catchily in-your-face tunes power this lean, mean Chicago trio, which here found its perfect producer in glam survivor Mike Chapman. Numbers like "Goin' Through Your Purse" and "Help Me Land" suggested an unholy alliance of the Sweet, Cheap Trick, and AC/DC.

**The Plimsouls,** *The Plimsouls,* **1981.**

While this much-loved L.A. quartet's debut doesn't include their defining near-hit "A Million Miles Away," singer/songwriter Peter Case and co. deliver a grittily melodic gem that suggests the Flamin' Groovies gone new wave.

**The Records,** *The Records,* **1979.**

These London-based, jangly craftsmen's debut (released in slightly different form in the U.K. as *Shades in Bed*) isn't brilliant all the way through, but with tunes as wittily infectious as "Teenarama," "Affection Rejected," and the mighty "Starry Eyes," it more than holds its own against any new wave album of its era.

**Shoes,** *Tongue Twister,* **1981.**

Earlier efforts by Zion, Illinois's finest may have contained higher highs, but this release, their third full-blown LP, is their most consistently perfect work.

**20/20,** *20/20,* **1980.**

Originally hailing from Oklahoma but based in L.A., this quartet got it absolutely right on their first try. With boyishly Beatlesque vocals, darkly intense songs and a vague rockabilly undercurrent, 20/20 debuted with a perfect balance of vision and craft.

# The Ten Most Important Hardcore Bands, Then and Now

## by Jim Testa

Jim Testa is editor and publisher of *Jersey Beat*, a fanzine he describes as "an ongoing excursion through the punk-rock underground, with occasional detours into the mainstream." He experienced his first mosh pit in 1982 and has been ducking ever since.

In the beginning (and, just for the sake of argument, let's begin at 1975) there was punk, as exemplified by the eclectic, groundbreaking and altogether breathtaking array of talent that emerged in New York City—the Ramones, Blondie, Television, and Talking Heads, among others. These bands had little in common musically beyond a raw honesty and a desire to strip away the artifice and pomposity of seventies arena rock. Rather than simply rejecting the mainstream rock world, these groups sought to reinvent it in their own image.

What punk rock suggested—and the message its bands sent to a thousand garages and practice spaces across the country—was that it was possible to produce viable rock & roll outside the mainstream, to ignore the bloated consumerist culture that produced *Frampton Comes Alive* and *Saturday Night Fever*. Sure enough, within a few years, a new generation of bands began to emerge, bands who were younger, louder, faster, and infinitely more pissed off than their older brothers and sisters in punk rock.

This new music—which first sprang to life in the late seventies and was in full flower by the time the eighties dawned—fed off the frustrations and runamuck emotions of adolescence. They called it hardcore, and it became the soundtrack to a new youth subculture, a never-never land without grownups or grownup rules, where you could get away with anything—including beating one another up—without mom or dad looking over your shoulder. The hardcore kids didn't want any part of corporately owned record labels, stadiums, or mainstream radio. Their rallying cry was "Do It Yourself," so bands formed their own labels, organized their own shows and published their own fanzines to carry the word from city to city.

Today hardcore has become an accepted—and, not incidentally, commercially exploitable—part of mainstream American culture. Nowadays it's commonplace to go to a rock show—even one in an arena—and encounter a mosh pit full of reckless daredevils tossing themselves around like crash-test dummies. Bands like Green Day and the Offspring—who once toured the country in small vans, playing all-ages basement gigs for audiences often numbering in the double digits—now fill arenas and sell millions of albums. And that skein of indie labels, makeshift venues, and homemade fanzines has grown into a vital national network that allows even the rawest young band with nothing more to its credit than a humble self-released seven-inch single to tour the country. Here is a list of ten bands that helped make the current punk explosion possible, followed by ten more who are keeping the hardcore tradition alive today.

# Hardcore Then . . .

**1. Minor Threat.**   Led by the charismatic Ian MacKaye, who first articulated the no-drugs, no-drinking philosophy known as straight-edge, Washington, D.C.'s Minor Threat epitomized the rapid-fire emotional assault of early hardcore while helping to define its DIY philosophy. Dischord Records, founded by MacKaye and drummer Jeff Nelson to release Minor Threat's early singles, has since grown into one of the most influential and successful independent labels in America, launching such notable bands as Dag Nasty, Soulside, Jawbox, and MacKaye's current group, Fugazi. Essential listening: *The Complete Minor Threat* (Dischord).

**2. Misfits.**   The Misfits, who grew up in the industrial wasteland of suburban New Jersey, began with a simple concept—combining the anthemic three-chord punk of the Ramones with the trashy horror graphics of comic books and horror movies—and turned it into an enduring legacy. Lead singer Glenn Danzig continued to refine the formula through the sinister goth-metal of Samhain, and currently reigns as the barrel-chested leader of the popular death-metal group Danzig. Essential listening: *Misfits* (Plan 9/Caroline), *Walk Among Us* (Ruby/Slash).

**3. Black Flag.** Arguably America's first hardcore band, Black Flag's enduring contributions cannot be overstated. The Los Angeles-based group gave us seething, bare-chested, tattooed frontman Henry Rollins, who has since become the preeminent media icon of nineties punk, not to mention guitarist Greg Ginn's influential SST label, which in the eighties released seminal work by such crucial combos as Hüsker Dü, the Minutemen, the Meat Puppets, and Sonic Youth. Just as important, though, was the fact that Black Flag was one of the first hardcore groups to tour beyond its regional base, thereby spreading the DIY doctrine to small towns and cities across America. Essential listening: *Damaged* (SST), *Wasted . . . Again* (SST).

**4. Dead Kennedys.** One of the most political of all American hardcore bands, San Francisco's Dead Kennedys tackled issues as far-ranging as U.S. military intervention ("Holiday in Cambodia"), the new age politics of then-governor Jerry Brown ("California Über Alles") and rock & roll self-immolation (their deadpan take of Elvis Presley's "Viva Las Vegas"), while helping to found the East Bay punk scene. Singer Jello Biafra remains one of punk's most articulate provocateur spokesmen, and his Alternative Tentacles label still provides a valuable forum for both dissidents and dissonance. Essential listening: *Fresh Fruit for Rotting Vegetables* (I.R.S.), *Bedtime for Democracy* (Alternative Tentacles).

**5. Agnostic Front.** The undisputed leaders of New York's hardcore scene for much of the eighties, Agnostic Front brought a flag-waving, right-wing polemical stance to punk, in sharp contrast to the anarchist ravings of the L.A. scene or the personal politics of the D.C. corps. Agnostic Front's anthems for scene unity often stood in sharp contrast to the bloody, violent mosh pits they inspired. Essential listening: *Live at CBGB* (In-Effect/Relativity).

**6. Hüsker Dü.** The banshee guitar and psychotic vocal wail of burly frontman Bob Mould, coupled with the catchier, more melodic sensibility of drummer Grant Hart, made this Minneapolis trio a double-barreled threat. While the threesome's earliest recordings (on the DIY labels New Alliance and Reflex) set the standard for bracing 100-MPH hardcore, the Hüskers' later, more sophisticated albums for SST rank among alternative rock's most influential recordings. Essential listening: *Everything Falls Apart* (Reflex), *Metal Circus* (Reflex/SST).

**7. Dave Smalley/DYS.** Boston's DYS brought the D.C. straight-edge message to New England, thanks to transplanted Virginian Dave Smalley. Though DYS only recorded two forgettable albums, both long out-of-print, the group's image—hooded sweatshirts, sweatpants tucked in at the calf, and a sweaty, testosterone-heavy athleticism—defined straight-edge style, enormously influencing subsequent, more popular groups like Youth of Today, Bold, and Gorilla Biscuits. Smalley would continue to be an important figure in the punk world, fronting such seminal combos as D.C.'s Dag Nasty (which also included Minor Threat guitarist Brian Baker), L.A.'s All (with three quarters of the Descendents, forerunners of the more melodically oriented pop-core movement) and, most recently, Down by Law. Essential listening: Dag Nasty's *Can I Say* (Dischord), Down by Law's *Punkrockacademyfightsong* (Epitaph).

**8. SSD.** The most important hardcore band to emerge from New England. Like DYS, SSD were disciples of straight-edge—and one of the earliest hardcore groups to make the transition to a more heavy metal-oriented sound. Essential listening: *Break It Up* (Homestead).

**9. Bad Brains.** The Bad Brains began their musical odyssey as gifted jazzbos from the suburbs of Washington, D.C., but soon moved on to carve out a revolutionary blend of lightning-fast speed metal and slinky, syncopated reggae rhythms. The impressive physical presence of lead singer H.R., coupled with the free-ranging guitar assault of Dr. Know (Gary Miller), made the Bad Brains one of punk's most eclectic, electrifying, and durable bands, as well as one of the few African-American groups to make a mark in the predominantly white enclave of hardcore. Essential listening: *I Against I* (SST), *The Youth Are Getting Restless* (Caroline).

**10. Minutemen.** Most hardcore bands simply sped up rock & roll's standard verse/chorus/verse structure. But this uniquely gifted trio from the backwater town of San Pedro, California, virtually reinvented punk, incorporating jazz and funk influences while creating their own free-form style. Many Minutemen songs clocked in at under two minutes (hence the band's name), their only unifying thread being the band's humanist politics and their try-anything embrace of eccentricity. The group's career ended prematurely with the 1985 death of singer/guitarist D. Boon, but bassist Mike Watt and drummer George Hurley continued the Minutemen's freewheeling legacy into the Nineties with fIREHOSE. Essential listening: *Double Nickels on the Dime* (SST), *3-Way Tie for Last* (SST).

# And Now . . .

**1. Fugazi.** Virtually a synonym for punk integrity and commitment, Fugazi continue to record for their own Dischord label and play only low-priced, all-ages shows, long after achieving the sort of popularity that would have goaded other bands to pursue the major-label brass ring and distance themselves from the DIY scene. More importantly, though, ex-Minor Threat frontman Ian MacKaye and former Rites of Spring guitarist Guy Picciotto continue to create music that burns with conviction and seethes with rage, trading the breakneck speed of their early bands for fractured rhythms and anguished vocals. Essential listening: *13 Songs* (Dischord), *Repeater* (Dischord).

**2. Bad Religion.** These L.A. veterans (who released their first album in 1982) have mined an aggressive, melodic, and fiercely intelligent brand of hardcore that's been echoed by a number of young bands who record for Epitaph, the label that guitarist Brett Gurewitz created to release Bad Religion's early recordings. In 1993 the band left Epitaph for a major-label deal and Gurewitz quit the band to concentrate on running Epitaph, which has blossomed into a thriving example of DIY entrepreneurship. Essential listening: *No Control* (Epitaph), *Stranger Than Fiction* (Atlantic).

**3. Sick of It All.** One of the few current bands who remain loyal to the "Old School" style of NYC hardcore, Sick of It All meld punishing metal riffs to angry lyrics tackling social ills and street justice. Brothers Lou and Pete Koller were joined in the band's most recent incarnation by ex-Agnostic Front bassist Craig Setari. Essential listening: *Just Look Around* (In-Effect/Relativity), *Scratch the Surface* (EastWest).

**4. Shelter.** As the guiding force of the Connecticut (later New York) straight-edge group Youth of Today, the charismatic Ray Cappo and guitarist John Porcell wielded considerable influence, refashioning New York's mid-eighties hardcore scene in their own image. Porcell went on to form Judge while Cappo subsequently converted to the fringe religious cult of Hare Krishna (which also claimed other members of the early-eighties NYC hardcore scene) and continued playing the same aggressive style of moshcore in Shelter, replacing his old straight-edge and posi-core sloganeering with Krishna consciousness. Essential listening: Youth of Today's *We're Not in This Alone* (Caroline), Shelter's *Attaining the Supreme* (Reveleation).

**5. Bikini Kill.** Hardcore had always been an exclusive boys' club until a group of angry, articulate young women from the Pacific Northwest began to make their voices heard. With an agenda that included traditional feminist concerns as well as a more aggressive call for female empowerment, the "riot grrrls" (as they came to be known) staked out their own turf in the hardcore scene. Bikini Kill, fronted by the outspoken Kathleen Hanna, helped found the movement and provide some of the genre's most impassioned music. Essential listening: *Bikini Kill* EP (Kill Rock Stars).

**6. 7 Seconds.** Originally from the desert resort town of Reno, Nevada, 7 Seconds continue to fight the good fight, recording for independent labels and touring midsized venues, playing energetic, positively themed punk rock with a melodic bent. Lead singer Kevin Seconds (né Marvelli) may be the band's only remaining original member, but 7 Seconds has never lost its reputation as a terrific live act. Essential listening: *Walk Together, Rock Together* (Better Youth Organization), *New Wind* (Better Youth Organization).

**7. Drive Like Jehu.**    This talented group not only spearheads the burgeoning San Diego punk scene, but is helping to change the complexion of hardcore with exquisitely rendered nine-minute compositions whose convoluted arrangements and intricate rhythms defy the conventions of punk songwriting. Essential listening: *Drive Like Jehu* (Headhunter/Cargo), *Yank Crime* (Interscope).

**8. Operation Ivy/Rancid.**    If any band can claim to have helped change the face of hardcore from a scowl to a smile, it was Operation Ivy, the Berkeley-based combo whose slap-happy, upbeat ska-inflected punk tunes helped put the Lookout! label (which would later sign and release two albums by the Operation Ivy-influenced Green Day) on the map. Operation Ivy members Matt Freeman and Tim Armstrong later formed Rancid, whose bouncy, up-tempo tunes continue in the Op Ivy tradition. Essential listening: Operation Ivy's *Energy* (Lookout!), Rancid's *Let's Go* (Epitaph).

**9. All.**    When Descendents lead singer Milo Aukerman decided he would rather pursue a graduate degree in botany instead of a postgraduate degree in punk rock, the rest of his band formed All, named after the title of the Descendents' last album. Dedicated in equal parts to catchy pop tunes and drummer/songwriter Bill Stevenson's fondness for quirky album concepts, All has continued to tour incessantly and record its simple, tuneful songs with a succession of lead singers (including the aforementioned Dave Smalley). Essential listening: *Allroy Sez . . .* (Cruz), *Allroy for Prez* EP (Cruz).

**10. Green Day.**    Long before Green Day made platinum-punk history with the massive sales of the *Dookie* album and high-profile appearances at Lollapalooza '94 and Woodstock II, the Berkeley trio redefined the sound of hardcore by eschewing metallic riffage in favor of happy, hummable songs about girls and growing up. Essential listening: *1039/Smoothed Out Slappy Hours* (Lookout!), *Kerplunk* (Lookout!).

"I write a lot about being a loser because I was conditioned to think that way. I was brainwashed to think that I was nothing compared to those people who are so-called geniuses that were teaching me this crap. So I was like, 'Okay, that'll be my art form: being a fucking idiot, being a loser.' And I'm going to do it the best way I possibly can."

—BILLIE JOE ARMSTRONG, GREEN DAY

# One Dozen
# Outstanding
# Roots-Rock Combos

## (and their state of origin)

---

The Beat Farmers (California)

The Blasters (California)

The Blood Oranges (Massachusetts)

The Del-Lords (New York)

Green on Red (California)

Jason and the Scorchers (Tennessee)

The Jayhawks (Minnesota)

The Long Ryders (California)

Los Lobos (California)

Rank and File (Texas via New York via California)

The Silos (New York)

Uncle Tupelo (Missouri)

# Top Ten Goth Acts

by Katherine Yeske

Athens, Georgia–based Katherine Yeske writes about Goth and other musics for a variety of publications.

**Siouxsie and the Banshees.** Frontwoman Siouxsie Sioux has always vehemently resisted the Goth label, but her black-clad loyalists still regard her as the reigning queen of the genre. True, the original, circa-1976 Banshees lineup (which grew out of a clique of fanatical Sex Pistols fans called the Bromley Contingent, and featured none other than Sid Vicious on drums), was largely punk-inspired. But the subsequent albums, *Juju* (1981) and *Hyaena* (1984), along with the string-saturated 1982 single "Fireworks," carved out a darker, more distinctive lyrical and musical identity to match Siouxsie's theatrical stage persona. Nearly twenty years after their emergence, the Banshees still claim a loyal international following.

**Bauhaus.** In 1979 "Bela Lugosi's Dead" raised this London quartet to near-deity status: The epic-length song's creepy atmospherics and vampire imagery perfectly encapsulate Goth's sinister intentions. Peter Murphy's deep, sinister vocals, guitarist Daniel Ash and bassist David J's inventive, intertwining melodies, and drummer Kevin Haskins' technical precision reinvented the genre with each new album. The group's relatively brief lifespan (it disbanded in 1983) hasn't lessened its influence; posthumously, Bauhaus is more popular than ever. Ash, J, and Haskins remain together as the less-menacing Love and Rockets, while Murphy's solo work continues to explore increasingly commercial terrain.

**Christian Death.** Upon its 1982 release, this band's debut album *Only Theatre of Pain* shocked even hard-core Goths with its grisly imagery, slashing instrumentation, and all-around unflinching morbidity. When the rest of his band jumped ship soon after, frontman Rozz Williams regrouped with members of L.A. death-rockers Pompeii 99. The newcomers continued to use the Christian Death name after Williams exited in the mid-eighties, with guitarist Valor taking the vocal and conceptual reins on a lengthy series of albums that continued the band's traditional thematic obsessions. Since then, the Christian Death name has been assumed at various times by factions led by Valor and Williams, but no matter who's using the venerable monicker, the songs remain the most unsettling compositions in the genre. Williams also led the equally scarifying Shadow Project, which he recently dissolved to form the somewhat more accessible Daucus Karota.

**Red Lorry Yellow Lorry.** Depressing even by Goth's formidable standards, Leeds, England's Red Lorry Yellow Lorry explores the bleakest soundscapes imaginable. Starting with 1984's *This Today* EP, the band cultivated a dismal but strangely addictive approach, with Chris Reed's mournful vocals and portentous lyrics smothered in slinky, distorted guitars and punchy rhythms. Unfortunately, Red Lorry Yellow Lorry seems doomed to remain a cult item. RLYL's catalogue is well worth seeking out, though, if only because it inspired so many subsequent gloomsters.

**Sisters of Mercy.** Difficult, brooding bastard or not, Sisters mastermind Andrew Eldritch is snarling Gothic sensuality personified, and his continued influence on the genre cannot be overstated, inspiring legions of worshipful imitators who've tried (mostly in vain) to replicate his musical inventiveness and disdainful personal charisma. Countless lineup changes have left Eldritch the only fulltime Sister, but that's okay since his deep, shiver-inducing voice, stingingly sarcastic lyrics, and distinctively danceable, hard-hitting electronic rock soundscapes are what really count here.

**The Mission (U.K.).** Former Sisters of Mercy Wayne Hussey and Craig Adams formed the Mission in the mid-eighties after a bitter legal battle/publicity war with former bandmate Eldritch. The rift created a deep division among fans that's resulted in many listeners' instant dismissal of the Mission's work. That's unfortunate because at their best the Mission created carefully crafted songs whose impassioned vocals and energetic guitar work flirt with straight hard rock.

**Sex Gang Children.** Emerging in the early eighties as the darlings of London's early Goth scene, this glam/punk-influenced outfit (later based in L.A.) created powerful, intelligent epics. The band's bass-dominated din is something less than instantly accessible, but its addictive properties become apparent with prolonged exposure. Frontman Andi Sex Gang's feline, androgynous raving slashes apart typical Goth rumblings, while dizzying tempo changes and bizarre lyrical content complete the gloriously unsettling effect. Their last releases found Sex Gang's sound grown increasingly ambitious, with intricate string arrangements and other classical touches. The band broke up in 1994.

**Alien Sex Fiend.** Possibly the most cheerful Goth combo in existence, Alien Sex Fiend creates weird, irresistibly danceable tunes with titles like "My Brain is in the Cupboard Above the Kitchen Sink" and "Wild Green Fiendy Liquid." Starting with 1983's *Who's Been Sleeping in My Brain?*, the band's gleeful disregard of Goth's gloom-doom rules has resulted in an abundance of rollicking, irreverent material. Nik Fiend's Alice Cooper-esque appearance and Cockney ranting provide a striking focal point, backed by Mrs. Fiend's quirky synth accompaniments. In its spare time, the band extends its influence by composing video game soundtracks.

**Fields of the Nephilim.** England's Fields of the Nephilim never *looked* like typical Goths; band members sported cowboy hats and Western gear instead of the usual black lace and silver jewelry. But the music consistently delivered, hinting at things far more sinister than the musicians' appearance would suggest. Carl McCoy's distinctively ragged vocals added to the band's sometimes rugged, sometimes atmospheric approach, creating one of the most recognizable sounds of the genre. In the late eighties, the Fields moved toward a more exploratory, ambient style. No matter how it's played, though, this band's sound is always as big as the desert sky.

(tie) **Rosetta Stone** and **Nosferatu.** These young English bands represent Goth's continued survival in the face of an often hostile mainstream environment. Liverpool's Rosetta Stone inject Goth's scarier lyrical aspects with a majestic musical aura. The band's relatively lush material is inventive and forward-looking, and many observers have tipped Rosetta Stone as successors to the dark throne previously occupied by the Sisters of Mercy. In contrast, Nosferatu reaches into the past for inspiration, combining strong classical influences with modern technology to create chilling, textured soundscapes that feature intertwining harpsichord parts, acoustic/electric guitars and synths curling around sensual, sinister vocals. Both bands' conviction and originality signal Goth's impending reintroduction into mainstream culture.

> "I despair when I pass Oxford Street and see bondage and leather and studs everywhere. It's become quite acceptable to go to work like that. It's disgusting."
>
> —SIOUXSIE SIOUX

# Ten Acts That Could Fall Under the Amorphous, Hybrid Tentacles of Alterna-Rap

by MC G-Money

MC G-Money (a.k.a. Greg Emmanuel) once scratched a record, but it was purely by accident and he wishes he hadn't.

**Arrested Development:**   Social commentary was never this danceable.

**Basehead:**   The lovechild of Chuck D and Liz Phair.

**The Beastie Boys:**   Funk, hardcore, rap—the coolest white boys this side of William Shatner.

**Cypress Hill:**   Purveyors of the pipe and some dope beats.

**De La Soul:**   Peace, love, and goofin' around—what's this shit doin' in rap?

**Digable Planets:**   Knew there was a reason for holding on to those Miles Davis records.

**The Goats:**   And you thought Cypress Hill smoked a lot!

**The Pharcyde:**   Mike D. likes them, so we do.

**PM Dawn:**   They sample Spandau Ballet, 'nuff said.

**A Tribe Called Quest:**   They sample Lou Reed; wait, who was he again?

# The Fifty Most Significant Indie Records

## (in chronological order)

by Rob O'Connor

Rob O'Connor, the tyrannical publisher and editor of *Throat Culture* ("the only magazine in the world"), a fanzine given over to his every whim no matter how financially disastrous the results, has contributed to ROLLING STONE, *Musician, BAM*, and various other publications.

This is not a list of personal favorites. Rather than recounting the records that changed my life (you have every right not to care), I have attempted to compile a list of fifty records that have profoundly influenced and reinforced the creativity of the independent rock scene.

It pains me greatly that records like *Palace Brothers,* Guided by Voices' *Bee Thousand,* the Leaving Trains' *Well Down Blue Highway* and countless others didn't make the cut, but fifty, unfortunately, means fifty.

This list is by no means definitive, but I hope that I've managed to highlight some important recordings for the benefit of listeners looking for a challenge. To my peers, who are certain to look at this and find something missing, I can only offer an empathetic nod.

Nearly every one of these records is still in print at the time of this writing, and whenever possible I've attempted to make note of their availability on CD. Happy hunting.

### 1. *The Fugs,* the Fugs (ESP, 1966)
By the mid-sixties, the spirit of the Beat movement had made its way into rock & roll. Bob Dylan's "Subterranean Homesick Blues"—whose promo-

tional film clip featured Beat godhead Allen Ginsberg—borrowed from the rambling, rough-hewn beatnik spirit of Ginsberg and Kerouac. The Fugs were a cruder version of this. Led by second-generation beats Ed Sanders and Tuli Kupferberg, the Fugs churned out raw, unexpurgated, relentlessly satirical meditations on sex, politics, sex and the Lower East Side. The musicianship is decidedly raw, presaging punk by over a decade, but the performance is what matters here.

Despite their uncompromising politics and copious use of four-letter words, the Fugs eventually signed to a mainstream label, Reprise, and while some of those releases held fast to old glories (check out the live *Golden Filth,* which illuminates what the Butthole Surfers aim to be), the band's reputation is based on their 1965 debut *First Album* and this, their second. In the nineties, Fantasy reissued both on CD with bonus tracks.

**2. *Contact High,* the Godz (ESP, 1966)**
In the days before the mainstream music industry discovered the commercial viability of progressive hippie rock, New York's ESP label had a virtual lock on high musical weirdness, mainly because nobody else was interested. Critic Lester Bangs championed the Godz early on, stating that whenever he got sucked into an argument over what was the worst album of all time, he would win because he had *heard* it. "It" is *Contact High,* the aural equivalent of an Ed Wood flick. The Godz didn't care about tempo. They didn't care about tuning. They simply didn't care. And why should they? Sounds like they're having a great time without all that high-falutin' stuff. Punk rockers the world over now detune to this primitive masterpiece. It has since been reissued on CD by a German company, ZYX.

**3. *Philosophy of the World,* the Shaggs (Rounder Records, 1969)**
The world was never ready for the Shaggs. The Fugs were raw, the Godz rawer, but the Shaggs. . . . The three Wiggin sisters, from Fremont, New Hampshire, wanted to rock, and they weren't about to be stopped by the fact that they didn't know how. Nowadays, bands deliberately play incompetently or don't want to learn their instruments, but the Wiggins' enthusiastic amateurism wasn't deliberate. They wanted to be a better band, they just couldn't be. As a result, this is the record that renders all future incompetency irrelevant. Half Japanese and Jandek may be able to build careers on this sort of thing, but in the end only the Shaggs will be counted. *Philosophy of the World* was reissued in 1980, at the behest of NRBQ's Terry Adams, by Red Rooster/Rounder.

**4. *Free Your Mind and Your Ass Will Follow,* Funkadelic (Westbound, 1970)**
Before Sly and the Family Stone made *There's a Riot Goin' On,* and before funk was a genre, George Clinton and Plainfield, New Jersey's finest made

this seminal classic. Though the band aimed toward music apropos to their name, something else occurred with this record. A quick look at the insert photo says it all. These guys weren't out to funk up your life, just to escape the mess of their own. *Free Your Mind* is one weird record; like more than a few others on this list, nothing else sounds quite like it.

### 5. #1 Record, Big Star (Ardent, 1972)

Quirkier than the Raspberries and more aggressive than Badfinger, Big Star aspired to Beatlesque pop at a time when everyone else seemed to be getting heavy, slick, or progressive. Chris Bell and Alex Chilton were both adept tunesmiths and harmonists, and their thorny pop sensibilities combined to make the band's debut a seminal classic. Bell would depart after this album, leaving Chilton to carry on through *Radio City* and the sublimely melancholy *Sister Lovers*. Big Star's albums never made any commercial impact upon their original issue, though the band soon became a rather luminous cult item, profoundly influencing a couple of generations of jangly pop combos. *#1 Record* and *Radio City* have been paired on a single CD by Fantasy. *Sister Lovers* was reissued by Rykodisc.

### 6. *Meet the Residents*, the Residents (Ralph, 1974)

Here is the first band to build an entire industry on an abstract formula. The Residents get by on an anonymity so strong that one suspects that even their parents don't know what they do. *Meet the Residents*, their first full-length release, was originally issued with a cover that was a dead-on parody of The Beatles' first U.S. album, before threatened lawsuits inspired them to tone down the artwork. The Residents' music, an ironic mélange of rock, polka, jazz, music concrete, and other atonalities, makes much of what we think of as "cutting edge" sound about as challenging as Foreigner.

The Residents' most inspiring achievement, however, remains the continuing self-sufficiency of their label, Ralph Records. Somehow, through bypassing the original channels of artistic development, Ralph was able to promote the unusual Residents to a cult audience that's enabled the label to continue releasing one ambitious product after another, without any noticeable decrease in quality.

### 7. "Piss Factory"/"Hey Joe" (seven-inch single) Patti Smith (Mer, 1974)

Nineteen-seventy-four was a great year for rock & roll—if you were Bad Company or Emerson, Lake and Palmer. Since you probably weren't, 1974 was a horrendous year for rock & roll. The music had lost touch with the essentials and misapprehended its own history. Patti Smith, meanwhile, had grown up wanting to be an amalgam of Arthur Rimbaud, Bob Dylan, and Jim Morrison. By the time of this, her debut release, she was already much more.

"Piss Factory" is an amazing, piano-driven account of what it was to be young and misunderstood, to be exploding with so many ideas that you resembled a film projector with reels and reels of film but no lens. Focus being out of the question, you ramble on.

Smith's take on "Hey Joe," meanwhile, is majestic. Beginning with a timely reference to Patty Hearst, Smith reinvents the much-covered folk song, balancing both the emotional connection to the song's truest elements and the intellectual exercise of reinventing an already classic structure. This self-released single would subsequently inspire many others to do the same.

"Piss Factory" can be heard on the ROIR compilation album *Singles: The Great New York Singles Scene*.

### 8. *Blank Generation* EP, Richard Hell and the Voidoids (Ork, 1976)

Though by definition punk rock was more concerned with spunk than precision, it couldn't hurt if you had both. Recorded mainly as a demo to procure major-label interest, *Blank Generation* includes early versions of the title track and "Another World," both of which would figure on Hell's major-label debut LP (also titled *Blank Generation*), released the following year. While Hell's untutored whine is spotlighted, the real stars of this record are guitarists Robert Quine and Ivan Julian; solos are traded, rhythms trampled, notes bent in and out of key at will. If twenty years ago it was important to give off the impression that anybody could do it, maybe now it's time to admit to ourselves that while anybody can do it, the correct mix of chops and abandon is what makes most shit kick.

### 9. *The Modern Lovers*, the Modern Lovers (Beserkley, 1976)

John Cale has produced many a fine record: Nico's *Marble Index,* Patti Smith's *Horses,* etc. But whatever Cale did here—provided he did something—this must qualify as the least intrusive production job of his career. Essentially demos recorded for Warner Bros., who passed, *The Modern Lovers* represents the full flowering of rock & roll's perennial adolescent, Jonathan Richman. The singer/guitarist—joined here by David Robinson (later of the Cars), Jerry Harrison (later of Talking Heads) and Ernie Brooks (later of the Necessaries)—created an album that went directly against the grain of seventies rock's propensity for excess. Minimalist in the best sense of the word, every sound on this album seems tailored for maximum effect. Richman's nasal-drip vocals, Harrison's rinky-dink organ, and the intimate drums and guitar decisively reject rock's arena impulses and bring it all back home to the den. *The Modern Lovers* has been reissued on CD by Rhino, whose version includes two songs produced by Kim Fowley ("I'm Straight" and "Government Center") along with the Cale tracks.

### 10. *Phonography*, R. Stevie Moore (Vital, 1976)

By the mid-seventies there was enough rock and pop music around that an artist with the right combination of gumption and talent could make interestingly personal music by mixing and matching styles at will. Finding other musicians with similarly eclectic inclinations, however, could prove frustrating. Nashville-raised, New Jersey-based iconoclast R. Stevie Moore never bothered looking for others to fill out his sound. Instead, he did it himself, overdubbing with two reel-to-reel tape recorders in his bedroom until it sounded like he'd just jammed with the hottest band in town. Nowadays, with home-recording technology vastly improved and more accessible, it's not such a big deal, but at the time it took a lot more effort. Couple that with the fact that Moore launched his own mail-order cassette club, which now boasts over two hundred titles, and you have the man who can safely be credited with bringing home recording to the forefront.

*Phonography*, Moore's first longplayer, is a neat little record ranging from rudimentary experimentation to adventurous compositional sophistication. Pressed up twice in limited-edition vinyl runs, it's currently available only through Moore's cassette club (429 Valley Road, Upper Montclair, NJ 07043).

### 11. *Motörhead*, Motörhead (Chiswick U.K., 1977)

Hawkwind would certainly be on this list if their most important records hadn't been issued by United Artists, so former 'wind bassist Lemmy Kilmister's metallicized offshoot will have to suffice. In 1977, the year that saw the rise of British punk, Motörhead was busy inventing a punk-metal hybrid that was at least a decade ahead of its time. When *Motörhead* was released, the band was an island unto itself. Uninterested in the politics of punk or the pomposity of heavy metal, Motörhead tore it up loud and fast with no apologies to either.

Roadrunner reissued the album on CD in 1990.

### 12. *Suicide*, Suicide (Red Star, 1977)

Keyboardist Martin Rev and vocalist Alan Vega's minimalist, synth-space performance-art-rock was not generally well liked when the pair first hit the New York scene as Suicide, and one doubts that it would go over well today. What made the pair so difficult probably has something to do with the average human being's attention span. Simply put, most people cannot stand in a club and listen to the same two or three notes played over and over on a buzzy synthesizer while the singer shrieks about the end of Western Civilization or some variation thereof. Suicide's music was never meant to be accessible, but liking it doesn't make you a better person. Understanding it just means you're patient.

Red Star reissued the album with additional tracks in 1981. England's Demon label released it on CD in 1986.

### 13. *Datapanik in the Year Zero* EP, Pere Ubu (Radar, 1978)

Pere Ubu's early indie releases on Hearthan, collected in England on this twelve-inch disc, represent some of the most impressive indie singles ever made. Swinging between the Stooges and their own more conceptual aesthetic, Ubu created a music more literal than most. David Thomas (a.k.a. Crocus Behemoth) shrieks atop a propulsive rhythm section where the bass guitar has carte blanche to lead the band when it's in the mood. Teen angst meets adult assimilation.

The original singles are long out of print, but they were reissued domestically on the 1985 TwinTone compilation *Terminal Tower*.

### 14. *Second Annual Report,* Throbbing Gristle (Industrial, 1978)

Apparently, England isn't a very happy place. Rains a lot. Perhaps that's why so much of their music is either overweeningly happy in an exaggerated, overcompensating kind of way, or cold and machinelike. Guess which Throbbing Gristle is. *Second Annual Report* is their debut album. With droning synth, annoyed-sounding vocals, and little actual *music* to speak of, it set the tone for all the life-is-pain bands who would subsequently hijack Throbbing Gristle mastermind Genesis P-Orridge's concepts and apply them to melody. However, misery hates melody; it soothes over the rough spots, and rough spots are what this stuff is all about. There's something entertaining here, too, a certain charm that wraps itself around these dismal dreamscapes. Welcome to the end of the world.

### 15. *Singles Going Steady,* Buzzcocks (I.R.S., 1979)

The Ramones toured England and everyone went home and formed a band, or so the story goes. At least Pete Shelley did, and a good thing too. This singles collection offers the best representation of Shelley's pointedly poignant songwriting and his band's loud-fast-and-extremely-melodic attack. Their other long-players suffer from album filler, but there's none of that here, just singles. . . .

### 16. *Songs the Lord Taught Us,* the Cramps (Illegal/I.R.S., 1980)

Rock history constantly reinvents itself, and since the definition of rock multiplies regularly, endless permutations result. The Cramps combine rockabilly with a deep and abiding love for sixties surf and garage rock. But unlike many of the bands they inspired, the Cramps add their own B-movie sickness to the voodoo jive. The CD adds four alternate versions and a bonus cut.

### 17. *Totale's Turns (It's Now or Never),* the Fall (Rough Trade, 1980)

Reportedly, Fall leader Mark E. Smith is tone-deaf, which would explain much about his band's approach. Spewing propaganda, poetry, and stream-of-consciousness nonsense against an imposing clang that bears more than a passing resemblance to the sound of a garbage truck, Smith makes the sincere politics of his contemporaries seem like the naive posturings and utopian pipedreams they probably were.

Since the Fall's 1979 debut *Live at the Witch Trials,* the personnel-change-prone band has been nothing if not prolific, often turning out several releases a year. *Totale's Turns* is a live album that displays the strength and humor of the band's early days.

### 18. *Closer,* Joy Division (Factory, 1980)

The fact that singer Ian Curtis hung himself before this album was released casts a definite pall over the proceedings. From the barren packaging to Curtis's soul-on-edge vocals and lyrics to the sepulchral music contained within, *Closer* redefined sonic disturbance. Martin Hannett's production creates an otherworldly musical zone, but to call this music otherworldly hardly does it justice. Drumbeats plod in mechanized fashion, bass riffs fall off rhythm and take the lead, and keyboards swoosh and swish into the ether, while guitars grind as if a million miles away.

### 19. *Negativland,* Negativland (Seeland, 1980)

Better music through science? Media-terrorist pranksters Negativland have quite an ear for isolating absurdity and looping it into your head. Samplers before sampling was cool, Negativland juxtaposes "found" objects with the band's own instrumental punctuation, until it often resembles a newscast gone awry. The group's more recent work is a good deal more sophisticated, but herein lies the genesis of Negativland's great art war.

### 20. *Los Angeles,* X (Slash, 1980)

Their raucous power denoted punk rock, but it was the raw, slightly off-key harmonies, rhythmic asymmetry, and anecdotal notebook poetry that made this quartet's music so special. Arty but never pretentious, X took on their hometown's decadence and spun it into something far more appealing. The band's second album, *Wild Gift,* is a bit more accomplished than this, their debut, but this is where the band's power is shown off most impressively. Delivering nine songs (including a cover of "Soul Kitchen" by the Doors, whose keyboardist Ray Manzarek produced this and their next three records) in under thirty minutes, *Los Angeles* has nothing to do with the hardcore movement that was brewing in L.A. at the time; it's far too emotionally advanced for that. *Los Angeles* has since been reissued by Slash on CD in tandem with *Wild Gift.*

### 21. *Prayers on Fire,* the Birthday Party (Thermidor, 1981)

Australia's greatest musical export? No, not Men at Work, the Birthday Party. Featuring the undisciplined feral howl of Nick Cave and the glass-shard histrionics of guitarist Rowland S. Howard, the Birthday Party took lurching rhythms and frenetic abandon to new peaks of mania. But this ain't no *Trout*

*Mask Replica.* The chaos encompassed here sounds not like a conscious af-fection, but rather a natural result of the fact that the participants were on a self-destructive collision course. They were young and *wanted* to burn out. The band's live recordings, particularly their *Peel Sessions,* reveal an even more energetic side of the band, but *Prayers on Fire* remains their most fo-cused work.

### 22. *Damaged,* Black Flag (SST, 1981)

Recorded before frontman Henry Rollins had completely found his footing, *Damaged* remains an extremely powerful remnant of the early-eighties hard-core movement. Side one works swiftly past with a suite of songs half-paro-dying and half-rejoicing in the power of bored suburban rebellion through beer, TV, and loud guitar. Side two, however, is much more tortured, sound-ing off existential rants that no amount of alcohol could ever quell.

Unfortunately, outside circumstances would slow the seminal combo's progress shortly after this disc's release. A lawsuit would prevent them from releasing an album for two years, by which time they were a changed (and less compelling) band. This remains their primal peak. The CD version ap-pends the band's 1980 EP *Jealous Again.*

### 23. *Signals, Calls, and Marches* EP, Mission of Burma (Ace of Hearts, 1981)

In this CD age, you'd be well advised to pick up Rykodisc's eighty-minute-plus compilation *Mission of Burma,* which includes this EP, the band's first album *VS.* (no relation to Pearl Jam) and various other singles and etc. But in the old (pre-CD) days, one had to be content with consuming the music in smaller portions—which is actually the best way to hear this stuff. In short staccato bursts that suggest more than they produce, you get a sense of the ur-gency that this EP—and others of the period—produced upon their arrival in the more interesting record stores of the day. The band's insistence on volume prompted guitarist Roger Miller to leave after his hearing was seriously jeop-ardized. Fortunately for us, we can always turn the stereo down.

### 24. *Album—Generic Flipper,* Flipper (Subterranean, 1982)

Hardcore's loud, fast rules quickly backed the genre into a corner, and since the music's truest adherents were iconoclasts at heart, it would only figure that somewhere a band would slow it all down to the point of the slowest grind short of stop. "Sex Bomb" is eight minutes of mesmeric downer rock, while "Life" is some poor soul's idea of daily affirmation. The album was rerereleased on CD in 1992 by Def American (now American Recordings).

### 25. *Chronic Town* EP, R.E.M. (I.R.S., 1982)

The little band from Athens that did. How? Fairly slowly, actually. *Chronic Town* (the band's second release, following a now-classic seven-inch on Hib-

Tone) was released at a time when synths and oversized drumbeats were beginning to dominate American rock. The EP's modest jangle and oblique lyrics struck a chord with fans who pined for the days of quirky, catchy guitar-based rock. It sounded like a bit of an anachronism at the time, and it wasn't clear whether the band would be heard from again. Though originally a vinyl-only release, *Chronic Town* was subsequently appended to the CD version of the odds-and-ends compilation *Dead Letter Office*.

### 26. *Drawings of Patient O.T.*, Einstürzende Neubauten (Some Bizarre, 1983)

This is true industrial music—not just loud guitars, but machinery. Not as accomplished musically as their subsequent work and not as aimless as their earliest, *Drawings of Patient O.T.* is an eerie, unsettling record that'll never be played on mainstream rock stations no matter how big Nine Inch Nails get. It was released in the U.S. in 1985 with a bonus EP containing four extra cuts.

### 27. *Out of Step* EP, Minor Threat (Dischord, 1983)

This is what's called ethics. D.C. hardcore trendsetters Minor Threat and the label they founded, Dischord, have never overcharged for anything. On the cover of this EP it says "$3.50 postpaid from Dischord," lest a fan find it in a store for more. The music inside is extremely proficient hardcore, played at supersonic speed yet very tuneful. Frontman Ian MacKaye writes it as if he were a member of Up with Youth, and that intensely positive approach remains true to the band's straight-edge credo (sample lyric: "I don't smoke, I don't drink, I don't fuck.") *Out of Step*'s contents are available along with the rest of Minor Threat's recorded output on a single CD, *Complete*. Available for six bucks from Dischord, natch.

### 28. *Show No Mercy*, Slayer (Metal Blade, 1983)

Some might opt for Metallica, but to these ears the reliably over-the-top Slayer stand as the true keepers of the flame that Black Sabbath lit way back when. It must be said, though, that *Show No Mercy* is one of the *clumsiest* albums ever made, with the band playing so fast that they have no chance to pay attention to what they're playing. Riffs slam headfirst into drumrolls, like barreling ninety miles per hour down a dead-end street. But every metal and crossover punk worth anything in the eighties paid attention to this record. The CD adds the band's 1984 EP *Haunting the Chapel*.

### 29. *Violent Femmes*, Violent Femmes (Slash, 1983)

If you were a college DJ in the eighties you could scarcely avoid this record, or the endless requests for "Blister in the Sun." Combining Jonathan Richman's nasal delivery with Lou Reed's narrow range, Gordon Gano sounds drenched in teen irony. But it's the "unplugged" production—acoustic guitar, stand-up bass, and a fat snare—that makes this alt-rock's greatest campfire album. The CD adds two cuts.

### 30. *Zen Arcade,* Hüsker Dü (SST, 1984)

This double album is indie rock's *Quadrophenia,* boasting a story line concerning a kid getting up one day and leaving home. Recorded mostly live and very quickly, with the vocals buried so deep that the printed lyrics are a must. Bob Mould's wall of guitar is immense, and the songwriting by Mould and drummer Grant Hart is amazingly strong. If only there had been a way to get this on the radio at the time, history might have been different.

### 31. *Double Nickels on the Dime,* the Minutemen (SST, 1984)

Feeling the friendly competition from their above-mentioned labelmates, the Minutemen offered up a double album of their own. Chock full of Mike Watt's chunky bass, George Hurley's frenetic drums, and singer/guitarist D. Boon's stream-of-cut-up-consciousness lyrics, *Double Nickels* represents a creative high point for the trio, who'd previously kept most of their songs to a minute or less. The forty-five songs that comprise the four-sided vinyl edition could not all fit on the CD.

### 32. *Let It Be,* The Replacements (Twin/Tone, 1984)

The little band from Minnesota who couldn't. The Great American Rock Band of the eighties who could never pull it together long enough to pull it off for good. Too true to their ethics, too full of the renegade rock & roll vibe (not to mention copious quantities of beer), and too afraid of being eaten alive by the business, when the 'Mats finally crashed and burned it was in many pieces that will never again be put together in quite the same way. Their records only capture part of the magic, but the magic *Let It Be* captures is considerable. Paul Westerberg's heart-on-sleeve songwriting and shining, shoddy voice, the goofy throwaways, the odd cover, Bob Stinson's over-the-top guitar, and the bumblingly brilliant rhythm section—it's all here.

### 33. *Cop,* Swans (K.422, 1984)

Turgid, churning rhythms and a singer who sounds like he took voice lessons from Leonard Cohen and *then* had his larynx removed—that's the ugly ugliness of these New York yuksters. The band's relentless adherence to this mind-dulling formula either causes people to leave the room in fear or keeps them entranced and wanting to hear how the whole thing turns out. Frontman Michael Gira may not be the most miserable person alive, but he's the most dedicated member of the misery club to make a record. Some find his self-pity overbearing, but that's exactly the point.

### 34. *L.A.M.F. Revisited,* Johnny Thunders and the Heartbreakers (Jungle, 1984)

When it was originally released in 1977 as *L.A.M.F.* (i.e., like a motherfucker), it was one of the worst-sounding rock albums of all time. Normally, that'd be no big deal, except that in this case, underneath the murk rested a pure piece of rock & roll heart. Drummer Jerry Nolan apparently knew it, since he quit the band over the horrendous original mix. Nolan's fellow ex-New York Doll Johnny Thunders had already junked and clowned his way into underground legend, but a deadly mix of heroin and ego would keep his post-Dolls projects from reaching full fruition. But this album beautifully captures Thunders's guttersnipe swagger and devil-may-care guitar heroics.

*L.A.M.F. Revisited* has been paired on CD with 1982's live-in-London *D.T.K.—Live at the Speakeasy* as *D.T.K. L.A.M.F.*

### 35. *Life's a Riot Etc.*, Billy Bragg (CD Presents, 1985)

Often described as a one-man Clash, Billy Bragg began his career carrying his electric guitar on his back and playing gigs as a highly politicized electric folk singer. Enamored with the raw power of a lone voice and a single electric guitar, Bragg recorded his earliest sides unaccompanied, and their stark sound conveys a sense of loneliness that no sidemen could ever convey. *Life's a Riot Etc.* is a U.S. vinyl compilation of Bragg's first two British EPs, *Life's a Riot With Spy vs. Spy* and *Between the Wars;* in 1987, Elektra combined its contents with that of his first full album, *Brewing Up With Billy Bragg,* on the CD comp *Back to Basics*.

### 36. *Frankenchrist,* Dead Kennedys (Alternative Tentacles, 1985)

Known more for their provocative political antics than their music, Dead Kennedys nonetheless represent eighties hardcore as well as anyone. By 1985, the band's velocity needed to simmer for frontman Jello Biafra to more clearly enunciate his political ravings. The music that evolved in that process was considerably more intricate than slowed-down hardcore. East Bay Ray emerges here as a smart, distinctive guitarist with a knack for screeching chords and low, surflike solos.

Still, some people took the Dead Kennedys as a joke. Certainly, the inane court battle over the H.R. Giger poster included with this album should have been viewed as one, but instead it destroyed the band. And, while Biafra's smirk could be as annoyingly self-righteous as anyone's, the band's music stands bravely apart.

### 37. *King of Rock,* Run-D.M.C. (Profile, 1985)

Any accusations of tokenism re this entry will not be taken seriously, since *King of Rock* is as much a rock album as it is a rap album. Those guitars in "Rock Box" could only have come from mid-eighties metal. That Run-D.M.C. managed to bring the beat back to college radio proved that it wasn't that indie-rock didn't want to dance, it had just forgotten how.

### 38. *Atomizer,* Big Black (Homestead, 1986)

Bringing the beat back, not to make you dance but to give you a headache, was Big Black's mission. Utilizing a drum machine and leader Steve Albini's considerable studio expertise, these Chicagoans forged an immense noise that in conjunction with Albini's sociopathic lyrics makes for extreme alienation rock. Through the band's unflagging bombast, the music is both charged and static, simultaneously an expression of hate and (unintentionally) a parody of it. *Atomizer* was combined on CD with the band's subsequent release *Headache* and an additional single as *The Rich Man's Eight-Track Tape.*

### 39. *Enjoy!,* the Descendents (New Alliance/Restless, 1986)

With all the talk about Nirvana's perfect meshing of pop and power, it's as if the Descendents never existed. Actually, even in its earliest days punk rock embraced the melodic influence of AM radio, and nowhere was that clearer than on the Descendents' last two albums, *Enjoy!* and *All.* While the band's early records were loaded with jokes and fast, amateurish playing, on *Enjoy!* the band fashioned a sound that spoke plainly from the heart while remaining true to punk's puerile nature. Even Bill Stevenson's intrusive, over-the-top drumming somehow fits.

### 40. *Element of Light,* Robyn Hitchcock and the Egyptians (Glass Fish/Relativity, 1986)

Overtly influenced by Syd Barrett and his loopy mode of lyricism, ex-Soft Boys leader Robyn Hitchcock is the virtual embodiment of the eighties college-radio star. He appeared on magazine covers, received glowing reviews and recorded a series of albums that borrowed from rock's past while adding a uniquely personal point of view, yet was never able to break out of cult status. There's not much consensus on which Hitchcock album best defines his essence. The acoustic *I Often Dream of Trains* (1986) is a favored pick, but *Element of Light* (recorded with the versatile Egyptians, a.k.a. the Soft Boys' old rhythm section) merges Hitchcock's stylistic influences and lyrical vision into his most cohesive, seamless work. Rhino's updated CD reissue features additional tracks.

### 41. *Exile on Main Street* (cassette), Pussy Galore (no label, 1986)

The jury may be forever hung on Pussy Galore. Depending on who you ask, they were either an ahead-of-their-time conceptual juggernaut or the most preening, pretentious assholes ever to make a record. This cassette, a limited-edition release of the band "deconstructing" (i.e., playing poorly) the entire Rolling Stones album of the same name, was recorded in response to Sonic Youth's never-executed threat to cover the Beatles' entire White Album. Pussy Galore's incompetence may or may not be deliberate, but the band's approach seemed partially a matter of the indie-rock clique playing itself out and partly a concerted effort to further alienate rock traditionalists. The original cassette is extremely difficult to come by, and bootleg LP pressings usually don't include the whole thing. Four *Exile* tracks also appear on the compilation *Corpse Love*.

### 42. *EVOL*, Sonic Youth (SST, 1986)

Originally a late entry in New York's No Wave scene, Sonic Youth have more recently emerged as forerunners and overseers of the current alternative community. If guitarist Thurston Moore shows up for your gig, watch out; the kids and cognoscenti will soon follow. When *EVOL* was recorded, Sonic Youth were still pretty much a noise band with a vague rock pedigree. While its acclaimed predecessor *Bad Moon Rising* suffered from the band's obvious discomfort with the imposed structure of the rock "song," *EVOL* staked out a workable comfort zone and came charging with a best-of-both-worlds attack. The band's subsequent albums, particularly *Sister* and *Daydream Nation,* may have firmed out the sound in greater detail, but *EVOL* is where it came together. The CD includes a cover of Kim Fowley's "Bubblegum."

### 43. "Touch Me I'm Sick"/"Sweet Young Thing Ain't Sweet No More" (seven-inch single), Mudhoney (Sub Pop, 1988)

Mudhoney's debut single epitomizes the soon-to-be-ubiquitous grunge aesthetic. Jack Endino's production is bargain-basement, the guitars' distortion from the cheesiest of distortion pedals and Mark Arm's singing flat-out raw. The band's next release, the EP *Superfuzz Bigmuff,* continued the glory, but it was "Touch Me I'm Sick" that best encapsulated the band's power. It appears with several other early singles on the import CD *Boiled Beef & Rotting Teeth,* and on CD pressings of *Superfuzz Bigmuff*.

### 44. *Surfer Rosa*, the Pixies (4AD/Rough Trade, 1988)

Brainy yet ballsy, the Pixies took song structure and stood it on its head, somehow leaving the song intact and stronger for the ordeal. At a time when college radio had found its formula, the Pixies took that formula and tilted it a hair. Not the most groundbreaking rock music ever made, but a virtual textbook for every new band who want to know how to rock "alternatively." The CD adds the band's debut EP, *Come On Pilgrim*.

### 45. *Metallic 2xKO*, Iggy and the Stooges (Skydog, 1988)

Not to be confused with plain old *Metallic K.O.,* released a dozen years earlier, this is the Stooges' hate-filled final show with some additional material. In either version, the live set remains a seminal document, since never before had the sound of breaking glass become so integral to a band. The chaotic atmosphere is the perfect counterpoint to the drugged-out dead end that the music evokes. Iggy's personalized pyrotechnics, of course, inspired a generation of wannabes.

**46. *Double Live,* Butthole Surfers (Latino Bugger Veil, 1989)**
Through most of the eighties, there was virtually no way for indie bands to gain mainstream radio play, so bands had little reason to tailor their sound one iota. Hence, the Butthole Surfers made loud, violent music that spit forth psychedelia, blues, heavy metal, and free jazz with little consideration for who might actually want to hear it. All of the band's early studio albums have definite singular vibes about them, but to really experience the way this group changed people's lives, you had to see them live. Armed with dancers, multiple drummers, lights, and some really disgusting films, the Buttholes updated the Fugs/Velvet Underground multimedia experience while remaining true to their own twisted Texan roots. *Double Live,* their official double CD bootleg, captures every phase of the group's career and includes a relatively straight version of R.E.M.'s "The One I Love."

**47. *California,* American Music Club (Grigter-Frontier, 1990)**
While most of the innovations on this list fall in the louder/faster spectrum, American Music Club is, in its own quiet way, as radical as just about any band listed here. Inspired more by the sort of luminous sadness that drove Hank Williams, Billie Holiday, and Nick Drake, AMC creates restrained, melodic music that doesn't need volume to convey the force of its passion. Singer Mark Eitzel writes songs that go out of their way to examine how the world treats its ugly and unwanted. *California* is the band's third album and remains their most breathtakingly austere. Look for the Demon import CD that pairs *California* with the band's fourth album *United Kingdom,* which, true to its title, is unissued in the states.

**48. *Liar,* the Jesus Lizard (Touch and Go, 1992)**
The production is pure Steve Albini, but the rhythmic drive is pure Jesus Lizard. Frontman David Yow possesses a singular yowl, and his stage antics have made the band's live shows notorious; but it's the band's screwy atonal guitar chords and angular rhythm shifts that have made the Jesus Lizard more than just another "alternative" put-on, and *Liar* is the band's most powerful work.

**49. *Watery, Domestic* EP, Pavement (Matador, 1992)**
Much like the Band before them, Pavement knowledgeably assimilate the elements of their tradition and use them to highlight their own personality. Originally a bicoastal recording group with several indie singles and EPs under its belt, Pavement eventually solidified its lineup and recorded a proper album, *Slanted and Enchanted,* and this EP, which is less wearing (thanks to its brevity) and contains some of the band's brightest moments.

**50. *Take the Guitar Player for a Ride,* Peter Laughner (Tim Kerr, 1994)**
Underrecorded underground legend Peter Laughner died in 1977. This two-record set (or one long CD with three tracks lopped off) consists of work

tapes—his work with the early Pere Ubu aside, he never recorded in a real studio—and attempts to encapsulate Laughner's sweet, sorry life in one fell swoop. Some of his songs are Dylanesque, others wear their Velvet Underground influence in the feedback, but all represent the work of a professional rock & roll fan who tried to pull his life together through the music that spoke to him. By turns frustratingly amateurish and surprisingly eloquent, Laughner's music was created for the same reason as every record on this list: out of the sheer need to say what he felt had gone unsaid for too long.

"Today, you see Pavement and Superchunk clones but you won't ever see Guided by Voices clones. It would be too hard to do. They'd have to have too good a knowledge of rock history."

—ROBERT POLLARD, GUIDED BY VOICES

# Heroes

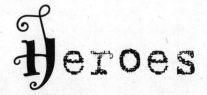

## PART 2

# and Villains

# Gimme Danger:
# The Stooges Saga

## by James Marshall

James Marshall, a.k.a. the Hound, has contributed to
*High Times, The New York Times, L.A. Weekly, The Vil-
lage Voice,* and worse. He is best-known through his
long-running radio program on WFMU, broadcast in East
Orange, New Jersey.

et us begin by stating that much of what occurs in the
name of Alternative Rock is an outgrowth—or, perhaps more accurately, a re-
hash—of what the Stooges and the Velvet Underground had achieved in the
late sixties and early seventies. To many ears, these two seminal groups still
represent the peak of a genre that has added relatively little to their respective
legacies.

The Stooges were the most despised band of their day and perhaps the most
esteemed band of *our* day. They had no hit records, received virtually no airplay and were met with indifference and outright revulsion by a youth culture
that preferred the solipsistic good vibes of Crosby, Stills and Nash or the
hackneyed blues rehashes of Ten Years After to the Stooges' "three-chord
train to hell."

Whatever else they were, the Stooges were above all a great rock & roll
band; they did what all great rock & rollers have done—create a magic that
can't be explained by fools who write about such things. The whole was
greater than the parts, and the parts themselves were a pretty unlikely bunch.

The Stooges straddled the Darwinian and great-man theories of history perfectly. They were a product of a time and place, they inherited a specific set
of musical influences, a collective sense of humor, irony, and sound. And they

were an integral part of what, for lack of a better term, we will call a scene, based in the Detroit–Ann Arbor, Michigan, axis.

Until Motown came along to sanitize it, the popular music created in and around Detroit was deliberately crude, ugly, and distorted. John Lee Hooker, with his brooding, hypnotic one-chord stomps, was the reigning blues king. The Fortune label served up its singular form of R&B exotica via Andre Williams, Nathaniel Mayer, and the Diablos. Rockabilly was accounted for by local greasers like Johnny Powers and Danny Zella. Detroit had also been the home base for more mainstream (though still decidedly oddball) talents like androgynous pop star Johnnie Ray, Hank Ballard and the Midnighters, and Jackie Wilson (the latter two were discovered on the same talent show by Johnny Otis in 1951).

By the early 1960s, a large suburban scene that had absorbed all these influences was breaking out all over Michigan, most noticeably around the college town of Ann Arbor, forty miles west of Detroit, where there were plenty of frat parties and teen mixers to provide work for budding players.

Ann Arbor's musical community encompassed Billy Lee and the Rivieras (later Mitch Ryder and the Detroit Wheels), the Fugitives, the Underdogs, the all-girl Pleasure Seekers (led by Suzi Quatro), the Del-Tinos (whose repertoire included numbers by Robert Johnson and the Trashmen), transplanted Texans, the Chicano-band ? and the Mysterians (who would score a monster hit with the garage-punk standard "96 Tears"), local DJ Terry Knight and his Pack (that band would later mutate into Grand Funk Railroad, while Knight himself would eventually end up in the federal witness relocation program), the Last Heard (led by future MOR star Bob Seger), the Rationals and the Motor City Five (later the MC5).

Enter James Osterberg, the son of a schoolteacher and a blue-collar Bendix Aerospace employee. Reared in an Ypsilanti trailer park, he transferred into Ann Arbor Pioneer High School in 1963. In an attempt to compensate for his working-class roots in an upper-middle-class school, Osterberg was soon pounding drums in a primitive two-man band known as the Megaton Two. That duo grew into the Iguanas (in which James rechristened himself Iggy, first with the surname Stooge, later amended to Pop) and hit the local circuit, eventually landing a summer stint at a northern Michigan resort in Harbor Springs playing five sets a night, six nights a week, serving up renditions of "Louie, Louie" (a tune Iggy would continue to perform in the decades to come), "Mona" (which the band cut as a 45), and other garage-band standards of the era.

In the summer of 1965, after graduating from high school, Iggy, enamored of the blues, quit the Iguanas and joined a white blues combo, the Prime Movers. Soon he got his high school pal Ron Asheton to join that band on bass, but neither lasted in the group for long. Iggy, at the invitation of Butterfield Blues Band drummer Sam Lay, soon headed for Chicago to apprentice drumming under blues greats like Walter Horton, Johnny Littlejohn, and

J.B. Hutto. Meanwhile, Asheton—whose only previous experience was in a basement punk band called the Dirty Shames—was soon demoted to roadie by the Prime Movers. Still, they let him rehearse with them, and soon he was accomplished enough to land a gig playing bass in the Chosen Few, a Stonesy local outfit led by singer Scott Richardson and guitarist James Williamson.

In Chicago Iggy spent time hanging around blues clubs and the basement of the Delmark Record Store. After eight months there, he had a brainstorm, Iggy told me a while back: "I was smoking a joint by the Chicago River one night, first joint I ever had in my life, and I thought, man, you don't belong here, get yourself some young guys who are unimpressed and make your own sound. I could take blues chords E to G, sometimes a D, sometimes a minor chord, sometimes to A, never to a B, 'cause then it's rock & roll. I could take them and it would be Detroit blues, young person's blues, use the 4/4 instead of the 6/8, and I was excited! I came back to Detroit and formed the Stooges."

Soon Iggy was back in Ann Arbor and rehearsing with the Dirty Shames, which included Ron Asheton, Ron's brother Scott and their neighbor Dave Alexander, all teenage misanthropes from the Division area of Ann Arbor. Only Ron had any real musical experience, but they had attitude and *that* impressed Iggy greatly. In short, they were the perfect raw, malleable material from which Iggy could construct his dream band.

Having yielded his drum stool ("a bad seat to drive from") to Scott Asheton, in early rehearsals Iggy tackled steel guitar and several homemade instruments including an amplified vacuum cleaner. These noise/art experiments were not as incongruous as they might now seem. For one thing, jazz critic John Sinclair had been managing the MC5 and had turned them and their scenemates on to avant-garde jazz, booking the likes of Sun Ra and Pharoah Sanders around Ann Arbor. And the Velvet Underground, themselves highly influenced by avant-noise of both the jazz and classical varieties, had passed through Ann Arbor in 1966 as part of Andy Warhol's Exploding Plastic Inevitable. Iggy had had an affair with the Velvets' beautiful Teutonic chanteuse Nico, and the Velvets' open-tuning drone and use of extreme feedback provided much inspiration for the Stooges, as did the aforementioned MC5, who by 1967 had created a powerful, loud sound that fused hard rock and free jazz. Other non-Detroit influences included Bob Dylan, the Rolling Stones, and Jim Morrison, and the auto-destructo pop-art sounds of the Who, the Yardbirds, and the Creation.

Other, nonmusical realities impinged themselves in the Stooges' development. The Vietnam War was raging, and the specter of the draft hung over the band members' heads. Ann Arbor was a hotbed of political activism, led by Sinclair, whose White Panther Party became a focal point for radical thought and action. At the same time, the area surrounding Detroit had moved from relative affluence to slow, steady economic decay. In other words, conditions were ripe for the sort of nihilistic, violent rock & roll that the Psychedelic Stooges (as they had initially dubbed themselves in early '67) were offering.

The band members began living together in a farmhouse, practicing every day. Their first gig was on March 3, 1968, at Detroit's Grande Ballroom, in the unlikely position of opening act for Blood, Sweat and Tears. Wearing golf shoes, Iggy played an electric washboard and Ron Asheton beat on an oil drum with a microphone inside. Soon the Stooges were playing small clubs all over Michigan, often on double bills with the MC5, with whom they would become close friends and musical allies. The MC5 had an incredible propaganda (i.e., hype) machine working for them, thanks to Sinclair's savvy string-pulling; without a record deal they'd even managed to get on the cover of ROLLING STONE.

In the fall of 1968, Elektra Records publicity director Danny Fields caught the MC5 and the Stooges at the Union Ballroom in Ann Arbor, and was impressed enough to drag Elektra's president, Jac Holzman, back to Michigan a week later to see the band play the Fifth Dimension teen club. Iggy, who had a 104-degree temperature at the time, appeared wearing whiteface and a maternity dress. By this point, the experimental instruments were gone, and the band had settled on the lineup of Iggy on vocals, Ron on guitar, Dave on bass, and Scott on drums. The Stooges were signed to Elektra in October 1968, and in June of '69 the band headed to New York's Hit Factory to record their first LP, with ex-Velvet Undergrounder John Cale producing.

The Stooges entered the studio with only five original songs in their repertoire: "Little Doll" (based around the bass riff from Pharoah Sanders' "Upper Egypt and Lower Egypt"), "Ann," "No Fun," "I Wanna Be Your Dog" and "1969." "Real Cool Time" and "Not Right" were written the day before the sessions, and the filler cut "We Will Fall" was created in the studio. The resulting album, *The Stooges,* was an ultra-crude masterpiece of teenage hard-on music. Ron Asheton's unrefined wah-wah/fuzztone-driven fifth chords and Iggy's snotty delivery of lyrics so dumb they transcended their own banality formed the basic blueprint for all the punk rock that followed.

*The Stooges* was issued in August of 1969, and immediately polarized the rock press. The album garnered rave reviews in *Creem, Circus, Rock,* and Britain's *New Musical Express.* More typical, however, was Ed Ward's ROLLING STONE piece, which ended with "So, cats and kitties, if you want to have a real cool time, just bop on down to your local platter vendor and pick up the Stooges' record, keeping in mind, of course, that it's loud, boring, tasteless, unimaginative, childish, obnoxious. . . ."

For the first time, the Stooges hit the road, soon appearing in New York City at the old World's Fair pavilion, where Iggy leapt off a ten-foot-high stage, cut his chest with a broken drumstick and scared the shit out of the entire audience. Promoter Howard Stein blamed his wife's miscarriage on seeing the Stooges.

The band spent the next year either touring or rehearsing in their farm-house, where they quickly became a tight, professional bunch of rank ama-teurs, their sound bubbling over in fury and violence. Iggy, 5 feet and 7 inches of wiry muscle and barely contained fury, made a nightly ritual of flying face-first into the audience, demolishing clubs and stages, and refusing to be ig-nored at any cost, even (especially) his own skin. Whatever members of the audience weren't appalled or terrified by Iggy's acrobatic assault became loyal fans, and the Stooges' cult began growing steadily.

Although the album's sales were less than staggering, Elektra—which re-putedly saw Iggy as a possible successor to the label's out-of-control meal ticket Jim Morrison—allowed the band to record a second LP. With ex-Kings-man Don Gallucci in the producer's chair, the band—which by now included a fifth member, Steve Mackay, on saxophone—entered an L.A. studio eleven months after the recording of the band's first album. The band's sophomore effort, *Funhouse,* displayed remarkable growth in execution and still stands as one of the greatest rock LPs ever made. The Stooges' bracingly ugly vision was fully realized, with Ron Asheton's brutal guitar chording setting up a re-lentless wash of distortion. Iggy's vocals—recorded through a cheap PA set up in the studio—are fierce and bruising: "I'm dirt/and I don't care" went the dirge that closed Side One, and with one listen anyone could tell that he meant it. Side Two, with Ron Asheton's pounding wah-wah pedal set against Steve Mackay's honking sax, is so ferocious that by the time it peters out into the free-form squall "L.A. Blues," the listener is left breathless and drained.

Meanwhile, the Stooges were playing bigger clubs and halls, including a legendary gig at the Fillmore West with the Flamin' Groovies and Alice Cooper (who'd moved from L.A. to Detroit in part to cop the nasty vibes the Stooges were giving off), and various rock festivals, including a 1970 Cincin-nati fest later broadcast on NBC that featured a dramatic clip of Iggy in prime punk-messiah form walking across the audience's hands and then smearing peanut butter all over his body.

At the same time, the Stooges' personal habits were changing along with their music. The drug choice at the farm had gone from pot and acid to speed, coke, and most tragically, heroin. Dave Alexander, who had been drinking heavily, froze up onstage at a rock festival and afterwards was fired by Iggy. With the departure of Alexander and then Mackay, 1970 saw a series of per-sonnel changes, with roadies Zeke Zettner and Bill Cheatham filling in on bass and rhythm guitar until bassist Jimmy Recca and guitarist James Williamson could be recruited. With the addition of the technically accomplished William-son, the Stooges reached their musical peak. They played a triumphant gig at Ungano's in New York, cementing the band's reputation as critics' darlings (and destroying their credibility with Elektra by refusing to play until label VP Bill Harvey forked over $400 for cocaine). At a subsequent show at Manhattan's Electric Circus, Iggy, encrusted in silver glitter, wowed the Warhol crowd and other Big Apple hepsters by barfing into the audience.

Despite their musical brilliance, the band was falling apart, with Iggy, Scott, and James having developed full-blown heroin habits. Manager Jimmy Silver had quit (he went on to become a millionaire health-food mogul in California), leaving baby-sitting duties to Danny Fields, who simply wasn't up to the task of managing this notoriously unmanageable band.

The new lineup auditioned for Elektra's Harvey and producer Gallucci a set of songs—at ear-splitting volume—for a proposed third album, including tunes like "Big Time Bum," "Searching for Head," and "Fresh Rag." But the label passed, releasing the band from its contract. Fields had by this time moved to Atlantic, where he managed to secure a deal for the MC5 (who'd been dropped by Elektra over the band's use of the word "motherfucker") and was attempting to do the same for the Stooges when, in June 1971, Iggy abruptly quit. Drained psychically and financially, the singer entered a methadone program to detox from his heroin addiction. Scott and James also went into detox. One roadie, a Vietnam vet, reenlisted so he could get back "in country," where smack was cheap. He died in 1975.

After rehab and some time spent mowing lawns for a living and playing golf, Iggy set out for New York, where he crashed on Fields's couch for several weeks before being offered a management deal by MainMan boss Tony DeFries, whose main client was Stooges fan David Bowie. With few options other than a less-than-promising offer to front Rick Derringer's new band, Iggy jumped at the opportunity. DeFries got Columbia Records president Clive Davis to sign Iggy for a reputed advance of several hundred thousand dollars. Iggy recruited latter-day Stooge Williamson, and in March 1972 the pair flew to England to record.

The decision to keep the Stooges moniker (now expanded to Iggy and the Stooges) rankled the spurned Asheton brothers, but after several weeks of auditioning British players, Iggy invited his old chums to rejoin the band in England, with Ron moving to bass since Williamson wanted to be sole guitarist. With the condition that Bowie would mix the LP, Iggy had secured the right to produce it. In the summer of 1972, the band laid down demos for such songs as "I Got a Right," "Sick of You," and "Tight Pants," which would later surface on a bewildering variety of quasi-legal albums. While still retaining its primal edge, the band—anchored by Williamson's screeching guitar work—was now a tight, professional-sounding rock band. The group played its only U.K. show on July 15, to a small but stunned crowd at London's King's Cross Cinema, with the *NME* reporting, "The total effect was more frightening than all the Alice Coopers and Clockwork Oranges put together, simply because these guys weren't joking."

After one complete LP was rejected by Columbia (where are those tapes today?), the final version of *Raw Power* was completed by the fall. Recorded on twenty-four tracks with a multi-layered assortment of guitar overdubs, it represented another substantial leap forward for the Stooges. Despite Bowie's unnecessarily arty mix (which removed most of the drums), *Raw Power* remains a masterpiece. More than ever, Iggy's lyrics fit his impetuous persona; "the world's forgotten boy/the one who searches and destroys . . ." was shrieked to an audience more attuned to the poetic banalities of James Taylor and endless boogie of the Allman Brothers. Like twin peaks of inspiration, all of Iggy's narcissism and self-hatred had welled up like an ugly boil, which erupted in songs like "Death Trip," "Hard to Beat" (later retitled "Your Pretty Face Has Gone to Hell"), and "Penetration." Elsewhere, the band expanded its musical scope by including its first straight blues, "I Need Somebody," and the Jim Morrisonesque ballad "Gimme Danger," which offered a telling look inside Iggy's tortured soul (where "there's nothing in my dreams/just some ugly memories"). Williamson's churning guitar spew picked up where Ron Asheton's had left off on *Funhouse*. The culmination of the Stooge's style, *Raw Power* represents a rock & roll milestone that has never been equalled.

Returning to the States and under DeFries's orders to "act like stars," Iggy and the Stooges relocated to Los Angeles, where they rented a huge house in the Hollywood Hills that became the site of some still-legendary parties. After numerous delays (and, according to some sources, deliberate sabotage) from the MainMan camp, *Raw Power* was issued in May 1973 to rave reviews and unspectacular if slightly improved sales (it cracked the Top 200—barely). With little hope of radio play, touring was the Stooges' main shot at album promotion. But hassles with MainMan, which reportedly tried to force Williamson out of the band, kept the group cooling its heels in Hollywood for many months. After freeing themselves from DeFries, the band finally hit the road in late July, by which time *Raw Power* was, commercially speaking, a dead issue.

The trek, which Iggy called "my blows-against-the-empire tour," went ahead anyway. The band, now a quintet with the addition of Scott Thurston on piano, wowed 'em at New York's Max's Kansas City (where Iggy belly-flopped onto a broken bottle), the Whisky in L.A., and other Stooges strongholds. The months spent holed up in L.A. had given the band plenty of time to write, so the tour's sets found the *Raw Power* material augmented by newer numbers like "Open Up and Bleed," "Head on the Curb," "Cock in My Pocket" and "Wet My Bed." In retrospect, Iggy must have been delusional to think that the teens of 1973 would want to hear such ditties, but the Stooges carried on, playing to an audience that heard rumors of greater and stranger atrocities occurring at each show. Fueled by a variety of substances ranging from vodka to heroin, Iggy grew progressively wilder and more out of control ("Whatever Iggy did, he did a lot of," said one former Stooges associate). Columbia attempted to record the band's show at New York's Academy of

Music on New Year's Eve 1973, but Iggy was so out of it that he could barely sing, falling off the stage repeatedly and introducing the same tune five times in a row. No one was surprised when Columbia dropped the band.

Things looked even less promising after a particularly nasty series of gigs in and around Detroit, where Iggy's onstage confrontation with a motorcycle gang led to the blood feast captured on the quasi-bootleg album *Metallic K.O.* Those gigs proved to be the Stooges' last shows (their farewell tune was an appropriately filthy rendition of "Louie, Louie"), with Iggy once again the first one to throw in the towel; without a record label or management and with little hope of getting either, standing onstage in a G-string while being pelted by bikers with debris hardly seemed worth the trouble.

Iggy returned to L.A. where, after a period spent mostly wandering around Hollywood in Jim Morrison's leather pants, he checked himself into UCLA's Neuropsychiatric Institute to detox. Thanks to a jump start from the still-faithful David Bowie, by 1977 Iggy had jumped headlong into an erratic solo career. The Ashetons returned to Division and still play music. James Williamson is a computer programmer in San Francisco. Scott Thurston is a high-priced session player (he played on Iggy's best solo disc, 1979's Williamson-produced *New Values*). Dave Alexander drank himself to death in 1975.

These days, everyone loves the Stooges. From the Sex Pistols to Guns n' Roses, their songs have become standards for anyone looking for that ever-elusive punk credibility. Unbelievably, "1969" even appeared on an MCI TV commercial. Every low-fi scrap of live performances and rehearsals have found their way to bootleg CDs and cassettes. Stooges T-shirts can be spotted in every city from America to Japan. Iggy, meanwhile, is now almost fifty and a revered rock institution, still diving into the audience, breaking mike stands, and looking for that elusive hit record. As the title of one bootleg EP went, "Jesus Loves the Stooges." Amen.

# On Roky Erickson and Mexican Food

## by King Coffey

King Coffey has been playing drums with the Austin, Texas-based Butthole Surfers since 1983. Roky Erickson's first new album in over a decade, *All That May Do My Rhyme,* was released in 1995 by Coffey's Trance Syndicate label.

About fifteen years ago I went to a Pancho's in Fort Worth, Texas, with my best friend, Phil Flowers, and we met Lorna Hicks for the first time. All three of us were punk rockers, in high school, living in Texas, enduring the death of the seventies. We became friends for life right there on the spot.

Tonight, November 15, 1994, Phil and Lorna (now married) and I went to Pancho's with Roky Erickson (his suggestion). Roky, former lead singer of the legendary Thirteenth Floor Elevators, has been credited with singlehandedly inventing psychedelic music. For some reason, I feel like I'm back in high school. To paraphrase Roky, we have always been here before.

Pancho's is a chain of Mexican restaurants serving blobs of starch coated with Velveeta cheese. The food is not good. The decor is garish. Mexican Muzak plays in the background. Why do we go there? It's cheap and all-you-can-eat. When you want more Velveeta, you raise a little Mexican flag on your table and a waitress scurries over bearing more Velveeta.

As teen punks, we ate there a lot. When bands came through town, we'd take them there. Why? Because it was cheap and all-you-can-eat.

One time Hüsker Dü (my favorite band on the planet) were crashing at my house (my dad is a patient man), and they bought me a piñata—in the shape of a duck dressed like Santa Claus—at Pancho's. It was a significant moment in my life.

So flash forward and here I am, back at Pancho's, dining with Roky Erickson. We have been joining him for dinner every Tuesday for about seven months now. In a few months my record label, Trance Syndicate, will release Roky's first new studio album in almost a decade.

Trance Syndicate was started about five years ago as a way to put out records by Texas bands who I thought needed to be heard. Since then, we have spewed forth wonderful (to me) records by Bedhead, Cherubs, Crust, Ed Hall, johnboy, Pain Teens, and other greats. Trance Syndicate is a labor of love. I haven't made any money doing it. I do it because it is fun and because, to me, it is the very essence of punk rock.

But now we're putting out a new Roky Erickson album. The label has just been profiled in *Billboard* magazine. All of a sudden the label seems serious. We have a real office. We all have ever-increasing responsibilities. While ignoring the plate of Velveeta in front of me, I'm thinking about all this as I'm staring at the devilish twinkle in Roky's eyes.

I think about what brought me here, with this group of people, at this time in my life. I think about how punk rock forever changed my life by making me appreciate almost anything that was out of the ordinary or strived to defy the mainstream. It allowed me to appreciate things of value that most people reject outright.

I think about how *punk rock* the Elevators' big hit "You're Gonna Miss Me" seemed to me when I first heard it. Roky screams in the song, his voice oozing with distinctively Texan soul. There's also a weird electronic bubbling sound made by the band's electric jug player, Tommy Hall. And there's Roky playing harmonica like his life depended on it. The song is timeless.

I think about all the acid I've taken. I think about how Texan punk rock, like Texas's psychedelic garage rock a generation earlier, has always been a little weird compared to its counterparts from other regions of the country. I think about how many times the band I play in, the Butthole Surfers, listened to the Elevators' *Easter Everywhere* album while spending much of the eighties crossing the country in a van. I look at Roky and think about all the acid *he's* probably taken, being at LSD ground zero in San Francisco in the late sixties (the Elevators were virtually chased out of Texas and found a temporary home in the Bay Area), and how vehemently Roky hates illicit drugs now.

When I first met Roky, I was starstruck. I had trouble speaking. I never get starstruck, but this was *Roky Erickson*. After the Elevators split up in the early seventies, Roky made some amazing records that were as raw and vital as any punk-rock recordings of the time. Songs like "Bermuda" and "Two Headed Dog" still send chills down my spine.

But the main reason I couldn't speak was how damn loud Roky's house was. He always has various TVs, radios, and police scanners hooked up to a complex, ever-changing series of amplifiers and speakers strewn throughout the house, and Roky is genius enough to follow every single transmission.

There's never a dull moment with Roky. He's always making off-the-wall comments. Once we were driving around and I asked him, half-jokingly, if he planned to vote in the upcoming election. Without missing a beat, he replied "I'm voting right now!" I believed him.

Sometimes Roky laughs and it's such an intense laughter that it causes you to laugh. Then he laughs harder. Then you laugh back even harder.

Sometimes when I look at Roky, though, despite his charming smile and his gentle nature, I get angry. I get mad because he has been treated so poorly by the industry he's contributed so much to. He is, to many, a singer as great as Janis Joplin, a songwriter as influential as Buddy Holly, yet he has seen shockingly little money for his incredible body of music.

If the record business has been unkind, even downright mean, to Roky, the U.S. legal system has been worse. Roky was sentenced to three years in a state-run hospital for the criminally insane because he made the mistake of being caught with a couple of joints in 1969 in the state of Texas. While there, he formed an all-inmate band, the Missing Links, read hundreds of books, was given electroshock and experimental drug treatments, and wrote a book of poetry entitled *Openers*. He now survives through Social Security and the kindness of friends and family.

Despite the multiple cruelties that life has dealt him, Roky still has his amazing musical soul. I've seen him casually pick up an acoustic guitar and belt out a Bob Dylan cover that'll leave my jaw on the floor. Just as abruptly, he'll stop, put down the guitar and tell you that he's "just relaxing."

I look at Roky again and think what an immense responsibility it is to be releasing a Roky Erickson LP. This is a chance for him to catch up financially with some of what the music business owes him. And it's a chance for me to do something good for a true pioneer, a musical genius, someone whom I love. The responsibility seems so huge that I get overwhelmed thinking about it and my body tenses up.

I then remember what Casey Monahan, the coproducer of Roky's new album, told me after he managed to talk Roky back into the studio for the first time since he retired from the business in disgust in 1984. "Okay," Roky said, "as long as we have fun."

Roky then raises the little Mexican flag at our table and I smile.

# Why Hawkwind Is the Greatest Band in the Universe

by Jim Green

Los Angeles-based freelance scribe and Hawkwind scholar Jim Green—who has actually appeared on *Beverly Hills 90210*—is a veteran of the pages of the late-and-lamented *Trouser Press*. His esteemed résumé also includes stints as a syndicated-radio producer and rock & roll musician.

If your notion of "alternative" is defined by a bunch of shoegazers, pop-punks, high-speed retro-rockers, and attitude-casters in funny clothes, then please consider that veritable institution of otherness that is Hawkwind.

Hawkwind has heard the complaints pretty much since Day One (the band released its first album in 1970): too loud, too hard, too fast, too drone-y, too many over-the-top sci-fi lyrics—and they go on too damn long. Hawkwind has long been taken to task for being, in a word, excessive. But that epithet indicates a fundamental misunderstanding of the band's essential charm. Indeed, Hawkwind (under the leadership of its founder and sole charter member, guitarist/singer Dave Brock) has built a career on making excess a virtue: shaping the music early on with too many drugs (and getting busted for it too), getting their songs heard the best way they knew how, by playing nearly every benefit gig attached to any cause they fancied. Recording vast numbers of albums as musicians, join, leave and return in baffling succession (to say nothing of the formidable if nonmusical Stacia who, after undulating in varying stages of undress at early gigs, was eventually inducted as a fully accredited member).

Hawkwind has always been alternative to whatever has been generally considered "alternative" at any given time during the band's history. It was never enough for Hawkwind merely to raise the hackles of "the establishment"—nay, they've managed to estrange themselves (intentionally or not) from the cognoscenti of nearly every musical movement that's held sway since the band's inception in 1969 (or 1968, if you want to count former blues busker Brock's Group X, which became Hawkwind Zoo, which became . . . ).

And how's *this* for alt cred: 1970's historic Isle of Wight festival was a star-studded celebration of the "hip" rock culture of the day (Dylan, Hendrix, etc.), so naturally Hawkwind played there—but they played for free, outside the festival grounds. The British press, who'd figured the fest would supply plenty to gawk at anyway, were tickled by the sight of the 'wind's legendarily flamboyant sax player, Nik Turner, who'd painted himself silver for the occasion (in later years, Turner would continue his tradition of sartorial eloquence by dressing up as a frog).

And how about the way Hawkwind scored their first (and only) hit? In early 1972 Hawkwind played a benefit for an alternative music organization called the Greasy Truckers, and the occasion was documented on a double live LP that featured a full side of Hawkwind. But it was an *outtake* from those tapes, a previously unreleased ditty called "Silver Machine," that soared to Number Three on the U.K. singles charts (Guinness *British Hit Singles* identifies Hawkwind as a "male vocal/instrumental group with female dancer"!). Typically, the follow-up, "Urban Guerilla," was no mere flop—it was withdrawn by the band's label for being "in poor taste"!

Brock (the one constant in the band's dizzying family tree) and recurrent member Robert Calvert (who died in 1988) explored all manner of cosmic/futuristic lyrical themes, but the band took its sci-fi connections to a new peak in 1973, when noted author Michael Moorcock began writing and occasionally performing with them (and proceeded to make the band members the protagonists of the "Black Sword" mythos in a trio of novels he wrote with Michael Butterworth).

Few of their peers have been willing to acknowledge Hawkwind's style and influence, then or now. Early on, critics greeted Hawkwind's hard-charging guitar, blaring sax, and obnoxious synthi-squeaks with great skepticism, yet eagerly lapped up a not-dissimilar sound when Roxy Music debuted a year or two later (is it a coincidence that Brian Eno hailed from Ladbroke Grove, as did the 'wind's own original electronics elf Dik Mik?). And didn't it seem obvious on Lollapalooza '94's Second Stage (i.e., the alternative stage at the alternative festival), that whole chunks of Stereolab's set could've passed as Hawkwind Lite—and that they'd be utterly mortified at the thought? And what about the band's undeniable influence on the ambient/

trance/rave scene? While the Grateful Dead (hippie-era contemporaries whose communal ideals, penchant for endless live jams, and rabidly devoted cult following parallels Hawkwind's) have belatedly won grudging respect from hipsters, Hawkwind have remained consistently unfashionable among rock's intelligentsia.

(It's also worth pointing out Hawkwind's role in spawning Motörhead, a band that's long stood as a paragon of ear-splitting iconoclasm on the hardrock/heavy-metal scene. The band's name came from a song that early Hawkwind bassist Ian "Lemmy" Kilmister wrote as the B side of the Hawks' "Kings of Speed" single; he was soon booted out of Hawkwind after being busted for amphetamines while on tour in Canada, and the rest is history.)

Hawkwind has released an absurdly large number of albums, about five dozen at last count (although, to be fair, many consist of live material issued years after the fact, with no participation or authorization from current lineups—but that sort of thing's hard to control when more than two dozen musicians have passed through a band). Studio efforts like *Doremi Fasol Latido, Hall of the Mountain Grill, Warrior on the Edge of Time,* and the uncharacteristically poppy *Quark Strangeness and Charm* and undeniably pretentious *Chronicle of the Black Sword* may stand out, but, not surprisingly, so do (legit) live albums like the vintage *Space Ritual,* the eighties-vintage *Live Chronicles* (featuring live renderings of the Black Sword material), and *Zones.*

At the time of this writing, the latest Hawkwind album—incorporating elements of the ambient and techno movements the group helped inspire—is *It Is the Business of the Future to Be Dangerous,* but by the time you have read this the band will have undoubtedly released several more. Whatever the nature of Hawkwind's future excursions, it's a matter of record that the band, in its various incarnations, has already spent more than a quarter-century rubbing everybody but hardcore devotees the wrong way. And if that's not "alternative," I don't know what is.

# Alex Chilton: Grandpappy of Power Pop

The enigmatic singer/songwriter/guitarist Alex Chilton could lay claim—but, of course, he never would!—to influencing two generations of alt-popsters via his early-seventies combo Big Star (which he co-founded with singer/songwriter/guitarist Chris Bell): from the dB's, to R.E.M., to the Replacements, to Primal Scream, to Teenage Fanclub . . . the list goes on and on. What does Mr. Chilton have to say on the subject? Here's a sprinkling of his thoughts on his work as a songwriter and with Big Star. (Thanks to Epic Soundtracks for some of the following quotes, originally published in an extensive 1984 interview in the London 'zine, *What a Nice Way to Turn Seventeen*.)

"Big Star was gotten together to sound like the Beatles. We did our best and succeeded pretty well too. The concept of the group was to be like a mid-sixties British group and the Beatles were the most among them. Until the Beatles came along in the mid-sixties, I really wasn't much of a rock & roll fan. I was listenin' to my dad's jazz records. . . . Chet Baker was my first inspiration to start singing."

"Led Zeppelin and all those bands that went into those ten-minute long solos, they were the big things around in those days [when Big Star started]. We used to say 'Hey Chris, let's get jammin'!' and he'd go . . . 'Bleeeagh!' "

"[While recording the third Big Star LP, *Sister Lovers*] I was gettin' pretty crazy, and into some pretty rotten drugs and drinkin' a lot, and I just wasn't thinkin' in any practical terms at all—after having the first two Big Star albums go pretty much unsought. Somewhere along the line I figured out that if you only press up one hundred copies of a record, then eventually it will find its way to the one hundred people in the world who want it the most."

"[In] 1973, predrugs . . . when I was getting really intense, wondering just why I was so unhappy. . . . I'd learned to write all these confused nonsensical lyrics from Chris [Bell] and [bassist] Andy [Hummel]. For whatever good confusion is worth, I think it's more important to tell people they don't have to be confused rather than to console them in their confusion . . . it is possible. To me, my best songs are more positive sorts of things. The really maudlin things I don't think are my best songs, just cause I don't see any reason to play music that makes people feel bad.

"Ever since '76 or '75 or sometime, I realized how to go about writing some lyrics and writing a tune and actually being able to put down succinctly what I wanted to say, in the most economical terms. I began to realize how to do that, and as soon as I did, then I said to myself, 'Well, okay, what kind of a song do I want to write?' I realized that I didn't wanna write about things like I'd been writing about, suffering and what have you. I wanted to write about positive things to send out into the world, not things that really just coddled peoples' maudlin sensibilities. Even though now, I guess, I still write in a kind of negative way."

"I've never considered myself to be much of a great songwriter. I mean I've written maybe five tunes in my life, or maybe it's between five and ten that I think are pretty good, and of those, I think five of them are worth doing. There are a couple of Big Star songs—one called 'In the Street,' one called 'When My Baby's Beside Me,' one called 'September Girls' that's fair. The best song I've ever written is [from] one of my solo recordings . . . called 'I've Got a Thing for You.' "

"It doesn't surprise me that there's such a big following [of Big Star], but I sorta think [the band is] overrated. It's the sort of music that appeals to young guys who are picking up guitars and don't really know much about playing them. And they hear this kind of stuff and it's music made by somebody in a situation much like they are. I was the same kind of twenty-year-old kid when I made those recordings, and I think it just sorta strikes a resonant chord with people who are in the same boat—you know, confused, twenty-year-old college students with a guitar in their hands."

"For me, the best group of the last few years has been Teenage Fanclub. I'm sort of a big fan of theirs. The Replacements were a great group, but I tell you, not much of new music appeals to me very much."

# The dB's: What Happened?

## by Peter Holsapple

Peter Holsapple sang, wrote, and played with the dB's from 1978 until 1988. He is presently a member of the Continental Drifters and a solo artist. He has also recorded and performed live with such acts as R.E.M., Juliana Hatfield, Hootie and the Blowfish, the Indigo Girls, the Troggs, the Cowsills, and Giant Sand, and has had his songs recorded by various artists. He now lives in New Orleans with his wife and band mate Susan Cowsill and their daughter Miranda.

These days, it seems that the position my former band the dB's hold in the pantheon of rock is in flux. In the rosy glow of hindsight, the group has taken on an almost grandfatherly aura in the eyes of its fans, some of whom are participants in present-day alt-rock success stories. The dB's never attained the level of visibility and acceptance achieved by some of our contemporaries, i.e., R.E.M., the Bangles, and the Replacements. It would even be a stretch to say that we earned a regular living from our records and tours, though certainly not from lack of effort (or quality) on our part. Let's just say that the dB's—Gene Holder, Will Rigby, Chris Stamey, Jeff Beninato, and myself—never seemed to be in the right place at the right time. Consequently, the overwhelmingly positive retrospective judgment of our contributions strikes me as slightly bizarre—though somehow fitting for a group that was either way ahead or way behind the time and tide of public sentiment.

It kind of makes sense, since we were all avid Big Star fans. That band's lack of worldwide success was always the Great Mystery to us. Once at Irving Plaza in New York, Alex Chilton played a show with the dB's. I commented innocently to Alex that I couldn't believe that *he* was opening for *us*. Alex may have misinterpreted that for gloating, but it was simply my sincere belief that in this world, that billing would never happen.

Welcome to the parallel world of the dB's. Virtually every conscious move (and there were many) that we believed could open doors and help us become a more popular band blew up in our faces. It was like having a curse on our professional life. While we did eventually ascend to some level of acceptance, the dB's never became the household abbreviation we'd hoped it would. Writing this seven years after the band's dissolution, I still can't come up with a convincing answer to "What do you think went wrong?" It's nearly as hard to respond to as "What kind of music do you play?" I don't know, I just write it and live it

In considering the factors at work in the band's career, we could start with our name. That's capital-T-h-e-space-lower-case-d-capital-B-apostrophe-s. Six little letters and a common punctuation mark gave people more problems than we could have ever imagined. I think that we saw, at one time or another, every possible mathematical combination of those letters. We would make gentle suggestions to club bookers as to the correct spelling, then would tool into town and find misspellings everywhere. We even told the folks putting up the letters on the marquees in front of clubs to use an inverted capital P for the lower-case d, and they would look at us like we were arrogant jerks for even mentioning it. At one point we even put a $100 fine into our contract rider for misspellings, but nobody ever paid up, since we never went on the road with signed contracts anyway. Somewhere toward the end of the band's ten-year lifespan, I think Will was trying to rally us behind a name change; but, ever the positive thinkers, we felt that we might stand to lose the groundwork we'd made under our original appellation.

The dB's made good records, some of which I can still listen to today. We tried to be creative without being obnoxiously clever; we attempted to make easily enjoyable music that would yield new levels of musical and emotional content through repeated listenings. Our efforts getting it to sound right could border on the pedantic. Painstaking and exacting on ourselves, it's amazing we didn't second-guess ourselves out of existence early in our recording career. Instead, I felt, and still feel, that our output was, on balance, distinctive, intelligent, and worthy of pride.

On the other hand, the mechanics of getting those records released was a constant source of distress. Our first two albums, *Stands for deciBels* (1981) and *Repercussion* (1982)—both recorded for the hopeful and imaginative British label Albion—went unreleased in the U.S. Albion did as much as they could from across the pond. The cassette version of *Stands for deciBels* came packaged in a bean can, requiring an opener to extract the music. Albion even attached a free cassette copy of *Repercussion* to vinyl copies of that album, ostensibly to prevent home taping of the record.

But in the case of those two albums, home taping was probably one of our best sources of exposure. I was working in a Manhattan record store at the time—knowing enough not to quit my day job until earthshaking success caught up with the dB's—and I found it unconscionable to recommend my own high-priced import albums to shoppers when there were cheaper domestic copies of XTC and Squeeze albums on hand. And, since the first two albums were not released here, that meant that they weren't serviced to radio stations. The college DJs who played the dB's had to bring in their own copies of the records. Commercial stations didn't even figure in. We were strangers in our own market.

So we went to Europe, just in time to be lost in the synthesizer-driven dance-pop craze ignited by bands like the Human League and Orchestral Manoeuvres in the Dark. Guitar-oriented pop rock was decidedly out of fashion in England, as was made clear when we found ourselves playing a huge club in Liverpool to a total of six people, three of whom were members of the Yachts. Sweden was a different story. We were gladly accepted there, got wined and dined by our licensees and felt fleetingly like kings. Returning to New York to gigs at half-empty clubs quickly jolted us back to the proletariat.

It took forever, but the dB's eventually did get a deal with an American label, Bearsville. We thought that was a cool move, considering the company's past associations with Todd Rundgren, Sparks, and Bobby Charles. After mixing "Love Is for Lovers," we frolicked around the studio control room, convinced that the track would be the key to our as-yet-unborn children's trust funds. By this point, Chris had left for a solo career, and for the first time I was responsible for coming up with an entire album's worth of songs on my own. I rose to the occasion and we made what I still consider a wonderful record—not to mention one that seemed relatively well-suited to the needs of American radio. Will, Gene, and I were finally in a position to be heard and wanted in the United States.

Or so we thought. The week of the scheduled release of *Like This,* Bearsville ended its longstanding distribution arrangement with Warner Bros. That pretty much meant that our record couldn't be shipped to stores until Bearsville got a new distributor—something that they didn't seem to be in any great rush to do. Review copies did go out to the press, but a large number of those turned out to be *Like This* sleeves containing the latest smooth soul offerings from Harold Melvin and the Bluenotes. A tour with R.E.M., who were beginning to take off commercially, proved relatively fruitless since there were no records in the stores.

The obvious next step was to get out of our Bearsville contract, but as we were negotiating with Bearsville's notoriously hardball owner Albert Grossman, he died on an airplane bound for France. Albert, a savvy man in most respects, left no provisions of what to do in the event of his demise. It ended up taking us a couple of years to escape our Bearsville deal, but there were some acts signed to the label that never even got to make a record, and they were even more stuck than us.

Meanwhile, we had watched our pals R.E.M. gather momentum on I.R.S. Records, the label that had previously launched the Go-Go's to stardom. Peter Buck lobbied long and hard for us at I.R.S. and the label eventually agreed to sign us, but not without my signing a copublishing deal with I.R.S. Music, the label's music-publishing arm. The time-honored wisdom in the music business is that you don't give your song publishing to the same company you record for, but I was willing to fly in the face of convention (and common sense) in order to get another dB's album out. We felt positive about our new affiliation and plowed ahead.

Our I.R.S. debut, *The Sound of Music,* was an all-out attempt on our part to make an album that radio could not ignore. But once we finished the record, it was as if our involvement in it was finished. I.R.S. insisted on releasing a ballad—not particularly representative of the band or the album—as the first single. It stiffed, as did the second single, which was even accompanied by a fairly arty promotional video. Another tour with R.E.M. (this time without Gene, who'd bowed out shortly after we recorded *The Sound of Music*) created nary a stir, and we found ourselves back in the same clubs we'd been playing for years. It was very demoralizing.

Our live shows were probably where a lot of impact was lost. We were not fashion plates, nor were Chris, Will, or I blessed with what you'd call particularly robust voices. Our carefully planned harmonies would fray microtonally to the point that instrumental passages were greatly looked forward to by both audience and band. Even then, we were consistently beset by mechanical gremlins in the form of broken-down amps and untuneable guitars. That's the usual stuff of live bands, I realize, but as with so much in our little world, it occurred with nearly epidemic frequency and totality. While we did have our share of fine, energetic, and tuneful shows, they were probably the exception, I'm afraid. Most of the live tapes of us that I've chanced upon have been pretty awful, which might explain the dearth of any dB's bootleg albums.

Our tribulations extended to our efforts in the still-emerging medium of music video. The video for our song "Amplifier," directed by Walter Williams, was a darkly funny romp through the jolly land of suicide, a subject I was quite familiar with. This may have made it appear even darker to my closest friends and relations, but I thought it was a scream. It was a step forward for me, to help move past earlier emotional lows and not take things so seriously. The censors at the major music video network were not amused, however, so Walter graciously edited in a "don't try this at home" introduction featuring his famous and pathetic clay hero Mr. Bill (who may be seen as an appropriate personification of our band's history). Even with the prologue, MTV told us that it was a nice try, but no dice. This was infuriating and depressing, considering some of the tasteless, violent, and misogynistic stuff they've put in heavy rotation before and since. We had better luck with smaller local video channels. A New Jersey station played "Amplifier" a lot, and I corresponded with one of that station's viewers for years after she first contacted me to say that the video had helped her rethink her own suicidal desires.

So the dB's did affect people, even if on a much different level than we'd first envisioned. The majority of the world never heard—or heard of—us, but we apparently did mean a lot to the small segment of the world that did. We were blessed that our songs struck some nerve in people in different parts of the world, particularly in our fellow musicians, whose praise often provided the temporary validation we needed. Our press kit grew into an unwieldy mountain of plaudits, but I knew from my record-store experience that good press doesn't necessarily translate into commercial success.

We thought we were just being melodic, tasteful, and smart, but maybe we thought it was better than it actually was (although we were self-effacing to a fault—one interband joke had us taking the stage with a casual "Hi, we're the dB's, and we're sorry" to atone in advance for any disasters to come). And nowhere does it say that a rock band has to be popular. There have been Haystacks Balboas and Helmet Boys for every generation of rock so far. My friend Dave Catching once told me, "Don't think of it as failure, think of it as moderate success." Dave's a wise man.

I can't dwell on where the dB's went wrong. Life's too short to be mired in the swampy past. I even consider us lucky in having gone from up-and-coming to also-rans to posthumously wonderful in a comparatively short period of time and without substantial radio play. When our pals R.E.M. took off for the stratosphere, we hoped we might follow suit, but not everyone can fly.

In the last few years, Big Star, Television, and the Velvet Underground have reformed for the benefit of an apologetic public that missed them the first time around. The one time Chris, Gene, Will, and I reunited—for a benefit show in the band's original home state of North Carolina—some overzealous union stagehands cut our power in the middle of "Amplifier." Although I'm not a big one for premonitions and such, that certainly doesn't bode well for any more dB's shows in the future. That's fine, too. We parted as friends, still love each other dearly and have moved on to other projects. I don't think I could face another assault on the merry-go-round.

It's peculiar to write about one's own history and try to make some objective sense of why it all turned out the way it did; it's also weird to be called upon as something of an expert on falling through the proverbial cracks. I'd like to believe that out of our individual endeavors, we ex-dB's (as the stickers attached to said projects inevitably refer to us) might have something more than an illustrious and damaged past to call our own. After all, we're not dead yet, nor are we retired. There is no sign of a boxed set or tribute album on the horizon—although at the time of this writing my present band, the Continental Drifters, finds itself in competition for sales with a hastily assembled batch of latter-day dB's demos, *Paris Avenue*. I can only hope that the ghost of a good band will not haunt the present of an equally deserving (and physically extant) one.

In the parallel world of the dB's, though, anything could happen.

"Basically, I hate pop stars unless they're me or personal friends of mine."

—SHANE MACGOWAN

# The Alt-Rock Book of the Dead

**G. G. Allin,** d. June 28, 1993, age 36. The notoriously confrontational über-punk, whose stage act often included violence, defecation, and self-mutilation—and who had often threatened to commit suicide onstage—died of a heroin overdose in New York City. The day before, the much-arrested performer and his band, the Murder Junkies, had played a Manhattan show that ended in a mini-riot, with Allin escaping from police by diving through a plate-glass window.

**Lester Bangs,** d. April 30, 1982, age 33. The seminal work of this much-beloved rock critic (and occasional recording artist), which appeared in *Creem,* ROLLING STONE, and *The Village Voice,* almost singlehandedly changed the face of music journalism. Bangs died from complications of a Darvon overdose, apparently accidental.

**Stiv Bators,** d. June 4, 1990, age 37. The Cleveland-bred Stiv Bators fronted CBGB regulars the Dead Boys and the London-based punk supergroup the Lords of the New Church. Bators was run over by a bus in Paris, walked away from the accident—reportedly because his drug use left his system so inured to pain—and died later that night of his injuries.

**Chris Bell,** d. December 27, 1978, age 27. Long-troubled singer/song-writer/guitarist Bell, who founded Memphis power-pop pioneers Big Star, was killed in his hometown when the car he was driving hit a telephone pole. Bell's only solo album, *I Am the Cosmos,* wasn't released until fourteen years after his death.

**Marc Bolan,** d. September 16, 1977, age 29. The T. Rex mainman's infectious glitter pop and pixieish persona influenced numerous contemporaries and countless later artists. He was killed when his car crashed into a tree, while he and girlfriend Gloria Jones were driving home from clubbing in London.

**D. Boon,** d. December 23, 1985, age 27. As singer/guitarist of the adventurous agit-punk trio the Minutemen, Dennes Dale Boon eloquently merged raw punk catharsis with articulate political and personal expression. He was killed in a van accident in the Arizona desert. His fellow Minutemen Mike Watt and George Hurley eventually formed fIREHOSE.

**Kurt Cobain,** d. April 5, 1994, age 27. The Nirvana leader's suicide by gunshot is alt-rock's answer to the JFK assassination, or at least the killing of John Lennon, defining-moment-wise. For nearly three years prior to the singer/guitarist's death, reports of his heroin use and fragile mental state persisted, but were consistently explained away by band, management, and record company.

**Joe Cole,** d. December 19, 1991, age 30. Cole, son of TV actor Dennis Cole, onetime Black Flag roadie, boyfriend to original Babes in Toyland bassist Michelle Leon, and close friend and roommate of Henry Rollins, was shot to death after he and Rollins were accosted by a pair of armed men while en route to their L.A. home.

**Darby Crash,** d. December 8, 1980, age 22. Crash, born Paul Beahm, hyperactive frontman of the early L.A. hardcore combo the Germs, died of a heroin overdose shortly after the band released its debut album.

**Ian Curtis,** d. May 18, 1980, age 23. Considering the bleak lyrical visions favored by Joy Division frontman Curtis, few were shocked when he ended up taking his own life. Curtis hanged himself just four days before his band was scheduled to begin its first U.S. tour. His bandmates eventually regrouped as New Order.

**Pete Farndon,** d. April 14, 1983, age 29. Just ten months after being ousted from the Pretenders for various personal habits including his heroin addiction, Farndon died of a heart attack resulting from drug-related complications—thus becoming the second original Pretender to suffer a drug-related demise.

**Rick Garberson,** d. July 15, 1979. The drummer with the Akron, Ohio, Bizarros died from carbon monoxide poisoning, apparently accidental.

**Martin Hannett,** d. April 18, 1991, age 42. English producer Hannett—whose resume included influential work with Joy Division, New Order, Buzzcocks, Magazine, U2, the Stone Roses, Happy Mondays, and Kitchens of Distinction—died in his sleep at home, from health problems related to his long-standing drug use.

**Hollywood Fats,** d. December 8, 1986, age 32. This acclaimed L.A. guitarist, born Michael Mann, died of a heart attack shortly after replacing Dave Alvin in the Blasters.

**James Honeyman-Scott,** d. June 16, 1982, age 24. Ironically, two days after the Pretenders fired bassist Pete Farndon over his drug use, the band's guitarist, James Honeyman-Scott, died in drug-related circumstances. Apparently, Honeyman-Scott had been detoxifying his system in order to kick an addiction to cocaine and suffered a fatal reaction after accepting a strong dose of coke at a party.

**Doug Hopkins,** d. December 5, 1993, age 32. Guitarist/founder of Arizona's Gin Blossoms, Hopkins wrote much of the material for the band's break-through album *New Miserable Experience,* before being ousted from the band in April 1992 as a result of his alcoholism. Feeling increasingly despondent as his ex-bandmates achieved commercial success, Hopkins shot himself in the head in his Tempe apartment.

**Peter Laughner,** d. June 22, 1977, age 24. This Clevelander was writing for *Creem* when he cofounded the innovative art-punk combo Pere Ubu with fellow critic David Thomas in 1975. Laughner, a long-standing drug user and alcohol abuser, played guitar and cowrote the band's first two singles but left in 1976 to start his own band, Friction. He died the following year of acute pancreatitis.

**Billy Murcia,** d. November 6, 1972, age 21. Original New York Dolls drummer Murcia suffered an overdose on the band's first tour of England. Rather than seeking medical help, Murcia's girlfriend attempted to keep him awake by pouring black coffee—on which he either choked or drowned—down his throat.

**Nico,** d. July 18, 1988, age 50. The German chanteuse (née Christa Päffgen), whose distinctively ghostly vocal presence was a feature of the Velvet Underground's first album, also appeared in Fellini's *La Dolce Vita,* worked as a fashion model in Europe and worked with Brian Jones, Jimmy Page, and Jackson Browne prior to her involvement with the Andy Warhol–era Velvets. She subsequently pursued both a culty solo recording career and an ongoing relationship with heroin. She suffered a fatal brain hemorrhage the day after falling from her bicycle while on vacation in Ibiza.

**Jerry Nolan,** d. January 14, 1992, age 45. The former New York Dolls drummer, who had replaced the ill-fated Billy Murcia and proceeded to fight his own painful battles with substance abuse, died of a stroke after being treated for pneumonia and meningitis.

**Charlie Ondras,** d. July 22, 1992, age 26. Ondras, drummer with New York's Unsane, died of an accidental heroin OD.

**Malcolm Owen,** d. July 14, 1980. The raw-throated singer with England's underrated punk-reggae Ruts died of a heroin overdose in a bathtub at his mother's home. His bandmates continued without him as Ruts D.C.

**Kristen Pfaff,** d. June 16, 1994, age 27. The bassist in Hole (and, previously, Janitor Joe) suffered an apparently accidental heroin overdose, just over a month after the drug-shrouded suicide of Kurt Cobain, husband of Hole leader Courtney Love—and a month after the release of Hole's *Live Through This,* Pfaff's first album with the band.

**Paula Pierce,** d. August 31, 1991, age 31. Singer/songwriter/guitarist Pierce, leader of L.A.'s all-girl garage-punk Pandoras, died of cardiac arrest. She had a history of health problems.

**Stefanie Sargent,** d. June 28, 1992, age 24. Sargent, guitarist with Seattle grunge gals 7 Year Bitch, died of a heroin OD, just as her band was beginning to gain national exposure.

**George Scott III,** d. August 5, 1980. Bassist Scott was one of the preeminent players on New York's late-seventies punk scene, working with James White and the Blacks, John Cale, the Raybeats, and Lydia Lunch's band Eight Eyed Spy. He died of a heroin overdose.

**Will Shatter,** d. December 9, 1987, age 31. Shatter, born Russell Wilkinson, was the singer and bassist of San Francisco hardcore godheads Flipper. He died of a heroin overdose.

**Hillel Slovak,** d. June 25, 1988, age 26. The Red Hot Chili Peppers' Israeli-born, Hollywood-raised founding guitarist, also played with What Is This and James Chance between stints with the Peppers. After Slovak's death from a heroin overdose, his devastated bandmates pulled themselves together and subsequently became superstars.

**Fred "Sonic" Smith,** d. November 4, 1994, age 44. The former MC5 guitarist and leader of Sonic's Rendezvous Band died of heart failure. Since 1980, he had been married to Patti Smith, collaborating on her 1988 comeback effort *Dream of Life.* At the time of his death, the couple, who had two children, had been working on songs for a new album.

**Snakefinger,** d. July 1, 1987. The British-born avant-guitarist, a.k.a. Phillip Lithman, had played with London pub-rockers Chilli Willi and the Red Hot Peppers before moving to the Bay Area to work as a solo artist and collaborate with avant-popsters the Residents. He died of a heart problem.

**Stacy Sutherland,** d. 1978, age 31. The Thirteenth Floor Elevators' guitarist/founder was shot to death by his wife.

**Johnny Thunders,** d. April 23, 1991, age 38. The former New York Dolls guitarist, Heartbreakers leader and solo artist (né John Genzale), long a paragon of junkie cool, was found dead of a drug overdose in his New Orleans hotel room.

**Rob Tyner,** d. September 17, 1991, age 46. Tyner, whose hearty howl fronted controversial late-sixties Detroit politico-punks the MC5, died of a heart attack.

**Manuel Verzosa,** d. November 14, 1993, age 30. The guitarist/singer, who had previously recorded with the New England-based Walkers, was killed while on tour with the Silos, when the band's van skidded on an icy road in Wyoming.

**Sid Vicious,** d. February 2, 1979, age 21. The Sex Pistols' perpetually trouble-prone bassist (whose real name was John Simon Ritchie) suffered the last of several heroin overdoses, shortly before he was due to stand trial for the stabbing death of his girlfriend and drug partner Nancy Spungen.

**Ricky Wilson,** d. October 12, 1985, age 32. The B-52's guitarist/founder, whose distinctively cheesy guitar sound was a crucial element in the Southern party combo's early sound, died of AIDS.

**Andrew Wood,** d. March 19, 1990, age 24. Wood, singer with the Seattle Green River spinoff Mother Love Bone, had reportedly been clean of his heroin habit for more than three months, but unexpectedly died of an overdose a month before the band's debut album was released. His bandmates Stone Gossard and Jeff Ament went on to mainstream stardom with Pearl Jam.

**Mia Zapata,** d. July 7, 1993, age 27. Zapata, lead singer of Seattle's Gits, was strangled to death in the poor Seattle neighborhood of Capitol Hill. Her friends and scenemates 7 Year Bitch paid tribute to her with the title and cover art of their sophomore album *Viva Zapata!*

*"I figure forty-five is a good age to go. Quick heart attack, something like that . . . or a nice, clean decapitation in a car crash."*

—LEMMY, MOTÖRHEAD

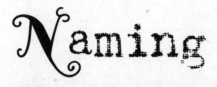

Naming

PART 3

Names

# How Bands Got Their Names

**ABC.** The urbane English popsters chose their name for its generic quality, and because it would put them at the beginning of alphabetical listings (like this one).

**The Angry Samoans.** L.A. rock critics turned punk satirists Mike Saunders and Gregg Turner named themselves in tribute to their favorite wrestlers.

**Anthrax.** The New York metal/hardcore crossover quintet got its handle from the name of an infectious cattle disease.

**Antietam.** This New York trio, which rose from the ashes of Louisville, Kentucky's Babylon Dance Band, took its moniker from the location of one of the Civil War's bloodiest battles.

**The Aquanettas.** The all-female New York quartet named itself after exotic 1940s B-movie actress Acquanetta.

**A.R. Kane.** A combination of acronym and pun. The "A" is for Alex (Ayuli), the "R" is for Rudy (Tambala), and the "Kane" makes the whole thing a play on the word "arcane."

**The Art of Noise.** These English dance experimentalists borrowed their moniker from a 1913 essay by Italian futurist Luigi Rossolo.

**The B-52's.** Southern slang for beehive hairdos, which singers Kate Pierson and Cindy Wilson wore in the band's early days.

**Bad Brains.** This influential black punk/reggae foursome named itself after a Ramones song.

**Band of Susans.** This New York avant-rock outfit's original lineup actually included three Susans—Lyall, Stenger, and Tallman. By the end of the eighties only Stenger remained, but the group did not change its name to Band of Susan.

**Bauhaus.** Named after the German design and architecture institute.

**Biff Bang Pow!** Alan McGee named his influential label after the great sixties English cult band the Creation, so it made sense that he would name his own group after one of the Creation's songs.

**Big Audio Dynamite.** Ex-Clash member Mick Jones liked the acronym B.A.D. and built the band's name around the initials (other candidates supposedly included Before Alien Domination and Black And Decker).

**Big Black.** Irascible indie-noise-rock vet Steve Albini has said that he was looking for a name that was "large, scary (and) ominous," and Big Black filled the bill. He later learned that an African-American jazz percussionist had recorded under that name during the sixties. Albini's subsequent band, Rapeman, was named after the title character of a rather misogynistic Japanese comic book.

**Big in Japan.** Future Frankie Goes to Hollywood frontman Holly Johnson, future Teardrop Explodes manager and JAMS/the KLF mastermind Bill Drummond, future big-name producer/Lightning Seeds leader Ian Broudie and future Siouxsie and the Banshees drummer Budgie invoked a hoary music-biz cliché to come up with a handle for their unsuccessful but historically significant early outfit.

**Big Star.** The influential Memphis power-popsters named themselves after a popular Southern supermarket chain.

**The Birthday Party.** Nick Cave's old band borrowed its name from a Harold Pinter play.

**Black Flag.** This seminal California hardcore group's name offered a nod to both the power of anarchy (of which the black flag is the international symbol) and the noxious qualities of insecticide (Black Flag being the brand name of a popular bug spray).

**Blake Babies.** As a tongue-in-cheek tribute to nineteenth-century English poet William Blake.

**The Boomtown Rats.** From a gang of teenage outsiders in Woody Guthrie's autobiography, *Bound for Glory*.

**The Boo Radleys.** Named after a character in *To Kill a Mockingbird*.

**The Breeders.** Ex-Pixie Kim Deal named her mostly female quartet after a gay slang term for heterosexuals.

**The Butthole Surfers.** Previously known as the Dick Clark Five, Nine Foot Worm Makes Own Food, the Vodka Family Winstons, Abe Lincoln's Bush, the Inalienable Right to Eat Fred Astaire's Asshole, Ashtray Baby Heads, and Independent Worm Saloon, these Texas avant-goofballs received their permanent appellation one night at a show in Austin, when Chris Gates of the Big Boys introduced the band as the Butthole Surfers, which had previously been the title of one of their songs. Because that show marked the first time the band had been paid, they kept the name.

**Buzzcocks.** From a British magazine's review of the TV show *Rock Follies,* which ended with the line "Get a buzz, cock."

**Cabaret Voltaire.** In honor of a cafe in Zurich that was the center for Switzerland's pre–World War II dadaist movement.

**Camper Van Beethoven.** A nonsensical but meaningful-sounding phrase concocted by early band member David McDaniel.

**Celibate Rifles.** This long-running Australian band's name was a back-handed tribute to the Sex Pistols.

**Chequered Past.** This name of this would-be new-wave supergroup— Michael Des Barres, Steve Jones, Clem Burke, Nigel Harrison, and Tony Sales—refers to the resumés of its members.

**The Circle Jerks.** From a messy male-bonding ritual whose details we shan't go into here.

**The Cleaners from Venus.** The name of this English DIY pop combo combined leader Martin Newell's interest in science fiction with the fact that he was working as a washer-up in a restaurant when he started the band.

**Cocteau Twins.** These influential Scottish etherealists (actually a trio) namecheck French surrealist filmmaker/artist/writer Jean Cocteau.

**The Communards.** Former Bronski Beat singer Jimmy Somerville named his next band after a party of French revolutionaries who ruled Paris for ten days in 1871.

**The Comsat Angels.** This darkly atmospheric foursome from Sheffield, England, named itself in honor of the ComSat communication satellite; trademark conflicts eventually forced them to amend their moniker to C.S. Angels on their U.S. releases.

**Concrete Blonde.** Michael Stipe suggested that Johnette Napolitano and her bandmates change their name from Dream 6 to Concrete Blonde. He never explained why, but they did it anyway.

**Crowded House.** Neil Finn's Antipodean trio was originally known as the Mullanes, until they were inspired otherwise by their experiences living in a cramped Los Angeles rental home while recording their debut album.

**The Cure.** A shortened version of the band's original name, Easy Cure, which was the title of a song written by then-drummer Lol Tolhurst.

**Das Fürlines.** This all-female New York punk-polka quintet, which began life covering songs by Germany-based American proto-punks the Monks, wanted to give themselves a German name in honor of that inspirational group, and ended up settling on "Fürlines," a nonsensical corruption of frauleins.

**Dash Rip Rock.** After a character—Ellie May's movie star boyfriend—from TV's *Beverly Hillbillies*.

**The dB's.** As the band's 1981 debut LP spells it out, *Stands for deciBels*.

**The Dead Kennedys.** Friends of singer Jello Biafra had come up with the name years before but, according to Biafra, "didn't have the nerve to use it." He adopted the name for his San Francisco-based agit-hardcore combo because, of all the names suggested, it provoked the most extreme responses.

**Death of Samantha.** This Cleveland art-punk quartet took its name from a Yoko Ono song. When three of the members subsequently regrouped, they rechristened themselves Cobra Verde, named after a film by German director Werner Herzog, who supposedly suggested it personally.

**The Del Fuegos.** The Boston quartet's name makes reference to Tierra del Fuego, the southernmost place on earth aside from Antarctica, because the name signified something "as low as you could get."

**The Del-Lords.** Ex-Dictator Scott Kempner's urban-roots quartet's name was borrowed from prolific Three Stooges writer/director Del Lord.

**Depeche Mode.** The band's name, taken from a French fashion magazine, literally translates to "fast fashion."

**Destroy All Monsters.** Former Stooge Ron Asheton's late-seventies band got its name from an all-star Japanese monster movie.

**Die Kreuzen.** The respected Milwaukee hardcore ensemble's name is a German phrase meaning "The Crosses," but the band claims they just liked the way it sounded.

**The Dils.** The name of this now-legendary punk band (led by Chip and Tony Kinman, later of Rank and File and Blackbird) was an abbreviation for Cosmic Dilrod Troubadours, the name of a fictional band in a poem written by Tony.

**The Donner Party.** These surrealist Bay Area pop-folk bohos share their band name with that of a group of nineteenth-century settlers who, stranded during a brutal winter, resorted to cannibalism to survive.

**Downy Mildew.** These L.A. folk-rockers named themselves after a cabbage fungus.

**The Dream Syndicate.** Steve Wynn's Velvet Underground-influenced band borrowed its name from Faust member Tony Conrad's solo album *Outside the Dream Syndicate*—not knowing that album title was a reference to an earlier band called the Dream Syndicate, an arty outfit whose membership included Conrad, influential avant-garde composer LaMonte Young, and future Velvet Undergrounder John Cale.

**Drivin' and Cryin'.** A reference to the band's original repertoire, which was a combination of rock (drivin') and country (cryin') songs.

**Droogs.** Futuristic slang for gang members in *A Clockwork Orange*.

**Durutti Column.** Guitarist Vini Reilly named his avant-garde/jazz/classical band after an anarchist brigade in the Spanish Civil War.

**Easterhouse.** This Manchester quintet named themselves after a working-class area of Glasgow.

**Echo and the Bunnymen.** Echo was the name of the band's drum machine, which kept the Bunnymen's beat until human drummer Pete DeFreitas signed on. Echo's name remained, though.

**Einstürzende Neubauten.** This German destructo ensemble's name (translation: "collapsing new buildings") gives a fairly good description of the group's sound.

**Eleventh Dream Day.** This Chicago combo's first bassist, Shu Shubat—an amateur-numerologist—deemed eleven to be the band's number and drummer Janet Beveridge Bean's days of unemployment yielded many dreams.

**EMF.** Reputedly an acronym for Ecstacy Mother Fuckers, although these English rave-popsters have gone to great lengths to deny it.

**Eyeless in Gaza.** This English duo appropriated the title of an Aldous Huxley novel.

**The Fall.** From Albert Camus's novel of the same name.

**The Fatima Mansions.** Ex-Microdisney member Cathal Coughlan named his subsequent band after a notoriously squalid housing project in his hometown of Dublin.

**Fine Young Cannibals.** Named after the 1960 movie *All the Fine Young Cannibals,* starring Natalie Wood and Robert Wagner.

**The Fleshtones.** Former art student Peter Zaremba named his band after a favorite Crayola color.

**Frankie Goes to Hollywood.** Supposedly from a vintage poster touting Frank Sinatra's first film.

**Fugazi.** Ian MacKaye, leader of this uncompromising and influential D.C. hardcore band, found the term (meaning a "fucked up situation") in *Nam,* a book of Vietnam veterans' war stories.

**Game Theory.** Computer terminology—not surprising given leader Scott Miller's day job designing computer software. The name of Miller's next band, the Loud Family, was a double-entendre on the cinema-verité clan featured in the seventies PBS series *An American Family* (one of whose sons, Lance, fronted New York punks the Mumps).

**Gang of Four.** These politically precocious English postpunks named themselves after a quartet of Red Chinese government officials (including Mao Tse-Tung's widow) accused of counterrevolutionary activities following Mao's death.

**Generation X.** Billy Idol's former band was named after a sixties book studying the sociology of British teens—not after the nineties novel of the same name.

**Giant Sand.** An abbreviation of the band's original name Giant Sandworms, which referred to the desert-dwelling creatures described in the cult sci-fi novel *Dune.*

**The Go-Betweens.** After director Joseph Losey's 1971 film.

**Golden Palominos.** The name for Anton Fier's avant-garde supergroup was actually what Fier wanted to call that other downtown New York band, the Lounge Lizards.

**Green River.** This Seattle band, which included future members of Mudhoney and Pearl Jam, was named in honor of a never-apprehended serial killer who dumped the victims in the Green River south of town.

**The Hangman's Beautiful Daughters.** This psychedelically inclined London quartet named themselves after a 1968 album by the similarly trippy Incredible String Band.

**Heaven 17.** From a fictitious pop group mentioned in *A Clockwork Orange*.

**Hole.** Courtney Love took her band's much-misinterpreted name from a line in Euripides' *Medea*, "There's a hole burning deep inside me."

**The Honeymoon Killers.** This New York group got its name from the 1970 film-noir cult classic.

**Human League.** From a computer game.

**Hüsker Dü.** After the name of a board game popular in the band's home state of Minnesota. Translates literally to "Do you remember?"

**The Icicle Works.** From sci-fi author Frederick Pohl's short story "The Day the Icicle Works Closed."

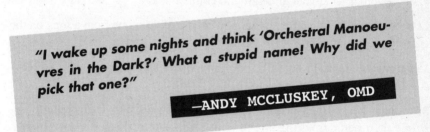

"I wake up some nights and think 'Orchestral Manoeuvres in the Dark?' What a stupid name! Why did we pick that one?"

—ANDY MCCLUSKEY, OMD

**The Jam.** Because the band originated with its members jamming during their school lunch hour.

**Jane's Addiction.** In honor of a Hollywood hooker who was an acquaintance of Perry Farrell and his bandmates.

**Japan.** These upscale English New Romantics, whose music bore no noticeable Asian influence, were so titled because of singer David Sylvian's interest in Japanese society.

**The Jody Grind.** This Atlanta-based band chose its name from World War II–era slang for adultery.

**Joy Division.** From the bitterly ironic name applied to the prostitution wing in Nazi concentration camps. After singer Ian Curtis's suicide, his bandmates continued under another Nazi-inspired handle, New Order.

**Killdozer.** The title of a 1974 TV-movie about a rampaging bulldozer possessed by an extraterrestrial intelligence.

**King Missile.** After a Japanese comic-book character.

**KMFDM.** This German industrial group's name is usually translated to "Kein Mehrheit Für Die Mitleid," which means roughly "No pity for the majority," although a radio station competition once yielded such candidates as "Kill Mother-Fucking Depeche Mode."

**L7.** The term L7 was hipster code for "square" (the term was also cited in Sam the Sham and the Pharaohs' "Wooly Bully").

**Let's Active.** From a magazine article read by band leader Mitch Easter, regarding Japanese misuse of the English language. The phrase "Let's Active" was apparently spotted "on somebody's jacket or something."

**The Lightning Seeds.** English producer Ian Broudie found the name for his one-man band after mishearing a lyric in a Prince song.

**Love and Rockets.** These three former Bauhaus members named their band after a popular American underground comic book.

**Love Battery.** This Seattle grunge-pop band took its name from a song on the Buzzcocks' debut album, *Love Bites*.

**Luscious Jackson.** From a TV sports announcer's mispronunciation of NBA star Lucius Jackson.

**Madness.** These English ska-revivalists-turned-beloved-pop-institution borrowed their name from the title of a hit by Jamaican ska star Prince Buster. The band covered the song early in its career.

**MC5.** Short for "Motor City Five," which is how this seminal late-sixties Detroit combo was originally known.

**MC 900 Ft. Jesus.** Mark Griffin borrowed his stage name from TV evangelist Oral Roberts, who once supposedly described himself as a "900 Foot Jesus."

**Meat Puppets.** The Arizona threesome's name reflected the band's contention that they often felt like their music was controlled by an unknown outside force.

**The Mekons.** The original Mekons were villainous aliens featured in the fifties English comic strip *Dan Dare*.

**The Men They Couldn't Hang.** Named in tribute to John Lee, who in nineteenth-century England was convicted of a murder charge, yet survived three trips to the gallows.

**The Minutemen.** Named in honor of the brevity of the band's songs. After the death of guitarist D. Boon the band dissolved; bassist Mike Watt and drummer George Hurley named their new band fIREHOSE, inspired by a placard held by Bob Dylan in the "Subterranean Homesick Blues" sequence of the documentary *Don't Look Back*.

**The Modern Lovers.** So named because leader Jonathan Richman considered his compositions to be "modern love songs."

**The Motorcycle Boy.** This name was actually shared by two bands—one an L.A. glam-punk outfit, the other an English garage-pop duo fronted by ex-Shop Assistants vocalist Alex—both of whom borrowed their name from a character in Francis Ford Coppola's 1983 film *Rumble Fish*.

**Motörhead.** Slang for "speed freak."

**Mudhoney.** Named after filmmaker Russ Meyer's tawdry white-trash cult classic.

**My Bloody Valentine.** This influential Irish noise band named itself after a low-budget Canadian slasher movie.

**Ned's Atomic Dustbin.** From the title of an episode of the English radio comedy series *The Goon Show*.

**New Model Army.** This politically committed English group got their name from the equally zealous seventeenth-century revolutionary army led by Sir Thomas Fairfax and Oliver Cromwell.

**999.** The late-seventies Brit punk band took its name from the English police emergency phone number.

**Nine Pound Hammer.** From Merle Travis's classic country song.

**Pere Ubu.** After the title character of Alfred Jarry's play *Ubu Roi*.

**The Plimsouls.** Peter Case's L.A. power-pop combo indulged its Anglophilia by naming itself after a variety of canvas, rubber-soled shoes popular in England.

**The Pogues.** Short for Pogue Mahone, Gaelic for "kiss my ass."

**The Police.** Apparently a tribute to band drummer Stewart Copeland's and manager Miles Copeland III's father, Miles Copeland II, who was instrumental in the formation of the CIA.

**The Pooh Sticks.** From a game invented by Winnie-the-Pooh in A. A. Milne's series of children's books.

**Prefab Sprout.** As a child, leader Paddy McAloon misunderstood the words "pepper sprout" in Nancy Sinatra and Lee Hazlewood's hit "Jackson."

**Public Image Ltd.** So named because of John Lydon's original desire to present a corporate, nonrock & roll face to the public.

**Pussy Galore.** From the ill-fated femme fatale in the James Bond book and film *Goldfinger.*

**Pylon.** This ahead-of-its-time Athens, Georgia, quartet named itself after a William Faulkner novel.

**Ramones.** Supposedly inspired by Paul McCartney's early stage name "Paul Ramon." Bassist Dee Dee Ramone was the first to use the name.

**Redd Kross.** These L.A. kitsch-rockers (who originally spelled their moniker Red Cross until the *other* Red Cross threatened to sue) named themselves in honor of a scene in *The Exorcist* in which Linda Blair masturbates with a crucifix.

**R.E.M.** Although the acronym stands for Rapid Eye Movement, the band has always maintained that they chose it not because of its dreamlike implications, but because they wanted a short, nonspecific name.

**The Residents.** The mysterious avant-garde group—or rather, its spokesmen—claimed that one of the group's early demo tapes, sent to Warner Bros. before the band had settled on a name, was returned addressed to "the residents."

**Scritti Politti.** Italian for "political writing."

**Sex Pistols.** Manager Malcolm McLaren (who ran a clothing boutique called Sex) chose the name for its juxtaposition of sex and implied violence.

**Sham 69.** The "Sham" comes from the band's hometown, the London suburb of Hersham.

**Shoes.** These Illinois power-pop godheads took their name from a comment once made by Beatle John Lennon, who, when asked about his band's name, looked down at his feet and replied, "Well, we could have just as well named ourselves the Shoes."

**Shonen Knife.** From the name of a Japanese toy knife ("shonen" means "little boy" in Japanese).

**Siouxsie and the Banshees.** The queen of Goth uses a corruption of her Christian name (née Susan), and the rest of the group's name was inspired by a viewing of the Vincent Price movie *Cry of the Banshee.*

**Sister Double Happiness.** From a dish spotted on a Chinese menu.

**The Sisters of Mercy.** From the title of the Leonard Cohen song.

**Skinny Puppy.** This Canadian industrial combo has claimed they took their name from the fact that they view the world from the vantage point of a starving, abused dog.

**The Smithereens.** Not from Susan Seidelman's punk-inspired cult movie *Smithereens,* but from the band's fondness for Looney Tunes character Yosemite Sam, who was always threatening to blow someone to smithereens.

**The Smiths.** Chosen for its implications of anonymity.

**The Sneetches.** From the Dr. Seuss book of the same name.

**The Soft Boys.** In naming his old band, Robyn Hitchcock combined the names of two William Burroughs books, *The Soft Machine* and *The Wild Boys*. He says that he envisioned "Soft Boys" as mysterious, vaguely omniscient creatures of indeterminate species.

**Sonic Youth.** Thurston Moore has claimed that his band's name was a tribute to ex-MC5 member Fred "Sonic" Smith and reggae dub master Big Youth.

**Soundgarden.** The Seattle grunge-metallurgists named themselves after an avant-garde outdoor sculpture park in their hometown.

**Sparks.** Brothers Ron and Russell Mael were originally known as Halfnelson. When their first LP under that name didn't sell, Albert Grossman, the head of their label, Bearsville, suggested reissuing the album with a new band name. He redubbed the pair the Sparks Brothers (as in the Marx Brothers), which the Maels insisted on shortening to Sparks.

**The Specials.** The biracial London ska revivalists' name refers to the "special" one-off discs produced for early Jamaican sound systems.

**Squeeze.** When the band members couldn't agree on a suitable handle, each member put his personal choice into a hat, and Squeeze was chosen at random. The band claims not to remember which member picked Squeeze, although there is some speculation that it was the suggestion of Velvet Underground fan Chris Difford (*Squeeze* was the title of the Velvet's final album).

**The Stone Roses.** The band was known for a while as English Rose, after a song by the Jam, before altering its moniker to acknowledge an equal fondness for the Rolling Stones.

**The Stooges.** Originally known as the Psychedelic Stooges, Iggy and friends christened themselves in honor of Moe, Larry, and Curly.

**Talking Heads.** TV slang for news anchorperson.

**The Teardrop Explodes.** From a line in a Marvel comic book.

**Tears for Fears.** Inspired by psychiatrist Arthur Janov's book *Prisoners of Pain*. Same goes for the dance-din band Primal Scream.

**10,000 Maniacs.** A variation on Herschell Gordon Lewis' sixties gore film *2000 Maniacs*.

**That Petrol Emotion.** Intended as an evocation of the frustrations of growing up in Northern Ireland.

**The The.** Matt Johnson gave his one-man-band a name that seemed certain to carry no preconceptions.

**They Might Be Giants.** From the 1971 film of the same title, starring George C. Scott as a modern man who believes that he is Sherlock Holmes. However, the phrase originally comes from Cervantes's *Don Quixote*.

**The Three Johns.** A bit of a no-brainer here, as the band's three members are John Brennan, John Hyatt, and moonlighting Mekon Jon Langford.

**Token Entry.** These New York hardcore rockers got their vaguely menacing name from a sign found at every subway turnstile in their hometown.

**Tom Tom Club.** Chris Frantz and Tina Weymouth, Talking Heads' husband-and-wife rhythm section, named their dance-oriented side project after their rehearsal space at Nassau's Compass Point Studios.

**Too Much Joy.** As teens, this foursome from Scarsdale, New York, ingested some psychedelic mushrooms, intending to jot down the flashes of brilliance that the trip would undoubtedly bring. When they awoke the next morning, the only thing written down was the phrase "Too Much Joy," which they immediately adopted as their band name.

**U2.** A double-entendre built around the name of the American spy plane piloted by Francis Gary Powers, who was shot down over the Soviet Union in 1960, a few days before Bono's birth.

**The Velvet Monkeys.** From leader Don Fleming's desire to "ape" his favorite band, the Velvet Underground.

**The Velvet Underground.** From the title of a trashy paperback novel, which is now a collector's item thanks to the band's subsequent notoriety.

**Veruca Salt.** From a bratty character in the book *Charlie and the Chocolate Factory*.

**Wall of Voodoo.** A low-budget variation on Phil Spector's legendary Wall of Sound.

**The Waterboys.** Would-be Celtic neo-mystic Mike Scott got the name for his band from a line in "The Kids," from Lou Reed's *Berlin* album.

**Ween.** This daffy twosome combined two of their favorite nouns, "wuss" and "peen."

**White Zombie.** From the 1932 Bela Lugosi horror film.

**The Wonder Stuff.** Leader Miles Hunt has claimed that John Lennon was a family friend during Miles's childhood, and that the band name comes from a phrase frequently used by Lennon. There are, however, some who believe him to be lying.

**XTC.** When Andy Partridge and friends christened their eclectic pop combo in the late seventies, they were playing on the word "ecstacy," though no drug reference was intended.

**Yo La Tengo.** Spanish for "I've got it"; more specifically, the name refers to a famous anecdote involving 1962 New York Mets outfielder Elio Chacon's problems with the English language.

# Ten Alt-Rock Bands Forced to Change Their Names, Sorta

by Michael Krugman

Freelance writer Michael Krugman lives in Brooklyn and is currently working on a novel or two.

**1. The Charlatans U.K.** These Manchester baggy-boys got their visa stamped onto their name, out of deference to Dan Hicks's sixties cult combo. (See also: Wham! U.K., The Mission U.K., U.K. Squeeze.)

**2. The London Suede.** A Washington, D.C.–area folk singer who nobody ever heard of had been calling herself "Suede" for years, so Britain's biggest next-big-thing of the early nineties took on this region-specific prefix, which makes them sound like a trench coat manufacturer.

**3. Dinosaur Jr.** J Mascis' fuzz-happy trio Dinosaur were sued by the Dinosaurs, a touring outfit comprised of ex-members of the Quicksilver Messenger Service, Country Joe and the Fish, and various other Bay Area fossils. The name change was an ironic homage to the geezers' seniority.

**4. Yaz.** Vince Clarke's post-Depeche Mode partnership with soul belter Alison Moyet, known throughout the rest of the world as Yazoo, got their vowels chopped off in the colonies in recognition of the Mississippi-based Yazoo Blues Band.

**5. The Verve.** Legendary jazz label Verve Records feared that some beret-wearing hepcat might mistake the work of this English spaceweird combo—originally known simply as Verve—for *Bird: The Original Recordings of Charlie Parker*. And what if you're looking for a classical record on the Angel label and end up with remastered rarities by Punky Meadows and Gregg Giuffria?

**6. The English Beat/the Paul Collins Beat.** In the late seventies, two bands from opposite ends of the Western Hemisphere spotted a great band name sitting unused, dropped the "-les" and christened themselves the Beat. This time, both groups were forced to modify their cognomina.

**7. The Bangles.** This briefly wonderful L.A. girl-group started out with the same moniker as doofy New Jersey bar-band the Bangs, whose career course would suggest that they should have called themselves the Whimpers.

**8. The Reivers.** Just as the Austin foursome known as Zeitgeist were set to release their second (and first major-label) album, they discovered a new age choral ensemble who'd been in touch with "the spirit of the times" a bit longer. For their new sobriquet they turned to William Faulkner.

**9. Redd Kross/the Three O'Clock.** A suit from the *real* Red Cross forced the seminal L.A. kitsch-punkers to appear to be functional illiterates. Meanwhile, their Paisley Underground contemporaries the Salvation Army had a similar crisis, but "Salvashun Armee" didn't have quite the right ring to it, so they took on this chronological *nom de rock*.

**10. Superchunk.** As there was already a Chunk—a New York avant-jazz combo led by drummer Samm Bennett—Chapel Hill's answer to the Buzzcocks asserted their supremacy with this peanut butter–like alteration.

# Noms de Punk: Alt-Rocker Stage Names (And the Real Ones)

Adam Ant (Stuart Goddard)

Jello Biafra (Eric Boucher)

Frank Black/Black Francis (Charles Michael Kitteridge Thompson IV)

Marc Bolan (Mark Feld)

Bono Vox (Paul Hewson)

Sonic Boom (Peter Kember)

David Bowie (David Jones)

Boy George (George O'Dowd)

Captain Beefheart (Don Van Vliet)

Cheetah Chrome (Gene Connor)

Tré Cool (Frank Edwin Wright III)

Elvis Costello (Declan McManus)

Darby Crash (Paul Beahm)

Howard Devoto (Howard Trafford)

The Edge (David Evans)

Exene (Christine Cervenka)

Perry Farrell (Perry Bernstein)

Flea (Michael Balzary)

Foetus/Clint Ruin (Jim Thirlwell)

Richard Hell (Richard Myers)

Lux Interior (Erick Lee Purkhiser)

Lemmy (Ian Kilmister)

Lora Logic (Susan Whitby)

Annabella Lwin (Myant Myant Aye)

"Handsome" Dick Manitoba (Richard Blum)

Moby (Richard Melville Hall)

Nico (Christa Päffgen)

Mojo Nixon (Neill Kirby McMillan, Jr.)

Nivek Ogre (Kevin Ogilvie)

> "Just because you call yourself psychedelic doesn't mean you are psychedelic."
>
> —RICHARD BUTLER, PSYCHEDELIC FURS

Iggy Pop (James Osterberg)

Kid Congo Powers (Brian Tristan)

C.J. Ramone (Christopher Joseph Ward)

Dee Dee Ramone (Douglas Colvin)

Joey Ramone (Jeffrey Hyman)

Johnny Ramone (John Cummings)

Marky Ramone (Marc Bell)

Ritchie Ramone (Richie Beau)

Tommy Ramone (Thomas Erdelyi)

Lou Reed (Louis Firbank)

Poison Ivy Rorschach (Kristy Marlana Wallace)

Johnny Rotten (John Lydon)

Rat Scabies (Chris Miller)

Captain Sensible (Ray Burns)

Will Shatter (Russell Wilkinson)

Siouxsie Sioux (Susan Dallion)

Snakefinger (Philip Lithman)

Epic Soundtracks (Paul Godley)

Joe Strummer (John Mellor)

Poly Styrene (Marion Elliot)

Nikki Sudden (Nicholas Godley)

Suggs (Graham McPherson)

Johnny Thunders (John Genzale)

Tom Verlaine (Thomas Miller)

Sid Vicious (John Simon Ritchie)

Jah Wobble (John Wordle a.k.a. Dan MacArthur)

Rob Zombie (Robert Straker)

# Riders on the Storm: Members of the Golden Palominos

Masterminded by drummer Anton Fier (Pere Ubu, the Feelies, Lounge Lizards), the sonically adventurous Golden Palominos have consisted of a constantly shifting membership since its inception in 1981. For performances and recordings, the New York–based ensemble has for the most part included players with underground credentials, though some "members" have high-profile careers. The common ground of this eclectic bunch has been a yen for experimentation and improvisation; songs range from originals written by members to unusual arrangements of well-known covers.

So, without further ado, we give you the Golden Palominos:

Michael Beinhorn, keyboards

Peter Blegvad, vocals, guitar

Carla Bley, keyboards

Jeff Bova, keyboards, programming

Jack Bruce, vocals, harmonica

T Bone Burnett, vocals, guitar

Lori Carson, vocals

Knox Chandler, guitar

Bootsy Collins, guitar

Tony Coniff, bass

Aïyb Dieng, percussion

Don Dixon, guitar, vocals

Anton Fier, drums

Fred Frith, guitar

Mike Hampton, guitar

Jody Harris, guitar

Lisa Herman, keyboards

Henry Kaiser, guitar

Lydia Kavanaugh, vocals

Robert Kidney, vocals, guitar

Sneaky Pete Kleinow, pedal steel

Amanda Kramer, vocals, keyboards

Bill Laswell, bass

Chuck Leavell, keyboards

Arto Lindsay, guitar, vocals

John Lydon, vocals

Mark Miller, vocals, turntables

David Moss, drums

Bob Mould, vocals, guitar

Larry Saltzman, guitar

Nicky Skopelitis, guitar

Chris Stamey, guitar, bass

Matt Stein, programming

Michael Stipe, vocals

Syd Straw, vocals

Matthew Sweet, vocals, bass

Jamaladeen Tacuma, bass

Mick Taylor, guitar

Richard Thompson, guitar

Pal Thrall, guitar

David Van Tieghem, percussion

Bernie Worrell, keyboards

John Zorn, saxophone, clarinet

# A Dozen
# Really Pretentious
# Band Names

A Drop in the Gray

An Emotional Fish

A Popular History of Signs

Balaam and the Angel

Electric Blue Peggy Sue and the Revolutionions From
    Mars

Fields of the Nephilim

Mary My Hope

Mussolini Headkick

Orchestral Manoeuvres in the Dark

Our Daughters Wedding

Spear of Destiny

We Are Going to Eat You

# 100+ Alt-Rock Supergroups We Hope Never Happen

**J**f alt-rock's late-blooming mainstream breakthrough demonstrates anything, it's the music industry's boundless capacity to transform iconoclasm and nonconformity into nonthreatening commercial fodder. The charts are currently loaded with putatively alternative artists, who were once presumed to be above such things, unironically retracing their musical forefathers' footsteps and doing the same stupid, desperate, embarrassing things that made their predecessors—you know, the ones they were supposed to be alternative *to*—worth rebelling against. Chief among these clichéd careerist moves is the once-discredited phenomenon of the supergroup—i.e., bands comprised of survivors of prior notable endeavors, generally coasting on the participants' past achievements rather than their current output. The following is a list of some particularly nightmarish potential linkups that, with any luck, we will never live to see come to fruition.

**Agnostic Front Line Assembly**

**Aldo Nova Mob**

**Anti-Nowhere League of Gentlemen**

**Average White Band of Susans**

**Bauhouse of Love Battery**

**B.B. King Crimson**

**Big Black Sabbath**

Bikini Killdozer

Black Flag of Convenience

Blind Idiot God Street Wine

Blood, Sweat & Tears for Fears

Boomtown Rats of Unusual Size

Bronski Beat Rodeo

Christian Death of Samantha

Cindy Lee Berryhillbilly Frankenstein

Clarence Carter the Unstoppable Sex Machine

Courtney Love Tractor

Crowded Housemartins

Dash Riprocket from the Crypt

Debbie Gibson Bros.

Diamanda Galaxie 500

Drive Like Jayhawks

Echo and the Bunnymen Without Hats

Fabulous Thunderbirdsongs of the Mesozoic

Faith No Morrissey

The Family Cat Stevens

Fire in the Kitchens of Distinction

Flaming Lipps Inc.

General Public Image Ltd.

Generation X-Mal Deutschland

Gentle Giant Sand

Grant Lee Buffalo Tom Tom Club

Grateful Dead Kennedys

Green Day La Soul

Guns n' Fish & Roses

Henry Cowboy Mouth

Hothouse Flowerhead

Hüsker Doobie Brothers

Ian Hunters and Collectors

Iggy Pop Will Eat Itself

Innocence Mission of Burma

Inspiral Carpetbaggers

Jad Fairport Convention

Joan Jett Black Berries

John Cougar Mellencamper Van Beethoven

Johnny Winter Hours

Jonathan Richman & the Modern Love of Life Orchestra

Kate Bush Tetras

Kevin Salem 66

Kool & the Gang of Four

Kool Moe D Generation

Kurtis Blow Monkeys

Leaders of the New School of Fish

Lee "Scratch" Perry Farrell

Levon Helmet

Little Richard Hell & the Voidoids

L.L. Cool JFA

Luscious Jackson Browne

Maggie's Dream Academy

Magnapopsicle

Martin Reverend Horton Heat

Marvin Gaye Bykers On Acid

Matthew Sweet Honey in the Rock

MC 900 Foot Jesus Jones

Me Phi Mekons

Millions of Dead Cop Shoot Cop

Mink DeVillage People

Modern English Beat Farmers

Mooseheart Faith Healers

Mr. Big Star

My Dad Is Dead Can Dance

Naked Raygun Club

Neil Young Fresh Fellows

Nice Strong Army of Lovers

Nick Cavedogs

Of Cabbages and King Missile

Pere Ubu Radleys

Peter Murphy's Law

Pete Shelleyan Orphan

R.E.M. Speedwagon

Rage Against the Machines of Loving Grace

Ryuichi Sakamotörhead

The Schoolly dB's

Scruffy the Cat Heads

Shelia EIEIO

Shocking Blue Aeroplanes

Simply Red Hot Chili Peppers

Sly & the Family Stone Roses

Smashing Orange Juice

Snatches of Pink Floyd

Soul II Soul Asylum

Steely Danzig

Stetsasonic Youth

Swing Out Sisters of Mercy

Syd Strawberry Alarm Clock

That Petrol Emotional Fish

Thelonious Monster Magnet

The The Police

Too Much Joy Division

Trip Shakespeare's Sister

U2 Live Crew

Uncle Green on Red

When People Were Shorter and Lived Near the Waterboys

XTC + C Music Factory

Yellow Magic Orchestral Manoeuvres in the Dark

Zodiac Mindwarp and the Love and Rockets

# Fan
# Club

## PART 4

# Footnotes

# U2 Firsts

**First band name:** Feedback.

**First public appearance:** three-song set at Mount Temple school student talent show in Dublin, autumn 1977, performing Peter Frampton's "Show Me the Way," a Bay City Rollers parody and a Beach Boys medley.

**First appearance as U2:** spring 1978, at Howth Community Hall, Dublin.

**First disastrous high profile gig:** September 9, 1978, opening for the Stranglers at the Top Hat Ballroom, Dun Laoghaire.

**First demo:** "Street Mission," "Shadows and Tall Trees," and "The Fool," recorded November 1, 1978, at Keystone Studios, Dublin.

**First press feature:** March 1979, in the Irish music paper *Hot Press*.

**First record deal:** With CBS Ireland, March 1979.

**First record release:** *U23* three-song single including "Out of Control," "Boy-Girl," and "Stories for Boys," released by CBS Ireland in September 1979.

**First New York show:** December 6, 1980, at the Ritz.

**First U.S. tour as opening act:** with J. Geils Band, spring 1982.

**First U.S. gold album:** *War,* certified July 15, 1983.

**First U.S. platinum album:** *The Unforgettable Fire,* certified February 7, 1985.

**First ROLLING STONE cover:** March 14, 1985.

**First U.S. Number One single:** "With or Without You," entered the charts March 21, 1987.

**First U.S. Number One album:** *The Joshua Tree*, entered the charts April 4, 1987.

**First Grammy Award:** Album of the Year (for *The Joshua Tree*), 1987, and Best Rock Performance by a Duo or Group with Vocal.

"It would be wrong for me to say, 'Yes, we can change the world with a song.' But every time I try writing, that's where I'm at. I'm not stupid. I'm aware of the futility of rock & roll music, but I'm also aware of its power."

—BONO

# R.E.M. Firsts

**First rehearsal:** January 1980.

**First performance:** party at deconsecrated church turned University of Georgia student residence, April 5, 1980.

**First paid gig:** at the Koffee Klub in Athens, Georgia, April 19, 1980.

**First print review:** in University of Georgia student paper, *The Red and the Black,* for second gig, May 6, 1980, at Tyrone's in Athens, opening for the Brains. Headline: "Underdog R.E.M. Upstages the Brains".

**First headlining gig:** May 12, 1980, at Tyrone's.

**First van:** green 1975 Dodge Tradesman, purchased for $1250.

**First demo:** eight songs—"Dangerous Times," "I Don't Want You Anymore," "A Different Girl," "Narrator," "Just a Touch," "Baby I," "Mystery to Me" and "Permanent Vacation"—recorded on four-track facility at Tyrone's, Athens, late 1980.

**First dispute over original material:** Bill Berry initially threatened to refuse to play "Carnival of Sorts (Boxcars)" onstage.

**First theater gig:** December 6, 1980, opening for the Police at the Fox Theater in Atlanta.

**First record released:** single, "Radio Free Europe"/"Sitting Still," on Hib-Tone Records, July 1981.

**First live radio broadcast:** May 14, 1982, show at Piedmont Park, Atlanta, broadcast on WRFG.

**First arena appearance:** opening for the English Beat and Squeeze at Nassau Coliseum, Uniondale, New York, November 24, 1982.

**First stadium appearance:** opening for the Police and Joan Jett at Shea Stadium, Flushing, New York, August 18, 1983.

**First overseas gig:** the Effener, Eindhoven, Holland, April 6, 1984.

**First officially released side project:** single by the Hindu Love Gods (Peter Buck, Mike Mills and Bill Berry, with Athens friend Bryan Cook on vocals and special guest Warren Zevon on piano), "Gonna Have a Good Time Tonight"/"Narrator," released by I.R.S. on June 16, 1985.

**First U.S. gold album certification:** *Life's Rich Pageant,* certified gold January 23, 1987.

**First U.S. Top Ten single:** "The One I Love," entered charts September 19, 1987.

"It's amazing how far you can get in this business just by showing up for your appointments on time."

—PETER BUCK, R.E.M.

**First platinum album certification:** *Document,* certified platinum January 25, 1988.

**First officially released solo project:** single, "My Bible Is the Latest TV Guide"/"Things I'd Like to Say," by 13111 (a.k.a. Bill Berry), released September 1989 on R.E.M. manager Jefferson Holt's Dog Gone label.

**First U.S. Number One album:** *Out of Time,* entered charts March 30, 1991.

**First Grammy:** Best Pop Vocal Performance by a Duo or Group with Vocal (for "Losing My Religion"), 1991. R.E.M. also won Best Alternative Music Album (for *Out of Time*), 1991, and Best Music Video, Short Form (for "Losing My Religion"), 1991.

# ᴥᴀlias R.E.M.

From their early days on the Athens, Georgia, club scene through their more recent adventures as honest-to-goodness rock stars, the members of R.E.M.—both individually and collectively—have always found time to engage in a variety of extracurricular and pseudonymous projects of varying degrees of seriousness. Here are a few of them:

**1066 Gaggle O' Sound.** In May 1981 frontman Michael Stipe used this name for a one-off one-man show he performed at Athens' 40 Watt Club. The set reportedly consisted of nonmusician Stipe making improvised sounds on an old Farfisa organ against prerecorded backing tracks, while photo slides were projected onstage. This show, incidentally, also marked the debut performance of Athens' Oh-OK, which included Stipe's sister Lynda and future Magnapop leader Linda Hopper.

**Gangster.** During the summer of 1981 Stipe served time in this cover band, which often appeared onstage in mobster attire. After quitting, Stipe reportedly swore friends to secrecy about his dalliance with the group.

**Tanzplagen.** A few months after the 1066 Gaggle O' Sound gig, Stipe continued his avant-noise experiments, singing and making Farfisa noise as part of this short-lived Athens-based project, which made a handful of club appearances before folding. In its brief lifespan, Tanzplagen recorded a pair of studio tracks for a never-released single, as well as three live tracks at the 40 Watt; these were released a decade later as the CD *Tanzplagen*. Also in 1981 Stipe was an occasional participant in another local art-noise combo, Boat Of.

**It Crawled from the South.**   On Halloween 1983 R.E.M. adopted this un-wieldy monicker for a surprise set opening for the Cramps at New York's Peppermint Lounge. The It Crawled set consisted entirely of cover songs, many of them learned specifically for the occasion.

**Hindu Love Gods.**   In January 1984 R.E.M.'s instrumental axis—guitarist Peter Buck, bassist Mike Mills and drummer Bill Berry—teamed up with singer Bryan Cook (of Athens' Time Toy) to form this casual cover ensemble, whose local club sets consisted of a selection of glam-rock covers as well as several early R.E.M. compositions that the parent band no longer performed. Hindu Love Gods also did some recording (with guest Warren Zevon on pi-ano) at John Keane's local studio, with a pair of tracks—the early R.E.M. original "Narrator" and a cover of the Easybeats' "Gonna Have a Good Time Tonight"—eventually released by R.E.M.'s then-label I.R.S. as a 1986 single. A few years later the Hindu Love Gods monicker was revived for Buck, Mills, and Stipe's one-album collaboration with Zevon (see below).

**Adolf and the Casuals, featuring Raoul.**   During a break from R.E.M.'s 1984 Little America tour, Peter Buck and the members of the Dream Syndi-cate (the tour's opening act) played an impromptu set of covers at an Athens bar, after the originally scheduled act—a local synthesizer band that had had its synth stolen—was forced to cancel. "We were so drunk we played 'Ghost-busters' twice," Buck later reported.

**The Southern Gentlemen.**   After backing Roger McGuinn on a 1984 MTV broadcast and being joined onstage by the ex-Byrds leader on some subse-quent shows in McGuinn's home state of Florida, McGuinn and R.E.M.'s three instrumentalists convened under this *nom de stage* for an Atlanta show on May 11, 1988, on which the combo performed a selection of Byrds clas-sics.

**Hornets Attack Victor Mature.**   In spring 1985 R.E.M. played a low-key show at Athens' Uptown Lounge under this name, borrowed from a defunct L.A. combo that Buck had read about in a *Trouser Press* article on silly band names. That group had taken the unusual handle from an old newspaper head-line reporting an incident in which the eponymous actor was set upon by an-gry insects during a golf game. According to Buck, the band booked the show reasoning that "anyone who'd pay a dollar to see a band with a name that silly is our kind of person."

**Full-Time Men.**   In early 1985 Peter Buck, in tandem with Keith Streng of New York's long-serving Fleshtones, recorded a low-budget EP, *Fast Is My Name,* in Athens (released by Coyote Records) under the Full-Time Men han-dle. Buck later joined Streng and various other Fleshtones for one Full-Time

Men set in New York that December. Three years later Buck contributed guitar to two tracks on the 1988 Full-Time Men album, *Your Face My Fist*. Streng continued to use the Full-Time Men name occasionally for various live gigs, minus Buck.

**The Community Trolls.**   In the mid-eighties this Athens-based, looseknit ensemble, which included Matthew Sweet, featured Michael Stipe's vocals on a handful of tracks. One of these, "Tainted Obligation," was originally slated for but did not eventually appear on the 1986 Demon compilation album, *Don't Shoot,* but did eventually surface on various R.E.M. bootlegs.

**The Corncob Webs.**   In March 1986 Mike Mills and Bill Berry launched this loose, sporadically active covers ensemble, which specialized in ragged renditions of the seventies hard-rock tunes they'd grown up with.

**Monkey Wash, Donkey Rinse.**   In February/March 1987 Buck, Mills, and Berry contributed to the sessions for Warren Zevon's *Sentimental Hygiene* album. Toward the end of the sessions, Zevon and the three R.E.M. members quickly recorded an album's worth of old blues tunes (and Prince's "Raspberry Beret") under the name Monkey Wash, Donkey Rinse. The material was eventually released by Giant/Reprise in 1990—to a decidedly mixed reception in the R.E.M. camp—as a Hindu Love Gods album.

**The Nasty Bucks.**   In 1987 when Georgia Satellites leader Dan Baird decided to revive his late-seventies/early-eighties group, the Nasty Bucks, to record an albumful of the defunct band's repertoire, Buck volunteered his guitar services. With Buck in tow, the reconstituted Nasty Bucks recorded enough material for an album that, as of this writing, has yet to see release.

**Worst Case Scenario** and **Nigel and the Crosses.**   During R.E.M.'s 1989 *Green* tour, Buck, tour sideman (and former dB's leader) Peter Holsapple, and various members of opening act Robyn Hitchcock and the Egyptians formed Worst Case Scenario to play Beatles and Byrds covers. The casual cover combo hastily assembled shows in Chicago and Minneapolis, the latter with Mike Mills added to the lineup. By the time the *Green* tour reached England in May, Worst Case Scenario had been renamed Nigel and the Crosses (in honor of *Bucketfull of Brains* 'zine editor Nigel Cross); under that name, they played a show at London's Borderline club and recorded a version of "Wild Mountain Thyme" for the Byrds tribute album *Time Between*.

**13111.**   In March 1988 Bill Berry recorded a cover of the New Colony Six's early-seventies hit "Things I'd Like to Say" and the original composition "My Bible Is the Latest TV Guide" at John Keane's studio in Athens. It was released as a twelve-inch single the following year on R.E.M. manager Jefferson Holt's Dog Gone label, under the enigmatic monicker 13111 (which, if you hold it upside down and look at it in a mirror, reads "Bill," sort of).

**Field Recordings.** Michael Stipe's aborted solo album project was to feature several of his musician friends and was slated for release on the independent Texas Hotel label in 1990. Reportedly, although *Field Recordings* was completed, its release was cancelled because the timing conflicted with R.E.M.'s activities.

**Bingo Hand Job.** During a spring 1991 trip to London to promote the album *Out of Time*, R.E.M. (with auxiliary member Peter Holsapple and guests Billy Bragg and Robyn Hitchcock) performed two acoustic shows at the Borderline under this name. The handle was chosen by Stipe, after his earlier suggestion of Storage Box Hand Job had been rejected ("I think he just likes the idea of people waiting in line to ask for Bingo Hand Job," Buck theorized). For the occasion, Stipe, Buck, Mills, and Berry were individually rechristened Reverend Bingo, Raoul, Stinky, and the Doc, respectively, while Bragg, Hitchcock, and Holsapple were redubbed Conrad, Violet, and Spanish Charlie for the occasion.

**William.** In June 1991 the band played a ragged eleven-song acoustic set at Athens' 40 Watt Club, donating the take from the $5 cover charge to a local animal shelter. Mike Mills barely made the show, having just arrived home from a trip to London.

**Automatic Baby.** In celebration of Bill Clinton's January 1993 Presidential inauguration, Stipe and Mills (playing acoustic guitar) took the stage with U2 members Adam Clayton and Larry Mullen for an acoustic performance televised as part of MTV's inaugural festivities. The ad-hoc foursome played U2's "One." The same night, Stipe guested with 10,000 Maniacs on a pair of songs.

# ℓighty-five Songs Covered by R.E.M.

## LIVE OR ON RECORD

(Each cover is listed with the artist whose version R.E.M. copped)

---

"Academy Fight Song" by Mission of Burma

"Afterhours" by the Velvet Underground

"All I Have to Do Is Dream" by the Everly Brothers

"All Right Now" by Free

"Arms of Love" by Robyn Hitchcock

"Baby Baby" by the Vibrators

"Behind Closed Doors" by Charlie Rich

"Born to Run" by Bruce Springsteen

"Broken Whiskey Glass" by Jason and the Scorchers

"California Dreamin'" by the Mamas and the Papas

"Chicken Train" by Ozark Mountain Daredevils

"Crazy" by Pylon

"Dallas" by Jimmie Dale Gilmore

"Dark Globe" by Syd Barrett

"Deck the Halls" (traditional)

"D.O.A." by Bloodrock

"Does Your Mother Know?" by Abba

"Eight Miles High" by the Byrds

"Femme Fatale" by the Velvet Underground

"Fever" by Little Willie John

"First We Take Manhattan" by Leonard Cohen

"Funtime" by Iggy Pop

"Ghost Rider" by Suicide

"Ghost Riders (in the Sky)" by Vaughn Monroe

"Gloria" by Them

"God Save the Queen" by the Sex Pistols

"Good King Wenceslas" (traditional)

"Have You Ever Seen the Rain" by Creedence Clearwater
    Revival

"Hello in There" by John Prine

"Hippy Hippy Shake" by the Swinging Blue Jeans

"Holiday in Cambodia" by the Dead Kennedys

"Hootenanny" by the Replacements

"I Can Only Give You Everything" by Them

"I Can't Control Myself" by the Troggs

"(I Can't Get No) Satisfaction" by the Rolling Stones

"I Got You Babe" by Sonny and Cher

"(I'm Not Your) Stepping Stone" by the Monkees

"In the Year 2525" by Zager and Evans

"I Walked with a Zombie" by Roky Erickson

"King of the Road" by Roger Miller

"Last Date" by Floyd Cramer

"The Lion Sleeps Tonight" by the Tokens

"Little Girl" by the Syndicate of Sound

"Louie, Louie" by the Kingsmen

"Love Is All Around," by the Troggs

"Love Is All Around," Mary Tyler Moore Show theme

"Midnight Blue" by Lou Gramm

"Moon River" by Henry Mancini

"Needles and Pins" by Jackie DeShannon

"Nervous Breakdown" by Eddie Cochran

"Paint It, Black" by the Rolling Stones

"Pale Blue Eyes" by the Velvet Underground

"Pills" by Bo Diddley

"Radar Love" by Golden Earring

"Rave On" by Buddy Holly

"Red Rain" by Peter Gabriel

"Road Runner" by Jonathan Richman and the Modern
    Lovers

"Route 66" by Bobby Troup (the Rolling Stones
    version)

"Secret Agent Man" by Johnny Rivers

"See No Evil" by Television

"Sex Bomb" by Flipper

"Skin Tight" by Ohio Players

"Sloop John B" by the Beach Boys

"Smokin' in the Boys' Room" by Brownsville Station

"So You Want to Be a Rock 'n' Roll Star" by the
    Byrds

"Spooky" by the Classics IV

"Strange" by Wire

"Summertime" by George Gershwin

"Superman" by the Clique

"Sweet Home Alabama" by Lynyrd Skynyrd

"Sweet Jane" by the Velvet Underground

"There She Goes Again" by the Velvet Underground

"Tighten Up" by Archie Bell and the Drells

"Tom's Diner" by Suzanne Vega

"Toys in the Attic" by Aerosmith

"Tusk" by Fleetwood Mac

"20th Century Boy" by T. Rex

"Wayward Wind" by Gogi Grant

"We Live As We Dream Alone" by Gang of Four

"What's New, Pussycat?" by Tom Jones

"Whole Lotta Love" by Led Zeppelin

"Wipe Out" by Surfaris

"With a Girl Like You" by the Troggs

"Word Up" by Cameo

"You Ain't Goin' Nowhere" by Bob Dylan (Byrds version)

# Nirvana Fun Facts

**First punk rock album purchased by Kurt Cobain:** the Clash's *Sandinista!*.

**First punk rock show attended by Kurt Cobain:** Black Flag at the Mountaineer Club, Seattle, August 1984.

**Contents of Kurt Cobain's pocket in police report on his first vandalism arrest, according to Aberdeen police report:** one guitar pick, one key, one can of beer, one mood ring, one Millions of Dead Cops cassette.

**First band Kurt Cobain auditioned for:** the Melvins, sometime in 1984. He failed because he was so nervous that he forgot the songs.

**Early Cobain bands:** Fecal Matter, with Melvins drummer Dale Crover on bass, and drummer Greg Hokanson, opened for the Melvins at the Spot Tavern in Moclips, Washington, in early 1986, and recorded a seven-song demo on a four-track deck owned by Kurt's Aunt Mary. A subsequent lineup featured Melvins member Buzz Osborne on bass and Mike Dillard on drums. Cobain subsequently fronted Brown Towel, a.k.a. Brown Cow, with Melvins members Buzz Osborne (bass) and Dale Crover (drums), which played one show at GESCCO Hall in Olympia, Washington.

**First band Kurt Cobain and Krist Novoselic played together in:** the Stiff Woodies, an informal Melvins spinoff whose lineup included Novoselic on vocals and Cobain on drums. The two subsequently formed the Sellouts, a Creedence Clearwater Revival cover band, with Novoselic on guitar and Cobain on drums.

**Early names of Nirvana:** Skid Row, Ted Ed Fred, Bliss, Throat Oyster, Pen Cap Chew and Windowpane.

**First Nirvana demo session:** on January 23, 1988, at Reciprocal Recording in Seattle, with Dale Crover on drums. The band recorded and mixed ten songs in six hours, namely "Floyd the Barber," "Paper Cuts," "Downer" (those tracks ended up on the band's debut album *Bleach*), "Beeswax," "Mexican Seafood," "Hairspray Queen," "Aero Zeppelin" (later included on *Incesticide*), plus "If You Must," "Pen Cap Chew" and an early version of "Spank Thru."

**First album stats:** *Bleach* is recorded in six days for $606.17 during December 1988 and January 1989.

**The band's influences, according to early Sub Pop bio:** *"H.R. Puffnstuff, Speed Racer,* divorces, drugs, sound effects records, the Beatles, rednecks, hard rock, punk rock, Leadbelly, Slayer and, of course, the Stooges."

**First national tour:** beginning on June 22, 1989, at the Covered Wagon in San Francisco and ending (prematurely) at the Pyramid Club in New York City on July 18 for the New Music Seminar. This was the band's only tour as a quartet, with Chad Channing on drums and Jason Everman on second guitar. The band cancelled the seven remaining tour dates, returned home and never played with Everman again.

**Labels that tried to sign Nirvana before Geffen did:** Capitol, Charisma, Columbia, Island, MCA, Slash.

**Hitting the big time:** *Nevermind* hits Number One on the *Billboard* charts the week of January 11, 1992, the day the band plays *Saturday Night Live*.

**Interesting sounding side band that never saw the light of day:** Lithium, an informal blues-inspired combo with Kurt Cobain on guitar, Krist Novoselic on bass, and Screaming Trees members Mark Lanegan (vocals) and Mark Pickerel (drums).

# Five
# Ex-Nirvana Drummers
# Who Aren't
# Dave Grohl

**Aaron Burckhard.**  The band's first drummer, who joined in the winter of 1987, was a trouble-prone local "stoner" and metal fan who was apparently chosen mainly for his availability but generally considered too straight and not committed enough for long-term service. He drifted away from the band when Kurt Cobain and Krist Novoselic moved out of Aberdeen, returned briefly in the spring of 1988 but got thrown out again after getting arrested for verbally abusing a cop who'd pulled him over for driving drunk.

**Dale Crover.**  Crover, a member of Cobain's influential Aberdeen pals the Melvins, rehearsed with the band in early 1988 and played on its first demo session (three tracks from which ended up on the *Bleach* album) before relocating to San Francisco with the Melvins. He returned briefly to help out on a short West Coast tour in August 1990.

**Dave Foster.**  A hot-tempered metalhead friend of the Melvins who was also considered too normal for permanent duty, Foster joined for a few months in early 1988, but got squeezed out after being jailed for beating up the guy his girlfriend was seeing on the side.

**Chad Channing.**  Elfin, eccentric Channing joined in May 1988 and played on most of *Bleach*. He toured the U.S. and Europe with the band and played on the demos of the songs that would end up on *Nevermind,* before musical and personal tensions between him and Cobain came to a head, resulting in his departure early in 1990.

**Dan Peters.**　Peters, a member of seminal Seattlites Mudhoney, briefly replaced Channing while Mudhoney were on hiatus in 1990. He played on Nirvana's 1990 Sub Pop single "Sliver" and played one Seattle gig with the band that September, before the band deemed Dave Grohl to be the man for the job.

# Sibling Rockers of the Alternative Kind

---

Dave and Phil Alvin (the Blasters)

Ron and Scott Asheton (the Stooges)

Kerry and Keith Brown (Catherine)

Tracy Bryn and Melissa Brooke Belland (Voice of the Beehive)

Richard and Tim Butler (Psychedelic Furs)

Manny Caiati (Del-Lords) and Albert Caiati (World Famous Blue Jays)

Bob and Jerry Casale (Devo)

Gary Lee and Van Conner (Screaming Trees)

Peter and Chris Coyne (Godfathers, Syd Presley Experience)

Mike and Tim Cross (Sponge)

Curtis Crowe (Pylon) and Rhett Crowe (Guadalcanal Diary)

Pete DeFreitas (Echo and the Bunnymen) and Frank DeFreitas (Woodentops)

Dean and Robert DeLeo (Stone Temple Pilots)

Vincent and Keith DeNunzio (the Feelies)

Steve and Joe Doerr (LeRoi Brothers)

Alejandro and Javier Escovedo (True Believers)

Jad and David Fair (Half Japanese)

Tim and Neil Finn (Split Enz, Crowded House)

Brian and Ken Foreman (Thrashing Doves)

Chris Frantz (Talking Heads) and Roddy Frantz (Urban
    Verbs)

Liam and Noel Gallagher (Oasis)

Howe Gelb (Giant Sand) and Ricky Gelb (Low Max)

Phil and Paul Hartnoll (Orbital)

David J. and Kevin Haskins (Bauhaus, Love and
    Rockets)

Noel and Mike Hogan (the Cranberries)

Tom and Chris Hooper (Grapes of Wrath)

Kirk, Kraig, and Kyle Johnson (Run Westy Run)

Steve Kilbey (the Church) and Russell Kilbey (Crystal
    Set)

Lou and Pete Killer (Sick of It All)

Chip and Tony Kinman (the Dils, Rank and File,
    Blackbird)

Curt and Cris Kirkwood (Meat Puppets)

Gerard and John Langley (Blue Aeroplanes)

John and Evan Lurie (Lounge Lizards)

John Lydon (Sex Pistols, Public Image Ltd.) and Jimmy
    Lydon (4 Be 2)

Kirsty MacColl (solo) and Neill MacColl (the Bible,
    Liberty Horses)[half sister and brother]

James Mastro (Bongos, Health and Happiness Show) and
    John Mastro (Tiny Lights)

Ken and David McCluskey (the Bluebells, McCluskey
    Brothers)

Jeff and Steve McDonald (Redd Kross)

Maria McKee (Lone Justice) and Bryan MacLean (Love)

Michael and Amy McMahon (Last Roundup)

Mike Mills (R.E.M.) and Mitch Mills (Three Walls Down)

Marc and Bruce Moreland (Wall of Voodoo)

Mark, Jim, and Des Morris (Balaam and the Angel)

Mark and Bob Mothersbaugh (Devo)

Jeff and John Murphy (Shoes)

Nic and Oliver North (Comateens)

Seán and Damian O'Neill (the Undertones, That Petrol Emotion)

Andy and Jonathan Paley (Paley Brothers)

Andy and Ivor Perry (Easterhouse)

Debbi and Vicki Peterson (Bangles)

Joey Ramone (Ramones) and Mickey Leigh (Rattlers, Birdland)

Charlie and Craig Reid (the Proclaimers)

Jim and William Reid (the Jesus and Mary Chain)

Billy and Tommy Robertson (Polyrock)

Dexter Romweber (Flat Duo Jets) and Sara Romweber (Let's Active, Snatches of Pink)

Shaun and Paul Ryder (Happy Mondays)

Mike and Ali Score (A Flock of Seagulls)

Chuck and Glen Stilphen (Gang Green, Mallet-Head)

Bob and Tommy Stinson (the Replacements)

Michael Stipe (R.E.M.) and Lynda Stipe (Oh-OK, Hetch Hetchy)

Nikki Sudden and Epic Soundtracks (Swell Maps)

David Sylvian and Steve Jansen (Japan, Rain Tree Crow)

Margo, Michael, and Peter Timmins (Cowboy Junkies)

Seth Tiven (Dumptruck) and Jon Tiven (producer/critic)

Cindy and Ricky Wilson (the B-52's)

Dan and Matt Wilson (Trip Shakespeare)

Andy Wood (Malfunkshun, Mother Love Bone) and Kevin and Brian Wood (Devilhead, Fire Aunts, Hater)

Janet, Doug and Tricia Wygal (Individuals, Wygals, Splendora)

Naoko and Atsuko Yamano (Shonen Knife)

Dan and Warren Zanes (Del Fuegos)

Miki and Paul Zone (the Fast)

"It's just me and me brother having arguments in a band. If we weren't in a band, we'd be havin' it in the house."

—LIAM GALLAGHER, OASIS

# Digging

## the Scene

# Coulda Been the Right Place . . . Musta Been the Wrong Time

## A GUIDE TO RATING A LOCAL MUSIC SCENE

**by Josh Grier**

A veteran of the Chapel Hill/Athens alt-rock axis, Josh Grier is currently an attorney in New York City.

It may seem simple enough to spot a good local alt-rock scene. Are there a few decent clubs? Is there a college radio station with a flexible playlist? Have any local musicians been signed and gone on to national prominence? Etc., etc. But veteran scenemakers know that the analysis is not that easy. This year's Seattle can easily become next year's Cleveland. A music scene is like a tapestry, constantly being rewoven, ripped apart and even burned. But if the foundation of a good scene is present, the music (and the musicians) will somehow survive and reinvent itself (and themselves). A network of elements, both musical and nonmusical, must combine to build the ideal scene.

To facilitate the process of analyzing the long-term vitality of a local scene, as a guide for those wishing to rate their own town, or evaluate another area where one may be contemplating relocation for educational, career, or other more compelling reasons, the following rating system has been compiled. Before you jump in and start scoring, however, note a few ground rules that generally apply:

(a) The system is time sensitive. Don't rely on last year's score today.

(b) The system works best on medium to small communities, the most likely spots to find legitimately developed scenes, anyway. To judge the physical dimensions of the scene in question, find the epicenter (your home, the center of campus, or whatever location seems to make sense) and calculate how far out in all directions you can ride on a bicycle in two hours. That's your geographic range and should be applied when racking up points. For example, if you're looking at Urbana, you can include Champaign, but if you live in Raleigh you can't include Chapel Hill.

(c) Major cities don't count. Suffice to say that big cities usually don't have that much great local rock, it's just too expensive to keep a band intact. If you simply *must* live in an urban center, skip the scoring and try Boston or San Francisco, two major metropoli that always have had and always will have great local music scenes. New York and Los Angeles are permanently tainted by the proximity of music industry professionals and their parasites; if you're planning on moving to either of these towns forget any comparisons, base your entire decision on what quality of apartment you can afford and buy a good set of headphones, because that's the only way your neighbors are going to let you listen to music anyway.

(d) A college or university within the bounds of the scene is imperative. Today, virtually every decent rock music scene seems to need at least one worthwhile institution of higher education as its anchor. Think of a music scene without this element like a mall without a J.C. Penney or a Sears; you just don't get enough citizens in the zone to make anything interesting happen. The size or nature of the school does not seem to have a consistency of impact; the music scene in Carbondale, Illinois (Southern Illinois University, student body over 30,000), can't touch Bloomington, Illinois (Illinois Wesleyan, student body under 10,000).

(e) Canadian towns don't count. Canada has distinguished itself, thanks to the ascendancy of such groundbreaking acts as Loverboy and Bryan Adams, by becoming the only entire country constituting a single bad music scene.

(f) The system is designed for use by musicians and music fans alike. The consumers of the music are as important to the weave as the purveyors.

Keeping all this in mind, start your evaluation with a personal visit to the scene, during the regular school session if possible. One full weekend is ideal. An ability to walk up and ask questions to locals in bars, clubs, and record stores will speed up the research. In an effort to simplify the evaluation process, the scoring system has been categorized, more or less in order of importance.

# EDUCATIONAL INSTITUTIONS

Start by identifying all the universities and colleges ("schools") within the boundaries of the scene. A solidly entrenched undergraduate presence in the community is a major advantage. Note all evidence of student dominance.

O  Add 500 points for every public college or university in the scene.

O  Add 250 points for every private college or university in the scene.

O  Subtract 100 points for every Ivy League college in the scene, except for University of Michigan add 500 points.

O  Add 100 points for each instance of a local university or college basketball team playing in the NCAA Final Four since 1977, including men's and women's squads.

O  Subtract 250 points per school if more than 40% of the student body commutes.

# RADIO

Decent radio is essential. Great radio is too much to ask, but there needs to be at least one station that you can listen to for more than fifteen minutes without reaching for the Prozac.

O  Add 500 points for each college radio station that devotes at least 50 percent of its broadcast time to music programming.

O  Add 200 points for each college station that is staffed entirely by matriculating students.

O  Add 100 points for each commercial station that has an ongoing policy of playing local music that is not released by major record labels.

O  Subtract 100 points for each college station where the music director or program director is over thirty and graduated at least five years ago.

O  Add 500 points for each commercial radio station that has a rock format and can be picked up clearly on a Walkman radio without an antenna.

O  Subtract 200 points for each commercial station that plays "classic" tracks by Foghat, Asia, or REO Speedwagon more frequently than twice per day.

# LIVE PERFORMING

The availability of continual live performances by all types of musicians can create the basis of a quality scene all by itself. Note drinking laws (which affect the economic viability of clubs), cover charges at the most popular venues (which affect the economic viability of the clubgoers), and proximity of the clubs to the scene epicenter (which affect the viability of having to own a car). Performances by major acts alone, however, does not seem to make as much of a difference to the permanent local music culture as one might expect. The Grateful Dead, the most popular touring act of all time, regularly plays the campus of Duke University. This has done nothing to help the dismal music scene in Durham.

O Add 500 points for each club that primarily features bands that perform original material.

O Add 250 points for each club that books an average of at least one all-ages show per week.

O Subtract 500 points for each club that regularly books cover bands; subtract an additional 100 points if the club also books "tribute" cover bands.

O Add 150 points if your scene can support at least one rock venue that holds more than 1000 people and books at least thirty shows per year.

O Add 100 points for each time that Hüsker Dü played the scene between 1983 and 1988.

O Subtract 100 points for each time that Toto played the scene between 1983 and 1988. Subtract an additional 100 points if they sold out a venue larger than 10,000 seats.

# RECORD STORES

Radio stations, clubs, and records stores are the three basic food groups of any scene. Make a list of albums you might buy on a particular day and see how many stores you have to visit to find the whole list.

O Add 125 points for each store in the scene specializing in the sale of new albums.

O Add 175 points for each store in the scene specializing in the buying and selling of used records and CDs.

O Subtract 50 points if the store is in an enclosed mall.

O Add 25 points if the store is within walking distance of campus.

O Add 100 points if the store regularly carries vinyl copies of new releases.

O Add 75 points if the store has a permanent seven-inch single section.

O Add 75 points if the store carries all local independent releases.

O Add 50 points if the store regularly posts flyers and/or schedules of local live venues.

O Subtract 50 points if the store still racks Lynyrd Skynyrd's *Gold and Platinum* on an end-cap.

"Seattle's a weird place—it's really boring."

—KEVIN MARTIN, CANDLEBOX

# MUSICAL EQUIPMENT STORES AND STUDIOS

If there aren't at least three stores selling instruments, amps, and the like present in the scene, something is definitely wrong. These shops are usually hidden off the beaten paths. The people that shop these places know where to find them. Once you've spotted a location, act like you want to buy a Sears Silvertone guitar. They won't have one, but they won't throw you out either. While you're at it, find out how many recording facilities are operating full time (more or less) in the area. You might have to turn over some rocks to find these places, too.

O Add 175 points for each specialized musical instrument store in the scene.

O Add 100 points if the store buys and sells used instruments and equipment.

O Subtract 50 points if the store is owned by a guy that plays in a wedding band on the weekends.

O Add 50 points for each recording studio with at least a sixteen-track board within a two-hour drive of the scene.

O Add an additional 50 points for any studio with a daily lockout rate under $500.

O  Subtract 25 points for any studio that advertises using a four-color brochure.

# RECORD LABELS

Most thriving music scenes eventually spawn homegrown record labels. The trick is to find labels somewhere in the twilight zone between the bona fide amateur operations and thinly disguised tentacles of the evil major label distribution empires. When visiting the local record stores, ask about regional imprints.

O  Add 50 points for each record label based in the scene.

O  Add 125 points if the label releases more than five titles per year.

O  Add another 50 points if the label releases more than twenty-five titles per year.

O  Add 100 points if the label has an actual office in the scene.

O  Subtract 50 points from any label that is all or partially owned by a major record label or a chain of record stores.

O  Add 50 points if the label presses vinyl copies of its releases.

O  Add another 50 points if the label *only* presses vinyl copies of its releases.

# OTHER MEDIA

The availability of films, television, museums, dance companies, and the like can all add to and be indicative of the health of the local arts scene in general; around the music scene and its populace they should be firmly entwined.

O  Add 25 points for each commercial theater screen in the scene.

O  Add another 100 points for each theater that regularly books independently distributed or financed films.

O  Add 25 points for any theater that changes programs more than once each week or has late shows.

O  Subtract 25 points for each multiplex screen that is showing the same program as another screen in the same complex.

O Add 100 points for each campus-operated screen that shows more than twenty black-and-white films per year.

O Add 1 point for each channel available on basic local cable service and an additional 5 points for each public access channel.

## PUBLICATIONS

Another important ancillary indicator of the solidity of the scene is its ability to sustain printed media. The existence of local fanzines, entertainment weeklies, and independent monthlies indicates both the existence of something to write about and the existence of enough people willing to read what's written to entice elusive advertising dollars away from the daily papers and real-estate pulps. Find these publications at records stores, on the floors of local clubs, and in street racks in front of diners.

O Add 75 points for each local publication that features the local music scene on a regular basis.

O Add 25 points if the publication publishes more than once each month.

O Add 50 points if the publication is owned and edited by one of its regular writers.

O Add 25 points if the publication is distributed free.

O Subtract 25 points if any title on the masthead of the publication uses the word "critic."

## LOCAL MUSICIANS

It may seem obvious that a music scene needs musicians, but musicians are everywhere so you've got to peer deeper into the pedigree. Don't be fooled if one band was signed out of the market, was all over MTV for six months and looks to have struck it rich. That single event might have been enough to kill the whole creative dynamic in a town, especially if these guys turn into obnoxious celebrities and come back on tour breaks to haunt the locals and bum everyone out. Still, success can sometimes breed more than just contempt, as any visit to Athens, Georgia, will reveal.

O Add 10 points for each local artist or group performing original compositions that play at a club or party in the scene during an average week of the spring or fall semester.

O Add 25 points for every band or solo artist that was a resident of the scene when they/he/she was signed to a major label record contract in the past five years.

O Add 50 points if any of the above are still signed and are still residents of the scene.

O Subtract 100 points if any of the above have begun purchasing restaurants, apartment complexes, and other key real estate in the scene.

O Subtract 50 points if any recording artist living in the scene has sold more than 2 million records.

# GEOGRAPHICAL LOCATION

Obviously, some attention should be given to climate and general geographic location, even though this seems to be among the least reliable indicators. Minneapolis maintains a vibrant combo scene even though most groups have tour vans that are buried in snow five months a year. You'll see more good music in Grinnell, Iowa, in one month than a whole year in Jacksonville, Florida. Maybe the isolation helps.

O Add 50 points if the scene is south of the Mason-Dixon Line.

O Add 25 points if the scene is within 300 miles of Graceland.

O Add 50 points if good surf is within four hours night driving.

O Add 50 points for each minor-league baseball team based within a forty-mile radius.

O Subtract 75 points if the average yearly temperature is less than 60 or more than 75 degrees Fahrenheit.

# FOOD AND CLOTHING

A proliferation of decent eateries and food merchants is another useful indirect indicator of a thriving scene. Music folk need plenty of cheap places to graze with round-the-clock service. Scene participants will also need plenty of waitperson and food-delivery employment opportunities to supply the income necessary to cover band operational deficits and finance record purchases.

O Add 50 points for each twenty-four–hour restaurant in the scene.

O Add 50 points for each locally owned grocer.

O Subtract 10 points for each fast-food chain with more than one location.

O Add 50 points for each Salvation Army or similar used-clothing store in the scene.

O Subtract 100 points for each used-clothing store in the scene that sells any item of clothing for more than its original cost or carries distressed leather jackets with bogus W.W.II logos on the back.

O Add 25 points for each Gap store. Subtract 100 points for each Gap store in a location that used to house a record store or music club.

Now, add it all up and compare. Subtract a final 1000 points if your scene has been singled out in the "What's Hot" issue of ROLLING STONE at any time in the past five years. If the score totals over 5000 points, move in right away and buy a house. If you're in the negative numbers, make sure to arrive with all your own records, sign a short lease and have sufficient funds to finance numerous road trips across the state to the place you should have moved to in the beginning. If you're still in doubt, move to Austin.

# People One Must Seek Out and Question About the L.A. Punk Underground Rock Scene of the Seventies

## by Fred D. Patterson (a.k.a. Phast Phreddie)

In a previous life, Mr. Patterson was known as Phast Phreddie, founding editor of *Back Door Man*. Beginning in 1975, *BDM* was the first national rock & roll magazine to feature local acts on a regular basis. His editorials in *BDM* not only prophesied the coming of the New Wave, but they demanded that it happen! As he spent a good deal of the seventies intoxicated (he tipped glasses with many of the people mentioned in this piece), his memory may be a tad weak, and he therefore begs the forgiveness of any person he may have missed or dissed. Currently he is a poet living in reclusion in Brooklyn.

Sometime in the near future—or maybe it has already happened and the author has not yet been informed—someone is bound to write a book and/or article about the Hollywood punk and new wave scene of the late seventies. (Why not? Every year publishers seem to issue books that concern themselves with subjects that are a lot more stupid.) If the following folks are not questioned extensively, there is no way a concise history can be looked at with any kind of credibility. Observe:

**Kim Fowley:** If you remember him for his work with Helen Reddy and Steel Breeze, you shouldn't be reading this at all. If you remember him as the Man Who Assembled the Runaways (and is reportedly now being sued by them), you are getting closer. As a songwriter, producer, artist, etc., his career goes all the way back to "Alley Oop" by the Hollywood Argyles. But it is his activity during the seventies that is of interest here.

The first topic of discussion will be the Runaways. Kim conceived of the idea of an all-girl band as a vehicle for the Teen Poet and songwriter Kari Krome. Legend has it that guitarist Joan Jett (who later produced the Germs' album) was discovered hanging out at the Rainbow parking lot after hours. Lead guitarist Lita Ford was brought to Mr. Fowley's attention by one D.D. Faye—a writer for the fanzine *Back Door Man*. The original bass player and singer, Michael Steele, was sacked for a blonde—but had the last laugh when she turned up in the eighties with the Bangles (a band that actually had Hit Records). Anyway, as the Runaways became popular and toured the world, something was burning in Hollywood.

Adding kindling to the fire was Kim Fowley. He sponsored some shows at the Whisky-a-Go-Go even before the once-hallowed club started booking punk rock regularly. He would let any band play that showed up for the afternoon soundcheck. As many as ten bands played per night. The Germs, Berlin Brats, and the Zippers all got their starts there. Many of these bands never played in Hollywood again.

Often neglected is the fact that Kim tried to duplicate his (relative) success with the Runaways by putting together another band: Venus and the Razorblades—a coed group. But few took that band seriously—including members of the band. Chalk Mr. Fowley up as a guy who tried to make a buck off punk? You bet. However, should one contact him, one should fasten his or her seat belt and be prepared for a good story or two.

Insider information has him recently moved to Austria—no doubt gearing up to launch the Now Sound of Vienna.

**Rodney Bingenheimer:**   At the time (as now and ever shall be) Rodney was a DJ on KROQ. After his theme song—the Phil Spector-produced "This Could Be the Night" by the Modern Folk Quartet—*anything* could be heard on his show. Local do-it-yourself punk records and trendy English imports were aired to the biggest market in the country. Many listeners heard "God Save the Queen" and "London's Burning" for the first time on his Sunday night show.

During the sixties Rodney made a name for himself as the Mayor of the Sunset Strip. His main claim to fame was that he was rumored to have been beaten up by Brian Jones. Also, he once substituted for David Jones on the Monkees' TV show.

In the early seventies he ran Rodney's English Disco (that's Gary Glitter records, not Village People), where touring English Rock Stars would come, drink and pick up hot young girls who were out to be picked up by English

Rock Stars. Led Zeppelin, David Bowie, and Mott the Hoople all made the Scene. The New York Dolls, Iggy, and Lou Reed were also photographed in the joint.

Rodney is best known for his radio show, on which he would feature guests like the Ramones, Blondie, or any hot band from New York or London on tour. Homegrown acts like X, the Plugz, the Weirdos, and the Go-Go's (Rodney *loved* the Go-Go's) all were interviewed in depth. If you didn't know Alice Bag's fashion secrets, you were not listening!

The Pasadena radio station also sponsored the Cabaret Club in Hollywood, where local bands faced their audience and Rodney was the MC. The Quick, Van Halen, and Quiet Riot played there. It didn't last long and apparently bills were not paid, so electricity was cut off. Later, Rodney sponsored two nights a week at the Starwood club, where he invited the bossest bands in town to play. That lasted until the Starwood, too, closed down.

The Cabaret and the Starwood are just memories, but Rodney Bingenheimer is the Duracell bunny rabbit of rock & roll—he just keeps on going and going. One can safely bet that he can still be seen on any afternoon at the Denny's on Sunset Boulevard, pounding down salads and Tab, accompanied by a Sweet Young Thing and some band's hotshot manager doing the Hollywood Hustle.

**Joanna "Spock" Dean (née Popkin):** Spock (the nickname revealed her devotion to *Star Trek*) is one of the few people in a legitimate band who the author deems necessary to mention in this arena. She played in Backstage Pass, formed by a handful of groupies who wanted to Rock with the Rock Stars in more ways than one. Backstage Pass's punk credentials included playing on a bill with the Weirdos and the Screamers at the Starwood, and being the first band to rehearse at the Masque. As a band, Backstage Pass didn't exactly tear it up, but individually they made their share of noise: Holly Beth Vincent (as leader of Holly and the Italians) had a minor hit called "Tell That Girl to Shut Up." Genny "Body" Schorr could have been the new-wave Dolly Parton/female Elvis Costello—her songs were that good. Keyboard player Marina Del Rey was later in Vivabeat, who cut the likable new-wave song "Man From China." Spock's musical legacy can be heard in the film *Desperate Teenage Love Dolls,* where she sings her song "Legend" backed by the really young Redd Kross.

Spock seemed to know everybody. She knew record company people (later becoming one herself), she knew rock critics (later becoming one herself), she knew video production people (guess what she does now?). She could walk into any club in Hollywood knowing full well that she was on the guest list.

Mainly, she knew Jake Riviera who managed Costello, Nick Lowe and the Damned, and ran Stiff Records. When he was in town, Jake was KING! Jake couldn't walk into a room without a dozen or so people waiting there to shake his hand, and anybody who didn't *know* wondering: Who is this obviously important person? Spock would be sitting at his table, drinking on his bar tab. Jake even married one of Spock's best friends. It was this connection that got Backstage Pass on the most coveted bill of 1977—the opening slot for Elvis Costello's first L.A. show at the Whisky-a-Go-Go.

Spock achieved Groupie Nirvana by actually marrying an English Rock Star—Rob Dean, guitarist for Japan.

As this goes to press, Spock can be found as an assignment editor at VH-1.

**Art Fein:** During that period of depravity known as the seventies, Mr. Fein cruised the county in his yellow VW ragtop (license plate: SO FEIN) to report on all happenings of the Night Club Scene for the *L.A. Free Press*. Louis Jordan at the Blue Velvet Room in Encino; Bruce Springsteen at the Troubadour; Joni Mitchell at McCabe's; the Ramones/Flamin' Groovies show at the Roxy; Tom Waits passed out at the Tropicana Motor Inn—Art was there and has the photos to prove it!

Art would find later notoriety as manager of the Blasters and the Cramps. Today he is the producer, director, and host of the Hippest TV talk show ever—*Li'l Art's Poker Party*. Guests on his show have ranged from Bullmoose Jackson and Screamin' Jay Hawkins to Peter Buck and Jeffrey Lee Pierce. Where else can you watch R. Meltzer smoke a cigar and make up card games? Where else can you watch people—who actually *know*—make corrections of the reporting of the *L.A. Times* entertainment section and *Billboard*? Where else can you watch people actually say what's on their mind and remain interesting? Naturally, it's on Public Access TV.

**Don Waller:** This gentleman is a rock & roll-ologist in the First Degree. This gentleman knows Music the way most people breathe. For example, at a class he cotaught with the author at UCLA's Experimental College in 1974 (subject: Rock & Roll Theory), he made the seemingly extreme claim that *Raw Power* by Iggy and the Stooges would become the most important album of the seventies. In retrospect he is more on-target than he could have imagined. That record, more than any other, laid the groundwork for the punk-rock movement that is generally considered to have begun two years later and is still being felt to this day! Nirvana, Pearl Jam, and the Offspring owe their careers to that record—ask Henry Rollins!

Waller's own band, the Imperial Dogs, were the first band to put *Raw Power* to use. As a frontman he was as outrageous as Iggy. The band was Hard, Loud, and Fast. Unfortunately, the I-Dogs rarely played outside of its hometown of Carson, a working-class community south of the L.A. Airport along the San Diego Freeway. Suffice it to say that people tend to remember the few times the Imperial Dogs played in Hollywood: The Gazzari's gig when Waller's pants split at the crotch; the shows at Rodney's that incorporated switchblades and whips.

Waller was so on top of the Scene that he can boast to have witnessed the first-ever L.A. shows by the following acts during the decade at hand: Aerosmith, Black Flag, Blondie, Blue Öyster Cult (who later recorded one of his songs), Boomtown Rats, Buzzcocks, the Clash, Elvis Costello, the Cramps, the Crawdaddys, the Dead Boys, Del Fuegos, the Dictators, the Feelies, the Fleshtones, the Furys, the Gun Club, Richard Hell and the Voidoids, Iggy and the Stooges, the Jam, Magazine, Bob Marley and the Wailers, Mink DeVille, Mott the Hoople, the New Order (the one with Ron Asheton of the Stooges, not the English new-wave disco band), the New York Dolls, the

> "I wish we were simple enough people to be able to write something like Hank Williams. We know too much for our own good."
> —JOHN DOE, X

Pandoras, Pere Ubu, Tom Petty and the Heartbreakers, the Plimsouls, the Pop!, Suzi Quatro, the Ramones, the Runaways, Slade, Patti Smith, Soul Asylum, Squeeze, the Sweet, Talking Heads, Television, Thin Lizzy, Johnny Thunders and the Heartbreakers, the Unclaimed, Roy Wood's Wizzard and ZZ Top.

He continued to be Where It's At in the eighties, and even today he has been known to phone his friends to discuss the merits of some new band— like the Revenants, That Dog, or Baby Lemonade. (What? Haven't heard of 'em? You will!) In reality, Mr. Waller applies pen to paper regarding musical experiences. Since the demise of *Back Door Man* (where he was a driving force), he has written for the *Los Angeles Times* and the *L.A. Weekly*. Also, he writes for *BAM*, when that mag is bright enough to ask him. He has written a book about the Motown label. As this is typed he is the senior editor at *Radio & Records*, a Music Industry trade-zine. Earth would be better served if Major Label Records were to hire him as an A&R cat.

**The Plungers:**  To the uninitiated eye, these four young ladies would appear to be groupies. However, they were just out for that illusive Good Time. The reason they were known collectively as the Plungers remains a mystery—

they may have formed a band, even though none of them owned or played an instrument, so it is doubtful that they ever performed a gig. Whoever the Plungers were, Hollywood would not have been the same without them.

Singularly known as Trudi, Helen, Trixie, and Mary, they were so On the Scene: If you saw them at a show, you knew you were at the right place at the right time. Somehow they seemed to be on the guest list for all the cool events—the Masque, the Whisky, the Starwood, you name it, if it was Happening, they were there. Very few photographs from the time seem to exist that do not show at least one of them.

For a while, a couple of them lived in an apartment next door to a twenty-four–hour adult bookstore and across the street from the Starwood on Santa Monica Boulevard. For several months the Plunger Pit was Party Central for the Spiked-Hair crowd. Members of every punk band, as well as other Fringe Scenesters, were seen there at one time or another—a required stop in Tinsel Town. Be assured that Fun was almost definitely had when one was there.

The Plungers were so Happening that two of them married into the Screamers—Hollywood's ulta-hip punk band (so hip that they graced the cover of the very first *Slash Magazine* before they had even played a gig!).

**Brendan Mullen:**  If it weren't for this Scottish-born individual, Hollywood would not have been the punk Hot Spot that it was in the seventies. Brendan ran the Masque—truly an underground club, located in the basement of the Pussycat Theater on Hollywood Boulevard. To get in, one had to enter from the alley, go down some stairs and tromp through about an inch of spilled beer and other liquids (perhaps bodily fluids). It may have been a deep, dark dinge but many would rather be there on a Saturday Night than anywhere in the world.

Dig this litany of bands that played there: the Alley Cats, the Avengers (San Francisco's *only* great Punk band), the Bags, Black Flag, Black Randy and the Metro Squad, the Controllers, the Dickies, the Dils, the Eyes, F-Word, the Flesh Eaters, the Germs, the Go-Go's, Hal Negro and the Satintones, the Mau Maus, the Nerves, the Randoms, the Screamers, the Skulls, the Last, Wall Of Voodoo, the Weirdos, X, the Zeros—all played there. If you weren't there, you were nowhere. It was *the* place to be seen throwing up.

After the Masque became renowned, Brendan started hosting Masque nights at the Whisky, where some of the more popular bands could play to a crowd in relative comfort. When fire marshals forced the Masque to close, he opened The Other Masque, a larger place near the corner of Santa Monica Boulevard and Vine Street, where the usual bands played, along with touring acts such as the Dead Boys, the Cramps and Bad Brains. But that place was soon gone, too, and Brendan continued to work the name by staging several

"Masque Benefits." Although the benefits seemed successful, another Masque never materialized.

In the eighties Brendan booked acts into the Club Lingerie, thereby putting the joint on the map. He brought in the Replacements, Big Joe Turner (backed by the Blasters), R.E.M., the Fleshtones, Queen Ida, Sun Ra and His Astro-Infinity Arkestra, and Los Lobos, to name a few.

Mr. Mullen has not yet made his presence felt in the nineties—but he really doesn't need to. If you were to ask the author, he would say Mr. Mullen has done enough!

There are a few others who should be mentioned:

**Greg Shaw:** A neat guy whose *Who Put The BOMP!* magazine started as a sixties rock collectors' fanzine and soon mutated into a new-wave digest. He also ran BOMP Records—a store in Burbank (Lisa Fancher, who brought you the Suicidal Tendencies and the Circle Jerks on her Frontier label, and Jeffrey Lee Pierce of Gun Club fame both worked the counter there) and a label that issued discs by the Flamin' Groovies, the Weirdos, and the Zeros. By the time the seventies were over, Greg was back hustling his first love—sixties records.

**Chris D.:** Another neat guy who sang in a band called the Flesh Eaters (*A Minute to Pray, a Second to Die* is the band's most fabulous record). He also wrote for *Slash* and produced a lot of the early L.A. punk records.

**Claude Bessy:** Speaking of *Slash Magazine,* this man—a.k.a. Kickboy Face, Chatty Chatty Mouth, and a couple other names—was a chief writer and figurehead for the popular tabloid and one would quickly assume that he would be the most obvious source of information. Although this Frenchman is likewise a neat guy and a fine arbiter of good taste and fine music, he should NOT be consulted! During this period of time, word has it, he was drunker than anyone! He was often seen passed out at gigs that he later reported on in his column! Or, at least that is how some folks remember him. He was last seen sleeping it off in Spain. Second thought, he may be the perfect person to seek out. He's likely in Spain right now writing down the whole thing—efficiently and with good punctuation.

**Don Snowden:** This chap must be mentioned somewhere. He bought (as opposed to begged, borrowed and stole) *all* the groovy records. He was about the only writer from the *L.A. Times* to visit the Masque on a regular basis—a brave fellow. He probably kept notes. Catch him quick—he is threatening to keep Kickboy Face company in Spain.

**Pleasant Gehman:** Come to think of it, this woman should be the *only* one consulted. Not only was she at nearly every event noted above, but she knew everyone, did everything, was often quoted by the *L.A. Times* as an Official Teenager (which she was at the time), married a Swingin' English Rockabilly Star, lived in a crash pad for Wayward Punks known as Disgraceland AND SHE KEPT AN ACCURATE DIARY! Some genius should publish it. The eighties saw her singing in first the Screamin' Sirens (a cowpunk band), then the Ringling Sisters. At the present, she sponsors benefits for an orphanage in Hollywood and makes spoken word recordings that are worth listening to.

Well, that should do it. Talking to these people should give a person a pretty good picture of what went on. That is, if you REALLY want to know.

P.S.: Rest in Peace: Michelle Meyers and Craig Lee. Tomata Du Plenty, call me.

# New York's Music for Dozens, or, Alt-Rock Pioneers for a Buck a Band

by Michael Hill

As associate director of A&R at Warner Bros., Michael Hill currently works with Paul Westerberg, Luka Bloom and Soul Coughing, among other artists.

Early fall 1982: I'm an editor of the soon-to-be-defunct *New York Rocker,* a widely respected, narrowly circulated alternative-rock rag—hey, Michael Stipe told ROLLING STONE he used to read it—from an era when categories like "alternative" didn't exist, or at least didn't make money. Hence our eventual fiscal doom.

Then, improbably, I hear from the owners of Folk City, a Greenwich Village institution—in name at least—that continues to play host to a fluctuating folk scene. They're looking for something a little more cutting edge one night a week, sort of like CBGB unplugged. I was about to be in need of a gig and this wouldn't be too dissimilar to *Rocker* life: very little money and lots of what L.A. band X called "the unheard music."

Thinking I couldn't go it alone, I run the idea by fellow writer and editor Ira Kaplan. Ira not only wants to go for it, but he comes up with a suitably ambitious name: Music for Dozens. The simple credo of our series is three bands, three bucks, and a ten P.M. starting time, early by New York standards of the day. Ira is more the maven; I take to the role of maitre'd (and I confess that I occasionally broke our egalitarian rules by slipping in a few A&R execs ahead of the line so they wouldn't miss a band, though I always made sure to get their three bucks). Eighty percent of the door goes back to the bands; Ira and I split the remainder. Given that the club literally only fit dozens, and the number of musicians onstage could also number dozens, we could generally guarantee that we'd all go home relatively broke.

Herewith, five big bills that would have collectively set you back fifteen bucks, the average price of a CD today. By the way, hardly anybody unplugged, or even played softly. Also, we sometimes only booked, or only could find, two bands for a bill. But we still charged three bucks.

### 12/1/82: Meat Puppets/Sonic Youth/Hose

I suppose you could discern a certain folk element in the herb-hazy hardcore of the Meat Puppets, which perhaps made our room appealing to them so early in our series. I used to regard them almost as a Grateful Dead–style country band, at least in musical and sartorial contrast to SST labelmates like Black Flag. Sonic Youth, on the other hand, were purely about sculpted noise, and they attracted their own loyal dozens of fans from a downtown scene splintering into art and rock factions. Sonic Youth were dependable, they lived nearby, they liked to play a lot, and their fans always showed up—qualities that made them among the most attractive candidates for repeat performances. They played the series twice in the following year.

As far as I can recall, Hose only played Folk City and Maxwell's in Hoboken, New Jersey, a rare distinction for both clubs. Hose were led by a seemingly unlikely visionary, Rick Rubin, a baby-faced New York University grad who was about to surprise us all by becoming a Def Jam Records mogul and singularly successful record producer. Hose were unknown, yet they were truly the shape of things to come. They were trying to fashion a fusion of hardcore and funk—with lumbering versions of hits like Rick James' "Superfreak"—that kind of rocked and kind of swung in a primordially grungy way. Rubin returned to expand on his vision the following year, this time with DJ Jazzy Jay, who became the first Def Jam recording artist, and the aptly named Big Boys, an underappreciated Houston band that matched Hose in both physical size and sound. That night was the first—and perhaps only—time Folk City sported a mosh pit.

### 1/29/83: The Morells/The Violent Femmes

The Morells were, at first, the news of the bill, particularly for fans of obscure vinyl and rare appearances: a group of seasoned Midwestern garage-and-bar rockers whose members had been parts of two different cult bands, the Skeletons and the Original Symptoms. Led by the fatherly Lou Whitney, the Morells proved irresistible, playing rock & roll in the NRBQ manner, in which the simplest gestures can seem virtuoso—not to mention plain old fun.

Yet it was the Violent Femmes who became news. Known mostly from press reports of their performances as demented buskers on the streets of their native Milwaukee, the Femmes drew the largest crowd of the series, thanks in part to an advance rave from *The New York Times*. Their show was like some David Lynch version of a hootenany: the faded, flocked wallpaper on the wall of the club, the dated 8 × 10 glossies of folk artists past and near present, and the unsettling presence of the young Gordon Gano, dressed in a dirty old man's raincoat and with a face of angelic innocence, spinning darkly funny tales of unrequited lust and murder. Slash Records honcho Bob Biggs followed them to the dressing room; shortly after the gig the trio signed a deal with Slash and subsequently released *Violent Femmes,* a record that remains a coming-of-age indispensible, the aural equivalent of *Catcher in the Rye*. We were told that filmmaker Wim Wenders also followed the Femmes to the dressing room. We were never quite sure what he was doing there—or if he really was there—but dropping his name felt sort of cool.

### 4/13/83: The Replacements/Del-Lords/Del Fuegos

Both Del Fuegos and the Replacements were making their New York City debut this evening. Both bands had a reputation as cool lo-fi garage rockers with very loyal followings in Boston and Minneapolis, respectively. But the Fuegos would eventually come to musically share more with New York's Del-Lords, who were up-and-coming, Springsteen-influenced, mainstream rockers. The Replacements would remain, well, the Replacements. At the time, though, the Del-Lords intimidated both bands with their Lower East Side biker-type friends in the dressing room.

The 'Mats may have made it to Manhattan sooner, but fifteen-year-old bassist Tommy Stinson was still in high school, something he soon ditched, and manager Peter Jesperson had explained to us they could only tour during school breaks. Ira had suggested that perhaps singer Paul Westerberg, already becoming known for his songwriting, would consider doing his own acoustic set, but Jesperson assured us that Westerberg wouldn't come out alone. Which, of course, only added to his mystique.

I didn't know that much about them before they appeared; they had yet to spread their reputation far and wide. We had scheduled a profile of the group in the *New York Rocker,* but we folded before it could ever appear, an appropriately Replacements-like situation. But my impressions from that night remain as vivid as my first glimpse of the Femmes. This time, though, the room seemed less like some surreal coffeehouse than a ramshackle cocktail lounge, where everything, band included, was falling apart. The band played way too loud, the tinny speakers blew, yet the show went on, fans hanging onto Westerberg's every garbled word. The owners, as if to rescue their hapless sound system, turned up the houselights, which only served to cast the proceedings in a more garish light. I'd say that just about everyone in that room followed the band around New York that week, from the Great Gildersleeves to Danceteria, looking for an elusive epiphany. Three out of four members crashed at

Ira's house in Hoboken; his recollections of those hairspray-scented days are perhaps best left for his own memoirs.

The 'Mats returned to Music for Dozens in August, fresh from an East Coast tour with R.E.M. On the road, they had all developed a fondness for mascara, a dangerous predilection on a hot August night, particularly if it's not waterproof.

### 4/27/83: Hüsker Dü/The Ordinaires/Men and Volts

Unlike the Replacements, Hüsker Dü came to Music for Dozens with a serious hardcore rep. They weren't unveiling themselves, but, for a portion of the show at least, unplugging themselves. For them, the gig was truly a departure into then-foreign pop territory as they performed folk-rock–style covers of the Byrds' "Eight Miles High," the Stones' "Paint It Black" and the Hollies' "Look Through Any Window." In retrospect, their choices reflect the balance they later achieved between overt pop songcraft and more expansive guitar

"If I go to see a band now, it's like 'Oh God, Thurston's here' . . . I don't go to see bands as much because of that."

—THURSTON MOORE, SONIC YOUTH

excursions, as well as the singer/songwriter approach Bob Mould often took in his solo work. On that night, though, it was just a ferocious band taking advantage of an unlikely venue and turning in a performance that was playful, funny, intimate and revealing.

As for the rest of the bill, Half Japanese compatriots Men and Volts were led by David Greenberger, publisher/editor of *Duplex Planet*. The Ordinaires were a very downtown New York, very large, very avant combo, mixing up jazz, funk and noise in alternately amusing and irritating ways. There were so many of them onstage that, given their individual fans and friends, they could always ensure a good crowd—just one reason why they were welcomed back.

### 6/29/83: Jill Kroesen/10,000 Maniacs/The Young Turks

Yet another New York City debut: 10,000 Maniacs. They were a definite unknown quantity, but this was one of those nights when we struggled to pull together a cohesive bill and, probably, Sonic Youth or the Ordinaires couldn't make it. Jill Kroesen was aligned with the downtown music and performance-art scene, a collaborator of composer Robert Ashley, among others.

So Folk City was as much of a stretch for her as for a hardcore band. We were sort of counting on the art-space types traversing the few blocks uptown from Soho, so for the rest of the bill, instead of rounding up more avant-gardists, we cast our net wider: to Jamestown, New York, for the Maniacs and suburban New Jersey for the Young Turks.

I can't tell you what became of the Young Turks; as for the 10,000 Maniacs, they went on to the greatest commercial success of any Music for Dozens artist. Given their name, they certainly confounded my expectations that night—and the owners were probably relieved to find their speakers weren't about to be blown again by some hardcore band. Ira, who had heard some very indie stuff, had described them to the owners, I believe, as reggae-ish.

The band drove from way upstate to the gig in a van that at least got them to the show. I wish I could say that the fifteen dollars they earned from the paltry turnout that night helped them make it back. (No, the art-damaged hordes never came north of Houston Street.) The band's van broke down; I don't know where they wound up sleeping, but they had accomplished one thing: they had played New York City. Several years later Natalie Merchant recalled that night from the stage of Manhattan's Beacon Theatre, where the group was headlining a sold-out show. I was relieved to hear that she remembered that night fondly. What I recall was an adept group of musicians going off on tangents that intersected in odd but intriguing ways. Guitarist Robert Buck favored spacey washes of sound, while fellow guitarist John Lombardo concentrated on earthier rock riffs. The rhythm section of Jerome Augustyniak and Steven Gustafson was, yes, reggae-ish at times, and Natalie was in a world of her own, singing in a lovely but baffling manner that made Michael Stipe's seductive mumblings of the time seem a model of clarity. I thought she was singing in Portuguese. Keyboardist Dennis Drew seemed to be nominally leading the band. It was Dennis who got the fifteen dollars and whom I had to ask quietly to wind up the set when it had gone on well past the allotted time. And it was Dennis who later filled me in on their arduous trek back up north. That didn't deter them, though. Within a year, they were returning regularly to New York City, to play places like CBGB and Maxwell's, and they landed a deal with Elektra, a label that stuck with the band until the rest of the world found them.

There were many other great and preposterous shows, lines around the block and rows of empty tables. I landed an A&R job out of it and got to know the Replacements a lot better. Ira wasn't deterred from starting—with his future wife, Georgia Hubley—his band, Yo La Tengo, a dreamy/noisy combo that has toured the world and whose work has evocatively graced the soundtracks of Hal Hartley movies. Music for Dozens ended in 1984; Folk City closed a few years later. And the unheard music doesn't sound so strange anymore.

# Ten Reasons Why You Want to Be in Cleveland if You Want to Rock & Roll

by John Petkovic

Cobra Verde vocalist/guitarist John Petkovic is proud to call Cleveland home.

**Location.** "The Best Location in the Nation." Centrally located, Cleveland is only about an hour west of Youngstown, an hour-and-a-half east of Toledo, an hour north of Akron, and a short canoe ride from Canada. And the fact that most Clevelanders leave Cleveland isn't so bad either; it just means that virtually anywhere in the country you're likely to find an ex-Clevelander who'll put you up for the night.

**Lineage.** The term "rock & roll" was supposedly coined in Cleveland (by Leo Mintz in 1952). Unfortunately, the term "Classic Rock Tribute Band" was also coined in Cleveland.

**Terrain.** The industrial flats of Cleveland, a seemingly never-ending expanse of warehouses and bridges and mills belching smoke and fire into the sky. The flats have been the primary inspiration for both the Cleveland art community, and the noisy Cleveland rock groups of the seventies. They are the classic ruins of America.

**Fame.** Can you play a riff, man? How does that Sgt. Pepper suit look on you? Well, the Rock and Roll Hall of Fame opened in September 1995. By the end of the twentieth century, as millions of rock & roll fans visit Cleveland, they will want to see their Rock Hall heroes come to life in the Rock and Roll Hall of Fame Showbar. Attractions will include Burning Love: A Tribute to Elvis; Moondance (featuring ex-members of Counting Crows): A Tribute to Van Morrison; 2112: Rush Arrives (A Tribute); Lizard King: A Spoken-Word

Tribute to the Music of Jim Morrison; Rolling Zeppelin: A Tribute to Page/ Plant/Jagger/Richards; and Pete Townshend: A Tribute to Roger Daltrey.

**Celebrity sightings.** Example: Spotting Cleveland rock legend David Thomas of Pere Ubu at the local Wendy's Super Salad Bar with Wendy's founder and president Dave Thomas.

**Media coverage.** Rock writer and local legend Jane Scott of the Cleveland daily *Plain Dealer,* who recently celebrated her seventy-fifth birthday. Scott (who received birthday cards from Keith Richards and Phil Collins, among others) has covered rock & roll from Day One (earning her the title "The World's Oldest Teenager"). In a 1987 feature on Scott in *People* magazine, a photo pictured her with the Butthole Surfers backstage at Cleveland's Phantasy Theater (at the time, *People* refused to print the band's name because "its name is insufficiently wholesome to mention here"). Scott's lack of cynicism and ability to cover a local band playing its first show in the same way she'd cover a Rolling Stones concert is her gimmick. "Part of the secret behind my success is that I show up when no one else does," Scott says. "I just go and talk to the band—and put it in the paper."

**Cult-comic hipness.** Harvey Pekar, author of *American Splendor.* If you lend Harvey a buck you might find yourself in the next issue. Cleveland is also home to the venerable comic character Howard the Duck.

**Prerock credibility.** Bluesman Robert Jr. Lockwood. He's called Junior because he plays like the guy who taught him, his stepfather Robert Johnson. Lockwood's playing is less defiant than it is proud, but on some nights he still inspires.

**Little competition.** Baseball's perennial losers, the Cleveland Indians, managed in 1994 to be the odds-on favorite to win the pennant in a season that wasn't completed. There ain't much else happening.

**Glamour.** In the fifties, Cleveland was home to the country's first late-night horror host, Ghoulardi, who blended horror trash with beatnik hep. Unfortunately, Clevelanders also still fondly remember when Joan Jett played Michael J. Fox's sister in the movie *Light of Day.* They jammed together at the local Euclid Tavern. It was bad.

# All Roads Lead to the Emerald City, or, Why Your Favorite Seattle Bands Aren't from Seattle

by Erik Flannigan and Grant Alden

Erik Flannigan was born and raised in Tacoma and has written for *Musician*, *CD Review*, *ICE*, and *The Rocket*. Grant Alden lives near Woodland Park Zoo and is former managing editor of *The Rocket*. He's also written for ROLLING STONE, *Spin*, and *Guitar World*.

Sure, we tell the stories: "I saw Green River play in 1986 in front of nineteen people at an abandoned cannery." But you never hear anyone say Mudhoney covered "Love Plus One" at their senior ball. Why? Because there's another dark secret about Seattle beyond the revelation that most of the city's rock clubs opened well after "Smells Like Teen Spirit" brought grunge to the masses. As it turns out, a lot of Seattle's preeminent rockers didn't start out in Seattle. They're from places like:

**Aberdeen/Hoquiam/Montesano, Washington.** Somehow local band Metal Church got signed to Elektra, proving that it could be done. They sold several hundred thousand records and opened for Judas Priest before fading into the sunset. The Melvins (a trio) taught the entire region to play *slowly* first, then *loudly,* before decamping to San Francisco—but not before inspiring Matt Lukin (later of Mudhoney) and an unknown band of misfits called Nirvana (also a trio). The area's previous claim to fame was its once-thriving brothels.

**Bainbridge Island, Washington.** Blame much of this mess on the Wood family. Islanders Andy Wood and Regan Hagar became the guiding forces behind Malfunkshun, and crossed the bay to Seattle. Then Andy glammed up for bigger and better things with Mother Love Bone, which after Wood's death from a heroin OD mutated into Pearl Jam and conquered the known world. Regan, meanwhile, carried on the thick funk in Molasses, before teaming with remaining Wood brothers Kevin and Brian in Devilhead; in the interim the brothers played with ex-Nirvana drummer Chad Channing in the Fire Aunts and then in Hater with fellow-Islander Ben Shepherd (later of Soundgarden).

**Boise, Idaho.** Tad Doyle began the exodus from Boise with a thunderous band called H-Hour. When that group disintergrated, he started the equally daunting Tad, who refuse to break up even after being threatened with legal action from a gospel singer (who didn't like seeing a carelessly discarded photo of her ex-husband fondling her on one of the band's album covers) and a major international conglomerate (Pepsi, who didn't take kindly to the song "Jack Pepsi"). Tad was followed west by the Treepeople, who have since split.

**Bremerton, Washington.** Back when producer/guitarist Jack Endino still went by "Mike" and worked as an engineer in the Bremerton shipyards, he played bass in a Jonathan Richman–inspired band called Food. He moved through a few other bands before ending up as guitarist for Skin Yard and producing just about every important Sub Pop record. His Skin Yard bassmate Daniel House took over C/Z Records, whose first release was the seminal *Deep Six,* perhaps the earliest recorded document of the emerging Seattle scene.

**Chicago, Illinois.** When Hiro Yamamoto and Kim Thayil headed west to school (physics and philosophy, respectively) at the University of Washington, they ran into Bruce Pavitt, the nerd who'd made fun of Kim in high school. Pavitt soon launched Sub Pop; Hiro and Kim started Soundgarden. In 1988 Soundgarden became the first Sub Pop act to sign to a major label. In 1994 their album *Superunknown* debuted at Number One. Now Kim makes fun of Bruce. And they're both millionaires.

**Ellensburg, Washington.** The town where Van and Gary Lee Conner's dad was an elementary school principal—at least until he let his kids' band, then playing new wave covers under the name Explosive Generation, entertain at an assembly. Later, as the Screaming Trees, they signed to SST before there was a Sub Pop. Dad runs a video store these days, and the kids are heroes in this isolated college town east of the Cascades.

**Lake City, Washington.** If you ignore the Sonics and the Wailers, the Washington State rock timeline starts in 1980 with the suburban formation of the Fastbacks. Fifteen years after their high school origins, Kurt Bloch, Kim

Warnick, and Lulu Gargiulo remain best friends and bandmates. In that time, Kim and Lulu paved the way for regular girls like Kim and Kelley Deal to stay regular girls and still play. The Fastbacks' legendary revolving drum seat (which has been occupied by Mudhoney's Dan Peters and Guns n' Roses' Duff McKagan, among many others) accounts for the local maxim that you haven't really lived in Seattle until you've drummed for the Fastbacks.

**Missoula, Montana.**   So Jeff Ament's band drives all the way from Missoula to Seattle for a gig, only to find out that it's been cancelled. Some good samaritan puts them up for ten days, they find another gig, and they never go back to Missoula. Ament went on to play bass in Green River, Mother Love Bone, and eventually Pearl Jam. Missoula also spawned former Big Black/Rapeman leader Steve Albini, still conducting his reign of terror as a producer (sorry, *engineer*) in Chicago. Missoula also produced a pretty fair Seattle band called Silkworm, but that came later.

**Olympia, Washington.**   The college town where Bruce Pavitt went to school. Where Bing Crosby's boyhood home still stands. Where *Op* (later *Option*) magazine was born. Where the K and Kill Rock Stars labels were born. Where Beat Happening and the whole love-rock thing started. Where Kathleen Hanna and grrrl-punk hail from. The International Pop Underground too. And, coincidentally, about an hour's drive from Aberdeen if you speed.

**Seattle, Washington.**   Seattle bands. They all moved here. Okay, a few of 'em were born here, but don't tell anyone that. The rent used to be cheap. There was no place to play. Major rock tours skipped the market. But the beer was cheap and brewed locally. The pot was good. There were lots of jobs as bike messengers and espresso pullers. Thrift stores had plenty of Pendletons. Rehearsing was an easy choice with the bad weather. And only a couple of bands had been signed, both heavy metal. We were due. Deal with it.

# Love Battery's Top Ten Reasons to Live in Seattle

In addition to their tireless boosterism on behalf of their hometown, Love Battery have recorded three albums of noisily melodic rock tunes.

1. Friends' heated pools

2. Catered barbecues

3. Jason's tab at the Comet

4. Easy tee times

5. Twenty-four—hour flannel stores

6. Full complement of mediocre sports franchises

7. Courteous staff at needle exchange

8. Cheap Love Battery CDs in used bins

9. Rainy day women

10. Go Dawgs!

# What Henry Rollins Likes About Los Angeles

as Told to
Michael Rubiner

Henry Rollins moved from Washington, D.C. to Los Angeles in 1981 to join preeminent hardcore band Black Flag. Since that group's demise, he has pursued parallel careers as a spoken-word artist and leader of the Rollins Band. He also runs 2.13.61, which publishes his own and other writers' books, and 213CD, which specializes in spoken-word recordings. This is what he said in ROLLING STONE about L.A.:

"You can walk around on Hollywood Boulevard and look at the runaway boys and girls, the junkies sitting in front of Mann's Chinese asking for money. You can look at the Japanese tourists videotaping Michael Jackson's star like it's gonna jump up and do something. You can watch the police and liquor-store owners with their flashlights looking for spent bullet casings in the curbs in front of the liquor stores that have just been robbed. You can look up into the sky and see one of L.A.'s forty-four police helicopters going back and forth from the mother hive in the Hollywood Hills. . . .

"To me, L.A. is hairy. It's where civilization has gone to die. It's where Nietzsche and Darwin would be high-fiving each other, agreeing—going 'Yeah, see?' 'I know, I know!' "

"The nights can be very nice in L.A., especially if you live near trees, so you can get a lungful of jasmine at night. That's when I creep out of the cracks and steal a breath of fresh air.

"I've never really been able to connect with Californians. I'm not some elitist asshole—it's just that when someone says, 'Hey, dude,' I'm like 'No, please don't call me dude. I'm not a dude.' "

# Under

# the
# Influence

# The Residents' Favorite American Composers

██████████████████████████████████

The ever-mysterious San Francisco-based Residents have been avant-pop trendsetters since the early seventies, turning out a catalog of more than thirty albums while carefully maintaining a wall of secrecy around their individual identities. In 1984 the group began its American Composers Series, an ongoing multi-album project that has thus far interpreted the work of James Brown, George Gershwin, John Philip Sousa, and Hank Williams, with future discs planned to pay tribute to the remaining artists on this list.

**Nick Ashford and Valerie Simpson**

**Burt Bacharach**

**Tommy Boyce and Bobby Hart**

**James Brown**

**Dave Brubeck**

**John Cage**

**Aaron Copland**

**Steve Cropper**

**Willie Dixon**

**Bob Dylan**

Duke Ellington

Stephen Foster

George Gershwin

Philip Glass

Jimi Hendrix

Brian Holland, Lamont Dozier and Eddie Holland

Charles Ives

Michael Jackson

Scott Joplin

Stan Kenton

Jerome Kern

Carole King

Jerry Leiber and Mike Stoller

Charles Mingus

Meredith Monk

Randy Newman

Carl Perkins

Cole Porter

Perez Prado

Otis Redding

The Residents

Smokey Robinson

John Philip Sousa

Sun Ra

Allen Toussaint

Don Van Vliet (a.k.a. Captain Beefheart)

Tom Waits

Fats Waller

Muddy Waters

Barry White

Hank Williams

Brian Wilson

Frank Zappa

"Each morning I get up at about ten o'clock, and the first thing I do is put on a Motörhead single. I play it as many times as it takes for me to wake up, which on average is twice. If I've had a rough night, then it takes maybe four plays."

—EDWARD TUDOR-POLE, TENPOLE TUDOR

# Thirty-one Artists Who Influenced Julian Cope

**F**irst as leader of the Teardrop Explodes and subsequently as a reliably iconoclastic solo artist, Julian Cope has outlasted various pop-culture movements to emerge as one of rock's most talented eccentrics. The following musical influences were cited in Cope's autobiography *Head-On*.

Marc Bolan/T. Rex

Tim Buckley

Can

Captain Beefheart

The Chocolate Watch Band

The Clash

Country Joe and the Fish

The Doors

Nick Drake

Brian Eno

Faust

Funkadelic

Joy Division

Love

The Modern Lovers

The Mothers of Invention

New York Dolls

Pere Ubu

Prince Far I

Ramones

The Residents

The Seeds

Sex Pistols

Patti Smith

The Subway Sect

Suicide

Television

Thirteenth Floor Elevators

Traffic

The Velvet Underground

Scott Walker/the Walker Brothers

# Music That Moves Me

## by Epic Soundtracks

Epic Soundtracks (a.k.a. Paul Godley) began playing music in 1972 and made his first record in 1977 as drummer with the influential Swell Maps, which also included his brother Nikki Sudden. More recently, Epic has re-emerged as a singer, songwriter, and piano player, recording solo albums that reflect many of the influences discussed below.

The last time I sat down and wrote about music was in 1984. I interviewed Alex Chilton for the 'zine *What a Nice Way to Turn 17* and the now defunct *Sounds*. Before that I wrote a long sprawling article on Brian Wilson and the effect his music had on me.

Trying to put down on paper just exactly why you like a particular piece of music isn't the easiest thing in the world. I was planning to just jot down an enormous list of stuff I liked, but the editors of this book wouldn't let me do that. "You've got to say why you like it!" Okay, I gave in.

I also couldn't mention everything I like, so what you get are just the first things that came into my head. My favorite music changes according to my general state of mind, but hopefully there are a few different areas covered here. And there are other records I could easily have included: "I Just Wasn't Made for These Times" by the Beach Boys, "A Change Is Gonna Come" by Sam Cooke, "Babe I'm Gonna Leave You" by Led Zeppelin, "Gimme Shelter" by the Stones, "There Was a Time" by James Brown, "Let It Rock" by Chuck Berry, "Wailing Wall" by Todd Rundgren and "I'm Only Sleeping" by the Beatles.

Oh, yeah, I left out the Kinks, the Impressions, Aretha Franklin, Don Covay, Carole King, the Stooges . . . I better stop . . . this is becoming a list.

### T. Rex, "Baby Strange" (from *The Slider*) 1972

I first started buying records in 1972. At my school at the time you were either into "serious rock" or "teenybopper stuff!" Thing is, I liked music from both of these invented categories. I loved Free and Led Zep and I loved T. Rex also. I was either very broad-minded or very confused. I loved the Carpenters . . . hmmm . . . "Say You Don't Mind" and "I Don't Believe in Miracles" by Colin Blunstone . . . there was some logical thread running through my mind at the time, I suppose. Another amazing record that sticks in my mind is Kevin Ayers' "Song from the Bottom of a Well" with its eerie guitar sound that sonically captures the song title so well.

Anyway, I liked a lot of stuff then that sounds more than just a little ridiculous now, but I have certain affection for it in my own muddled way. Now if someone at school had had some Big Star or James Carr to lend me . . . pretty unlikely though. Whatever, I'm rambling, I mentioned T. Rex: *Electric Warrior, The Slider, Bolan Boogie*. Classic records with classic sleeves. T. Rex sound as fresh to me today as they did then. An aural melting pot for everything rock & roll had been up till that point but at the same time nothing like anything else. There were various elements cooked up by Marc Bolan and producer Tony Visconti in this particular musical stew: boogie rhythms, Sun slapback echo, deep strings, honking saxophones, cool guitar licks, handclaps, surreal backing voices, ever so slightly altered R&B riffs, and a few bricks borrowed from Phil Spector's Wall of Sound. On top of this there was Marc Bolan's nonmacho/macho vocalizing. Big Star had the taste to cover T. Rex's "Baby Strange" in the early seventies. Now that must mean something.

### Can, "Pinch" (from *Ege Bamyasi*) 1972

What is this music? Rock? Jazz? Avant garde? Who cares? Can never got hung up about labels so why should we? There's so much going on in this track. I must have heard it hundreds of times but I still hear new things. Can were formed in Germany in 1968 originally with black New Yorker Malcolm Mooney as vocalist, then between 1970 and '73 with Japanese former busker Damo Suzuki with his wonderful scat pidgin English vocalizing. This is my favorite period of Can, the albums: *Tago Mago, Ege Bamyasi, Future Days* . . . check them out. Unlike anything that had really gone before. Hypnotic, unfolding all the time. Can sure knew how to explore and exploit a good groove.

They soaked up a million different influences. There's bits of James Brown, V.U., musics from every time and every place, ancient and modern, but it all came out sounding like nobody else . . . except . . . Can.

### Faces, "Ooh La La" (from *Ooh La La*) 1973

Rod Stewart and the Faces seem to sound better with each passing year. You realize there'll never be another band quite like them. It's almost as if they were so busy having a good time that they didn't even realize just how great and lasting their music really was. There was nothing intellectual about the Faces, but they sure knew how to play it from the heart.

There's something so English about them and yet a lot of their influences were so obviously American, especially Rod's love of Soul legend Sam Cooke. Ron Wood's guitar playing from this period is so unique, just listen to his work on a track like "Just Another Honky" from *Ooh La La*. There's so much great music on the Faces and early Rod albums (which usually feature most if not all of the band). The title song of *Ooh La La* actually has Ron Wood handling the lead vocal and has been one of my favorite songs for a long time. There's something so down home and relaxed (but not laid back) about it. Try finding some bootlegs of Faces live shows. They overflow with good times. May their music live on forever.

### MC5, "Sister Anne" (from *High Time*) 1971

Total sonic overload. Truly one of the most transcendental moments in rock & roll. If I'm in the mood for a party, this is one of the records I grab for, crank up and kick out the jams to! Can't say much else . . .

### Alex Chilton, "My Rival" (from *Like Flies on Sherbert*) 1979

One of Alex's best songs from a much-maligned album full of songs dealing in sexual innuendo, jealousy, revenge, and so on. The lyrics of "My Rival" are to the point: "My rival, I'm gonna stab him on arrival, shoot him dead with my rifle." The backing by Memphis legend Jim Dickinson and his co-horts is sloppy in the extreme but raw and alive. The music threatens to fall apart at every moment, just teetering on the edge but somehow hangs together. Most people probably hear this stuff and just hear a chaotic din but when you're familiar with other records that these guys have made you'll know there's more to it than that. It takes a lot of talent to play music as badly as this! For those familiar with Big Star's *Sister Lovers,* I guess the musical missing link between the two albums could well be "Walking Dead," another controlled piece of mayhem that was recorded in 1975 and eventually surfaced on the *Lost Decade* album.

### Frank Sinatra, "Blues in the Night" (from *Frank Sinatra Sings for Only the Lonely*) 1958

To me, Sinatra's *Only the Lonely* album stands above all his other work, with the closest set being *In the Wee Small Hours*. This is a dark, bluesy, late-night album. The singing is emotional and expressive and Nelson Riddle's arrangements are suitably deep. Sinatra had recorded some of these songs earlier in his career but they never sounded quite like this. Basically he sings as if he's been there . . . which he no doubt had. "Blues in the Night" is one great performance on a record full of them.

**Laura Nyro and Labelle, "Desiree" (from *Gonna Take a Miracle*) 1971**
The essential Laura Nyro albums are her first, originally titled *More Than a New Discovery,* a self-composed set of pop/soul classics, and *Gonna Take a Miracle,* a perfect collection of soul covers showing the roots of her style.

Laura's voice harmonizes beautifully with those of Labelle, especially on gorgeous cuts like "The Bells" and "Desiree." We hear an evocative, sparse arrangement—the voices virtually carrying the whole track. A heavenly sound.

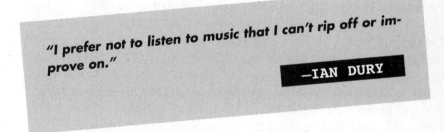

*"I prefer not to listen to music that I can't rip off or improve on."*

—IAN DURY

**Slim Harpo, "Tip On In" (from *Tip On In*) 1968**
Slim Harpo is one of the very best rhythm & blues artists. This is such a cool groove . . . the way the guitar works with the bass and drums. It's subtle and lazy but funky. I dig this stuff: "Te-Ni-Nee-Ni-Nu," "Shake Your Hips." Slim Harpo is an important figure in the scheme of things. Ask Alex Chilton . . . ask the Stones.

**The Replacements, "The Last" (from *All Shook Down*) 1990**
Paul Westerberg is my favorite songwriter from postpunk America. I like the way the Replacements came out of the hardcore scene but wore all their influences on their sleeves: bubblegum pop, R&B, Facesy rock & roll, Beatles, Led Zep and, of course, a little Big Star. There's not much about the 'Mats that was new wave, which is why they'll age a lot better than most of their contemporaries. Key songs are: "If Only You Were Lonely," "Swingin' Party" and "Achin' to Be." This is my favorite, however. From the last 'Mats album (although really the first Westerberg solo album), this song is a real heartbreaker. Right out there on the edge . . . but subtly so.

### Ike and Tina Turner, "Doin' It" (from *Come Together*) 1970

In the same way that "River Deep, Mountain High" wasn't a smash hit in America because it was too pop for the R&B charts and too R&B for the pop charts, Ike and Tina Turner seem to have been overlooked by a lot of people who should (and probably would) really dig some of their stuff. From 1970, the *Come Together* album is a red hot mixture of R&B, rock & roll, and soul styles. Alternatively rockin' and/or lowdown and dirty in all the right places, and always tight. *Come Together* kicks off great with "It Ain't Right (Lovin' to Be Lovin')" and ends with "Doin' It," one of the best sleazy tracks ever recorded (along with "Take It Off" by Groundhog Richardson). It would be nice if Ike Turner could go down in the history books for his contribution to music rather than all that other stuff. Underrated.

### Harold Smith's Majestic Choir, "We Can All Walk a Little Bit Prouder" (single), 1968

A totally over-the-top joyous sound: gospel-choir–drenched R&B. It kind of reminds me of the *Right On Be Free* album by the Voices of East Harlem from a couple of years later. This is the sort of record you put on really loud first thing in the morning to start the day off on the right track.

### Arthur Alexander, "Rainbow Road" (from *Arthur Alexander*) 1972

Written by the great Dan Penn and his sometime collaborator Donnie Fritts, this classic song is sung by the late Arthur Alexander as only he could have. Alexander had a beautiful country-tinged, soulful voice. It had a certain vulnerability which made it unique. You can feel the bad luck the man had in his life when you hear him sing. Record company rip-offs and bad deals made Alexander shy away from the music industry to the extent that he made relatively few recordings in his over thirty-year recording career. He was an important influence on more than a few, however, as John Lennon would no doubt have testified. Alexander was a great songwriter himself, giving the world classics like "You Better Move On," "Anna (Go to Him)," "Everyday I Have to Cry" and "Mr. John." In 1993 Alexander released his first record for years, and he hadn't lost his magic. Tragically, though, he died soon afterwards. "Rainbow Road," from the early seventies, sounds as achingly beautiful now as it did then. It was never a hit: in fact it was never even a single. But it was, and always will be, a classic.

### Gram Parsons, "She" (from *GP*) 1973

The late great Gram Parsons. A walking contradiction. An angel on one shoulder, a devil on the other . . . sounds like someone I could've related to. Gram's voice hangs on a thread on "She," a sublime country ballad with lilting melody, subtle rhythmic shifts and gorgeous chord changes. Just hearing the way Gram sings the word "Hallelujah" is enough to make the most fervent unbeliever put their faith in the Lord above. Gram's singing was always so assured and yet so naked and fragile. I once had the honor of meeting Keith Richards and asked him about Gram: "Man, I never been so angry about anyone checkin' out early as that guy . . . he was totally on the right track." Keith sounded sad when he said this, thinking of his friend who had slipped away in 1973. I guess Keith was made of stronger stuff than Gram, the visionary Southern boy who was blessed with good looks and charm as well as a burning love of soulful music particularly of the country variety. He also had a lust for hedonistic excess, but he wouldn't have been Gram if he hadn't. Listen to any number of songs: the good feeling of "Older Guys" or the heartbreakers, "A Song for You" or "Brass Buttons," and you'll know why Gram Parsons is one of the greatest artists ever.

### Dion, "Your Own Backyard" (from *Born to Be With You*) 1970

Such a powerful song. Such a powerful performance. An ex-junkie sings about how good he now feels to have kicked his habit. But nothing about Dion's song is preachy. He's telling you about his own experiences, he's not telling anybody what to do. When Columbia signed Dion DiMucci in 1962, he was still hot property. A seemingly clean-cut teen idol with just a hint of Bronx street suss. The label tried to groom him for the MOR market, but little did they know that he was going to veer off down his own idiosyncratic path, experimenting with and absorbing blues and folk forms. Initially Dion continued with the stomping doo-wop sound, which had given him smash hits like "The Wanderer" with the Belmonts for Laurie Records. He soon stopped having hits, however, and lost a large percentage of his audience, as his records became more and more "un-Dion." In 1967 he got back with the Belmonts for the bizarre reunion album "Together Again." Sort of like the missing link between the Velvet Underground and doo-wop (amongst other things). The *Dion* album from 1968 is strange, consisting of sparse, haunting arrangements of mostly other people's songs. "Your Own Backyard" dates from 1970 and was originally available only on a single, but a few years later was added to a bunch of mostly Phil Spector-produced cuts for the underrated *Born to Be With You* album (1975). I believe this song to be one of the best I've ever heard. The backing includes another of my idols, Jim Dickinson, uncredited on piano. This is an inspiring record. It's real. Try and hear it.

# Five American Artists Who Changed My Life

by Simon Bonney

Australian singer/songwriter Simon Bonney led the band Crime and the City Solution, before embarking on a series of solo efforts that draw more explicitly on his American influences.

### Bob Dylan

The literate oddball outsider who somehow managed to cross over into the mainstream of the American psyche and become a permanent cultural deity. He elevated the popular song lyric from the rigid teen formula to the semi-abstract narrative of, say, "Desolation Row." Yet his work was not marginalized into obscurity; it was truly popular music. Growing up with Dylan meant my concept of the song was of a *story,* first and foremost, being told through the medium of music. He's the only musician who could get up in front of thousands of people with nothing but an acoustic guitar and an "unusual" voice and have everyone spellbound. He made people want to hear the words and believe they were worth listening to.

### Lou Reed/The Velvet Underground

When I was fourteen, Lou Reed's songs gave me a connection to a world that I related to more comfortably than the world in which I lived. His songs allow you to see the humanity of his characters. To me, Reed is the great social historian of his time and place. He observes, writes it down and turns it into song, without venturing judgment.

### Willie Nelson

I heard his 1975 album, *Red Headed Stranger,* for the first time in about 1992, and it was one of the most captivating and moving records I had ever heard.

The song/chapters that comprise the album come at you like half-formed memories—familiar, yet disturbing. It truly captures the complexities of the American identity and is, in the very best sense, a great American record.

### Ronnie Van Zant/Lynyrd Skynyrd

Van Zant's "Simple Man," a very wise and uplifting song, is about the here and now, and about the innate worth that we are all born with. I find myself playing it over and over again.

### Jim Morrison/The Doors

A distinctive storyteller supported by one of the most inventive and dynamic bands of its time. The words affect me less now than they did when I was younger, but the band's improvisational, unorthodox approach to pop music will always be a big influence on me.

# My Ten Most Inspirational Pieces of Gear

by Matthew Sweet

The success of such albums as *Girlfriend, Altered Beast,* and *100% Fun* has allowed Nebraska-born singer/songwriter/multi-instrumentalist Matthew Sweet to indulge his weakness for snazzy gear.

Having always been a bit of a gearhead, I get a lot of inspiration from the instruments and various gadgets that I accumulate. When I get a new guitar, I'll start writing songs on it, and there'll usually be something unique about that particular instrument that will bring something out in me. When I first started making music, I was really into synthesizers and computers. But over the years as I've rediscovered loud guitars and real drums, I've come to appreciate certain things because they're so primitive. There's been kind of a movement toward using older things—or making new gear that's based on old principles. That's how it is with technology: People always want the newest thing because it has some advantage over the last thing, but there are always cool things that got tossed out the window when they invented the new thing. Anybody who's into this stuff will probably get mad at me for giving it more notoriety and driving the prices up . . . but here are a few of my current favorites:

**Gretsch guitars.** Growing up, I always thought Gretsches were kind of cheesy; they were aways warped and sort of gaudy looking. But since then, I've learned that Gretsches can be kind of gnarly and darker sounding, like a Gibson, but they can also be kind of twangy and trebly and out-of-phase like a classic Fender. What got me into Gretsches were the really good Japanese Gretsch reissues that were less expensive—and less warped—than old Gretsches. They've influenced me in so many different ways; I think the first one I used on a record was the picking, arpeggiated rhythm guitar on "I've Been Waiting" on *Girlfriend*.

**Fender Jazzmaster.** While we're on the subject of Japanese reissues, it's worth mentioning that Japanese Fender reissues are almost uniformly better than the American ones. I've got a Jazzmaster that was made in Japan in about 1983 that's been a big influence on me. Richard Lloyd's used it to play a lot of leads on my records; he makes amazing weird noises on it. I used to tour with it, but I don't take it out anymore because I don't want anything to happen to it.

**Mellotron.** What got me out of using synthesizers and MIDI was that I came to blame machines for zapping the energy out of music. The music I'm making now is really guitar-oriented, but lately I've been getting into a lot of weird old keyboards, including the Mellotron, a keyboard instrument from the sixties. The Mellotron has a piece of tape and a tapehead for each key, with a motor that pulls the tape across the tapehead, playing the sound of an instrument that's recorded on this piece of tape. In a way, Mellotrons were the first samplers, but they had a kind of unearthly quality about them because they were so low-fi. After I got out of high school, I had a Mellotron that cost about three hundred bucks; now they're worth a couple grand. The thing weighed about 300 pounds, and it was really hard to move around; a lot of my earliest recordings with Buzz of Delight used Mellotron pretty heavily. It's a lot easier to get them serviced now. When I had one before, I didn't know of anybody who knew how to fix them, which could be a problem because they'd usually need servicing as soon as you played more than three notes.

**Optigan.** The vinyl equivalent of the Mellotron, the Optigan uses these sort of floppy celluloid discs. It's more of a nonprofessional home-use piece of gear, though; in fact, it's about as low-fi as you can get. Each key on its keyboard corresponds to a groove on the record with that note recorded on it. Also, it's got the actual backing tracks of a band playing lots of different styles. The Optigan sounds like an old record playing, which makes it even cooler. It's cool because it's just so insane. The Optigan is not really usable as far as using it for overdubbing on modern recordings, because they break constantly and the motor isn't steady enough for it to stay in tune, but you can use it for little segues and things like that. Playing with it has inspired me to explore new sounds, and I've made up little instrumental pieces on it. You can also make some great outgoing phone-machine messages with the Optigan, and you could probably make a hell of a Muzak album with it.

**Altec and Ampex mixers.**    These are just old tube mixers from around the early seventies that were used to mix several sounds into one. You can make them distort, and if you run a sound source through one of them, the tubes cut off a lot of the high end and make it sound warm and old.

**Electro-Harmonix pedals.**    Electro-Harmonix was this amazing company—its heyday was the during the seventies—that just made tons of guitar effects and pedals. When I was growing up, their pedals were everywhere, and nobody took them seriously because they could be kind of noisy and odd sounding, but now they're becoming collector's items on the vintage market. Electro-Harmonix is really well known for the Big Muff fuzz pedal, which has been used a *lot* in Seattle over the past few years. They also have something called the Memory Man, which is an incredibly great analog delay pedal. It's a big favorite of mine, and Robert Quine has used it a lot on my albums, to fatten that twangy, thin Fender sound. Live, I've learned to make weird noises with the Memory Man. I also have this Electro-Harmonix thing called the Queen Trigger Wah, which is this huge wah-wah pedal thing that also has touch-sensitive wah's built into it. The company also made this thing called a mini-synthesizer, which was just a monophonic synthesizer with a few little knobs and a kind of fake keyboard that responds to pressure. Although I'm by no means into doing music by computer, I'm not averse to a weird sound here and there, and primitive synthesizers are really good for that.

**Baldwin electric harpsichord.**    This was made by the Baldwin company in the fifties. It's just like a regular harpsichord, only it has an aluminum frame and a Plexiglas top, so it looks really cool. It was used a lot by the Zombies in their *Odyssey and Oracle* period, and I think The Beatles used it on *Abbey Road*. The harpsichord's sort of complex, because it's a string instrument but it's also a keyboard. The way the notes sound is cool, and it's got a sort of baroque funereal Addams Family thing about it that I like.

**Hammond organ.**    I used to have a rule: No Hammond anywhere near my music, because in the past a lot of people used it in a generic, hokey way. But being a huge Brian Wilson fan, I eventually realized how many cool Beach Boys recordings had really weird, cool, creative sounds that were coming from a Hammond. Finally, I sat down at a Hammond with a big Leslie speaker, messed around with it and realized, This thing sounds really cool. Hammonds are very complex, they break a lot, they're too heavy, they take up too much room, and they're really expensive now. But if I ever own a house of my own, it will have a Hammond in it. There's also a thing called a Novachord that Hammond made for a short time in the early thirties; they're the really unearthly, weird-sounding organs you'll hear in old horror movies.

**Hofner bass.** When I started playing bass as a teenager, I didn't care at all about Paul McCartney or his bass playing, and I would frequently brag that I was a better bass player than he was because he didn't do anything fast or complicated. I wanted to be like Chris Squire, with a grinding trebly Rickenbacker bass sound. But one day a few years ago, Chris Harford came over with a Hofner bass and I was blown away by the way it sounded. So I got myself a trade deal on a Hofner bass, and since then it's inspired me a lot.

**Gibson 330 guitar.** It's kind of like Gibson's answer to the Gretsch Country Gentleman. Lloyd Cole had one, and I borrowed his for the longest time. I first picked it up at one of Lloyd's sessions, and I immediately wrote "Evangeline" on it. When I went to Atlanta to record *100% Fun* with Brendan O'Brien, he had about five of them. I got really covetous, so at the beginning of the sessions I bought one—a '59 Sunburst—from a vintage guitar dealer in Atlanta. I ended up using it a whole lot on the record; in fact, I wrote a song on it that we recorded.

# My Ten Biggest Influences

## by Kristin Hersh

Kristin Hersh is founder, guitarist, vocalist, and songwriter of Throwing Muses.

**1. Adelle Davis.** She was a scientist who said that you have to *kick hard* in order to breathe. Wow. I could never eat raw liver in the morning, but she gave me beautiful babies anyway.

**2. Marian Gail Hersh.** My grandmother. When I was six she had to be carried out of my tap dance recital because she was laughing so hysterically. She saved me from a career as a lousy tap dancer.

**3. Robert Johnson.** Scary, happy *blues* is a wild concept; it could never be faked. Selling your soul to the devil is *good*.

**4. Exene Cervenka.** Exene is my biggest Rock Dream. Teeny little combat boots, and a pretty guttermouth.

**5. Marge Simpson**. . . . for president. I can only aspire to Margeness. I even had blue hair for a while.

**6. Gordon Gano.** Gordon's brilliant, scary, whiny rat thing was American youth at its most pure.

**7. Gilda Radner.** The body of a ten-year-old, and the brain of a funny saint. At the top of the list of people who shouldn't die.

**8. Little Richard.** We need Little Richard, always have. Heart of gold with a hairdo on top.

**9. Sable.** My childhood cat. She stood about eight inches high, had twenty-seven children, and still found the energy to hunt and listen to me practice.

**10. James Herriot.** No philosopher learned more from sitting around thinking than James Herriot did from sticking his hand up cows' butts.

# $\mathcal{T}$en Men
# Who Inspired Me

by Matt Johnson

Englishman Matt Johnson has led his group, the The, through a variety of incarnations since its formation in 1978.

**Robert Johnson.** Little is really known about the details of Johnson's life, but his voice, words, and music live on through generations of black and white imitators. The granddaddy of them all.

**Hank Williams.** The original American "pop" icon and the first great white confessional songwriter. He died young, years before it was fashionable to die young. In death, he has defied time as well as national and cultural borders to ensure his legendary status.

**John Lennon.** I know people will find this odd, but I see Lennon as part of the same artistic lineage as Hank Williams. He had a huge impact on me.

**Bob Marley.** Marley was to reggae what Hank Williams was to country. One might say that both were bigger than the genres that spawned them. Marley's best work is timeless.

**Tim Buckley.** The greatest white singer of his generation. The first time I heard him was in the late seventies, when Johnny Rotten was playing his favorite records on a late-night radio show in London. "Sweet Surrender" came on and, then as now, I was stunned by the beauty of his voice.

**Howlin' Wolf.** What a voice! You have to earn a voice like that, so one can only wonder what kind of life Wolf (né Chester Burnett) must have led. Spawned a thousand imitators but never bettered.

**Muhammad Ali.** Even people who hated boxing loved Ali. A giant of a man who inspired love and affection from people worldwide, regardless of race or religion. He brought a rare and brief dignity to the sport. My favorite quote from him was "No Vietcong ever called me a nigger," when he refused to fight in Vietnam.

**Pelé.** Won his first World Cup for Brazil when he was seventeen. What Ali was to boxing, Pelé was to soccer. It's at the hands of men like these that sport transcends itself and enters the realm of art.

**Noam Chomsky.** For translating the hidden agendas and doublespeak of the U.S.A. Should be compulsory reading in all American schools.

**Woody Allen.** I know it's fashionable to knock Woody, but I'm one of those rare people that prefer his later "serious" films to his early slapstick. Also the way he films New York with such love, warmth, and affection was a factor in my moving there.

# Vernon Reid's Ten Essential Role Models, Musical and Otherwise

## (in no particular order)

In addition to his most visible role as leader of now-defunct Living Colour, guitarist/composer Vernon Reid has also earned widespread respect as a founder and guiding force in the Black Rock Coalition.

**Carlos Santana.**  He influenced me to pick up the electric guitar.

**Arthur Rhames.**  One of the greatest musicians I have ever heard. He died totally obscure.

**Ornette Coleman.** For the methodology of his musical freedom.

**James Baldwin.** For his heartfelt witnessing.

**Jimi Hendrix.** For none of the obvious reasons.

**Miles Davis.**  *Sketches of Spain, Miles Smiles, In a Silent Way, Agharta, Live-Evil, Bitches Brew* . . . incandescent beauty.

**James Brown.**  The Godfather.

**Sly Stone.**  One of the great poets of song.

**Ronald Shannon Jackson.** Taught me music as a way of life.

**Eric Dolphy.** Limitless beauty.

# Eleven Jazz Sessions at Which Page Hamilton Would Have Loved to Be Present

Not only the leader of the loud New York quartet Helmet, Page Hamilton is a graduate of the Music Masters degree program in jazz guitar from the Manhattan School of Music.

1. John Coltrane, *A Love Supreme*

2. Miles Davis, *Kind of Blue*

3. Charlie Parker, Dizzy Gillespie, Bud Powell, Charles Mingus, Max Roach, *Jazz at Massey Hall*

4. Bill Evans Trio, *Sunday at the Village Vanguard*

5. Duke Ellington, *Duke Ellington and His Orchestra at Newport*

6. Louis Armstrong, *West End Blues*

7. Wes Montgomery, *Full House: Live at Tsubo in Berkeley*

8. Miles Davis, *Miles Davis*

9. Thelonious Monk w/Sonny Rollins, "Think of One" on *Reflections*

10. Duke Ellington and John Coltrane, *Duke Ellington and John Coltrane*

11. Jim Hall, *Jim Hall Live!*

# The Things That Made Me Who I Am

by Tara Key

Louisville, Kentucky-bred singer/guitarist Tara Key is a founding member of the New York-based band Antietam, and also performs and records as a solo artist. Prior to that, she and Tim Harris, her husband and Antietam bandmate, were members of Louisville's much-loved Babylon Dance Band.

**1. Official press photo of the Mercury astronauts.** Seeing this still makes my stomach drop. I think I thought they were sexy before I knew what it meant. But instead of being in awe of them, I always assumed I'd be one of them. It never occurred to me that being a woman would be a problem.

**2. Transistor radio.** Through high school I probably fell asleep with a radio on most nights. One of my earliest memories (age five or six) is lying with one ear on my radio, pillow wrapped around my head so no one could hear how late I was up, hearing "Sugar Shack." I spent many subsequent nights DJ'ing on the AM band. It was exciting to hear weather and news from other places—there might be other places to go. Then I started getting into moving the dial between stations and playing with the static.

**3. Top Forty.** WAKY in Louisville, Kentucky, was a classic speed-talkin' hit-barrage mid-sixties Top Forty station—they broke "Wooly Bully" by Sam the Sham. Waiting to pick up the printed countdown each Friday from Vine Records . . . "star" bands *and* one-hit wonders . . . and the whole idea of regional hits. The fact that local bands like the Rugbys and the Oxfords could have Top Ten hits and still be playing a dance at my brother's high school was wild. It's amazing now to think about how vital music felt then.

**4. Band as gang.** In my neighborhood there were, including me, three tomboys. Always holding our own in sports and army, we were equal members of the gang. I beat up the boy next door and ripped his T-shirt and made him cry . . . probably because I liked him. Over the years, I've always wanted my bands to be like gangs to run with—living life like the moment when the band members, all holding hands, leap off the wall together and freeze in midair.

**5. Raiders and Monkees.** My bedroom, down to the square inch, was covered with pinups from *16* and *Teen Beat*. I transferred my identification with fame from astronauts to rock stars. I didn't like to sit around with other girls and moon over Fang from Paul Revere and the Raiders or Peter from the Monkees. I preferred being alone, dressed in my mother's scarves and suit jackets, singing along to the Raiders' "Steppin' Out" or "Words" from the Monkees. There are brilliant touches all over those groups' records—I first tuned into how moments could be manipulated: the beginnings of "Louie Go Home" or "Good Thing," the pause in "You Told Me," the moment before the drum roll or the handclaps on "Just Like Me" or the tom overdub on "Take a Giant Step." I also liked the fact that almost everyone in both bands got to sing leads.

**6. The pulse/stopping time.** There is a lineage for me from the Raiders' "Just Like Me" to Tommy James' "Draggin' the Line" to Buffalo Springfield's "Mr. Soul" to David Bowie's "Rebel Rebel." All of those songs feel like they will always be in my bloodstream. The grooves put me in the same bliss state as other time-stopping devices—like when you're not even aware of the flippers during multiball or like a night when it's five A.M. and *neither* of you cares about the time or is aware of it. . . .

**7. The moment.** A visceral transport to somewhere else because of a sound: heart being pulled taut like a high E string (the entry of the chorus of "Walk Away Renee"), the bottom dropping out (the single note solo on "Cinnamon Girl" *and* Neil's "whew" thrown in), that micromillisecond where Neil plays a note and it teeters toward feedback. (I told someone once that that was the spot where I wanted to live my life.) When Ronson plays the "vocal" guitar line on "Man in the Middle," I feel ecstatic.

**8. Belters and odd voices.** Betty Wright ("Clean Up Woman") or Freda Payne ("Band of Gold") or Honey Cone ("Want Ads") always made me wanna sing along. Joan Baez didn't. Dusty Springfield was more mannered, but craggy. One Sunday morning I was paralyzed by Linda Ronstadt singing "Long Long Time." I lay there for three and a half minutes unable to make a move to turn the station, physically pinned by her voice. She was belting, but I knew she was designing it. There are eight emotions in each waver and crack of Neil Young's voice. Patti Smith's voice gave definition to inexplicable rumblings inside me.

**9. Stones Over America—Freedom Hall.** I saw in person (from the third row) how it worked. I only understood the Stones after I understood more about sex, so I caught up on them—it wasn't a firsthand experience until that night. The obvious frontman had little effect on me—it was standing in front of Keith, seeing his sway and angles, that taught me where the chug and bravado of guitar come from. An *incredibly* seminal moment: Keith swigging down Jack from the bottle mid-set ten feet from me and wheeling around to *dive* into his guitar with a big grin.

**10. Bowie.** For the first time, I listened to music no one in my family understood. Music that was *never* on the radio. Those of us who understood seemed to find each other. It was the first time (of many) that music I listened to defined me—the first time I was part of a community formed by music *outside* of the norm. I knew then that a lot of the words were dumb, but the sonics were killer. And the image and the ambiguity were liberating to me at sixteen—it seemed like suddenly there were a lot of possible ways to live—I tried on a few. Ronson's Les Paul was sharp and growly—it totally slayed me: witness the end of "Moonage Daydream." Gotta say, though, Bowie's guitar on "Rebel Rebel" comes close to being my mantra.

**11. Patti.** At three A.M. when I was eighteen, I was in my room partaking, when the local FM station played *Horses* in its entirety. My head was blown off before "Gloria" was over. I'd never heard a voice so like mine before—that is, if I let myself go a little farther. I could absolutely not sleep until seven or so. . . . I rolled all my pennies, sold some old coins at the collector's store (I didn't have a job yet) and bought it the next day. Finally a woman who was sexy against the rules . . . dressed to look like a good version of herself—not as what someone else thought sexy *should* be—and that self-knowledge was the sexiest thing about her by far. She was a fan, like me, and identified with her heroes. She taught me about the beauty of collision—of words, sounds, thoughts—and, by her example, I gave myself permission to live passionately, permission to be an alien, permission to be self-confident. A few years later, at my first audition as an electric guitar player, I dressed like her (white shirt, tie, black coat). I bloodied my hands and shirt and guitar and joined my first band.

**12. Neil.** Quite simply: He taught me how girl and guitar can be one—inseparable—and how the slightest movement can change a sound. How to make emotion with a touch. How to cry and rail and caress and soothe and confront and get off with a finger on a string. He influenced me to go the Les Paul route—and, therefore, to find my translator.

# My Thirteen Most Memorable Celebrity Encounters

## by Dennis Diken

If you run into the Smithereens' Dennis Diken somewhere, ask to see his celebrity snapshots.

A very famous man once said, "Give me liberty or give me death." Another once told us, "You won't have Dick Nixon to kick around anymore." Yet another very well-known gent assured us that "Everybody must get stoned."

All points are well taken.

In this fast-paced world, we look to our leaders and heroes for inspiration, to set an example for our own lives. Such qualities as age, wisdom, and life experience on the bumpy road to the top endow these notables with a universal sympathy for life's woes. Their charisma and heightened media exposure present them to us as larger-than-life figures.

But, you know, they're only human.

Take it from me, playing in a touring rock & roll band affords one the opportunity to travel aplenty and meet the wackiest, *wonderfullest* sampling of humanity. Our occasional in-person encounters with a favorite celebrity or hero are icing on the cake.

Allow me to introduce myself. Diken's the name, drumming's my game. As a member of the Smithereens, I have the privilege of playing with three of my best friends. I'll be referring to these lads in the following tales, so let's introduce them:

Mike Mesaros is our bass player. He and I have been pals since the third grade. He is a good man.

Jimmy Babjak, a.k.a. Tex, plays guitar, sings and writes songs. We've been playing together since high school. He was my best man.

Pat DiNizio sings lead, plays guitar and writes songs. He's my main man.

Whenever I'm fortunate enough to find myself in the presence of a particular personage of personal importance, I still find myself entering "fan" mode. For this, I make no apologies. The inspired works of my faves continue to inspire me. Be it ever so.

**1. Allen Funt.** In January of 1990, the Smithereens were flying to Seattle from L.A. The four of us were walking through the airport with our tour manager, Wally, when I spied him standing by the ticket counter—Mr. Allen Funt of *Candid Camera* fame. Of course, we approached him for a photo. He was very gracious.

**2. The Kinks.** Mike, Jimmy, and I were dedicated, dorky, pubescent followers of the Kinks, and during the seventies we frequently pestered them outside the Capitol Theatre in Passaic, New Jersey, and in the lobby and bar of New York's Warwick Hotel. Never "tired of waiting," Ray Davies often took the time to chat or have a beer with us, and Mick Avory was very generous with his time as well, indulging my drum shop talk. Quite inspirational to a starstruck lad such as myself.

A few years back, Tex and I encountered them once again at a Don Kirshner party at the Hard Rock Cafe in New York City. A loud, looped, red-faced chap was palling around with Mick, and we were floored to make the acquaintance of Pete Quaife, the band's long-gone original bassist, reunited with his old mates for the Rock & Roll Hall of Fame awards.

In 1991 the Smithereens had the chance to back up Ray and Dave Davies on "You Really Got Me" during a benefit show at Boston Garden. During the soundcheck, Ray expressed concern over my casual flannel attire. Though I dressed that way all of the day, I dutifully spiffed up for that night's performance.

**3. Brian Wilson.** Brian is a lifelong hero of mine and a continuing source of inspiration. No matter what he's been through or shall go through in the future, I'll always keep my ears open for the moments of brilliance that I know are still in him.

I'd had the pleasure to say hello to Brian on several occasions. On the first, I overheard an assistant informing him of a seven-thirty A.M. call for an early-morning TV appearance. Bri's reply was: "You know it's hard, it's really hard to get up that early." I knew then and there that he was a kindred spirit.

My most recent encounter with B.W. was at a 1991 in-store appearance at Tower Books in New York. I gave him a cassette of some Four Freshmen material I'd heard he'd dug. He really lit up and was truly appreciative. A nice moment.

**4. Dennis Wilson.** Along with Dion, Dennis—"the only surfing Beach Boy"—embodied cool in my pre-Beatles youth.

New York's Plaza Hotel, 1979 (during the "Christine McVie period"): A friend was presenting some vintage film footage to Denny, who at the time was planning a career documentary on the Boys. He was very engaging, warm and "on." At one point I was leaning over a chair talking to someone in the crowded room when I felt someone drumming a rapid tattoo on my back. I looked up to see Dennis sprinting away across the floor. Dennis was a great drummer, singer, writer, and rock & roll spirit who, for my money, never received the respect he deserved. That evening at the Plaza was a gas.

**5. Hal Blaine.** Studio drummer extraordinaire. "Be My Baby," "California Girls," "Surf City," "Wichita Lineman," "Mr. Eliminator," "Mr. Tambourine Man," "Strangers in the Night" . . . I could go on and on. Any rock & roll drummer worth his sticks owes a blistered handshake of gratitude to the exalted Hal Blaine for showing us all how it's done.

In 1982 a friend got me Hal's home address and I dutifully wrote the great man a fan letter. I nearly pooped my jockies when, a few weeks later, the phone rang and H.B. and D.D. were actually speaking . . . to each other! The Smithereens were not a "name band" at the time. I was just some dweeb fan, but Hal would often call or write with a new joke or an encouraging word, and we became good friends.

In 1985 Hal borrowed my old Slingerland kit for a rare live appearance (with David Grisman) at New York's Bottom Line. I was his proud personal valet and roadie, chauffeuring him around the city in my '65 Chevy Apache truck. I'll never forget that day.

When I first started listening to records, it was as if they magically appeared, like manna from heaven. The notion of people going to work to create such greatness was beyond my comprehension. Okay, so maybe there ain't no Santy Claus. But when I hear Hal, I still feel like a kid.

**6. Arnold Stang.** The diminutive filling-station attendant in *It's a Mad, Mad, Mad, Mad World*. The voice of "Top Cat" and a million others. A prime example of the type of man who made an indelible dent in our youthful psyche. The type of man they just don't make anymore.

A cold November afternoon, midtown Manhattan, late eighties: Jimmy and I were on our way to a "business meeting." The avenue is quite crowded, but I see friggin' Arnold Stang! What luck! All my life I've wanted to meet Stang! And here stands Stang! For the asking!

I gripped my pocket idiot camera and shoved it at Tex, urging, "Jimmy, it's Arnold Stang! Take a picture!"

"What?!"

"That's Arnold Stang! Hurry!"

"Really?"

"Yes!!"

Subtle as a flying mallet. No hello, no excuse me, no nothing.

"Mr. Stang, may I take a picture with you?"

"Well, I don't think, uh, I . . ."

"I'm a big fan."

"Oh, uh, alright, I . . ."

Snap. Gone. Wow.

Sometimes you just gotta seize the moment.

**7. Del Shannon.** Del has been a mythical figure to me for all of my record-digging days. A quick handshake and an autograph preceded a 1982 appearance in New York City; that show was one of the most electrifying and riveting evenings of my life.

In 1987 I reached Del through an agent and invited him to sing on the Smithereens' *Green Thoughts* LP. He and I sang a part together on the same mic! I don't care what success you've experienced or how "pro" one considers oneself to be—meeting and/or working with a hero can still turn you into tapioca!

Jimmy and I added some backing vocals to some of Del's demos in 1988. A true honor. We also had him join us for an encore at the Roxy in L.A. I last saw Del at a taping of Bob Costas's New York talk show in 1989, not long before his death. He still had the fire. Wish he was here.

**8. Bud Abbott, Jr.** The Abbott and Costello TV shows loom large in the body politik of the Smithereens. Not that we don't enjoy their movies. The TV shows are just . . . *better*. With characters like Sid Fields, Mike the Cop, Stinky, Hillary Brooke, Mr. Bacciagalupe, and Bingo the Chimp thrown into the delirious mix of the boys' vaudeville routines, rehashed "plots," Costello's comedic genius and Abbott's inane non sequiturs, all of it spiced by an asylum-like laugh track, you've got yourself a surreal stew of circular dada/mayhem nonpareil.

Now don't get me wrong. We *love* and admire the unmatched brilliance of Lou Costello, but for some reason it's "straight man" Bud who holds a special place in our hearts. Maybe it's those caustic asides, or his sharp "con-guy" manner, or perhaps his occasional mustache. Sad to say, we never did manage to make Bud's acquaintance during his lifetime. But . . .

In the late eighties, a good friend was doing some archival film work with the estates of A&C, dealing closely with Bud and Lou's offspring. While visiting Bud Jr.'s house, he noticed a copy of our first album, *Especially for You*, in his record collection and brought "son of Bud" to one of our shows at the Roxy in L.A.!

Can you *imagine* your father being Bud Abbott? *Man* . . . Hopefully, we'll meet Bud Sr. in the great beyond someday. In the meantime, Bud Jr. is a swell guy. Life is good.

**9. David Mortlock.** You probably won't recognize the name. Here's another one you may not recognize: Percy Helton. Allow me to explain . . .

Ever since my toddlin' days I've always been quite taken with the short, hunched, balding, squeaky-voiced countenance of character actor Percy Helton, who appeared in numerous films from the late forties through the early seventies. Remember the drunken Santa Claus in the original *Miracle on 34th Street,* Mr. Brewster in *Jailhouse Rock,* or the greedy morgue attendant in *Kiss Me Deadly*? How about a recurring familiar face fitting the above description in *Superman, Green Acres, Alfred Hitchcock Presents* or, of course, *The Abbott and Costello Show*? This is Helton.

In 1986 the Smithereens appeared on MTV's *The Cutting Edge,* hosted by jocular Fleshtones frontman Peter Zaremba, who asked us about our favorite Hollywood celebrities. I made a reference to Helton. A month or two later I got a letter from a guy who caught the show by chance and tells me he's the late Percy's great nephew!

Well, it turned out to be absolutely true, and the proof was in the putting into my grubby mitts some honest-to-goodness Heltoniana—photos, scripts, even clothing! Dave visited "Uncle Perce" during a family vacation to Hollywood in the sixties. He would also send him his homemade 8 mm. monster movies for the actor's approval. Invariably, Percy would call and encouragingly tell him "Good picture, Dave."

In his own right, David Mortlock is a fine dude and a good friend. He even helped me move once.

**10. Otis Blackwell.** The Smithereens spent a good part of our scuffling younger days playing at Kenny's Castaways and the Other End (né Bitter End) on Bleecker Street in Greenwich Village. Through that scene, we became friends with ace keyboardist Andy Rosen, who chose us to be the backup band for legendary singer/songwriter Otis Blackwell. In addition to our regular Smithereens gigs, we'd do shows with the man, performing such Blackwell-penned classics as "Don't Be Cruel," "All Shook Up," "Fever," "Handy Man," "Great Balls of Fire," "Breathless," "Return to Sender," etc. etc. etc.

Otis made a lot of great music. He also made and lost a fortune in his day. During the period we worked with him, he was trying to give his career a second wind. Though he was well into his fifties at the time, he performed every set with the fire of an eighteen-year-old. Otis's songs were close to our hearts, and we rocked pretty hard—and loud—when playing them. And often too loud for Otis's ears: He would turn to us mid-song and holler, "I can't hear myself!" bellowing the command directly into his mic for all the audience to enjoy.

Onstage at Heartbreak in New York (probably in 1983), we beheld a sunglassed Jack Nicholson gawking up at Otis from the audience. After the show, Pat and Tex invited the Academy Award–winning superstar to visit Otis backstage, citing Mr. Blackwell's prodigious output of classic tunes. Jack demurred, declaring, "I'm sure we're all grateful to Otis."

Indeed we are. As I write this in January 1995, Otis's health is not so hot. Say a prayer for this genius.

**11. Sam Donaldson.** In the summer of 1992, the Smithereens appeared on *The Tonight Show* (with Jay Leno) for the first time. Jay's other guests that night were actress Katey Sagal and news stalwart Sam Donaldson. The man was cool. A friendly dude. Take a picture, Sam? No problem. The shot was so right-on that it graced our band's Christmas card that year. I sent him a copy and he sent me a handwritten thank-you note on his stationery. That's class.

At the end of the show we all got to sit on the couch while Jay said his "thanks" to everyone who appeared that night. This was an election year. As the outro music played, Sam turned to the four Smithereens and proclaimed in *that voice,* "I think *you* guys should run for president."

To know him is to love him.

**12. Leon Askin.** You know him as the haughty General Burkhalter on TV's *Hogan's Heroes*. In September of 1989, the Smithereens knew him as "Mr. Askin," an actor in our employ on location in Hollywood, U.S.A., for the shooting of the alternate (i.e. unused) video for our song "A Girl Like You."

In all honesty, our initial casting choices for the role of the band's domineering manager were Louis Nye and Ernest Borgnine. Neither of those exalted men could be swayed for love nor money. The late David White (Larry Tate of *Bewitched*) was also considered. But Mr. Askin did not disappoint.

It was a typical video shoot, lots of hurry-up-and-wait. Much of that downtime was spent pumping Mr. Askin for his insights into the inner workings of Stalag 13. Though he likened the cast to a family, he snapped, "Ivan Dixon (who played Kinchloe) wanted to be a director," and described Bob Crane's untimely murder as a "crime of passion." Unfortunately, no amount of prodding would produce the desired "Klink, you id-i-ot!"

This man was a legend to us. In our wildest dreams, we'd never envisioned an opportunity to meet, let alone work with, the remarkable Leon Askin. I trust he enjoyed his day with the Smithereens as well, though our unending praise and heaps of gratitude must have sounded patronizing after a while.

**13. Sam Butera/Keely Smith.** Sam Butera and Keely Smith are two of the finest entertainers known to humankind. Period. Both originally found fame in the employ of Louis Prima, the wild trumpeter/vocalist who was the high priest of Vegas-lounge musical mirth in the roaring fifties. Keely, his wife/straight person/vocalist, and Sam, his able saxman/sidekick, along with the crack combo the Witnesses, made the Prima entourage the solidest senders this side of the Sahara. Since Louis exited this bitter earth, these two gifted folks have kept on keepin' on in their own right, carrying Louis's rich legacy to new audiences.

My initial Butera experience occurred in '88 in Vegas, when Mike and I caught an early set by Sam and his wonderful group "the Wildest" at the Tropicana. For years I'd been waiting for a chance to see Sam, and when the moment of truth arrived, I was not let down. The man and his band rocked, swung and *entertained!* I've been to many a "concert" and/or "performance" in my day, but this gig gave new meaning to the word "show"! When we excitedly approached Sam after the set to score a handshake and purchase some of the albums he was hawking, he mysteriously sensed that we were in "the business" and graciously offered us a professional discount.

That summer, the wife and I swung down to the swank resorts in Atlantic City for the most glorious night of "show" we'd ever witnessed, with Sam and the Wildest alternating sets (three each!) on the same stage with the fabulous Treniers, another gregarious aggregation who in their younger days blessed us with records like "Rock a Beatin' Boogie," "Poontang" and "Hadacol, That's All." Neither group consisted of any spring chickens, yet many of today's "rock bands" would do well to take a cue from these guys' "sheer energy" (to quote one of Sam's LP titles) and vitality.

In true show-biz fashion, Sam introduced several other stars in the house that night—namely Tony Butala of the Lettermen and the great comic/impressionist George Kirby (two more photo ops!). Sam always goes the extra mile to meet his fans (especially those who buy records from him!)—no mean feat following the draining nightly spectacle of Sam's through-the-audience-romp on "When the Saints Go Marching In."

In May '93, the four Smithereens and their gals hit Vegas for a three-day swing, to celebrate Jim and Betty Babjak's ten-year wedding anniversary at the Graceland Chapel, and to catch a few shows. Tom Jones at the Sands, Allen and Rossi at Bob Stupak's Vegas World weren't bad, but the real treat was the historic reunion of Sam and Keely at the Desert Inn. Not since their days together in Louis's domain had they graced a stage together, and this was an all-Prima "tribute" set.

Our manager, Burt, greased the appropriate palm and wrangled us a primo table to better drink in the marvel of the exquisite voice of Ms. Smith, backed my Mr. B and his men. At one point between tunes Keely actually introduced *us* from the stage, claiming, "I think they're in town with their friends the Temptations"! After thirteen years "in the business," it felt like we'd finally arrived.

Do yourself a big, big favor. Go out of your way to catch Sam and/or Keely, together or separately. When they hang it up, there'll be no one to take their place.

**Honorable Mention:** A chance howdy outside the London EMI building with George Martin, fresh from a curbside meeting with former Beatles road manager Neil Aspinall. . . . Mike and I exchanging a telepathic nod with the Amazing Kreskin buzzing through Port Authority. . . . A wonderful all-night session at Les Paul's home/studio in Mahwah, New Jersey, listening to some of his own recordings that he hadn't heard himself in forty-odd years. . . . An audience with Dan Ingram, king of sixties New York City AM radio, who, when I gushed to him what an influence he'd been on my sense of humor, retorted, "You know, if you drink enough water, that'll go away." . . . Gabbing with fellow native New Jerseyan Danny DeVito about the many advantages of the White Castle on Route 1 in Rahway. . . . Jimmy and I meeting grown-up Little Rascals Stymie and Spanky at a midnight appearance at the Capitol Theatre in Passaic, in '74. . . . Sitting in a chock-full van after the Beach Boys' 1984 Washington Monument Fourth of July show, regretfully refusing Harry Nilsson a ride into town when his car was ripped off at the site—and earlier that day informing a grateful Carl Wilson, who'd just emerged from the men's room and was making his way toward the stage, that a hunk of toilet paper was hanging from his belt.

So what do you suppose we can learn from this? I think our friend Sam Butera sums it up best when he tells us at the end of every show: "It's nice to be important, but it's much more important to be nice!"

Well, thanks for coming along, and keep in mind that your favorite stars might be just a glance away. They shop, eat, fly and walk around all the time. Keep your eyes open!

# Advice

## PART 7

# and Anecdotes

# The Ten Commandments of Guitar Playing as They Were Handed Down to Moris Tepper by Captain Beefheart

## by John McCormick

Moris Tepper was born in Peashoot, Iowa, but currently resides in Southern California. He has an extensive discography, which includes work with Captain Beefheart and the Magic Band, Tom Waits, and Frank Black. A singer, songwriter, and painter, Tepper now plays and records with Eggtooth and the Moris Tepper Band. John McCormick is a screenwriter. His credits include *Living on Tokyo Time*, *Cliffhanger*, and the Russ Meyer film, *The Bra of God*.

**I**n the mid-1970s Jeff Moris Tepper was just out of Taft High School in Southern California's San Fernando Valley when he decided to move to Northern California to study marine biology. Two days after arriving in the coastal town of Eureka, which is approximately one hundred miles south of the Oregon border, Moris was in his car checking out one of the lush, ultra-green forests in the area when he saw what appeared to be a huge pumpkin flying through the woods. He followed the flying gourd through the forest and watched it ultimately come to a stop and transform itself into a bright orange Corvette Stingray. When he looked at the driver, he realized it was Don Van Vliet, a.k.a. Captain Beefheart, a musician whose music he had loved since he was first introduced to it by high school classmate, Erick Drew Feldman.*

---

*On Beefheart's *Trout Mask Replica* LP there is a cut entitled "Hair Pie: Bake 1," which features another of Tepper's high school classmates talking to Vliet in the latter's then Woodland Hills backyard. The point is raised to illustrate the multiple strange convergences

Wanting to say hello to Beefheart without bothering him, Moris quietly approached the orange Corvette, then very softly said, "Don?" The voice completely caught Vliet by surprise, causing him to jump in his seat, hit the interior of the car and put a large bump on his head.

Despite the egg Moris gave Beefheart, the two had a friendly conversation wherein Moris revealed that he was relocating to the area and was looking for a place to live. Vliet mentioned that that very morning he noticed there was a place for rent next to where he was living. Moris ended up going to Vliet's house that night where he saw two Hudson Hornets sitting in the driveway like massive sleeping beetles. Moris rented the place next door to Vliet's.

Not a serious musician when he met Vliet, Moris was inspired by his new neighbor. He began to figure out some Beefheart tunes on an electric guitar, which he played through a four-track tape recorder. Owing to the complexity of Beefheart's compositions, it took weeks for Moris to learn "Fallin' Ditch," "Dali's Car" and "When Big Joan Sets Up"; all songs which appeared on the album *Trout Mask Replica*. When he finally figured out the songs, he recorded the two distinct and complex guitar parts that were originally played on the record by Zoot Horn Rollo (Bill Harkleroad) and Antennae Jimmy Semens (Jeff Cotton), creating perfect transcriptions of the songs on tape.

One day when Vliet was visiting, Moris played him the tape. Vliet, who at that point was on hiatus from his musical career, was impressed with what he heard; so much so that he decided to get another band together. He called longtime associate Frank Zappa, who had among other things produced *Trout Mask,* and told him he wanted to get back into the music business. Zappa responded by taking Vliet out on the road with him on the Bongo Fury tour, but when that tour finished, Vliet called Moris and told him to get down to L.A., "We're doing this."

Moris went to the mountain and became an integral part of the Magic Band. From 1976 through 1982, the year Beefheart retired from music to devote himself entirely to painting, Moris handled guitar (or in Beefheart parlance "guitar, acoustic guitar, slide guitar, nerve guitar, spell guitar, steel appendage guitar") for Vliet, touring and recording four albums with him: *Bat Chain Puller* (unreleased), *Shiny Beast, Doc at the Radar Station* and *Ice Cream for Crow.*

---

of Moris's and Beefheart's paths, but also to reinforce a basic precept of biological survival; that is, in an adverse and hostile environment, like the San Fernando Valley, it's natural for like species to find each other and form a pack in order to feed and fend off natural enemies. Even though the meeting of Moris and Vliet ultimately took place some 1,100 kilometers north of their original habitat, some species, like the Tundra Wolf (*Canis lupus tundarum*), when hunted, are known to cover distances of 200 kilometers in a single day.

Moris subsequently brought Erick Drew Feldman to Beefheart's attention, and he became a keyboard and bass player with the Magic Band.

It was during his tenure with the Magic Band that Beefheart passed along to Moris the Ten Commandments of Guitar Playing: ten precepts that would enable a guitar player to stop wandering lost through the desert and step up onto a plane that was going somewhere. For years Moris carried this covenant with him, reticent to share the dicta with other plectorists for fear "it would pop the goo in their filaments." But he ultimately had a change of heart as he watched two California desert tortoise hatchlings (*Gopherus agassizi*) he had recently adopted. The baby tortoises, which are half-dollar sized, their carapaces walnut colored, their necks already full of ancient looking wrinkles, seemed to be bobbing their heads at him as they fed on hibiscus petals. The bobbing motion consisted of a figure-eight pattern similar to the waggle dance honeybees use for communication. Originally, Moris thought the tortoises were trying to tell him their sex (as one can't normally determine the sex of a tortoise for ten years). But after more careful scrutiny he realized they were simply nodding their heads "yes" to him. He understood. It was time to reveal the Commandments and make the world a safer place for all reptiles.

So herewith are the Ten Commandments of Guitar Playing as Given to Moris Tepper by Captain Beefheart. Though they bear numbers, they are not arranged hierarchically—each Commandment has equal import. Also, to help clarify their intent, each Commandment is followed by an exegesis.

**1. Listen to the birds.**
That's where all the music comes from. Birds know everything about how it should sound and where that sound should come from. And watch hummingbirds. They fly really fast, but a lot of times they aren't going anywhere.

**2. Your guitar is not really a guitar.**
Your guitar is a divining rod. Use it to find spirits in the other world and bring them over. A guitar is also a fishing rod. If you're good, you'll land a big one.

**3. Practice in front of a bush.**
Wait until the moon is out, then go outside, eat a multi-grained bread and play your guitar to a bush. If the bush doesn't shake, eat another piece of bread.

**4. Walk with the devil.**
Old Delta blues players referred to guitar amplifiers as the "devil box." And they were right. You have to be an equal opportunity employer in terms of who you're bringing over from the other side. Electricity attracts devils and demons. Other instruments attract other spirits. An acoustic guitar attracts Caspar. A mandolin attracts Wendy. But an electric guitar attracts Beelzebub.

### 5. If you're guilty of thinking, you're out.

If your brain is part of the process, you're missing it. You should play like a drowning man, struggling to reach shore. If you can trap that feeling, then you have something that is fur bearing.

### 6. Never point your guitar at anyone.

Your instrument has more clout than lightning. Just hit a big chord then run outside to hear it. But make sure you are not standing in an open field.

### 7. Always carry a church key.

That's your key-man clause. Like One String Sam. He's one. He was a Detroit street musician who played in the fifties on a homemade instrument. His song "I Need a Hundred Dollars" is warm pie. Another key to the church is Hubert Sumlin, Howlin' Wolf's guitar player. He just stands there like the Statue of Liberty—making you want to look up her dress the whole time to see how he's doing it.

### 8. Don't wipe the sweat off your instrument.

You need that stink on there. Then you have to get that stink onto your music.

### 9. Keep your guitar in a dark place.

When you're not playing your guitar, cover it and keep it in a dark place. If you don't play your guitar for more than a day, be sure you put a saucer of water in with it.

### 10. You gotta have a hood for your engine.

Keep that hat on. A hat is a pressure cooker. If you have a roof on your house, the hot air can't escape. Even a lima bean has to have a piece of wet paper around it to make it grow.

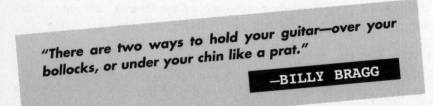

"There are two ways to hold your guitar—over your bollocks, or under your chin like a prat."

—BILLY BRAGG

# Wayne Kramer's Ten Tips for Electric Guitar Players

Wayne Kramer has been busting the sound barrier, expectations, and the status quo since his guitarslinging days in the seminal Detroit band the MC5. He has since written songs, played guitar, and sung in various bands, as well as releasing several solo albums.

**1.** Plug the thing in. I'm no technical wiz, but I've noticed that electric things always work better plugged in.

**2.** Wash your hands. You play better with clean hands.

**3.** If you have to sing and play guitar, practice by yourself before you do it at band practice; you don't want to bring down the rest of the band by making them watch you learn how to walk and chew gum at the same time.

**4.** Always wear your coolest clothes onstage. It's better to look good than feel good.

**5.** Work on developing your own sound.

**6.** Learn music—not guitar.

**7.** Write songs (with words!).

**8.** Watch other guitarists' hands and feet.

**9.** Breathe—don't hold your breath.

**10.** When smashing the guitar, keep a smile on your lips and a song in your heart.

# Kevin Salem's Do's and Don'ts for Aspiring Rock Stars

New York-based singer/songwriter/guitarist/producer Kevin Salem has gleaned the following advice from his character-building experiences as leader of his own band, guitarist with the likes of Dumptruck, Freedy Johnston, and Yo La Tengo, and producer for such bands as Scarce and Madder Rose.

**Do** accept free meals from record companies, even if you are not hungry. They'll starve you later.

**Don't** expect a royalty check, ever. I mean it.

**Don't** sign a record contract on the hood of a car.

**Don't** sing with an English accent—even if you are English.

**Do** turn up when the soundman says you are too loud.

**"Don't** squeal on the pusher" (see Ween's *God Ween Satan*).

**Don't** sell copies of your own CD to the local record exchange.

**Do** sell copies of your own CD to relatives at import prices.

**Don't** challenge J Mascis to a pot-smoking contest.

**Do** know the difference between Patti Smith and Patty Smyth.

**Don't** choose a musician for a lover unless you have a huge trust fund. On second thought, not even then.

**Don't** correct people when they refer to "Freddy Johnson." It's a useless, thankless task.

**Do** invite a *Billboard* photographer to capture the spectacle of an artist giving his/her attorney a swirlie in the restroom at CBGB's.

Speaking of CB's, if it is 8:00 P.M., **Do** know that you have time to run home and grab a bite to eat before your 8:30 set there—even if you live in Delaware.

# Paul Leary's Do's and Don'ts for Recording the Butthole Surfers

**Paul Leary is guitarist and founding member of the Butthole Surfers, and has produced records for the likes of the Meat Puppets and the Reverend Horton Heat.**

## Do:

**1.** Set up pool table in the best room.

**2.** Set up microphones in the kitchens, bedrooms, and bathroom.

**3.** Invent strange new games such as "Lose the quarter in the hole" and "Formula one roller chair racing."

**4.** Give traditional games new rules, e.g. "Stopwatch pool" and "no rules Ping-Pong."

**5.** Allow dogs to do their jobs.

**6.** Play like you are on glue.

## Don't:

**1.** Turn off the TV. Commercials have great music.

**2.** Record during *The Young and the Restless*.

# Jack Logan and Kelly Keneipp's Home Recording Tips

Jack Logan, Kelly Keneipp, and other musical pals have long been in the habit of killing time and tape in the comfort of Logan's Winder, Georgia, home. Their efforts have yielded *Bulk,* a forty-two–song double CD released in 1994 on the Medium Cool label, and a bunch of other unlistenable weird junk.

1. Distribute beer fairly.

2. Remove small furry animals, hair, and ash from the top of the mixing board.

3. Make sure the air conditioner is "in tune."

4. It's okay to giggle while others are screwing up their tracks.

5. Leave your shoes on.

6. Pitch control works just as good as tuning.

7. Recommend seasoning the drums underneath the house for a month or two.

8. Many things in the kitchen are not only good to eat but make great percussion instruments.

9. When equipment breaks, hit it, then take it apart.

10. Wear costumes whenever possible.

# The Top Ten Reasons for Being a Musician

## by Chris Randall

**Chris Randall is lead singer and conceptual mastermind of industrial rockers Sister Machine Gun, who have released three albums on the Wax Trax! label.**

**10.** The easy hours (noon to 3-ish . . . )

 **9.** All the kids think you're cool

 **8.** Free drinks at nightclubs

 **7.** You get to wear really stupid clothes and call it fashion

 **6.** Your girlfriend doesn't mind paying the rent now and then

 **5.** People always write nice things about you in all your favorite magazines

 **4.** People pay to see you jump around and act like an idiot for forty-five minutes every night

 **3.** You get to see the country

 **2.** People never seem to get tired of hearing you complain

 **1.** The money

# How the Search for the Ultimate Esoteric Recordings Has Made My Life in a Band Meaningful

## by Tim Gane

Guitarist Tim Gane designs sound structures for the hypno-pop, Britain-based Stereolab, whose first album cover depicted a phonographic needle dropping onto the vinyl platter of what was undoubtedly an obscure sound recording.

"What sort of people made this music? Who are they? And what planet are they from?" That was my first reaction upon hearing Cabaret Voltaire's 1979 record "Nag Nag Nag," and this has been the overriding factor and key influence upon my musical taste, preferences, and ideas ever since.

Generally speaking, this concept comes from the absolute opposite standpoint of the basic concerns of traditional community-based music—i.e., music that spoke to you directly and was understood implicitly. Sun Ra claimed to be from another planet, not because he was simply wacko but because it was the metaphor he chose for an outsider's identity—music from "out there," music maybe from a better place.

I was never really an outsider, but this metaphor means a lot to me— incredible excitement just beyond my grasp, mad and psychotic creativity. Mind-altering to the extent that once you "get it," you can never go back. This inevitably brings one to search for recordings that may contain these mad and psychotic creations: music of bizarre and visceral juxtapositions of sound and violence, beautiful otherworldly melodies, primitive electronic instrumentation run amok.

The problem is that this stuff tends to be quite difficult to track down—

which, of course, only increases its desirability. The anticipation of what these records may contain only adds to their potency. Unfortunately, these type of things sometimes disappoint (though many do not), only because they can't hope to compete with your own imagination. The trick is to use this imagination to fire your own creativity. The search for records that will sound like nothing you've ever heard, music that's been formed in a way you could never have previously conceived of, can only widen all horizons and lead to infinite possibilities in sound. These records should be used to fire the imagination of the listener, to create inspiration and exploration from within. And the best part is that you don't even need to have ever heard them.

As of this writing, my want list of obscurities includes recordings by Horrific Child (Faust-style early-seventies French avant-garde rock), Mutantes (way-out Brazilian psychedelia from the late sixties), Hans Lampe LP (Neu producer), Amon Duul (*not* Amon Duul II) and Cluster's albums as "Kluster."

# Sprechen Sie Rok?

## by John Petkovic

John Petkovic, formerly vocalist/guitarist for Death of Samantha and currently leader of Cobra Verde, wants it to be known that he can now talk the talk.

It was a few years ago, backstage at CBGB. I was in this band and we'd just finished our set. The bass player told me, "Man, we gotta get things rollin' and strike the stage, so I can start working the room."

Huh? I thought to myself. "*Strike the stage? Work the room?*" I wondered. I walked out of the dressing room, down the hall toward the rest rooms and into the janitor's closet, where I found a broom. I carried it back and handed it to the bass player. "Here you go," I said. "If you wanna work the room, you're gonna need this."

"No, man," he responded, "you don't *work the room* with one of those. Working the room is part of my *gig*."

I realized then that I was missing out on something. I remembered the thrill I got outta making the flier for my first show: cutting and pasting and lying at the copy shop about the number of copies I had made 'cause there wasn't any band fund to cover the cost of making 500 copies at five cents apiece (they didn't have a copy counter on the machine, which is why I always went there to get my fliers done). Maybe I'd been naive all along.

So I asked him, "What's your gig? How do you do it?"

"Well, first you start by putting that broom back where you got it," he answered. "This is the *backstage area*. You see, we gotta *strike the stage*—you know, move your shit out of the way for the next band. And then you want to *work the room*. You know, *meet and greet—network*. See, if you want to do rock & roll, you gotta *walk it like you talk it*. You gotta *put in your time* and *pay your dues*. You gotta *line up some gigs* so you can *get your stage legs* and *hone your chops*. And it ain't easy, 'cause you're gonna have to start small—*hump your own gear—advance your own shows—shitty per diems*—you're *all tapped out*—you're *low on coins*—you're *living hand to mouth* but you're *doing it*."

"I'm not sure I understand," I said.

"What's there to understand? While you're heading to the gig, you gotta *advance* it—call ahead of time to see if it's still happening. Then if it is, you go there. If it ain't, then you *shitcan the B.A.*—that's the Booking Agent. You see, you're really on your own. It's just you—the band is you—since you all gotta be one—*a band is like a family—you're in the trenches together*. Of course, you got the *L.D.*—that's Lighting Director—or, if he's a *top-notch team player,* the *Lighting Dude*—and the *driver* and maybe a *S.G.*—Sound Guy or *G.T.*—Guitar Tech."

"What about roadies?" I asked.

"No roadies. There's road work, but no roadies. You got the *Road Warriors*—they do some of the grunt work but they ain't roadies. . . . So what you gotta do is *advance the show*—tell 'em when you're in for soundcheck—and you *strike the stage*—that's move the gear to make room for the next band. If you wanna take it off the stage altogether, then you gotta *spike the stage*. So anyway, you *get your stage legs* and do some *support work*. Then you get the *buzz going on the street, build up your base, work the room,* and *hook up with a major player* who can help you *take it to the next level* and *get some momentum going* so you can get *the big push,* and before you know it you're *cranking units outta the box* and *blowin' 'em out the door*. Then you *recoup*. That's how you gotta do it."

# The Industrial Twelve-Step Program

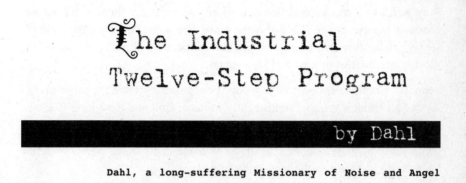

by Dahl

**Dahl, a long-suffering Missionary of Noise and Angel of Aggression, wishes you a painful journey.**

**Step 1.** Admit that you are powerless over pop music—that your life has become unbearable because of its existence. Repeatedly listen to the four sides of unadulterated feedback from Lou Reed's *Metal Machine Music*.

**Step 2.** Come to believe that only a dissonant sound greater than any other—i.e., those that can be found on the nefarious *Greatest Hits: Entertainment Through Pain* by Throbbing Gristle—can restore you to sanity.

**Step 3.** Make a decision to turn all your listening devices to the highest volume, and to turn your life over to the cacophonous cadence of Kraftwerk's *Trans-Europe Express* and *The Man Machine*.

**Step 4.** Make a searching and fearless sonic inventory of every Psychic TV live album (purportedly twenty-three exist), featuring Genesis P-Orridge's malevolent maneuvers.

**Step 5.** Admit to yourself and to another human being the exact power of noise by exposing them to Suicide's self-destructive, minimalist electronics and Chrome's frighteningly twisted epics.

**Step 6.** Now be entirely ready to have the epitome of Industrial, Einstürzende Neubauten, remove all the defects of character that pop music once thrust upon you. By thoroughly exploring all of E.N.'s work, from *Kollaps* to *Tabula Rasa,* popless purity can be achieved.

**Step 7.** Humbly immerse yourself in the violent intensity of Scraping Foetus Off the Wall's *Hole* and *Nail*, as it will further remove your shortcomings.

**Step 8.** Make a list of all persons you know who have been damaged by staid pop music and make amends by compelling them to listen to Front 242's *Tyranny for You*.

**Step 9.** Make direct amends to such people by exposing them to the aggro-chaos of Ministry (*The Land of Rape and Honey*) and Skinny Puppy (*VIVIsectVI*), wherever and whenever possible, especially when to do so would most injure their or others' melodic senses.

**Step 10.** Continue deconstructing your pop senses by taking a sonic inventory of all splinter groups, significantly Pigface, Coil and Revolting Cocks.

**Step 11.** Seek through noise and aggression to improve your conscious contact with Industrial, listening for the knowledge of its fierce power as it has been carried onward to the masses by Nine Inch Nails.

**Step 12.** Having had a brutal sonic awakening as the result of these steps, try to carry this message to other soulless, lost popsters, and practice these exemplary principles in all your affairs.

# J Mascis's Recipe for Toasted Cheese Sandwiches

J Mascis is the idol of millions as leader of Dinosaur Jr.

You will need:

12 slices of stale bread
4–6 thin slices of processed cheese
softened butter or margarine

Spread bread slices with butter. Place cheese slice between two slices of stale bread, with buttered side facing out. Toast in toaster until golden brown, about three to four minutes.

You may make variations of this sandwich by adding tomato slices or bacon strips between the two slices of bread.

# $\mathcal{F}$uck Songs, Sucker

by Howe Gelb

Since the mid-eighties, Howe Gelb has been singer, guitarist, songwriter, and sole charter member of the ever-mercurial Giant Sand, which has released a variety of albums on a variety of labels of varying sizes.

Fuck you very much, please.

The ravel. The ravel. Then the undoing. Love that undoing.

I don't care what you think you know. Even less what larvae hatches under your rocks of desire.

Because in all of the world, they still have not been able to define it . . .

And in all the time that's passed and/or been wasted like cut grass blowin' over cracked glass, there remains no other word for it other than "it."

So fuck it.

Never has there been anything so priceless and so disposable at the same time.

And therein lies the irk of its lifesavingness.

But how you make it by how you disregard the enchantment of where it will all end is the fucking fuel that festers finely.

You have to fuck with your songs. You have to come at them with a knife.

Dare them to fail. Toss them down the canyon and then settle down under a parasol of shade to savor the sound it makes hitting bottom after falling all that distance.

(That's called "an ending.")

244

But most of all, just see what it's made of. Because if that sucker can take all that set-up and trashing, and still stand up right beside you during said moment of impact, then you have a song for life.

Yes sir, that sucker really has IT.

And for crying out loud, don't sweat over what it is ever supposed to be.

IT is forever only CRYING OUT LOUD . . .
And you get to fuck with very much just by the toss.

So shut up and spew.

Blare, if you know what not to do.

And remember, don't buy in to the pressure of pleasing the micro or massive record label just because they yank you by the larvae of your own desire.

They should be able to sell anything you give them, YES EVEN AN ASHTRAY, because that's their purpose. They can only tell you what a good song is way after they were able to sell lots or not.

And then one day, you'll overhear one of them say, "Yes sir, that sucker really has it."

# Philosophical Musings

**PART 8**

## and Idle Chit-Chat

# Confessions of
# a Cult Artist

## by Russ Tolman

**Russ Tolman is a Los Angeles-based singer, songwriter, guitarist and, yes, cult artist who has recorded several albums, first as a member of True West and more recently as a solo artist. He is said to be quite popular in Europe.**

**C**ult artist. Not sure if I ever liked that term much. Conjures up too many images of ritualistic mumbo-jumbo and shadowy netherworld goings-on. Sounds like too much extracurricular image-building and maintaining for a guy who just wants to write songs, make records and play for people. Okay, so maybe if it were up to me I would have picked a different name for what I do. But, like Cher says, "If the shoe fits, buy a roomful."

I'm pleased to report that no dismembered chickens or crudely drawn pentangles have shown up on my front porch since I made the transition from Next Big Thing (that wasn't) to Cult Artist. I guess that being a cult artist means having a small but loyal audience. This is nice. Any kind of audience is nice.

Perhaps the most noticeable difference between being a Next Big Thing and being a Cult Artist is backstage after the show. In the old days, there were girls. Now, there are guys who want to discuss in length the liner notes of your third import-only double CD.

Things get better, though. My fellow singer/songwriter Steve Wynn has this theory that if you succeed in hanging in there for twelve or fifteen years, you get your "legend card" and people start covering your songs. It's sort of a dues-paying, rite-of-passage thing, kind of like getting a gold watch for your years of loyal service. I've got a couple more years to go before I qualify for my card, but if anyone's interested in beating the rush, I've got a fine catalog of songs for you to choose from.

Europe tends to be a place where many of us cult types ply our trade. Why? Is it the romantic Ernie Hemingway expatriate thing? Is it because nonnative English speakers seem to appreciate good lyrics more than Americans do? Is it because European promoters tend to wonder what *they* did wrong if show attendance is low, rather than be pissed off that you didn't sell the requisite amount of beer? Is it because European audiences just see it as "American music," unlike stateside where my music tends to fall between the cracks, industry-category–wise? Is it because being a critics' darling and getting good reviews and reams o'press actually help sell records there? Is it because the truck stops, McDonald's, and 7-Eleven's in Europe are more interesting than their domestic cousins? Is it because the geographical distance between Oslo and Rome is less than the distance between L.A. and Austin? Actually, it's all of these and more.

One of the biggest problems with being a cult artist is your cult. As soon as fans have an artist pegged, they tend to resent efforts by said artist to grow or change. And heaven forbid if you actually do threaten to achieve even a small measure of popularity, since cult audiences tend to want to keep you all to themselves. They've been known to bail if they perceive that you are beginning to reach a wider audience—whether or not this perception is actually true. A possible scenario: You get some radio play, and your core audience decides you've suddenly become Billy Joel and bolts for the cargo door screaming "Geronimo!" Meanwhile, your record company fails to translate aforementioned airplay into sales (either the CD isn't in the stores, or the mass audience just doesn't give a shit), leaving your humble cult artist one step forward and three steps back.

Now I can hear all of you moaning that a *real* artist wouldn't be fixated on such mundane business considerations. *Real* artists don't soil themselves with such earthly matters as commerce, *n'est pas? Au contraire!* Just to continue having the opportunity to make records and tour, we cult types have to wear a lot of different hats. As often as not, we are our own managers, negotiators, producers, road managers, or whatever the occasion requires, simply because there's not enough dough to pay anybody who might be better at the job.

So, if you've got your mind set on doing whatever your creative heart desires in music, give up that illusion that some sugar-daddy (or mommy) manager, record label, or whatever will come along and take care of you. A big part of this cult-artist gig is figuring out new ways of doing business, so that you can continue to eke out a living from this sod farm we call Art. Not only is it a tough row to hoe, it's generally considered uncool to be up-front about the cold practical realities of maintaining one's own small niche in the pecking order.

Okay, you're asking, why would anyone *want* such a depressing gig? A good question, and one that I find myself asking on a regular basis. I suppose that it comes down to either having some serious rocks in one's head, or having an unquenchable desire to make records and play for people, or some twisted combination of the two. I'm often reminded of the joke involving the circus worker, the incontinent elephant, and the punch line "What—and give up show business?"

So that's the job description. It ain't for everybody. The hours are long, the frustrations are many, and the material rewards are few. But if you're a certain sort of person, there is nothing in the world that will get your rocks off quite as satisfyingly. Even better than stripping naked, getting tattooed with pentangles and swimming in a cauldron of boiling goat's blood. Even better than dressing up in funny robes, dancing around a fire and biting the heads off chickens. And damn near as good as painting arcane alchemical symbols on wistful, willing virgins. *Bon chance!*

"You know that thing Andy Warhol said about everybody being famous for fifteen minutes? Well, I had twenty minutes, which was probably more than my fair share anyway."

—IAN DURY

# You Do What You Gotta Do, You Do What You Can: Notes on DIY

Austin, Texas-based Thomas Anderson has recorded three albums of his own songs, and has written for such publications as *Creem* and the *Bob*.

I never took DIY [Do It Yourself] as a personal credo. I still don't. If I had my way, I'd have legions of groveling underlings, who at the snap of my fingers would trample each other to get me a pack of cigarettes. Unfortunately, that kind of deferential butt-kissing has eluded me thus far, and anyway I don't smoke. So why DIY? Most musicians, myself included, sooner or later find themselves facing a situation where everyone who was supposed to come through hasn't. Which leaves two options: do it yourself, or go back to college.

I did my first album myself. After recording it in a guy's home studio during one of the coldest winters I can remember (every time the door opened an arctic blast knocked all the guitars out of tune), I wound up having the LPs manufactured in Arizona, the covers in Texas, and the lyric sheets in Oklahoma (where I was living at the time). It was expensive, it was a thousand headaches, it was being told every step of the way that I'd done all the previous steps wrong, it was people trying to scam money right and left, it was vanishing artwork, it was not knowing if the skips in the test pressings were due to faulty pressing or to the old turntables that were the only ones at my disposal. . . . You get the picture. But when I opened the first box of album covers and saw 200 sleeves, spine out, with my name on them, it was definitely one of life's little crescendos.

I made sure that the album got out to radio stations, the press, and all the

A&R people whose names and addresses I could get a hold of. In other words, I took 'em all to the post office myself (and patiently explained to the clerk that, yes, even though record albums weren't, strictly speaking, books, they could be sent "Book Rate"). I made follow-up calls on every one of them. Then someone reminded me that there was a place called Europe, so I did the whole thing all over again.

What I gained from this experience, I'm still discovering. It's given me a greater awareness of opportunities and some degree of business savvy, and it's led to me getting records out on both sides of the Atlantic. Every record deal I've signed I've negotiated myself, and presently I'm getting by without a manager or a booking agent. I even get fan mail occasionally, sometimes from places like Hong Kong.

Of the three albums I've recorded, the money for each came out of my own pocket. I never thought that it was supposed to work that way in rock & roll, and maybe it isn't. But like I said, if I'd waited for the limo to take me to Fantasyland, I'd still be asking "Do you want lids on these?"

So no, I'm not getting rich doing this. My savings account is currently at twenty-three dollars, and the "Check Engine" light on my car's dashboard, which used to flash on for fifteen seconds every once in a while, is now as steadfast and dependable as a loyal friend. Yes, I'd *like* to get rich doing this. It's hard to convince yourself that you're in it for the glory when you have a blowout in the Ozarks at five in the morning in January. And the thought does occur to me that this is the country that let Herman Melville and Lonnie Johnson die penniless. . . .

But it's like the old JBL speakers ad used to say, "Under pressure, most tweeters simply fail." When you do it yourself, you only fail when you choose to.

"We're living proof that you don't need talent or good looks to make it in music. People ask what it takes to become a successful rock band. I always say just fucking quit your job and live on the street. And when you get really hungry you'll come up with something good."

—PAUL LEARY, BUTTHOLE SURFERS

# Negativland's Tenets of Free Appropriation

![black bar]

**S**ince the late seventies—i.e., long before their much-publicized copyright battles with U2, Casey Kasem, and SST Records—the Bay Area satirical-experimental-conceptualist group Negativland has made extensive use of found sounds in their ongoing sonic explorations of contemporary culture. In the nineties, though, the band's disputes with the aforementioned parties—sparked by the group's punningly titled *U2* single—brought these veteran media provocateurs considerable (though not necessarily welcome) public attention, forcing the band to explicitly address the issues of ownership and appropriation that had always been implicit in their work. What follows is Negativland's definitive statement on the subject.

O  Free appropriation is inevitable when a population bombarded with electronic media meets the hardware that encourages them to capture it.

O  As artists, our work involves displacing and displaying bites of publicly available, publicly influential material because it peppers our personal environment and affects our consciousness. In our society, the media which surrounds us is as available, and as valid a subject for art as nature itself.

O  As artists, the economic prohibition of clearance fees and the operational prohibition of not being able to obtain permission when our new context is unflattering to our samples should not diminish our ability to reference and reflect the media world around us.

O  Our appropriations are multiple and *fragmentary* in nature; they do not include whole works.

O Our work *is* an authentic and original "whole," being much more than the sum of its samples. This is *not* a form of "bootlegging" intending to profit from the commercial potential of the subjects appropriated. The law must come to terms with distinguishing the difference between *economic* intent and *artistic* intent.

O There is no demonstrable negative effect on the market value of the original works from which we appropriate, or the cultural status or incomes of the artists who made the original works. Referencing a work in a fragmentary way is at least as likely to have a positive effect on those areas of concern. (Rap/hip-hop sampling played a big part in the renewal of James Brown's career, and he sued them for it!)

O The urge to make one thing out of other things is an entirely traditional, socially healthy and artistically valid impulse which has only recently been criminalized in order to force private tolls on the practice (or prohibit it to escape embarrassment). These now all-encompassing private locks on mass media have led to a mass culture that is almost completely "professional," formularized, and practically immune to any form of bottom-up, direct-reference criticism it doesn't approve of.

O The courts' often-espoused principle that "If it's done for profit, it can't be fair use" represents a thoughtless and carelessly misguided prejudice against the struggle of new art to survive. Making media—any media—is expensive. It requires substantial up-front investments in time and manufactured goods to create, duplicate and distribute anything. The courts' easy reliance on a not-for-profit standard for fair use ignores the reality that artists, no matter what they choose to do, need to support themselves and their work with a return on their investment just like everyone else. The currently applied "nonprofit only" standard simply assures that only the independently wealthy may dabble in fair use. If society values the challenging and reforming aspects of critical, fair use works that bubble up from independent, grassroots thinking, the law should not condone the smothering of such works by disallowing their economic survival in our "free" marketplace.

O We believe that artistic freedom for all is more important to the health of society than the supplemental and extraneous incomes derived from private copyright tariffs which create cultural climate of art control and Art Police. No matter how valid the original intent of our copyright laws may have been, they are now clearly being subverted when they are used to censor resented works, to suppress the public need to reuse and reshape information, and to garner purely opportunistic incomes from any public use of previously released cultural material which is, in fact, already publicly available to everyone. The U.S. Constitution clearly shows that the original intent of copyright law was to promote a *public* good, not a private one. No one should be allowed to claim a private control over the creative process itself. This struggle is essentially one of art against business, and ultimately about which one must make way for the other.

# The Reinvention of Inner Ear Disorder and Its Quest for Princess Dyslexia

## by Howe Gelb

Rampart: Part ramp. Part part.
Reinvention: Part ramp and another part.
Rant: The birth of the above combined.
Lucky: An excuse applied where no application is necessary.
Storm: The luckiest air on Earth.
Fleeting: Absolutely everything.
Fleet: More than one ride awaiting at curbside.
Flee: To lose what just was.
Fle: No such word yet.

Wisdom is something encased in a canlike perimeter with an attractive wrap-around label especially dedicated to its order of ingredients well displayed.

Only, either way, it's somebody else's. You're only choosing to buy theirs. You can disagree with it later, after the inability to digest.

Listen. Before you had to talk, you had things figured quite nicely.
From the time you began applying the luggage of language to qualify your every synapse, you began building your very own drainage ditch.
And now you suck on near every morsel of supernal sonicscape to recapture that which you already knew way back before you attempted to burden your exact feelings with a sticky display of malignant word *lypolma,* already half chewed at that.

And from only that to excite the powers that be, a royalty is paid out to equally incite.

Royalty: Not unlike the fair Princess Dyslexia.

It is from this scattering of points a myriad of games ensue. Small business wryly whilings. Cliché corporate politics. The luster and lusting of possible agendas.

But if you already knew something, then forgot it, then found it out again way later, a cycle is achieved. And since everything in nature is cyclical, then it is at least only natural.

And likewise, since a song is but a slice of reinvention, which in itself can only be had by an infinite number of perspective changes, then somewhere in your heart you know it's self-defeating to build your soul foundation on that which is lottery.

Lottery of birth. Lottery of defeat. Lottery of prejudice.

Lottery: A dull thudlike sound in your head. The absence of trajectory.

Trajectory: Everything that soars.

That's what the best records are made out of.
Excellence in trajectory. It still flies after twenty years.

Long live Princess Dyslexia, her Excellency, and her luted backdoor man.

# Cake Icing

## by Jean Smith

Jean Smith is one half (with guitarist David Lester) of Vancouver's Mecca Normal, who have released several albums since 1986. Smith's first book, *I Can Hear Me Fine,* was published in 1994.

**J** am sitting outside at a cafe table in Holland with David. Our traditional breakfast has arrived: salami and a white bun. I order a beer and use the salami to shine my boots.

"It seems like music and philosophy have cut themselves off from life. They ignore each other, they used to feed each other," says David, continuing our ongoing conversation.

"As far as music goes, there's an agreed-upon obligation to create replicas of what's already in front of us," I say. "It seems like the one thing necessary to make something of value is the thing we're encouraged to hide. Difference. The thing that makes us different from each other."

My beer arrives, filled with bubbling amber in the slant of morning sun. I am looking at the back of the cafe wondering what the rectangular black shapes on the far wall are. I realize they are other rooms.

"Success seems to be viewed in terms of ability to imitate. Who told us to stop making up life as we go along? It's funny how we've traded political rights for consumer rights, we've been reduced to buying and selling popular concepts, guzzling approval. Who's trying to create anything?"

"For me," I say, "change is improvisation, the point when new choices are made. Music, the news, life is always happening somewhere else. The camera decides what culture is, what our lives are like, and we watch."

I am ripping chunks off the white bun, chucking them at pigeons. They're not aware they're being attacked.

"My neighbor turns on the TV the moment she walks in and doesn't turn it off until she lies down to go to sleep. I think a lot of people are afraid to be alone," David says.

"The weird thing is," I say, "I don't think most people know there are parallels to conventional life where . . . well let's put it this way, it's like breaking into a pomegranate for the first time and trying to figure out where all the pockets of juicy seeds are, at first it's hard to find a pattern and a method of getting them out. It's unfamiliar, but it's there. Then there are the people who don't even know what a pomegranate is."

# Cobalt Blue Sonata

## by Robyn Hitchcock

A painter, writer and musician, Robyn Hitchcock is a founding member of the seminal avant-pop band the Soft Boys. Since the band's breakup in 1981, he has toured and recorded extensively both as a solo artist and with the Egyptians.

As the touring wore on, my guitar began to bleed paint. At first this was not a problem. Lumbering discreetly around the clustered cities of the Northeast, we were all still fairly unsoiled. The primal urge of rock musicians to become their own road-kill was there, all right, but it was still skulking in our spines. The black swarming darkness in the back chamber of the bus and in the tattered stencilled flight cases was pregnant with something, but none of us knew what. We trundled from city to city in a womb drenched in polish. Outside, the leaves turned orange.

"Morning, Mr. H," chimed the voice of Pinky, our tour manager. He gently laid a plastic lobster across my stomach. I was lying on my back with my hands folded on my chest like a dead knight. "This came for you last night, from Todd. Shall I put it with the others?"

"Vaguely," I drawled.

"Ooh, you're so abstract sometimes I wish I could hang you in the Guggenheim."

"You've missed your chance, Pinky-boy—we've played New York already."

"Not on this tour, sweetheart," said Pinky, ruefully platting his seaweed locks into something indecent. "That was last autumn. This year we started in

Boston." He fingered the lobster and then twirled it around so the pincers were facing my head. "Hmm . . . did life evolve from above or below the waist?"

I watched the plastic crustacean gaze blankly up from my crotch. "In your case, Pinky, it started in the rectum and migrated to the genitals. Typical Scorpio."

"I'm a Gemini, chief."

"That's what I mean—typical Scorpio trick, to be a Gemini." I thrust my hips upwards with uncharacteristic verve, sending the lobster spiraling up in the air. It came to roost in Pinky's locks. It peered, rather less blankly, out of his green smoky nest of hair.

"Oh," I cried, "it really suits you."

"Not me, chief." Pinky extricated the little plastic thing and examined it quizzically between his forefinger and thumb. "I'm a shrimps-only man myself," with which he flicked the lobster into the bucket in the corner, where it lay silently with all the rest. He stood up and wrinkled his nose.

"A fetching aroma. Been at the Chardonnay again, have we?"

Just then, an umbrella handle crooked itself around Pinky's neck, and he staggered back through the little maroon doorway, into the belly of the bus.

"Pinky! Come and play double-or-nothing with me and Mr. Spools." That was the voice of Ram, the bass player. I lay back and continued to bounce through New England.

Onstage that night at the Ritz in New York, we were churning into a new song I had just written, "Death to All Relationships." The middle section called for Dino, the percussionist, to strike a glass with a felt-encased mallet while humming a major ninth through his nose. The glass sphere was dangled in front of him by Retch, the guitar tech, who then had to whisk it smartly back and forth between two microphones to produce an eerie stereo keening noise. Mr. Spools, our soundman, could have achieved this by panning the knobs on the desk, but he disliked actually touching the board once the show had started. "That's what soundchecks are for," he would say.

"What's that, Mr. Spools?" somebody would invariably ask.

"For the sound."

As Retch was about to swing the glass orb within Dino's striking range, I struck a dark, portentous chord on my guitar. Or I tried to. My fingers seemed to pass through the strings, and I whirled around to check my amp—to look for the sound, as it were. Nothing came out of the amp, but from my hand arose the unmistakable odor of paint. Two Chinese boys in the front giggled, and a couple of rows back I saw Lori Quartz, a DJ from WNYU, wipe something out of her eye. Looking down again, I saw that my right hand was dripping with black paint.

To my left, Ram seemed oblivious, his hand to his ear and his eyes shut tight as a fetus, as he hummed a jagged harmony to Dino, and a great long tibia of a bass note oozed inch by inch out of his speaker cabinet. But I noticed that Dino was having problems. The glass sphere too was daubed with black paint, which had smeared itself all over Dino's felt mallet. As Retch haplessly swung the orb across Dino's face, it wiped paint across the percussionist's nose. The mallet slowly wilted in his hand and the smudged orb gradually stopped directly in front of his face, still suspended by the faithful Retch. With neither percussion nor guitar to accompany him, Ram stopped playing too. He glared inquiringly at me. I shrugged my shoulders and played an A chord. A coil of red paint shot out of my amplifier and burst against my back. The audience applauded wildly.

Two nights later in Chicago, it happened again. The roadies were primed and had a big bucket of turpentine by the side of the stage, but Ram got Cobalt Blue all over his Paul Smith jodhpurs and threw his bass down in disgust. Fortunately, this was near the end of the show, and we were able to finish with the a cappella number "Nobody Loves You Like the Phone."

Back on the bus, tempers were simmering.

"Look at them! They're ruined." Ram unfurled the stricken jodhpurs from a roll of turpentine-drenched newspaper. "Look at that fucking great smear. I'll never get that off."

"Ooh, it looks like Italy," said Pinky, laughing.

"Nah," said Mr. Spools flatly. "It's more like Sumatra."

"Actually," opined Dino, thoughtfully, "it's more like Cornwall than Italy."

"I'm glad somebody thinks it's funny," growled Ram, looking squarely at me. I hadn't actually said anything.

"Me?" I was outraged.

"It came out of your guitar."

"Yeah, but I didn't . . ."

". . . and it's all over my clothes."

"Ram," I said, steadily, "it's all over mine, too."

"Call that a stain?" Ram pointed derisively to my jacket. "It's only the size of Malta. You heard everybody say mine was like Italy."

"Sumatra, mate," said Mr. Spools, reaching for the turpentine.

"All right, all right!" I raised my voice, and looked at them all in the lurching maroon gloom of the tour bus. "I know it comes through my gear, but where is it really from?"

Dino shrugged and looked away.

"You're the artist," he said, almost inaudibly.

In Minneapolis the following night, Retch and Mr. Spools surrounded my amplifier with Chinese bathing screens. A huge mosquito net draped above them ensured that any paint that the amplifier might discharge would be directed toward me alone and wouldn't soil the others.

Despite that, after a few songs the gig was a shambles. Dino and Ram played beautifully. It was the first time that their skeletons of rhythm had struck the ear so clearly. But my guitar sound was gone, turned into paint. I could still sing, and nobody seemed to mind that. But when the jets of colored paint shot from my amplifier and burst like oily fireworks above the check-shirted crowd, they went wild.

"Hey, man, do some crimson!"

"Cobalt blue! Cobalt blue—ooh!"

I struck what would have been a growling E minor 9th, only to find a sea-green finger of paint spout from my Telecaster, to be joined by four others to make a giant oily hand that swept above the goggling audience.

"Way to go, Mr. H—sneaky green!"

That night, on the bus, the others avoided my gaze. Pinky had had a hard time of it from the promoter, whose floor was now an oily swamp of color. Pinky had pointed out to him that the show was a sellout. The promoter sighed, agreed, and handed over the money.

In Seattle Dino and Ram played for half an hour by themselves. When I took to the stage in a frogman's suit surrounded by Chinese baffles, the others slipped away. Mr. Spools put a Nine Inch Nails CD on the sound system, and the audience writhed in a slow frenzy of paint. I didn't bother to sing along.

When I got back to the dressing room, there was a pumpkin with a split gash of a mouth perched on top of my case. In it was a note from Dino and Ram.

"Be seeing you . . ."

Back at the hotel, I was pouring turpentine over my hands, taking care not to smoke, when the phone rang. It was Nattie Stootz, my A&R person.

"Hi," her voice waved up at the end. You could have hung a shirt on it. "Great sho-ow."

"Yeah? I didn't see you."

"Well, uh, Viper and Lee"—her bosses—"were kind of, you know, about the paint, so . . ."

"You stayed at the back?"

"Well . . . no, uh—we didn't actually come to the show per se, we talked to the promoter and . . ."

"And?"

"Listen, Mr. H, it's just that it's hard to sell music that you can't hear."

"Why not? You've been selling music that's unlistenable for years."

"Mr. H, you're not even making any sound."

"Maybe that's what the next big thing will be."

"What's that?" said Nattie, curious for once.

"Silence."

"Mmm . . . you could have something there."

So these days, I don't tour. I sit in a white tower by the edge of the sea. It once was a lighthouse, and up in its circular glass top, I get the best light for painting. If I need a plastic lobster, I have to walk down to the safe and get it. It's 528 steps both ways. Pinky doesn't work for me anymore. Mr. Spools is running a kite shop in St. Petersburg. Retch is on the road with Two Make a Frog. Dino and Ram opened a chain of delicatessens and have a residency in Las Vegas with Elvis Costello. And here I am, painting them all.

# Attitude

**PART 9**

## and

## Misbehavior

# $\mathfrak{E}$ight
# Really Dumb Things
# the Replacements Did

## by Chris Mars

Chris Mars spent a tumultuous decade as the Replacements' drummer. Since leaving the band in November
1990, he has pursued a solo recording career and won
considerable acclaim for his paintings, which have
graced the covers of his own albums as well as various other artists.

## 1. The Roxy

We played the Roxy in Los Angeles on May 1, 1986. It was brought to my
attention at soundcheck that there were going to be a lot of record-industry
muckety-mucks present that evening. The best tables in the house, close to
the stage, were reserved for these folks. So, after soundcheck I immediately
went to the nearest novelty store and picked up several bottles of stink juice
(a.k.a. fart perfume). I brought them back to the club and showed them to
Bob, who let out a good cackle at the possibilities. About midway through
our set, with the steamy club filled with a crowd of about 400, Bob came
back to my drum kit. I handed him about half of the bottles of stink juice.
He set them down on the edge of the stage. When the next number—one of
our most sensitive tunes, as I recall—started, Bob kicked the stink bottles
into the crowd. Then I threw the rest in as well. Within a couple of minutes,
the entire joint—which was packed to sardinelike capacity—was consumed
by this unimaginable stench. Me and Bob turned to each other, red-faced,
laughing so hard that we could barely play our instruments. As the over-
powering odor grew more dense, Paul and Tommy looked at us in bewilder-
ment—both from the smell and from me and Bob helplessly screwing up
the song. Meanwhile, the looks of befuddlement on the crowd's faces grew,

as people looked suspiciously at each other and all around the room. During the next few songs, the remaining bottles of stink juice were crushed, making the wafting reek even more horrific. It was the Replacements in odorama.

### 2. The Winnebago

Around 1986, we were traveling through Canada in a rented deluxe Winnebago with a porta-toidie, a little kitchen, and the whole nine yards. The trouble started with someone bringing a gallon can of white paint aboard. Inevitably, on the ten-hour-plus drives between Canadian provinces, boredom and road fatigue set in. We snapped. The paint ended up all over the walls. From that point on, it was straight downhill. Our roadie, Bill Sullivan, had the unfortunate position of driving, while the band members became a four-man wrecking team, kicking down all the walls and pretty much gutting the vehicle in less than fifty miles. There was nothing left but a pile of rubble in the back. Somebody succeeded in booting out the side and back windows, allowing the cold Canadian air to rush in. The Winnebago immediately became a wobbly shell of its former self, especially around turns. Even the passenger seat was ripped out. The only things remaining were Bill Sullivan sitting in the driver's seat and the front windshield (on which there was also an attempt made, which luckily failed). For the remainder of the tour, the rubble heap became a piss mound and refuge for beer bottles and other assorted garbage that—even with the radical ventilation—stunk. By the time we made our way back to the United States, the Winnebago had been in this state for a good couple of weeks (the paint still hadn't dried, thanks to the chilly conditions inside the vehicle). I remember the border patrol guy walking up to the Winnebago in his nice, freshly pressed uniform and police coat. He made us all go into the holding tank, and then proceeded to inspect the vehicle (for fruit or whatever, I guess). When he emerged a little while later, his face was crimson, obviously struggling to hold back his anger. He hadn't found any fruit, but he had paint all over his coat and piss on his shoes and he was pretty much speechless. He then left the room to gather himself, returning a while later to tell us to get the hell back to the United States and never set foot in Canada again. We then, of course, had to return the Winnebago to the rental place, but that's a whole other story. It ended up at about $5,000 or $6,000 worth of damage.

### 3. Electrocution in Kansas

We were in Kansas on one of our early tours, probably around 1984. It was about 100 degrees in the shade and very humid that day. We were to play a VFW hall. We were setting up for soundcheck with all the P.A. gear and Bob and I were alone on stage. He plugged in his guitar and adjusted the microphone. Upon gripping the mic stand, Bob somehow—from the humidity or whatever—grounded himself on it, sending all the voltage in the whole damned place through him. Pulling the mic stand to his guitar neck he scorched the skin on his left hand, leaving string-mark burns on it. The guitar neck then snapped, in two places, and the stand seared his right forearm. While all this was going on, I'd had my head down adjusting my drums, and I heard a stuttering moan coming from Bob; the shock was so great he couldn't even yell. As he fell down to his knees, I ran out from behind my kit. It seemed like forever, but I'm sure it wasn't that long. When I grabbed Bob by the shoulders to try to yank him away, I got a jolt like I'd put my hand into an electrical socket—obviously, there was a lot of electricity going through Bob. It was one of the most frightening things I've ever witnessed. All I managed to do was roll Bob on his back while he was still being electrocuted. By this point, I and the other people who had taken notice of Bob's predicament were yelling at the sound man, who cut the power. Bob—who I believe came within an inch of his life—was damned shaken up, but somehow the show went on. He recovered and everything was fine, but whenever the band was onstage or around the amps or P.A. gear, you can bet your life we were pretty damned cautious from then on—for at least a week.

## 4. Bouncer Riot in Boston

We were playing the Channel Club in Boston around 1985. It was a punk-fest; I can't remember exactly who else was on the bill, but it was us and a couple of hardcore bands. Anyone who played the Channel during that period will fondly remember the club's bouncers, who were real wise guy/wrestler/Mafia goon types. At the time, the Channel was in transition, moving from Top Forty cover-type acts to more alternative bands. The night we played, there was an obvious tension between the bouncers and the punkers. When the slam dancing started, the bouncers, with their limited experience dealing with this sort of thing, thought that something was wrong. Thinking that they were looking at some kind of fight, they tried to stop people from slamming. Pretty soon they were throwing kids out left and right. The kids then started moving onto the stage to get away from the goons. At this, the bouncers went even more berserk, and the overcrowded stage erupted in a volley of spit aimed at the bouncers, who started spitting back. I remember this shower of goober crossfiring from the stage to the dance floor. It sort of reminded me of the Battle of the Bulge, but instead of bullets it was loogies. At that point, I think, the rest of the slam dancers went up onstage. It was getting pretty scary now with the bouncers trying to get onstage to throw kids off, and the bouncers breaking chairs and whatever they could find to beam the kids with. I remember me and another band member hiding behind one of the bars to take cover from the ensuing riot. The band had long stopped playing and the only sound was thumping.The coppers soon came to break it up. Needless to say, we never got to play.

## 5. Shaving our Eyebrows in Seattle

In 1989 we kicked off a tour in Seattle. We were sitting at the hotel bar before the first show. Scott McCaughey and another member of the Young Fresh Fellows were there. We were all getting pretty toasty, so we made a pact to shave our eyebrows. First Paul went up to his hotel room, shaved his off, came back down and couldn't stop laughing. He looked like a Martian. Then we all decided to do it. First Tommy, then me, then Slim. The whole band was without eyebrows. Then for some reason Scott McCaughey decided to do his too. The rest of the night was spent bobbing around Seattle from bar to bar, and every time we looked at each other we would double over with laughter. There was no talking going on, just laughing; it was probably one of my most gut-wrenching laughs ever. For the rest of the tour, people would come up to us to say hello, and everyone would ask, "Are you feeling all right?" They couldn't quite figure out what was wrong with us. They knew something was different, and we did look kind of sick but no one could place it, and we wouldn't tell anyone what it was. We'd paint eyebrows on in the morning with a grease pencil, so we wouldn't look that goofy throughout the day. Of course it would wear off, and then we'd be back to looking pretty sickly at night. It takes a long time for your eyebrows to grow back; mine took a good three months. When we came home, about three weeks after we'd shaved our eyebrows off, I had a little stubble, and I started using chalk to fill them in—which led to a few embarrassing moments. One night I went to an East Indian restaurant and started sweating from the spicy food. My dinner partner began laughing at the little black trail running down my face—I was literally sweating my eyebrows off. I don't think I'll be shaving my eyebrows off again anytime soon.

## 6. A Running Joke

It had been a running joke for one of the band members, back at the hotel after shows, to grace the inside of the ice machines with bladder-fulls of beer urine. This went on for several tours in different parts of the country. On one special occasion, someone crapped in an ice bucket and sent it down in the elevator.

## 7. Atomic Drummer

We were playing a show in California, and they brought in Mexican food for us. There were two big bowls of green chili on the table. I'd had the flu and thought the chili would be a good way to clean out my system. I also wanted to make some money, so I said, "How much if I eat both of those bowls of green chili?" They said, "Aw, you're crazy. A spoonful of the stuff will put your mouth on fire." But they started putting money down. Someone put down a ten, then someone put down a twenty 'cause they thought there was no way I would finish it; I think the pool got up to forty-odd bucks. I picked up the two big bowls and ate the chili as fast as I could. And that was it. My mouth was on fire. I drank something, and we went out to play. I remember for some reason that Ian Hunter was in the audience that night—or maybe it was a delusion from my flu. There I was, sweating away like I usually do when I play, and about halfway through the set, this burning chili sweat began coming out of my pores and into my eyes. I had to play the rest of the set with my eyes closed. In my stomach there was a nuclear reaction going on. I didn't feel sick, but I felt like I was glowing—I had definitely cleaned out my system! I don't think it was worth the forty bucks, but I am thankful that I had eyebrows at the time.

## 8. Playing Chicken

In 1980/81, after a gig with our buddies Hüsker Dü, we went over to Bob Mould's house. We were drinking, and it got to be about three in the morning, so we decided to split. Paul got on the back of my dirtbike/motorcycle and we took off. There were no cars on the road so I was zigzagging around, back and forth, between lanes on the mostly empty street. When I saw headlights approaching, I decided to stay in the wrong lane and play chicken with the car. I was going to get out of the way at the last minute, which I did. But the car turned around and started chasing us. So, with Paul still on the back, I went speeding across lawns and yards trying to outrun this car. Still pretty drunk at the time, I thought that maybe it was a couple of people out to kick a punk rocker's ass or something. It didn't dawn on me that the car might have been an unmarked cop car, which is exactly what it was. Me and Paul were having a hoot, and I outran it for a good long time. After a while, though, Paul had had enough, and he jumped off and ran up to a house, pretending it was his. The cops stopped, handcuffed Paul, and threw him in the backseat of their car. Meanwhile, I knew by now that they were cops. But I was an out-of-my-mind-drunk punk, so I started circling the car and screaming obscenities and yelling at the cops to let Paul go. At this point, they were pretty pissed off. When one guy got out of the car, I'd taunt him and rev my engine. I'd let him get maybe within two feet of grabbing me and then I'd pop the clutch, aggravating him thoroughly. I repeated this little trick about four times. Obviously by this point, they'd called in for backup. So Paul's still in the back of the car and I'm still howling and riding around. Suddenly squads of cops came at us from all angles, from all corners of the block. They boxed me in, threw me against the car and that was it. They let Paul go, and I spent the night in jail.

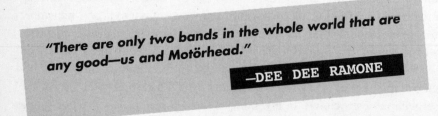

"There are only two bands in the whole world that are any good—us and Motörhead."

—DEE DEE RAMONE

# Fifteen
# Alt-Rock Feuds

John Lydon vs. Malcolm McLaren

Lou Reed vs. David Bowie

Elvis Costello vs. Bonnie Bramlett

Joe Strummer vs. Mick Jones

The A-Bones vs. the Gibson Bros.

U2 vs. Negativland

Negativland vs. SST Records

Meat Puppets vs. SST Records

Sinéad O'Connor vs. Frank Sinatra

Sinéad O'Connor vs. the Pope

Courtney Love vs. her dad, Mary Lou Lord, Kathleen
    Hanna, Kill Rock Stars, Trent Reznor, Pearl Jam,
    the Beastie Boys, Madonna

Steve Albini vs. Geffen Records

Smashing Pumpkins vs. Pavement

Kramer vs. Ann Magnuson

Oasis vs. Blur

# Substance Abuse Hall of Fame: Ten Alt-Rockers Who've Danced with Mr. Brownstone

Nick Cave

Kurt Cobain

Perry Farrell

Grant Hart

Anthony Kiedis

Richard Lloyd

Courtney Love

Lou Reed

Johnny Thunders

Sid Vicious

*"My mother isn't particularly impressed by my music, although I think she's relieved that I didn't overdose on drugs or become a full-fledged petty criminal."*

**—RICHARD HELL**

# Ten Consistently Depressing Alt-Rockers

G. G. Allin

Bauhaus

Nick Cave

Christian Death

Danzig

Diamanda Galas

Ministry

Missing Foundation

Nine Inch Nails

Skrewdriver

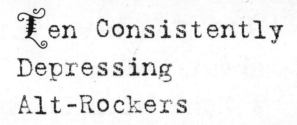

"It's so much easier to write about angst and anger and fear and darkness and fucked-up feelings than to write about intense happiness. Happiness just sounds dorky."

—MICHAEL STIPE, R.E.M.

# The Ten Best Things About Being in a Band with En Esch

by Sascha Konietzko

Sascha Konietzko and En Esch comprise the creative core of the Hamburg, Germany, quartet KMFDM, an acknowledged leader in the industrial/dance genre since 1984.

**1.** He jumps out of the fourth floor of a burning building in Chicago in the winter of 1990 and ends up in a hospital, almost dead.

**2.** He gets undressed backstage before a show.

**3.** He gets undressed backstage after a show.

**4.** He sits in a freezing cold tour bus clad only in a laminate.

**5.** He and I sit in front of a running video-camera for three hours without saying a word.

**6.** He says, "Nobody loves me."

**7.** His girlfriend, Isis, "plays" the violin in the back of the tour bus.

**8.** He cooks.

**9.** He has to show his ID. He doesn't have ID.

**10.** He has to go through a metal detector in an airport and his metal arm (see #1) sets it off and he starts arguing with the security guys.

# Joe Jack Talcum's Top Ten Reasons to Kill Your Boss

In between day jobs, Joe Jack Talcum plays guitar with the Dead Milkmen.

**10.** You forgot your uniform.

**9.** He told you to sweep the floor.

**8.** He has no sense of honor.

**7.** He won't double your pay.

**6.** You wanna test out your new Glock.

**5.** You hope to get a job as a postal worker.

**4.** You always wanted to see what sex in prison was like.

**3.** Your boss would probably kill you if he had the balls.

**2.** Waking up at five A.M. is not civilized.

**1.** Manson, Manson, Manson.

# Murray Attaway in Audio-Vérité Hell

**Murray Attaway was a founding member of the Georgia-based combo Guadalcanal Diary. After the band released its last album in 1989, singer/songwriter/guitarist Attaway embarked on a solo career that has thus far produced two albums.**

For years, among musicians and other similarly benighted souls, there has existed an alternative to music. In terms of pure listening enjoyment, this alternative has no peer. I speak, of course, about "the tapes." Much has been written about these audio-vérité masterpieces; the writing usually falls into the category of informative dissertations geared toward presenting these works to a larger audience (often for someone else's gain).

Perhaps the best known of these items are the notorious "Tube Bar" tapes, which preserve an unidentified prank-caller's persistent harassment of short-fused, Newark, New Jersey, bar owner Red Deutsch. These tapes have spawned God-knows-how-many higher-profile tributes, from a short independent film entitled *Red* (starring veteran B-movie icon Lawrence Tierney) to countless calls from cartoon hellion Bart Simpson to Moe's bar. Another well-known example is the immortal Troggs tape (capturing the protopunk Brit combo bickering during a desperate late-sixties recording session), which, after years of underground circulation, was eventually released on CD as part of a Troggs retrospective package. And then there's the near-household-name Jerky Boys—a couple of smartass New Yorkers making obnoxious but undeniably hilarious prank calls to an assortment of hapless victims—who've dragged the entire idiom kicking and squealing into the mainstream marketplace by releasing cleaned-up versions of their under-ground tapes on CD via a record company, which then spawned an actual film.

Therein lies the problem. What's always been cool about this stuff has been the grassroots network of listeners that interest in these tapes generated. If you knew someone who had a more pristine copy of Dean Martin and Jerry Lewis waxing obscene while attempting to record a radio spot for their fifties celluloid extravaganza *The Caddy* ("it'll make ya shit"), you might return the favor by introducing them to the nutty brilliance of "J & H Productions" (a long, *long* cassette letter to various vague entities in "the label industry" from a would-be concert promoter). I have seen groups of talented, literate adults reduced to giggling morons by these tapes. Powerful.

These things get under your skin—way under. I find myself, for alarmingly long periods of time, listening to nothing else. No music, just these strange lit-tle windows into various alternate realities. Sometimes nothing else will do but to turn the lights down low and put on that tape of Orson Welles lapsing into a profane tirade while recording voice-overs for a fish-stick ad. Or you might want to unwind with Billy Gibbons' amazing "Queen Bee BBQ" spots.

I have no doubt that this steady diet of strangeness has begun to seep into my own recording work. I suspect it's only a matter of time before I start interrupting my sensitive studies of spirituality and the human condition with vicious shouts of the vilest obscenities. The tapes have even begun to impinge upon my musings on the afterlife. If I am unfortunate enough to end up in hell or its equivalent, here is how I now envision my eternal torment:

I find that I am a bearded Australian musician, traveling through the gloomy, mid-1970s American night on what I instantly recognize as a tour bus. All around me are other young musicians, all of whom appear to be in a highly advanced state of nervousness. Before long, the source of their (and, soon, my) anxiety reveals itself. From a room in the back of the bus emerges a strangely familiar figure. It is a face I recall from album covers and countless episodes of *The Tonight Show Starring Johnny Carson,* only now the face is swollen with a hideous, incendiary rage that shakes me to my core.

It is my new boss, Buddy Rich.

Buddy advances slowly, uncertainly, up the narrow aisle of the moving ve-hicle, but there is nothing uncertain about the incredible stream of bile that is exploding from his sodden lips.

"I don't wanna see the fucking beards on you again. If I catch 'em on you, you're through! This ain't the fuckin' House of David baseball team. This is the Buddy Rich band—young people, with faces!"

My brain is swollen and feverish, temples pounding. I discover that, yes, several of the young men around me have wispy, newish beards, but nothing compared to the thick black Fidelista that hangs from my sweating jaw. I smell the noxious mix of Brut and Johnny Walker and notice to my horror that Buddy has paused directly behind me.

"How about you? You seem to be giving me more trouble than anyone else—you wanna do something about it?"

My heart takes off like a jackhammer. As I slowly turn to look up at the glowering figure of Buddy, I tell myself that there has been some horrible mistake. I am not a member of the Buddy Rich band—young people with faces. I am in fact not even a musician in Buddy's definition of the term. My trembling lips open and, in an Australian accent, this is what comes out:

"I strongly suggest that you not touch me."

My mind recoils in horror at the brazen threat that I have involuntarily hurled at this drunken black-belt psycho. Buddy wades in.

"Well, let me give *you* a suggestion. If I catch the fuckin' beard on you again, I'll THROW you off the fuckin' bandstand. Now THAT's a definite suggestion."

Surprisingly, my head is still attached. I marshall my thoughts and decide to try again. I don't know how I got here; I'm not the person he thinks I am. I'm a singer and songwriter from Georgia, not a horn player from Sydney, and I'd happily shave the beard off if he'd only point me in the direction of the nearest sharp surface. Instead:

"It's not coming off."

"What?"

"The beard's not coming off." WHAT IS COMING OUT OF MY MOUTH??? What do I care for some HAIR if it means salvation? I'm frantic, confused. I struggle for a way to clamp my lips shut.

"You're through! That's it! Pull this fuckin' bus over now. I want him off!!!"

Buddy's eyes are now narrow slits, like a viper's; his tongue quickly wets his lips in anticipation.

Slowly, as if possessing a deranged life of its own, my mouth begins forming more words. "Do you have two weeks' pay for me?" My mind is racing wildly now, as though trapped in a screaming missile headed for a stone wall. Buddy's face twists into a hideous smile.

"Two weeks' pay? I'll give you two weeks—time! And just TRY to take me to the fucking union. I'd love it! I'D LOVE IT!!"

And so on. Death be not proud.

# The Evening Before . . .

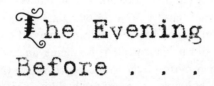

by Graham Parker

Graham Parker released his first album, the raw and compelling *Howlin' Wind*, in 1976. More than a dozen critically acclaimed LPs have followed. In his spare time, Parker writes short stories and has recently completed a novel.

Kreska and her husband, Dander Smith, were having dinner with my girlfriend and me one balmy Friday evening in our Chelsea loft, six floors up, in a monolithic building that once housed printing presses but now crawled with alleged artists, rich Eurotrash, and punk rockers like myself.

The property was purchased by an effete Lugano socialite two years before, and its cavernous, raw-space floors had been divided into units replete with massive industrial radiators, metal pipes the size of a man's chest, and rolling, wavy ceilings built to withstand the enormous weight of the presses. Where once those presses had hissed and boomed and squirted ink on long-dead publications, now the muffled strains of house, rap, and punk rock rumbled through the pipes, and lovers' quarrels in Italian, often fueled by cocaine—the building's drug of choice—could be heard echoing in bathroom vents at all hours of the night.

The four of us attacked a seafood gumbo and guzzled *pouilly-fumé* in the living space that stretched ninety feet from front door to back window, our voices accelerating in volume as the drink took hold and Kreska's spike heels clanked on the maple floor in an uneven tattoo. As soon as the dinner (which, although delicious, was merely a preliminary for the real dish) was finished,

Dander pulled out a gram of Peruvian, light on the mannite and zero on the speed, and the mirror and sterling-silver straw became our launching pad into those noxious heights of egocentric effluence so typical of late-seventies evenings. We enthused about our latest projects and guffawed over rumors of Stephen Stills' legendary steel nasal implants. We motor-mouthed about our teeth, as if they were a highly important topic.

As the night sped forward and Dander's Peruvian reduced accordingly, I offered up some Tribeca nonsense with a serious glass-splinters burn to it, just to keep us honest. Dander and I talked of doing a record together, something I, in soberness, would never consider, his being an overproducer of the worst type. The women moved over to the couch where they discussed the latest, most ridiculous hairstyle of one of the building's more famous female occupants, and began laughing so hard, I thought they would cough up blood.

It was then that I remembered the Evening Before Pills. Roughly a week before, the Evening Before Pills came to me, like many gifts of dubious merit, backstage at a New York club gig. There, my band and I, the Debilitators, had given a rip-snorting performance to a packed house of rabid, leather-clad lunatics whose sole reason for being at the show—it appeared from my view on the stage—was to project streams of beer and spittle into my mouth and to severely damage themselves either with substance abuse or the now-quaint ritual of mass pogoing.

The postshow backstage scenario was *de rigueur* for the period: hordes of liggers packed into a tiny, graffiti-daubed dressing room, chain-smoking, guzzling white Boucheron or beer, popping into the toilet in pairs only to reemerge chattering like wind-up toys, grinding their teeth as if plugged into the mains. It was within this parodic tableau that the Surgeon appeared as if from nowhere, hovering with an out-of-date Medusa hairdo, inches from my face.

"Hi, I'm Dr. Allfox!" he said forcefully, and I assumed that the exclamation mark was in fact a legitimate feature of his name, as normal as a Nordic umlaut.

"You know what happens next," he went on, his nostrils dilating like black holes in space. "You have to keep doing the coke 'til dawn, even though you feel like dogshit."

"Right," I mumbled.

"Ever feel like going back to that first line of the evening—the one that worked? You know what I mean?"

I knew what he meant all right. The junk was addictive and everyone seemed to be on it. Even your accountant would come backstage in those days and offer you a hit. The wretched coke craze raged through the music industry like a mutant virus, infecting every level with jived up superficiality, squeezing the talented, the talentless, the stupid, the intelligent—the whole gamut of the rock & roll firmament—into a narrow band of jaw-breaking, hungover banality.

In a way, we all became equal: You would think nothing of spending an entire evening of garbled, meaningless conversation with utter greaseballs who at the time seemed to be your friends, your bosom-buddy confidantes, with whom you would no doubt be tight for a lifetime—as long as their supply didn't dry up.

But at that time, nobody had any sense. We just wanted to keep on going.

"Yeah," I said, looking up at the wild-eyed Allfox! "It would be great to be able to take something that just . . . I dunno . . ."

"Takes you back to the beginning of the evening?"

"Exactly!" I said, seizing the idea with enthusiasm. "So that you could start again, cos you know—after four or five lines, you're not really enjoying the shit anymore, you're just . . ."

"Going through the motions? Doing it because you hate the crash?"

"Yep. Uh . . . what was your name again?"

"Dr. Allfox!"

"Right, right. What kind of doctor are you?"

"I'm a surgeon. And by the way, I'm a huge fan of yours. I always play your stuff when I'm operating. Do you ever feel like cutting people up? I mean, listening to your music, it sounds like you would."

I looked up at Allfox!, taking in the hawklike nose, the glassy, obsidian eyes, and the afro hair which resembled that freak at the party in *Midnight Cowboy* who has one line: "My hair is like tendrils, they reach into space."

The man was obviously a psychopath, but at the time, under the influence of three lines, half a bottle of Boucheron, and a couple hits of grass, he seemed like a pleasant, likable chap.

I explained to him that no, I hadn't really had the urge to cut someone up but saw no real harm in his unusual peccadillo—providing the intensity of my music didn't force any mistakes from the Allfox! scalpel, or its volume wake the hapless patient in the middle of a heart bypass.

"By the way," he said, his voice dropping and his birdlike gaze flicking around the throng to either side of us. "I've been working on something. A drug that'll do just what we've been talking about. A pill that will take you back to the beginning of the evening. Want to be in on its development?"

"Wow," I muttered, which he appeared to take for a yes.

"Yeah," he continued conspiratorially, and suddenly it seemed that Allfox! and I were in our own bubble removed from the thrum of chatter in the room. "Got a couple of boffins working on it now. Couple of rogue chemists. They did a nice little T.H.C. replicant last year. Wanna try a little?"

"Rather," I said foolishly.

Allfox! pulled out a folded piece of *Playboy* magazine right there in a room full of people and still no one seemed to notice. He unfolded it, revealing a heap of beautiful mauve powder. This stuff looked tempting enough to rub all over and when he handed me the top from a biro I didn't hesitate in scooping up two nostrils full. Where I had removed the powder, I noticed a tit staring up at me and I looked at the doctor with a grin. As soon as the gear hit my sinuses, it wiped out the effect of the poor quality coke I'd had earlier and bang! I was stoned as a twit.

"Nice," I said, feeling it to be a profound utterance.

"Right," said Fred, for that was indeed Allfox!'s Christian name.

"So," I said, trying desperately to hang onto the memory of what we had discussed moments before, "what about this other stuff?"

"If you're interested," said Allfox! pulling out his card, "call me tomorrow. It's almost ready for a test hop. They're getting close, just need a few guinea pigs."

And with that, the mad surgeon made for the door, and the party came crashing back into my senses in a big dread wave.

So the next morning I phoned him and over a beaklunch meeting he enthused about his chemists—Heckle and Jeckle he called them—and how near they were to perfecting the Evening Before Pill. A few field tests to get the bugs ironed out, and they'd have a perfectly marketable product on the street in no time.

"Bugs?" I ventured.

"Well . . ." he hedged. "You know, pill shape, color. The time it takes to come on. Nothin' to worry about."

All he required from me was to recommend the product to a few well-connected rock & roll business clientele whose voracious appetites for toot would ensure, Allfox! reckoned, instant success.

"Great!" I exclaimed, the beaklunch talking. "I'm in!"

"This is such an honor. I'm a huge, huge fan of yours," said the intense surgeon, smoothing his pale-green hospital gown and lurching off to the operating room, leaving me in his white office, wondering what the hell I'd gotten myself into.

And so, on that balmy summer evening, with Dander and Kreska giving each other little looks that pointed to a precipitous exit, and the clock edging toward two A.M., I bolted to the German mahogany cabinet in the gloom of an alcove in the living space, and quickly pulled out the vial of Evening Before Pills that Allfox! had had couriered over the previous day. And even though these people bored the living crap out of me—like so many people on so many ancient, terrible nights—I didn't want them to go. If they left, there would be little excuse to go on overindulging and I was determined to bore them with a video of a performance by the Debilitators at an obscure Essen kino, and Dander, I knew, had at least another gram and a quarter left, whereas my Tribeca nonsense was down to a few measly shards.

No, they were not going to leave my girlfriend and me chewing out the insides of our cheeks and slugging bourbon in a futile effort to attain unconsciousness. Oh, no. We were all going back. Back to about eight in the evening when we still felt fairly human, before our descent into the hoglike beings that now inhabited that cavernous, echoing Manhattan loft. Back, back, to that clean, anticipatory state, fresh of nostril and pink of tongue and ready to whack up white dusty train lines from a polished mirror through a sterling-silver straw.

"Ah . . . Kreska," yawned Dander, delicately trying to pry the girls apart with none too subtle body language. "It's . . . ah closing in on two A.M. I'm a little wiped," he said with a mock stretch.

"Wait!" I almost yelled, "We got to check this out. This doctor gave it to me."

I spouted on enthusiastically about the benefits of the product and without too much arm-twisting managed to convince the three of them—even though Dander halfheartedly waffled on about a mixing session the next day at noon—that the Evening Before Pills were well worth a bash.

Out came the Rebel Yell, and we washed down one plain white tablet each and returned to the dining room table to await results.

After about fifteen minutes miraculous changes occurred. We began, as one, to feel revitalized, straightened, normalized, unplugged in. Incredibly, that foul, thickened feeling of too much coke, booze, and tobacco was being erased at awesome speed; that normally irreversible experience of overstressed synapses, slurred speech, and the godawful density of what felt like a pair of leather trousers where the lungs used to be was going, going, decaying at a breathtaking clip. And then, as Allfox! had promised, we found ourselves back at the beginning of the evening! Oh, the clock still inexorably hurtled toward dawn, but the four of us no longer had the weight of hours of overindulgence in our systems.

Out in the street, car horns still blasted, people would be drifting from the Limelight to Danceteria; in the corridor a door clicked shut and a laughing couple headed to the elevator. Would we use the Evening Before Pills as a universal hangover cure while the night was still young? No, we would not! Whoopee! We yelled. We can start all over again!

But then, as Dander with gleeful eyes pulled out his coke and reached for the blade and mirror, something very odd began to simultaneously overtake our pregluttony senses.

We didn't stop there.

We kept going right on back!

Within minutes, our internal clocks, which moments before had clearly been signaling that before-coke anticipation, now indicated that before-dinner-first-glass-of-wine feeling.

It was at this point that I began to feel a sliver of apprehension as I perceived we were indeed, as one, experiencing the same thing.

"Do you feel . . ." I ventured, as yet another metabolic cycle flooded through us. But I never finished the sentence, and with frightening acceleration, I was back at lunchtime, the blood-sugar level of that very meal reversing, and the hangover of the night before inching its way into my brain and gut.

"Oh, dear," gulped Dander, as the results of Thursday night's bender at the Milk Club hit him like a curse, and before we knew it, the four of us with tired moans were draped over the furniture as we plummeted through the wee hours of Friday morning, back into the drug and alcohol stupor of Thursday night.

Outside, the traffic swelled to its usual Saturday morning volume and we slept on thickly, reliving the indulgences of two nights before.

We woke up backwards and retraced most of the week in the space of a few hours until finally we found ourselves ready for a late breakfast on Tuesday morning! Most of the week had gone . . . the wrong way!

Well, I had some excuses to make and swore I would get Allfox! to apologize to my girlfriend and our guests for this outrage; the mad surgeon would at least eat humble pie, and his boffins had to be warned of the terrible chemical bungle they had unleashed.

Dander and Kreska finally left albeit with somewhat stunned expressions.

"Nice . . . ah . . . nice dinner party, man," said Dander robotically as I showed him the door.

"Yeah, long night," I said. "Listen, Dander, I'll get that bastard doctor."

"Right . . ." he muttered, and I rushed back in to the phone and called the hospital.

"Yeah, sorry about that," said Doctor Fred Allfox! almost nonchalantly. "Uh, what day is it for you?" he asked, sounding distracted.

"Day? What fucking day?" I hissed. "Christ, I dunno," I continued irritably, "Tuesday, I think. At least that's what it feels like. We had sushi Monday night, and I can still taste it when I belch—always repeats on me, sushi. Look here, Allfox!, what went wrong? It's slowed down, thank God, but I'm still going back a tad here."

"Don't worry, it'll stop pretty soon," said Allfox! blandly. "Mmmm . . . you know these genius underground chemists, though. They don't tell you much. I think they left out a step in the process—the stuff came out like, a molecule short or something. Or a molecule too many. I think that was it. Happens all the time in drug development.

"Anyway—listen," he went on, "tell your friends I'll call them and apologize—I wanna talk to that Dander anyway, he ruined the last record by the Bloody Cavities. Overproduced the shit out of it."

"Right, right," I sighed, looking at my watch as the taste of bagels and lox from Tuesday's breakfast crept across my tongue. It was just after noon on Saturday.

"Anyway . . ." Allfox! went on, "the boffins know there's a problem, they'll brew up another batch by next week. I'll test it out and give you a call. I gotta run now. I gotta take some poor bastard's leg off—or was it a brain tumor? Shit, I can't remember, got my days all mixed up. I'm sure I'll figure it out when I get in there and get the Debilitators cranked up, heh, heh. Know what I'm saying? Catch ya later . . ."

And with that, Allfox! hung up. I could imagine him in a blood-spattered gown in the operating theater, leaning over some unfortunate with the scalpel floating betwixt brain and knee cap, my vicious songs bouncing around the white-tiled room as the surgeon tried to make up his mind. Allfox!, a wild gleam in his eye, unsure of what day of the week it was.

I never heard from him again, which was okay by me. And that white devil cocaine gradually slipped out of the pop music world and found its logical niche as crack and burrowed down into the substrata of society—right down there with the poverty-stricken blacks and Hispanics, leaving them to dream of the Evening Before Pill. Who knows, maybe Heckle and Jeckle got the formula right and it's out there now, being sold as a chaser to the little vials of rock. I'm not that interested anymore. Now a pill that could take you forward . . . hm, there's a thought . . .

"I truly relish natural acts of what people call disaster. To me, they're divine. . . . The visual beauty of a tornado just bowls me over. I also love hurricanes and floods and that kind of stuff. It's beautiful to me. . . . Not to be lighthearted about it, but it's very amusing to watch the world crumble."

—ANTHONY KIEDIS, THE RED HOT CHILI PEPPERS

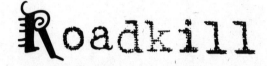

# Roadkill

**PART 10**

# Punk Rock Tours America, or, the Sex Pistols' Road to Nowhere

By the time the Sex Pistols undertook their one and only U.S. tour in January of 1978, the musical revolution that the English foursome had set in motion had taken Britain by storm, even if it had yet to make a large-scale impression on American audiences.

But all was not well in the Pistols' camp. While the band's four U.K. singles and their album *Never Mind the Bollocks, Here's the Sex Pistols* had been bestsellers as well as significant cultural events, the media firestorm stirred up by manager Malcolm McLaren's hype-mongering was spinning out of control, with the sensationalistic scrutiny that now accompanied the band's every move overshadowing the music.

Meanwhile, the band's internal chemistry had grown increasingly combustible. Though Johnny Rotten had had no prior band experience when McLaren recruited him to front the band, the singer, rather than falling into line as a compliant vessel for McLaren's media-terrorist vision, had quickly taken to his role as performer and songwriter. Rotten's fierce independence—and his growing disenchantment with his manager's increasingly cartoonish conceptual schemes—was proving to be a formidable threat to McLaren's dominance of the band.

While Rotten's less iconoclastic bandmates, guitarist Steve Jones and drummer Paul Cook, generally remained loyal to McLaren, Rotten, Jones, and Cook were united in their increasing frustration with bassist Sid Vicious. Though he could barely play his instrument, the trouble-prone Vicious—a longtime friend of Rotten's and a highly visible Pistols hanger-on who'd replaced original member Glen Matlock in March of 1977—had come to take his notoriety as rock outlaw a bit too seriously, developing a serious heroin addiction that was in full swing by the end of 1977.

So it was that the Sex Pistols seemed on the verge of self-immolation by the time its American record company, Warner Bros., prevailed on the band to tour the States to promote their album's U.S. release. From the start, the label encountered resistance from McLaren, who seemed curiously reluctant to have his band promote its product in the world's most lucrative market. McLaren initially insisted that the Pistols only tour in the southern United States. He eventually relented and allowed the band to be booked for shows in the eastern United States and in San Francisco, but still insisted that the band not play in the media centers of New York and Los Angeles (which also happened to be where most of the band's stateside fans were).

The tour's first date was originally scheduled for December 30th in Pittsburgh. But on the 29th, when the group attempted to board its flight at London's Heathrow Airport, the band members were denied U.S. visas due to their prior criminal records (Rotten for a minor drug charge, Jones for burglary, Cook for theft, and Vicious for assaulting a police officer). Warner Bros. hired a high-powered immigration lawyer to help, but by the time the affair was sorted out, it was too late to salvage the tour's first leg—which was to include dates in such northern cities as Chicago, Cleveland, and Pittsburgh, as well as a high-profile national TV appearance on *Saturday Night Live*.

This left only the second leg of dates in the South and Southwest, coinciding nicely with McLaren's original notions to have the band play exclusively in the South and prompting much speculation that McLaren (who didn't bother to apply for the band's U.S. visas until the 29th) intentionally engineered the situation. McLaren—whose prior involvement with the New York Dolls gave him experience dealing with junkie rockers—may have been desperate to keep Vicious away from the drug-related temptations he would be certain to encounter in New York and L.A.

Here is a capsulized account of the Sex Pistols' adventures on the road in America:

**Tuesday, January 3, 1978.** The Sex Pistols finally arrive at New York's JFK Airport, where sixty photographers and journalists await them outside of customs. Mindful of the group's contentious encounters with the English media, their handlers work to keep reporters as far from the musicians as possible. After shaking the unwanted press entourage, the band is ushered (in a plush tour bus rented for the occasion) to another terminal to catch a flight to Atlanta, site of the tour's first show. When the band arrives in Atlanta at one A.M. that night, only one journalist is on hand to greet them. A less luxurious tour bus takes the band to the Squire Motor Inn—a modest motel on the outskirts of town, its location chosen to keep the band members (particularly Vicious) out of trouble. Rotten and Vicious rebel and head for a nearby strip club, but the excursion is cut short by the pair's first encounter with redneck cops, who so intimidate them that they sheepishly return to the motel.

**Wednesday, January 4.** Despite Warners' efforts to keep the band away from the press, NBC-TV's *Today Show* has sent correspondent Jack Perkins to Atlanta to cover the tour's opening and interview the band. That afternoon, Warner Bros. publicity chief Bob Merlis rents a suite at an upscale downtown hotel for the occasion, but the band splits after Perkins refuses to give Jones the five dollars he demanded to do the interview. Later, Vicious is lectured for grabbing a female Warner Bros. publicist's crotch. Warner special projects director Ted Cohen's attempt to take the band to dinner at a local steak house devolves into an orgy of destruction. In the men's room at the restaurant, a drunken Vicious picks a fight with one of the burly bodyguards hired for the tour, who lets Vicious punch him before losing his temper and repeatedly slamming his head against the bathroom sink. The band still has yet to play a note of music in the United States.

**Thursday, January 5.** By the day of the tour's first show, Vicious, cut off from his usual drug suppliers, is suffering from the early stages of heroin withdrawal. At some point, he steals a watch from Rory Johnston, McLaren's U.S. management representative, to sell for drug money. Clearly Boogie Tiberi, the Pistols' English roadie entrusted with the all-important job of keeping tabs on the wayward bassist, needed reinforcements. Therefore, road manager Noel Monk (an American touring vet hired by Warner Bros. to minimize the chaos the tour is expected to engender) began posting a guard outside Vicious's room to keep him in and the rest of the world out.

While Vicious is wrapped up in his deteriorating physical condition, the rest of the band is nervous and excited about that evening's sold-out show at the Great Southeast Music Hall, a club located in a sterile shopping mall. Along with the fans, journalists, photographers, and TV crews that comprise the night's crowd, there's also a noticeable police presence—thanks to local moral watchdogs who've informed the vice squad that the band's set will include live sex acts and loaded guns. Also present are vice-squad cops from Memphis, the next city on the tour, and a camera crew led by *High Times* magazine founder and notorious political agitator/crackpot Tom Forcade, who will follow the band for most of the remainder of the tour, attempting— mostly unsuccessfully, but with increasingly bizarre levels of desperation— to bribe his way into gaining access to the band in order to shoot a documentary of the tour, and to exploit Vicious's drug dependency in order to get an interview with the bassist.

Despite the apprehensions of band, crew, and various outside parties, the show is a success and no one is injured. Afterwards, Vicious breaks away from his minders and disappears into the night, looking to score. Meanwhile, McLaren has arrived in town, but doesn't show up for the concert. For the remainder of the tour, he will keep his distance from the band, rarely attending shows and always traveling by plane rather than on the band's tour bus.

**Friday, January 6.** By the time the band is to catch its flight for Memphis, Vicious is still AWOL. They leave without him, in the hope that the road crew will dig him up in time for the night's concert at Memphis's Taliesyn Ballroom. Other band members visit Graceland. A barely conscious Vicious (who has indeed scored) does eventually turn up, with the words "I Wanna Fix" carved by self-inflicted knife wounds into his chest. That night, before the show, Vicious disappears again. He is eventually found at the hotel, engaging in fisticuffs with a hotel security man who pulls a gun on the disoriented bassist, once again suffering withdrawal. By this point, the rest of his bandmates (even his longtime friend Rotten) are refusing to speak to the unstable, violence-prone Vicious. Noel Monk refuses to provide him with heroin, and his attempts to enlist Warners' aid in procuring methadone go unheeded; Monk will attempt to placate Vicious with Valium to ease his withdrawal symptoms.

Meanwhile, the 725-capacity venue has been oversold by about 500 tickets, so city fire marshals bar several hundred kids from the show, sparking fears of a riot and prompting the police to call in a SWAT team. The show itself suffers from muddy sound and features a brief late-set guest appearance from the local SWAT team, which, having finally dispersed the crowds of turned-away fans congregating outside, bursts into the club and quickly leaves.

After the show, band and crew drive all night to Texas in their new tour bus, which fans have already spray-painted with Pistols slogans and song titles. McLaren opts to fly first-class to the tour's next stop, San Antonio.

**Saturday, January 7.** The band and crew spend their day off in Austin, Texas, rather than San Antonio as planned, because of death threats received in conjunction with the following night's San Antonio performance. This has the added benefit of throwing the press and the ever-persistent *High Times* posse—whom McLaren has decided are actually agents of the CIA or some other government organization sent to cause havoc on the tour. The band's night off in Austin is relatively quiet and uneventful.

**Sunday, January 8.** The evening's gig, at Randy's Rodeo in San Antonio— once again seriously oversold—is the tour's first show at which the threat of violence seems genuine. Numerous fights break out in the crowd, and audience members throw debris at the stage throughout the band's set; a local sheriff is hit in the head with a bottle. Rotten—who is suffering from bronchitis due to ubiquitous air conditioning—persistently taunts the crowd. Vicious twice throws his bass at a heckler but succeeds only in injuring both a photographer and Ted Cohen. Following the show, a backstage food fight breaks out before the band begins its all-night drive to Baton Rouge, Louisiana.

**Monday, January 9.** Vicious is unaccounted for when the band's bus arrives in Baton Rouge. He is eventually found passed out in the bus lavatory. Later, he bathes for the first time on the tour. At a press conference in his suite, McLaren bemoans Warners' supposed lack of support and claims that the band is making a film and live album of the tour and is planning to play in Puerto Rico. Most observers agree that tonight's show, at Baton Rouge's Kingfish club, is the first on the tour in which the band's growing internal friction has adversely affected its performance. At one point, Vicious brings a female fan onstage; she has his pants down before the crew removes her.

**Tuesday, January 10.** During a meal break at a truckstop en route to Dallas—one of the rare occasions upon which the security-conscious Monk allows the band out of the bus rather than bringing their food back to the bus—Vicious taunts a truckstop waitress and vomits all over the men's-room wall. After arriving at Dallas's Greenleaf Hotel, the less-than-hygiene-conscious bassist is given a bath under the supervision of the security crew, for fear that he'll pass out and drown if left to bathe himself. At the band's show at Dallas's Longhorn Ballroom—a club founded by Western Swing pioneer Bob Wills and once managed by Jack Ruby—the local police and fire departments are out in force. So is the health department, in order to prevent fans from spitting.

The show itself finds the band in fine confrontational form, with Rotten—decked out in his best cowboy duds—enthusiastically taunting the "cowboy" audience. During the set, Jolene Hack, who's driven from San Francisco for the show, headbutts Vicious, giving him a bloody nose. The bloodied bassist responds to the attack by smashing a beer bottle over his amp and cutting up his chest, in the process ripping open an earlier self-inflicted wound on his arm. The band's set is filmed by a three-man camera crew commissioned by Warner Bros., but the footage proves unusable due to poorly synchronized sound. After the show, the cops intercede when Forcade and some hired goons attempt to rough up the uncooperative Monk. Monk later has to move quickly to prevent Vicious from driving off with the aforementioned Hack.

**Wednesday, January 11.** Band and crew drive directly from Dallas to tonight's venue, Cain's Ballroom in Tulsa, Oklahoma. The tensions within the band—between the increasingly frustrated and distrustful Rotten and the Cook/Jones/McLaren faction, and between Vicious and virtually everybody else—are such that by now Cook and Jones are traveling by plane with McLaren, while Rotten and Vicious travel by bus with the crew. That afternoon a fight erupts between Rotten—accusing his bandmates of creative complacency—and Jones, who resents Rotten's increasing dominance of the band and isn't particularly fond of the new songs the singer has been writing (some of which will later end up as key tracks on the first Public Image Ltd. album). When they reach the club, in the midst of a hailstorm, the band is greeted by religious protesters handing out pamphlets reading "There is a Johnny Rotten inside each of us and he doesn't need to be liberated—he needs to be crucified." Nonetheless, onstage the band seems to be going through the motions.

Later, after getting into an argument with Rotten during an otherwise-harmonious party in the hotel room of John Holmstrom—editor of the For-cade-associated *Punk* magazine—Vicious storms out. Later, he goes upstairs with a groupie and accidentally starts a fire by leaving a lit cigarette on a couch; he subsequently suffers a diarrhea attack while she performs oral sex on him, with the expected messy results.

**Thursday, January 12.** After a hotel breakfast which finds Vicious tossing his meal across the room in a withdrawal-inspired hissy fit, Cook and Jones fly with McLaren to the tour's final show, in San Francisco, while Rotten and Vicious continue to travel by bus with the crew. On the flight, McLaren informs Cook and Jones of his plan to have the band travel to Rio de Janeiro to record with notorious British train robber Ronnie Biggs.

**Friday, January 13.** Rotten, Vicious, and the road crew spend a night off in Los Angeles, making a brief, noisy visit to the Whisky-a-Go-Go; next, they head down the Sunset Strip to the Roxy, where Vicious jumps onstage with Hunt and Tony Sales' band. Meanwhile, in San Francisco, Cook and Jones do a drunken, abusive late-night interview on the adventurous radio station KSAN, one of the few U.S. stations actually playing Pistols music. While recording some station IDs prior to the live interview, Jones angrily stomps on a pair of headphones. During the catastrophically out-of-control live studio segment that follows, the two drunken musicians curse, insult callers and attempt to solicit sex from listeners.

**Saturday, January 14.** At a truckstop between L.A. and San Francisco, a trucker attempts to engage Vicious in conversation by putting out a cigarette in his palm, but is silenced when Vicious responds by slashing his own left hand with a steak knife. While Cook, Jones, and McLaren are staying at San

Francisco's luxurious Miyako Hotel, Rotten, Vicious, and the crew check in at the decidedly downscale Cavalier Motel in San Jose, about fifty miles outside of town. That afternoon, Rotten and Vicious are interviewed on KSAN, still reeling from its encounter with Cook and Jones the previous night. Rotten and Vicious, who have been promised new leather jackets if they behave themselves, manage to keep the four-letter words in check, instead spending most of the interview muttering vague complaints about America.

Shortly before showtime, McLaren and promoter Bill Graham—owner of that evening's venue, the Winterland, which at 5,400 seats is by far the biggest on the tour, and one of the largest the Pistols have ever played—argue over the show's opening acts. Graham has booked prominent local combos the Avengers and the Nuns—the first support bands on the tour possessing legitimate punk credentials—but McLaren has other ideas. McLaren insists that Graham add Negative Trend—whom local DJ/scenester (and future 415 and Sire Records head) Howie Klein had earlier described to McLaren as the worst band in town—to the bill, immediately before the Pistols' set. While the Avengers are on stage, McLaren (actually attending his first U.S. Sex Pistols show) shows up backstage with the members of Negative Trend (who had been in the audience) and their equipment. McLaren informs Graham that the Sex Pistols will not take the stage until Negative Trend have played, but backs down when the formidable Graham strongly suggests that they compromise and have the band play after the Pistols.

The Pistols—who by this point are not speaking to each other—play a rousing if sour-spirited set, filmed by a Warner Bros. camera crew and broadcast live on KSAN (with Vicious's amp turned off in the interest of musicality). The set ends with the last words uttered by Rotten onstage as a Sex Pistol, "Ever have the feeling you've been cheated?" Needless to say, Graham manages to clear the house before Negative Trend has a chance to get to the stage.

A postconcert party is attended by no Sex Pistols; Rotten later will claim that he was refused admittance. The disgusted band members do find time for a shoot with *Rolling Stone* photographer Annie Leibovitz. At some point during the evening, someone casually mentions McLaren's Brazil scenario to Rotten, who claims that that's the first he'd heard of it. Rotten argues with Cook and Jones about the plan, refusing to participate and insisting that Vicious won't either. But the singer (who, like Vicious, has barely spoken with McLaren during the tour) encounters considerable difficulty in gaining access to the manager to register his disapproval. Meanwhile, Vicious, after a heated confrontation with McLaren, who refuses to give him drug money, disappears with Jolene Hack, who is back in San Francisco, and later that night is spotted by Klein at a party, half-conscious, in a closet.

**Sunday, January 15.** At Hack's apartment, Vicious suffers a heroin over-dose. He passes out and turns blue before Rory Johnston and Boogie Tiberi roust him into some semblance of consciousness. Johnston's attempt to get a local acupuncturist to treat Sid's drug dependency goes awry when Vicious (who seems unaware that the tour is over, or that the band has splintered) at-tempts to trash the acupuncturist's office.

That night, Klein interviews Cook and Jones on the San Jose station KSJO, but the session ends up much the same as the pair's profanity-laden KSAN interview. Half an hour into the show, Jones disappears with a groupie, leaving Cook to finish the interview on his own. The next day the station fires Klein.

**Monday, January 16.** Rotten finally gets the chance to confront McLaren about the Brazil plan, which the singer now suspects was concocted as part of a plan to oust him from the band. Rotten has already declared the Sex Pistols finished, though he does attempt to talk Cook and Jones into firing McLaren and attempting to keep the band together. But the drummer and guitarist re-affirm their loyalty to their manager.

**Epilogue.** Cook, Jones, and McLaren depart for Rio de Janeiro and their rendezvous with Biggs. Rotten is temporarily stranded in San Francisco with little money, no passport, no plane ticket, and without most of his posses-sions (which had been left on the tour bus and lost). Warner Bros. has to bail the singer out of the hotel and provide him with a plane ticket home. John-ston takes Vicious to L.A. where he is given two days' worth of methadone. Consuming all of the methadone on the flight back to New York, Vicious overdoses and spends a few days in a Manhattan hospital before returning to London and falling back into heroin addiction with girlfriend Nancy Spun-gen.

Cook, Jones, and McLaren's rendezvous in Rio with Biggs will yield the in-name-only Sex Pistols single "No One Is Innocent." The drummer and gui-tarist will (under McLaren's aegis) record several tracks under the Pistols banner for the soundtrack to the embattled film opus *The Great Rock 'n' Roll Swindle* and will briefly consider continuing with vocalist Edward Tudor-Pole (later of Tenpole Tudor). But the Sex Pistols are, for all intents and pur-poses, finished. The band never makes up the East Coast dates postponed from the first leg of the U.S. tour, and a Scandinavian tour that was scheduled to follow the North American trek never takes place.

Back in London, Rotten (who has reassumed his real name, John Lydon) will briefly attempt to involve Vicious in his new project, Public Image Ltd., but the bassist's drug problems make further collaboration impossible. Lydon will subsequently mount a successful legal challenge to the band's management contract, suing McLaren and his former bandmates to recover his share of the band's earnings. The events that will later befall Vicious in New York assured there would never, *ever* be a Sex Pistols reunion gig.

Compiled from issues of ROLLING STONE; *Rotten: No Irish, No Blacks, No Dogs* by John Lydon with Keith and Kent Zimmerman; and *12 Days on the Road: The Sex Pistols and America* by Noel E. Monk and Jimmy Guterman.

*"I never really liked the Sex Pistols because they were a heavy-metal band."*

—EDWYN COLLINS

# Country Dick Montana's Rules of the Road

On November 8, 1995, the unforgettable Country Dick Montana—drummer, vocalist and chief hell-raiser with San Diego's Beat Farmers—died with his boots on, on-stage in front of a sold-out crowd. This is the code that he lived by.

Hi! I'm Country Dick Montana and I get paid to act like I'm eleven! I just finished a six-week tour of Canada and the Midwest and I can't wait to get back out there in those un-airconditioned vans full of hung-over Beat Farmers filling the air with involuntary responses to the outrageously violent ride (bad roads, worse shocks) while constantly arguing about some music you hate that's distorting the crappy little speakers that cut out on every bump after zero sleep 'cause we had to leave real early to be interviewed on the radio by some dickhead that got stuck covering for the *one guy* who'd ever heard of us who split 'cause his dog was havin' puppies and he's got the only copy of our product that anyone's ever seen so we climb back in the van and Joey snaps the base of the passenger seat in half which inspires a cry of "I *told* you that would happen, you *fuck!*" and most of my fresh Whopper to miss most of his face and splatter 'cross the driver's side of the van Jerry washed just *this morning* as we head down to the border to enjoy our four-hour momentum break while the bastards rifle through every square inch a few times more than they need to make us miss the soundcheck for where we star tonight as the only "non-local heavy metal" band but Rolle, seeking more distinction, takes so much Valium he can't remember pushin' me into the black hole at the side of the stage where the stairs were on the other side but luckily the corner of the monitor board stepped in to break my fall and crack a rib which I knew bummed-out my kidneys 'cause they were workin' the first two weeks of this tour but had finished passin' the stone two days before I met this rib that just 'bout cried thinkin' of how much fun they all coulda had workin' me together in that van . . . Ahh. . . . But enough about me . . . *Let's get you packed!*

Crack open a beer. Grab that suitcase and listen up, 'cause *this is important*: always assume that *whatever you take out there will be lost, broken, or stolen*. So leave all precious items buried in the yard (and don't forget where).

All right, toss *all* your medical supplies, vitamins, lotions, sprays—whatever's in the bathroom—into the suitcase. Be *sure* to include *every single pain pill you can get yer hands on!* Don't ask—*take!* Trust me, it's worth the bitching out.

You will also need:

1 million cassettes and CDs (124,712 for misplacing; 91,039 for givin' away; 380,000 for thieves; 250,000 for breakage; 197,457 for throwin' out windows; 4 for playin'; rest for layin' 'round the floor)

*All* your clothes

1 cheap camera that your roommate probably won't even miss

2 rolls of duct tape

Most of a roll of somebody's stamps

1 rabbit's foot, 1 mojo bag, and 1 suitcase full of good luck candles

2 comfortable shoes

Everybody's sedatives

A copy of the "Beat Farmers' Bowl Report"—a detailed rating of North American rest rooms in categories ranging from acoustics to seat condition and water temperature. It'll become your best friend.

1 Swiss army knife

4 skin mags

An ice chest

2 pairs of sunglasses, 1 to hunt around for several times a day and 1 to replace the ones that just blew off when ya stuck yer dumb head out the van window

1 "Do not disturb" sign

5 international symbols for radioactivity

A condom

Some Super Glue and an *extra large, all-purpose rock-solid alibi.*

*Bonus tip—if you're flying, pack a load of liquor into your carry-on *before* arriving at the airport!

## Do:

**1.** Remember which states currently hold "immature" (under seven years of age) warrants for your arrest.

**2.** Drink the local brew—and *love* it!

**3.** Practice peeing in Bud bottles and shitting without sitting.

**4.** Know how to say "rest room," "bar," "taxi," and "hospital" in the tongue of wherever the hell you are.

**5.** Have the front desk refund you the $1.80 you may lose to that vending machine, now that you've got it.

**6.** Be in a country & western band whenever you get pulled over. It also helps to have an older brother suspended from the Chicago force for driving around town with his partner's suspected killer cuffed to the back bumper, *and dig this*: in the South, you can drink and drive naked in a carved ivory convertible with SATAN LOVES YOU painted on the sides and a senior citizen tied to the hood *if you're related to the quarterback*. So *be* that.

**7.** Save your receipts.

## Do not:

**1.** Write any songs about being "on the road."

**2.** Even *think* about driving or getting laid in England.

**3.** Open the mini bar.

**4.** Order spaghetti at Denny's.

**5.** Pee on toilet seats (I *will* find you!)

**6.** Tell Mojo Nixon your room number.

**7.** Direct morning rush-hour traffic in Omaha with your pants around your ankles.

**8.** Leave your crack pipe on the dash.

**9.** Take souvenirs from the crypt of a voodoo queen—remember that zombies are even worse drivers than drunks.

**10.** Ask a cop where the nearest drive-thru liquor store is, what it's gonna take to get a message through his thick skull, how long the Village People have been broken up, or for change back from your five dollar bribe.

**11.** Use someone else's bus sock.

# Random advice:

**1.** Harness the power of the guest list! It can cover your forgetful ass by being stocked with celebrities ("Of *course,* I put you on the list! Just tell 'em you're Nancy Reagan and John Wayne Bobbit!") and *save you money* ("How much would it be if I put you + 2 on the list?").

**2.** The party's in the roadies' room.

**3.** The sketchier you are, the better you'll look in artist's renderings.

**4.** You should be able to see more than just your face in the rearview mirror.

**5.** Onstage only play half of your most popular song and act all compromised about it in an English accent that's regularly dropped, and be clear about nothing except your genius and worshipability.

**6.** In interviews, remember to drift off in mid sentence, avoid eye contact by three to four inches, go to the bathroom for half an hour at least once, refuse to answer questions concerning your name, place, and date of birth, weight, height, and one more thing selected at random and emotionally produce a photo of a dog that died when you were four. In England you should be from Texas and animatedly hostile towards these "tea-timin', sync-lipped lard feeders" that won't let you have a gun 'cause they're "wimpy-whiny-wipers of royal weenie-wackage that couldn't handle a drive-by drum machine memory bank trashing!" In the rest of Europe, just be from Texas.

**7.** For a duration-length, maid-free environment, combine surprise and high volume with a pottymouth tizzyfit highlighted by aggressive nudity.

**8.** Even if you don't drink and hate tomato juice—start each day with a bloody Mary! You'll see.

## Dealing with your accommodations:

Always demand a room on the top floor, and quickly establish yourself as the biggest problem in the joint (minor and even *major* problems mean *nuthing* to a *total disaster!*). If you are *not* the biggest problem on the premises, then you're probably up against a preexisting condition of considerable nastiness.

It is *wrong to purposely damage your room or anything in it*. However, if management and staff are *evil,* or you realize that your room sits above *violated burial grounds,* then what you need is a project of *untraceable origin* to keep your mind clear of "bad things."

(Note: *Do not try this at home!*)

March to the market and pick up a zip-lock baggie and one whole, uncleaned fresh fish. Now, return to your room and place your uncleaned and securely zip-locked tight aquatic bomb behind the grill of the Time-Release Natural Disaster Storage Unit (a.k.a. the Heater Vent). Mother Nature will take over from here, as she proves that although Fishy may be quite *dead,* he's still not quite *done*! And sure enough, after a feverish week or so of supernatural gas-accelerated frenzy, the highly pressurized action becomes *uncontainable* in a dramatically explosive manner so sensorily devastating that even *evil* gets the hell out!

Of course, *you'll* be long gone by that time, or at least you'd *better* be!

It's checkout time, so *haul ass!!*

*"Cops would pull us over and instead of throwing us into jail, they'd feel sorry for us, shaking their heads."*

**—PAUL LEARY, BUTTHOLE SURFERS**

# Chris Connelly's Top Ten Shameful Onstage and Touring Indulgences and Mistakes

Both as a solo artist and as a member of such combos as Ministry, Revolting Cocks, Pigface, and Murder Inc., vocalist/multi-instrumentalist Chris Connelly has long been a familiar presence on the industrial-music scene.

**1.** Playing the song "Get Down" for forty-six minutes straight (Revolting Cocks, Paris, 1991)

**2.** Being so hungover I wept (Revolting Cocks, Amsterdam, 1991)

**3.** Band, crew, and audience melting into one (Revolting Cocks, Glasgow, 1991; my mother in attendance)

**4.** Tripping so hard onstage I was chased and surrounded by my own lyrics (Pigface, Toronto, 1991)

**5.** Hiccuping all the way through an encore (Revolting Cocks, Melbourne, 1990)

**6.** Falling asleep between verses (Chris Connelly/William Tucker, Eugene, Oregon, 1994)

**7.** Retiring onstage (Chris Connelly Band, El Paso, 1992)

**8.** Throwing up onstage after smoke-bomb attack (Revolting Cocks, San Francisco, 1990)

**9.** Asking fans to buy me drinks (Chris Connelly/William Tucker, any given show)

**10.** Whole band tripping too hard to play (Revolting Cocks, Chicago, New Years' Eve, 1988)

# Rodney Anonymous's Top Ten Reasons Why Touring Sucks

Road gripes aside, singer Rodney Anonymous has spent much of his "adult" life recording and touring with the Dead Milkmen.

**1.** You realize that those drooling idiots wearing Sonic Youth T-shirts were not just a local phenomenon

**2.** Your bass player hears, "Mah pah sez we gotta get married" at least three times a week

**3.** You know the number of times that the boom mic can be spotted in the movie *The Beastmaster*

**4.** The hotel night manager recognizes you as the one who pissed in the ice machine

**5.** Those women dropping their kids outside at the club look an awful lot like the Go-Go's

**6.** Your van only breaks down in small Southern towns

**7.** You find yourself playing on "Beer-drinking homicidal rednecks get in free with proof of gun" night

**8.** Marc Singer, star of *The Beastmaster,* hogs the mosh pit

**9.** You're joined onstage by Al "Year of the Cat" Stewart for a six-hour jam

**10.** HBO's *Beastmaster* marathon cuts heavily into your draw

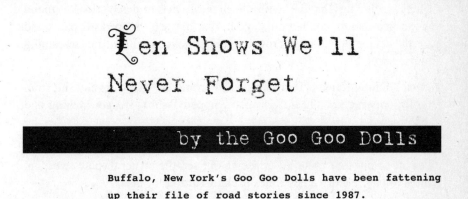

# Ten Shows We'll Never Forget

## by the Goo Goo Dolls

Buffalo, New York's Goo Goo Dolls have been fattening
up their file of road stories since 1987.

**International Hall of Fame,** Charlotte, North Carolina. Don't know if it's
still there, but if you meet the owner you'll know where they got the idea for
the banjo player in *Deliverance*.

**Church's Tip Top Cafe,** Huntsville, Alabama. Summed up by Buck Owens's
song "My Red Neck, White Sox and Blue Ribbon Beer." Don't know how
24-7 Spyz got out of this place alive.

**The Electric Banana,** Pittsburgh, Pennsylvania. After bar-backing at gun-
point, we were paid for one blistering punk-rock show with a case of circa-
1971 Schaefer's, a.k.a. "The One Beer to Have After You Drank Everything
Else." Only hope for this place is that it may fall off the cliff it's attached to.
P.S. Don't eat the Rude Judy Burger.

**Chuy's,** Tempe, Arizona. Very plush bar in a quaint historic district. Looked
like a padded cell for Merv Griffin.

**OKayz Corral,** Madison, Wisconsin. Accurate re-creation of the set from
*Bonanza*. Our dorky roadie fell through the stage.

**Some heavy metal bar,** Raleigh, North Carolina. After driving eighteen
hours to make the show, we find out we're opening for—get this—Extreme.
Undaunted by the angry jeers of the crowd, we play on valiantly, but to no
avail nor applause. Resorted to low vaudevillian jabs at the headliner to make
ourselves feel better.

**Some heavy metal bar,** Fayetteville, North Carolina. We were scheduled to open for Extreme again. When we showed up we were paid $200 and told not to bother playing. We removed letters from the marquee so it read TONITE IN CONCERT R E M.

**Max's on Broadway,** Baltimore, Maryland. Seven people showed up that evening, including The Guy with the Biggest Dick in the World. We found this out because he jumped on stage during our set, dropped his pants and gave the scarce but stunned crowd a genital helicopter, then ran screaming into the street.

**Y-Not,** Wichita, Kansas. Tour manager to promoter: "If I want any shit from you, I'll squeeze your head." He got a ripped T-shirt. We got nothing and liked it.

**Confetti's,** Albuquerque, New Mexico. Last-minute booking takes us 500 miles off of our tour route. After seeing our set, the owner displays weapon, refuses to pay. We drive 500 miles back to our tour route.

"I was an altar boy for four years. . . . I liked the suits. The black dress with the white thing over the tops. I figured if I had to go to church, I might as well be onstage."

—GREG DULLI, AFGHAN WHIGS

# The Smears' Top Ten Road Laxatives

The Smears are three young women from Bloomington, Indiana, who have been known to play "crotch-grabbing, beer-swilling punk rock."

1. Kansas
2. 10 minutes till set time
3. Passing the last rest stop for 20 miles
4. Potholes
5. Free keg beer
6. Locked bathroom doors
7. Unknown burrito
8. Well whiskey
9. Any warm foodstuff from a gas station
10. Truck stop coffee (hundred-mile brew)

# The Many Faces of Zuzu's Petals, or, Sybil Does Dallas

by Laurie Lindeen

Laurie Lindeen sings, plays guitar, and travels with the Minneapolis all-gal trio Zuzu's Petals, who've managed to record and release two albums between road trips.

Road stories—yawn—everybody's got them. Traveling musicians are always trying to one-up their peers with ever-more-shocking tales of arrests, accidents, breakdowns (vehicular and nervous), stolen gear, practical jokes, sexual exploits, scummy promoters, substance abuse, equipment abuse, and blown-up sound systems.

As for gender-specific experiences—snore—we've got thousands. Yes, our cycles sync up. Yes, we have been repeatedly patronized and discriminated against. And yes, we initially received a curious amount of attention by virtue of our voluptuous birthrites. Big hairy deal. It's not as if our perky breasts have been menacing the coveted pages of ROLLING STONE or anything. To hell with road stories and gender; they leave me catatonic with boredom.

To me, the real meat lies in the drama of self-preservation that occurs when subjected to less-than-ideal circumstances (i.e., straddling no-budget touring while in indie hell), in which one's quality of life often hinges upon the quality of public rest rooms. You are in the real external world, cold and harsh, without a safety net or a calling card. You struggle with the elements daily. Regardless of thunderstorm, blizzard, hurricane, or tornado, your livelihood depends upon getting to the next gig. Your van becomes a person with a name. You coo and cajole its dysfunctional innards, gently caressing the dashboard and cheering it on. You are at its mercy, and like most things born in

1979 (the year of the Knack), it needs a lot of love. You see, smell, hear, feel and—unfortunately—taste Detroit, Des Moines, Albany, and Tampa. Inhabitants wear their town's history in their faces, hands, but mostly in their eyes. You are performing every night, giving away pieces of your soul, and you are extremely vulnerable. You are not immune to your sixteen-year-old six-months pregnant waitress with the kind eyes, nor to the down-and-out alcoholic slumped over the bar as you arrive for soundcheck. You are a soldier at war—conquering one city, hobbling wounded and defeated from another. It's boot camp, and no amount of daydreaming about the officers club can filter out the ugliness.

Numbing yourself with vice and denial generally results in lost years, problems at home, and psychiatric problems that you cannot afford to remedy. Our band manages to cope, thanks to the development of nice healthy multiple personality complexes. Some of these personas have been useful in our day-to-day survival, some are entertaining, and some get us into a lot of trouble. As with all multiple personality complexes, we have no control over who is going to emerge, where, when, or why.

**The Hard-Boiled Wisecrackin' Good-Time Girl** is the one who got us into this mess to begin with. She was the dominant personality in the Petals' early years. She's bawdy, a little dumb, and in touch with her masculine side. She's been known to slap an ass or two, and has been overheard muttering, "Give mama some sugar." She bellied up to the bar, and stumbled onto the stage (she thinks she's in the Replacements circa 1983). She'll talk to anyone, especially if they're buying. She strikes ballads from the set in favor of New York Dolls covers. She wears cutoffs, ancient rock T-shirts, and cowboy boots. She has a filthy mind, a gutter mouth, orders bacon for breakfast and loves Zep. She's a Marlboro-smokin', gum-chewin' tough cookie that we don't see that much of anymore. I miss her spirit, not the hangovers. She lives on in our sarcastic sneers, raspy voices, and low throaty chuckles.

**The Phony** is our prevailing businesswoman. She flashes her fakey smile to the audience, lying through her gritted teeth, "Thanks a lot, you guys are the greatest." She speaks politely and articulately to promoters, managers, lawyers, record companies, and booking agents, and kisses the ass of anyone important (potentially helpful to our career). She pretends to listen to people who want to talk about themselves and acts like she's interested. The Phony says "good show" to the Pearl Jam Jr. band that just opened. She wears a lot of makeup and digs breathy-voiced little-girl singers who have eclipsed her success. In fact, she wishes ill on no one. Of course she does, she's a big phony.

**The Snot** was born on family car trips. She cut her teeth on the hyperhistorical bicentennial vacation when Tatum O'Neal in "Paper Moon" was the ideal role model. She's terminally bored, and refuses to get out of the van to look at Niagara Falls. She says "no thank you" in a disgusted monotone to everything whether she wants it or not. The Snot has been known to crinkle up her nose and pinch. She cannot be bothered with writing postcards to loved ones who think that her life is exciting (she'll assure you it's not). She's one of our best songwriters, so we have to endure her existence. She's mercilessly self-effacing, therefore entitling her to poke fun at everyone else. She knows that you'd like to kick her ass, but that does not deter her insolent scorn of all things mundane. She borrows money from the measly band fund to purchase items she doesn't really want. She is suspicious of the audience and jealous of her more-successful peers. She has a picky palate (a nightmare in England). She finds humor only in how much fun she isn't having.

**The Crab** is a shade darker than the Snot in terms of temperament. She has a chronically knitted brow and is asked repeatedly, "Are you mad?" Of course she's mad; last night she played in a bomb shelter that reeked of raw sewage, and in a concrete Motel 6 room, with the TV chained to the wall, laid her head down listening to a domestic brawl in the room next door. Not only that, the line is busy every time she tries to phone home, and she is starting to break out. The Crab is a defense mechanism against discomfort, which is generally experienced while getting too much attention—or none at all. The Crab also protects a very shy girl: No one wants to talk to a stone-faced sourpuss. Thus, when paralyzed with an attack of shyness, a scowl can deter potential social intercourse. The Crab is a lady of few words, thank heavens. She has been known to lie on her back prostrate during soundcheck, staring blankly at the spitball-covered ceiling while wondering aloud in a robotic monotone, "What am I doing here?"

**The Unapproachable PMS-Addled Skag** is a mean, ugly bitch. She is Cruella DeVille's soul sister, with ice water pounding through her veins and a lump of coal for a heart. She won't dress up for an audience, and she passes on a shower (it might make her feel better). In the darkest of all moods, she intends to fly with it, causing misery to all who cross her destructive path. She can easily go an entire day without uttering a single syllable. She piles black eye makeup on her pimply, greasy face. Basically, she is irrational and insane with a festering hatred for all humanity burning in her murderous soul. For her, nothing is funny or worth laughing at. Her inner dialogue reads simply, "Shut up, I hate you." It is far too late for that megadose of B vitamins, and her concerned and calmer sisters try to intervene as she rushes to the phone to torture her boyfriend. She has called the audience "a lovely group of corpses." Onlookers marvel at how much better she looks in photographs. I pity the fool who said that, now get me another burger before I kill you.

**The Midwestern Hick** is a breath of fresh air compared to her premenstrual sister, though she can be thoroughly embarrassing. She's a big bouncy what-the-hey farm girl with a toothy grin. She loves Nazareth, Deep Purple,

Head East, Heart, and John Denver, for that matter. You may have seen her on the back cover of *Kiss Alive*. While on dates, she drank blackberry brandy and threw up at rock concerts. She got hickeys at cheerleading camp, and Cheap Trick played at her prom. She knows every inch of the Wisconsin Dells intimately and is enthusiastic to eat at Hardee's. Bless her white-trash cracker heart, she's a stoner with a gut. She's itching to go to a mall and buy stirrup pants. She usually graces us at the most inappropriate of times (i.e., when a degree of elegance is required). She enjoyed an entire month on the road with Adam Ant ("What was it like on *Northern Exposure*?"). Hopefully, she has some degree of irresistible charm because we can't make her go away.

Deeply seated in denial, the **I-Feel-Alive Idiot** surfaces when we are faced with probable death. Death comes knocking at our door regularly in the form of severe weather conditions during long drives. Sometimes the Idiot wants to drive through the mountains during a blizzard, marveling at the vehicles ahead as they slowly career into a ditch. Usually she is not driving (the Crab is), though she is chatty, cheerful, and excellent company throughout the crisis. She may also grace us when her love life is in the toilet, her career is on a downward spiral, or it is about four weeks into a tour and she is suffering from severe road-burn. Face radiant with the glow of near-death, she could care less about being late, misdirected, or unappreciated. She feels alive and says so often, much to the chagrin of her cohorts. Many a lucky two-person audience have seen her perform magic onstage.

Everyone is a little jealous of the **Health Nut.** She is a strict vegetarian subsisting on sugar-free cereal, fresh fruit, and salads. She does sit-ups, stretches before a show, jogs, swims, or at the very least walks. She removes her makeup before bed and medicates, rather than mutilates, her blemishes. She creeps out of the motel room early for a jog, clears her mind by reading a little of the Tao, and then rids herself of venom by writing her morning pages. Devoted to her regime, she can go too deep and become frightfully vain. Regardless, she takes a mysterious array of vitamins and watches her cigarette intake. She seems smug and superior to her slovenly sisters because she has discipline. One rarely sees her late into a tour.

**Tallulah Bankhead** is pure showbiz in the classic sense. She doesn't feel stupid bellowing "Hello dahhhling!" She cackles "What a dump!" (a line stolen from her nemesis Bette Davis) upon entering each seedy venue. She has big red lips and chain-smokes while ordering around everybody on the payroll or anyone affiliated with her upcoming performance. She is a soundman's nightmare. She has greasepaint in her blood, and she's dying for a martini. Wardrobe is very important to her, as she'll explain that Frank Sinatra does not sit down before a performance for fear that he'll rumple his suit. Not destined to win a Grammy in the near future, she's a bit of a hack who looks great and has more stage presence than she knows what to do with. Favoring sleek casual chic by day, she is pure lamé and sequins by night. She is not averse to saying things like, "I can't work like this," because she so craves the big time. She abhors grunge, and modern audiences who have not heard of her and so don't get it. Oblivious to temporary trends, she is far too busy to be bothered—it's a large task just trying to look—and be—fabulous. She recently attempted—to no avail—to attend a private soiree hosted by the Rolling Stones in New Orleans. No amount of "Don't you know who I am" 's and "Get me Ron Wood" 's would penetrate those goons at the door. If anyone could appreciate white-girl hacks with a bad case of the blues while looking like a million show-biz bucks, it would've been the Stones.

Some think that **the Lady** doth protest too much, but the Lady is the most sensitive of all of her alter egos. She's uptight—naturally, because her mere existence is threatened daily. She went to a young girls' etiquette-training course entitled "White Gloves and Party Manners." She's very polite, very unrock and was not raised to survive these vulgar conditions. Hyper-articulate with a vast vocabulary, she escapes by reading or writing long, heartfelt letters. She obsesses over physical flaws (tweezers are her best friend) and is repulsed by filth under her nails and the state of her calloused, distraught hands. Preferring Joni Mitchell and Carly Simon, the Lady adores comparing their James Taylor-inspired songs, quietly speculating and summarizing, and then applying it to her own life. Yes, she's "such a girl," and she enjoys being one. Her gag reflex is hypersensitive, and road odors offend her. After purchasing cruisewear in a St. Augustine, Florida, secondhand store, she laments that there is no appropriate place in her life to don these fine threads. In the bowels of truck-stop magazine racks, she can usually find *Vogue* and *Elle* hidden behind *Beaver* and *Screw*. Senses bruised, she finds it in her heart to at least appreciate the fact that truck stops are now equipped with capuccino makers. She views herself as a professional entertainer with a responsibility to dress accordingly—or is that just an excuse to justify her shopping addiction? You may see her in Denny's with curlers in her hair (once again, a professional necessity). She's terribly disappointed when she has to haul gear, which is twice daily. She likes the sink on the outside of the bathroom in the motel room, while dreaming of a hotel room with elevators and bellhops. She cries in front of the TV no matter what is on, and gets horribly homesick. The Lady jumps for joy in the cities inhabited by rich relations or grown-up-friends-with-lives, for she is assured of all the comforts. She collects recipes and believes that knitting will aid her when it's time to quit smoking. Soundcheck is a pain that interrupts her shopping, and showtime has been known to interfere with a lovely dinner.

As you might imagine, the van can get a trifle overcrowded with all these women popping in and out at their every whim. There is nothing worse than the I-Feel-Alive Idiot butting heads with the Unapproachable PMS-Addled

Skag, or the Midwestern Hick rattling the Lady's cage. In psychology these personas are referred to as defense mechanisms, as I understand it, and if that is indeed what they are, they are highly effective. The truth of the matter is that we are all cracked in the head—which you have to be to be in this business. Anyway, I must go now, because it is a snowy late December morning in Minnesota, and the Child can think of nothing else but purchasing soaps-on-ropes and sipping egg nog. On days like today there are no show-biz tramps haunting my psyche, just the pure delight in being home.

"For some reason, it's more fun to watch girls playing music at this point. When you see women playing, you kind of don't know what's going to happen, and maybe that's because they're more willing to make themselves vulnerable. Or not. I can be like, 'Fuck you, you expect us to be vulnerable, and we're not.' But still, the context for vulnerability is set up, merely because you're looking at girls onstage."

—KIM GORDON, SONIC YOUTH

# Swell's
# Top Ten Reasons
# to Go on Tour

**San Francisco's Swell describe themselves as three guys who believe that freedom is a good name for a candy bar.**

1. Catch up on reading

2. Discover new types of cheese

3. See interesting parts of the world, like Wyoming

4. Collect hotel keys

5. See how many days you can wear the same socks

6. Learn how to play the songs on your record, really

7. Because someone makes you do it

8. Sleep deprivation makes you very creative

9. Loading the equipment is good exercise

10. Don't have to make your bed for months

# Swell's
# Top Ten Reasons
# *Not* to Go on Tour

**1.** Too many names to remember

**2.** It's too far

**3.** Do you really want to get to know the other guys *that* well?

**4.** It smells

**5.** See interesting parts of the world, like Wyoming

**6.** Driving intoxicated is illegal in all fifty states now

**7.** Gas station food

**8.** The equipment is too heavy

**9.** Truck stop bathrooms while they are full of truckers after breakfast

**10.** No one's ever heard of you anyway

# Some Sweet Memories You Gave to Me

## IRA KAPLAN FONDLY RECALLS THE TWELVE WORST YO LA TENGO SHOWS

Since 1985, Hoboken, N.J.-based singer/guitarist (and former rock critic) Ira Kaplan has sung and played guitar—alongside his wife, drummer Georgia Hubley—in Yo La Tengo.

**1. Down Under, Boston, June 15, 1985.** Our first-ever out-of-town weekend concludes at this short-lived nightspot in Government Center, and—Jonathan Richman to the contrary—there is little rockin'. Both of the other bands on the bill were also playing elsewhere *the same night*—at a benefit.

**2. The Electric Banana, Pittsburgh, December 6, 1985.** Cognoscenti could challenge this show's appearance on this list, because at no time did the owner pull a gun on us.

**3. The Living Room, Providence, Rhode Island, June 27, 1986.** We had set up in front of other bands' gear before and have set up in front of other bands' gear since. But only on this night did we set up in front of two bands' gear—both including exclusively electric drum kits.

**4. J.C. Dobbs', Philadelphia, August 8, 1986.** Our first-ever tour kicks off in grand style as we are asked to use the headliner's drums. Despite the fact that Georgia's a lefty.

**5. Exit/In, Nashville, August 20, 1986.** We bring ex-roommate/ex-Raybeat Danny Amis on stage to play a surf instrumental, lowering the attendance to zero. (To this day, Lambchop's Kurt Wagner claims to have been there, and though I'm not calling him a liar, I stand by my count.)

**6. CBGB, New York, October 17, 1986.** Our bassist Stephan Wichnewski calls from London on the morning of the show to tell us he missed his flight home. Having already been threatened with a ban from CBGB's should we cancel (a long story), we turn to Chris Stamey, who miraculously (A) is awake at six-thirty A.M. and (B) agrees to help out, despite being called at six-thirty A.M. With Dave Rick on lead guitar, the lineup plays for the first and last time during our very excellent set.

**7. No Bar and Grill, Muncie, Indiana, November 3, 1987.** Always August shows up for their date a whole week early, are added to the bill, and outdraw us.

**8. Dingwall's, London, December 13, 1987.** Our first European tour comes to a smashing conclusion with our English debut, on the Dingwall's equivalent of audition night. The house soundwoman, seemingly convinced that Georgia is claiming to be left-handed merely to make extra work for her, refuses to set up drum mics. Our scheduled 20-minute set clocks in at a minute and a half, 40 seconds with the DJ's record still on. I know, because I have a tape of it.

**9. Theater Gallery, Dallas, February 5, 1988.** A freak snowstorm in Dallas, and—just our luck—the club has no heat. Eight people watch us stretch five songs into an hour—and request an encore. The club closes for good the next night.

**10. Fat Chance, Albuquerque, February 9, 1988.** Can this really just be four days later? House soundman decides we're not heavy enough to get a soundcheck. Georgia and I argue onstage during the third song. Georgia storms off, returning minutes later. When the fourth song evaporates in a barrage of monitor feedback, the soundman launches his attack:

> HIM: "Your guitar is too fucking loud."
> ME: "I think that's why we needed a soundcheck."
> HIM: "No. You needed a soundcheck."

We turn our backs and play three more songs that last 45 minutes. Afterwards, opinions range from "You suck" to "The best concert I ever saw—better than Ace Frehley, as good as the Eagles."

**11. The Lingerie, Los Angeles, February 19, 1988.** Wow, what a tour. Georgia and I barely escape with our lives when we go for a walk after our set, violating what has to be the most severe all-exits-final policy ever.

**12. The Gallery, Normal, Illinois, April 11, 1988.** Monday night. Academy-award Monday. I can't take any more.

**P.S.** I should point out that, in a real sense, the worst shows are the ones that don't stand out in any way—in which case none of these qualify.

# Ellen Stewart Presents Touring Do's and Don'ts

Booking agent Ellen Stewart lives happily in Hoboken, New Jersey, and makes every effort to associate only with those who are smarter than she is, so that they make her try harder.

I love all my bands, not only for their musical prowess but also for their innate sense of smarts when it comes to touring. I asked some of them to draw on their road experiences to come up with a list of do's and don'ts for neophytes.

**Rebecca Gates, the Spinanes**
DO: Check your equipment *every night* after you load your vehicle to make sure you have everything, merchandise included.
DON'T: Go on a long trip on your very first tour. It's harder than you think. Figure out the dynamics of traveling before you commit to a cross-country tour.
DO: Travel in a reliable vehicle. A broken van has bummed out many a trip.
DON'T: Drive while falling asleep. It may seem obvious, but a lot of folks try to be macho. Don't be afraid to be pull over, or to wake up somebody else. Be a wuss; it's healthy.

**Jason Arbenz, Throneberry**
DO: Bring bats, balls, Frisbees, etc., so truck stops and rest areas can become arenas for pent-up energies.

DO: Soundchecks when they're offered. They'll remind you that your cables are bad, or that your hi-hat stands, batteries, strings, or whatever need replacing and give you enough time to do something about it.

DO: Pay attention to the names of soundmen, promoters, hosts, techies, etc., and review names when you're together in the van. It doesn't take much to separate yourselves from the pack, courtesy-wise.

DO: Remember that random acts of kindness are always good for morale, and people in your own band make worthy recipients.

DO: Check in frequently via phone with your agent, label, manager, etc. Opportunities slip by if you're incommunicado.

DO: Suck out the poison in the event of snakebite.

DO: Have a good time. There are lots of people who'd love to do what you're doing. It's a privilege to get to play your music around the world, and the second you lose sight of that you should quit.

DON'T: Invite suspicion by covering your van with stickers that proclaim "I brake for hallucinations" or "Child molester on board."

DON'T: Flaunt your limited knowledge of the city you're playing in by making onstage references to WKRP in Cincinnati, the wind in Chicago, or Hardee's Frisco Burger in San Francisco. I guarantee they've heard it before.

DON'T: Leave your gear in the van in New York. Park it at this place on Lafayette between 3rd and 4th where it's cheap and safe.

DON'T: Take merchandise like CDs, cassettes, or T-shirts to Canada unless you're playing several shows. The time lost during border crossings, coupled with duties, tariffs, and whatnot, cancels out any meager profits from their sales.

DON'T: Leave home without a good working knowledge of *Spinal Tap* and *The Jerky Boys*. Together they are like a Hippocratic oath for musicians, and you'll surely draw upon their valuable teachings.

DON'T: Joke about drugs or weapons in airports.

DON'T: Let minor points of contention accumulate between you and your bandmates. If you do, don't be surprised when a litany of grievances is thrown back in your face on the day you miss load out because you were talking to the Hooper triplets.

### Mark Robinson, Air Miami

DO: Remember to get paid.

DON'T: Travel in the same vehicle with anyone else in your band.

DO: Eat at the most expensive restaurants you can find.

DON'T: Eat at the restaurant the club recommends you go to.

DO: Remember to put gas in your van every chance you get.

DON'T: Paint your van so it looks like you're in a band or something.

DO: Drink as much beer as humanly possible.

DON'T: Get into fights with drunken audiences.

DO: Read lots of books and see lots of movies.

DON'T: Talk to any crazy people at your shows (i.e. anyone).

DO: Stay at very nice, sane people's houses (not at hotels because they kick you out at noon).

DON'T: Accept any tour support from your record label. It's your money and you could spend it on better things like rent and food when you get home. Only a dumb band could lose money on tour. If you do insist on receiving tour support, at least spend it on limousines and champagne.

DO: Split duties evenly. Everyone should help to load in and load out unless someone's doing payout, etc.

DON'T: Forget to say thank you.

DO: Use the girls' bathroom. Boys: station a girl outside.

DON'T: Forget medicine, a pillow, stamps, condoms, and the folks at home.

### David Steed, Afghan Whigs road manager

DO: Go to Bozeman Hot Springs for a swim and a skin-tingling, sulfur-enriching spa. It's a few miles south of I-90 on Rt. 85. It breaks up the long ride through Montana.

DON'T: Go anywhere near the thin state of Indiana.

DO: Go and see Devil's Tower in northeast Wyoming. It's visible by taking U.S. 14 north of I-90. Everyone who makes a living at night needs a little Satanic influence.

DON'T: Go anywhere near the El Paso border checkpoints. Search and seizure lives at the border.

DO: Go to the Big Texan restaurant. It's the home of the sixty-four-ounce butt steak; if you can eat it with all the trimmings, it's free. I'm not sure where the hell it is in Texas, but look for the tall neon cowboy on the north side of the highway. Or just ask your bus driver; they all know where it is.

DON'T: Drive through Kansas during the day. All there is to see are a few tumblin' tumbleweeds.

DO: Go to the Cheetah III or the fabulous Gold Club when you're in Hot-lanta, Georgia. It's by far the finest nude dancing in America. No excuses; they're open 'til four A.M.

DON'T: Go to Philadelphia. What's there: A dirty river, a broken bell, and cobblestone streets. I can't remember anyone having anything good to say about Philly.

DO: Go to Prairie Dog Town in Montana. It's about eighty-five miles west of Billings on I-90.

DON'T: Drive through North Dakota. All the trees there grow upside-down.

DO: Drive through South Dakota and stop at Wall Drug. It's about fifty-five miles east of Rapid City on I-90 in Wall, South Dakota. They offer free ice water and a ten-cent cup of coffee. The coffee's free if you're a Vietnam vet. It's also a great place to stock up on batteries, film, and condoms.

DON'T: Drive fast through mountain passes at night. Black ice is real. You just can't see it because it's black at night and so is the road.

DO: Schedule a day off in New Orleans. This should be obvious, especially if you've been there before.

DON'T: Stop at the Sloss Furnaces National Historic Landmark in Birmingham, Alabama.

DO: Take a detour and go to Las Vegas. This is best done on an overnight drive when leaving California. The casinos are open all night and the approach to the lighted strip of Las Vegas Boulevard is a shot of pure adrenaline.

DON'T: Stop at the Alabama (the band) headquarters in Fort Payne, Alabama. It's the band's museum, fan club, mail-order operation, promotion department, conference room, June Jam office, souvenir shop, warehouse, music room, rehearsal hall and truck bay area. It's just minutes off I-59, but if you're like me, don't go there.

DO: Attend a Cubs game at Wrigley Field in Chicago. Sit in the bleachers if you can get the tickets.

DO: Some snow skiing in the spring.

DO: See Niagara Falls in the summertime.

DO: Take a day off in Manhattan anytime.

DO: Return home to your loved ones disease-free.

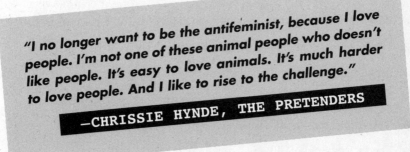

"I no longer want to be the antifeminist, because I love people. I'm not one of these animal people who doesn't like people. It's easy to love animals. It's much harder to love people. And I like to rise to the challenge."

—CHRISSIE HYNDE, THE PRETENDERS

# The Cranberries List the Best and Worst Things About Touring in America

On the road to pop stardom, Ireland's Cranberries have put in more than their share of U.S. mileage. We asked the foursome to share their most and least favorite aspects of stateside travel.

## Best:

1. People are generally friendly and open-minded.

2. The weather—lots of sunshine, no umbrellas or raincoats required.

3. Enthusiasm of gig-goers.

4. Wide variety of clothes, makeup, etc., and at half the price of home.

5. The education one can receive from a New York City cab driver.

6. (tie) Caesar salads and hotel swimming pools.

7. Pubs stay open all night (and that's handy when you're Irish).

8. *Beavis and Butt-head*, also *The Simpsons*.

9. The fact that people like our music over here.

10. The fact that Americans will never forget John F. Kennedy.

# Worst:

**1.** Roadside diners.

**2.** Truckers' waistlines.

**3.** New York City sandwiches are too big; you can't get your mouth around them.

**4.** Gun laws.

**5.** The importance of materialism, especially in L.A. (cars, cellulars, perfect teeth, silicone implants, etc.).

**6.** Bimbo women who misrepresent the intellect of women with brains, e.g. supermodels, titty-bar girls, and hookers.

**7.** Availability of hard drugs and the misperception of it being a cool thing to do.

**8.** Smells such as pretzels, hot dogs and other burning animals, and roadside fast-food restaurants.

**9.** The trendiness of the grunge scene.

**10.** The water gives you diarrhea (especially in New York City and L.A.).

# The Five Worst Rock-Club Rest Rooms in the United States of America

## ACCORDING TO THE MEN OF SUPERCHUNK

North Carolina indie-rock trendsetters Superchunk have spent plenty of time availing themselves of America's facilities.

**1. (tie) Trees, Deep Ellum, Texas; Galaxy Club, Dallas, Texas; Liberty Lunch, Austin, Texas**
The Monitor Guy at Liberty Lunch as much as told me that Texas men prefer to shit in front of other men. Trees in Deep Ellum is a sort of monument to this barbaric notion. The Galaxy Club down the street's no better.

**2. CBGB, New York City**
Kind of like Woody Allen's joke about life in *Annie Hall*. Impossible to reach and disappointing when you get there.

**3. Club Babyhead, Providence, Rhode Island**
I actually used this one in front of three grown men. None of us were Texans, however.

**4. Lake Boone Country Club, Raleigh, North Carolina**
Big room. No stalls. A nightmare from puberty.

**5. Twister's, Richmond, Virginia**
The toilet is inside a cell of chicken wire. This must be what jail is *really* like, Mr. Dulli.

# Going

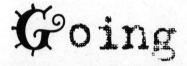

**PART 11**

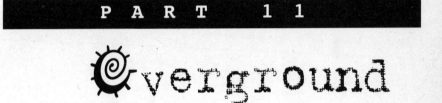

Overground

# $ub Pop Singles Club Releases

█████████████████████████████████████

From November 1988 to December 1993, the fledgling
Seattle-based Sub Pop label released a series of limited-edition subscription-only seven-inch vinyl singles that over the next five years proved to be a
revitalizing force in the grassroots American rock underground.

November 1988: **Nirvana,** "Love Buzz"/"Big Cheese" (pressing of 1000).

December 1988: **Mudhoney,** "Halloween"/**Sonic Youth,** "Touch Me I'm
Sick" (3000).

January 1989: **Flaming Lips,** "Strychnine"/"Drug Machine"/"What's So
Funny" (1500).

February 1989: **Les Thugs,** "Chess and Crimes"/"Sunday Time" (1500).

March 1989: **Helios Creed,** "Nothing Wrong"/"The Sky" (1500).

April 1989: **Afghan Whigs,** "I Am the Sticks"/"White Trash Party" (1500).

May 1989: **Mad Daddies,** "Alligator Wine"/"Take Me Back to Woodstock"
(1500).

June 1989: **Tad,** "Damaged 1"/**Pussy Galore,** "Damaged 2" (2500).

July 1989: **Das Damen,** "Sad Mile"/"Making Time" (1500).

August 1989: **Rapeman,** "Inki's Butt Crack"/"Song Number One" (2500).

September 1989: **Lazy Cowgirls,** "Loretta"/"Hybrid Moments" (2000).

October 1989: **Lonely Moans,** "Shoot the Cool"/"Texas Love Goat" (2000).

November 1989: **The Honeymoon Killers,** "Get It Hot"/"Gettin' Hot" (2000).

December 1989: **Fugazi,** "Joe #1"/"Break In"/"Song #1" (2000).

January 1990: **L7,** "Shove"/"Packin' a Rod" (3000).

February 1990: **Dwarves,** "She's Dead"/"Fuckhead" (3000).

March 1990: **Big Chief,** "Blowout Kit"/"Chrome Helmet" (3000).

April 1990: **Lubricated Goat,** "Meating My Head"/"20th Century Rake" (3500).

May 1990: **Babes in Toyland,** "House"/"Arriba" (3500).

June 1990: **Thee Headcoats,** "Davey Crockett"/"Time Will Tell" (4000).

July 1990: **The Rollins Band,** "Earache My Eye"/"You Know Me" (4000).

August 1990: **Sister Ray,** "The King"/"Push Me" (4000).

September 1990: **Unsane,** "Vandal X"/"Street Sweeper" (4000).

October 1990: **Poster Children,** "Pointed Stick"/"Thinner Stronger" (4500).

November 1990: **Poison Idea,** "We Got the Beat"/"Taken by Surprize" (4500).

December 1990: **Reverend Horton Heat,** "Psychobilly Freakout"/"Baby You Know Who" (6500).

January 1991: **The Fluid,** "Candy" (live)/**Nirvana,** "Molly's Lips" (live) (7500).

February 1991: **The Velvet Monkeys,** "Rock the Nation"/"Why Don't We Do It in the Road" (7000).

March 1991: **Unrest,** "A Factory Record" (7000).

April 1991: **Shonen Knife,** "Neon Zebra"/"Bear Up Bison" (live) (5000).

May 1991: **Urge Overkill,** "Now That's the Barchords"/"What's This Generation Coming To" (5000).

June/July 1991: (double single) **Sonic Youth/Gumball/These Immortal Souls/Laughing Hyenas,** "Alice Cooper tribute" (5500).

August 1991: **Come,** "Car"/"Last Mistake" (4500).

September 1991: **Gorilla,** "Detox Man"/"Sober" (4500).

October 1991: **The Gories,** "Give Me Some Money"/"You Don't Love Me" (4500).

November 1991: **Love Battery,** "Foot"/"Mr. Soul" (4000).

December 1991: **Green Magnet School,** "Singed"/"Slipper" (4000).

January 1992: **Tsunami,** "Left Behind"/**Velocity Girl,** "Warm"/"Crawl" (4000).

February/March 1992: (double single) **Tar,** "Deep Throw"/**Cows,** "My Girl"/**Helmet,** "Oven"/**Vertigo,** "Dynamite Cigar"/**Helios Creed,** "Hideous Greed"/**Boss Hog,** "Fire of Love"/**God Bullies,** "Bullet"/**Surgery,** "Our Demise" (5000).

April 1992: **Mecca Normal,** "You Heard It All"/"Broken Flowers"/**Kreviss,** "Going to Hell" (3500).

May 1992: **Pain Teens,** "Death Row Eyes"/"The Smell" (3500).

June 1992: **Rocket from the Crypt,** "Normal Carpet Ride"/"Where Are the Fuckers"/"Slumber Queen"/"Flip the Bird" (3000).

July 1992: **Codeine,** "Realize"/"Broken-Hearted Wine" (3000).

August 1992: **Crackerbash,** "Nov. 1"/"Halloween Candy" (2752).

September 1992: **Mono Men,** "Skin and Bones"/"Comanche" (2746).

October 1992: **Big Damn Crazyweight,** "Might As Well"/"Off That Cow" (2341).

November 1992: **Anti-Seen,** "We Got This Far (Without You)"/"Remember You" (2205).

December 1992: **The Jon Spencer Blues Explosion,** "Big Yule Log Boogie"/"My Christmas Wish to You" (2218).

January 1993: **Wolverton Brothers,** "My Assassin"/"Max Gomez Love" (2015).

February 1993: **Bewitched,** "Hey White Homey"/"Troll Doll" (2125).

March 1993: **Dead Moon,** "Dirty Noise"/"Dark Deception" (2125).

April 1993: **Royal Trux,** "Steal Yr Face"/"Gett Off" (2105).

May 1993: **SF Seals,** "Nowherica"/"Being Cheated" (2116).

June 1993: **Severin,** "Waste of Time"/"Powerplay" (2039).

July 1993: **Ween,** "Skycruiser"/"Cruise Control" (2039).

August 1993: **Snow Bud,** "Killer Bud"/"Third Shelf" (1550).

September 1993: **Combustible Edison,** "Cry Me a River"/"Satan Says" (2070).

October 1993: **Pigface,** "Empathy"/"Steam Roller" (1654).

November 1993: **Didjits,** "Dear Junkie"/"Skull Baby"/"Fire in the Hole" (1625).

December 1993: (double single) **Lou Barlow,** "I Am Not Mocking You"/"Survival"/"Helpless Heartbreak"/"Dirty Mind"/"Forever Instant" (1526).

# The Best/Worst Things About Owning an Indie Label

## by Jill Kalish and Steve Pilon

Jill Kalish and Steve Pilon live in Atlanta and run Long Play Records, which has released albums by the likes of the Big Fish Ensemble, the Opal Foxx Quartet and Smoke.

You get lots of free records, BUT they're never the records you want.

People are interested in what you do for a living and ask you lots of questions about it, BUT the next time you see them they ask "What's the name of that record store you work at?"

Once in a while one of your records starts to sell pretty well, BUT then your distributor goes out of business and you still manage to end up losing money.

Beer is tax deductible, BUT only if you remember to get a receipt.

It's pretty much your job to make fun of major labels, BUT . . . well, there's really no downside to that one.

You can work in your underwear if you want to, BUT . . . there's really no downside to that one either.

People always ask your advice on what new records to buy, BUT they go out and buy Smashing Pumpkins and Tori Amos anyway.

You feel confident that your records are the absolute best records being released anywhere by anybody, BUT everyone just buys Smashing Pumpkins and Tori Amos anyway.

# Twenty-five U.K. Hitmakers Who Never Meant Squat in the U.S.

Altered Images

Angelic Upstarts

The Associates

Bad Manners

Blancmange

The Bluebells

The Buggles

A Certain Ratio

Classix Nouveaux

Haircut 100

Haysi Fantayzee

Heaven 17

Japan

JoBoxers

Manic Street Preachers

Orange Juice

Pigbag

Rip Rig & Panic

Secret Affair

Sigue Sigue Sputnik

Tenpole Tudor

Theatre of Hate

Toyah

Transvision Vamp

Visage

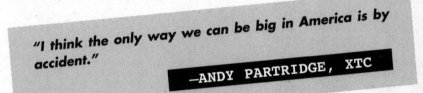

"I think the only way we can be big in America is by accident."

—ANDY PARTRIDGE, XTC

# The Mainstreams of Alt-Rock

ALT-ROCKERS WITH
ONE OR MORE
U.S. PLATINUM ALBUMS

(as of 1995)

Alice in Chains

Arrested Development

The B-52's

The Bangles

The Beastie Boys

Beck

Blondie

David Bowie

The Cars

The Clash

Elvis Costello

The Cranberries

The Cult

Culture Club

The Cure

Cypress Hill

Depeche Mode

Devo

Duran Duran

EMF

Erasure

Eurythmics

Faith No More

Fine Young Cannibals

The Fixx

Peter Gabriel

The Gin Blossoms

The Go-Go's

Green Day

Hole

Billy Idol

Indigo Girls

Jane's Addiction

Jesus Jones

Joan Jett

The Knack

Living Colour

Los Lobos

Mazzy Star

Natalie Merchant

Midnight Oil

New Order

Nine Inch Nails

Nirvana

Sinéad O'Connor

Offspring

Pearl Jam

Pet Shop Boys

The Police

The Pretenders

Radiohead

Rage Against the Machine

R.E.M.

Red Hot Chili Peppers

Roxy Music

The Sex Pistols

Silverchair

Smashing Pumpkins

Soul Asylum

Soundgarden

Squeeze

Stone Temple Pilots

The Stray Cats

Talking Heads

Tears for Fears

Temple of the Dog

10,000 Maniacs

Thompson Twins

A Tribe Called Quest

U2

Violent Femmes

Weezer

Yaz

# ALT-ROCKERS WITH ONE OR MORE U.S. GOLD ALBUMS

## (as of 1995)

Adam Ant

Bananarama

Belly

Big Audio Dynamite II

Big Country

Björk

The Breeders

Bush

Candlebox

The Church

Collective Soul

Concrete Blonde

Cowboy Junkies

Crowded House

Divinyls

Filter

A Flock of Seagulls

Foo Fighters

Frankie Goes to Hollywood

Debbie Harry

Helmet

Human League

Information Society

Annie Lennox

Live

Love and Rockets

Meat Puppets

Men Without Hats

Ministry

Missing Persons

Modern English

Oingo Boingo

Orchestral Manoeuvres in the Dark

Porno for Pyros

The Presidents of the United States

Primus

The Proclaimers

Psychedelic Furs

Lou Reed

Simple Minds

The Smithereens

The Smiths

Suicidal Tendencies

Matthew Sweet

Til Tuesday

Tom Tom Club

Tool

Veruca Salt

## ALT-ROCKERS
## WHO'VE WON
## GRAMMY AWARDS

# (as of 1995)

**The Art of Noise** (Best Rock Instrumental Performance, 1986)

**David Bowie** (Best Video, Short Form, 1984; Best Album Package, 1989)

**David Byrne** (Best Album of Original Instrumental Background Score Written for a Motion Picture or Television, 1988)

**Duran Duran** (Best Video, Short Form, 1983; Best Video Album, 1983)

**Brian Eno** (Producer of the Year, with Daniel Lanois, 1987, 1992)

**Eurythmics** (Best Rock Performance by a Duo or Group with Vocal, 1986)

**A Flock of Seagulls** (Best Rock Instrumental Performance, 1982)

**Green Day** (Best Alternative Music Performance, 1994)

**Living Colour** (Best Hard Rock Performance 1989, 1990)

**Los Lobos** (Best Mexican/American Performance, 1983)

**Nine Inch Nails** (Best Metal Performance, 1992)

**Sinéad O'Connor** (Best Alternative Music Performance, 1990)

**The Police** (Best Rock Instrumental Performance, 1980, 1981; Best Rock Performance by a Duo or Group with Vocal, 1983; Song of the Year, 1983; Best Pop Performance by a Duo or Group with Vocal, 1983)

**R.E.M.** (Best Pop Performance by a Duo or Group with Vocal, 1991; Best Alternative Music Album, 1991; Best Music Video, Short Form, 1991)

**Red Hot Chili Peppers** (Best Hard Rock Performance, 1992)

**Henry Rollins** (Best Spoken Word or Nonmusical Album, 1994)

**Ryuichi Sakamoto** (Best Album of Original Instrumental Background Score Written for a Motion Picture or Television, 1988)

**Soul Asylum** (Dave Pirner) (Best Rock Song, 1993)

**Soundgarden** (Best Hard Rock Performance, Best Metal Performance, 1994)

**Stone Temple Pilots** (Best Hard Rock Performance with Vocal, 1993)

**U2** (Album of the Year, 1987; Best Rock Performance by a Duo or Group with Vocal, 1987, 1988, 1992; Best Performance Music Video, 1988; Best Alternative Music Album, 1993; Best Music Video, Long Form, 1994)

**Tom Waits** (Best Alternative Music Album, 1992)

*"Exploiting yourself is much better than exploiting others."*

—MALCOLM MCLAREN

# Ad-Rock: Seven Punk and New Wave Songs That Have Been Used in TV Commercials

**The Ramones** (Bud Light) "Blitzkrieg Bop"

**The Pretenders** (Rover automobiles, England) "Brass in Pocket"

**The Stooges** (MCI) "1969"

**The Clash** (Levi's, England) "Should I Stay or Should I Go"

**Velvet Underground** (Dunlop tires, England) "Venus in Furs"

**Lou Reed** (Honda motor scooters, with onscreen endorsement from the artist) "Walk on the Wild Side"

**Buzzcocks** (Arthur's cat food, England) "What Do I Get"

# The Twenty Most Influential Alt-Rock Videos

**The B-52's,** "Love Shack"

**The Beastie Boys,** "Shadrach"

**David Bowie,** "Ashes to Ashes"

**Devo,** "Whip It"

**Thomas Dolby,** "She Blinded Me with Science"

**Eurythmics,** "Sweet Dreams (Are Made of This)"

**Peter Gabriel,** "Sledgehammer"

**New Order,** "Perfect Kiss"

**Nine Inch Nails,** "Closer"

**Nirvana,** "Smells Like Teen Spirit"

**Sinéad O'Connor,** "Nothing Compares 2 U"

**Pearl Jam,** "Jeremy"

**R.E.M.,** "Losing My Religion"

**Ramones,** "Psycho Therapy"

**Red Hot Chili Peppers,** "Give It Away"

**The Replacements,** "Bastards of Young"

**Sonic Youth,** "Kool Thing"

**Talking Heads,** "Once in a Lifetime"

**Talk Talk,** "It's My Life"

**U2,** "Mysterious Ways"

# The

## PART 12

# Printed
# Page

# A Mad Lib, or, a Make-Your-Own Alternative Rock Review

by Neil Strauss

Using the list of required words below in the fill-in-the-blank review, select adjectives, nouns, verbs, etc., of your choice. You, too, can be a rock critic! (If you already are one, just cut out and tape next to your computer screen, to use as a handy refererence when a nasty case of brain drain strikes.)

———

The __1__ __2__ , who performed at the __3__ Club yesterday, played a __4__ and __5__ blend of __6__ and __7__. With a wave of his __8__, lead singer __9__ __10__ invited the audience to __11__. And __12__ they did, turning the mosh pit into a sea of __13__.

The band opened with its __14__ anthem for the __15__ generation, "Don't __16__ the __17__," which built to a __18__ climax. __19__ the __20__, a former member of the influential group the __21__ __22__, played a __23__ __24__ solo on __25__, which was very reminiscent of a young __26__ on __27__.

The __28__ -person group was adept at exploring the territory between __29__ and __30__, though they tended to indulge in a __31__ -esque obsession with __32__. All in all, the performance was __33__ but not too __34__ and the audience left __35__.

———

| | | | |
|---|---|---|---|
| 1 | Adjective ending in -y | 19 | First name |
| 2 | Plural noun | 20 | Type of tool |
| 3 | Noun | 21 | Type of food |
| 4 | Adjective | 22 | Occupation (plural) |
| 5 | Adjective | 23 | Adverb |
| 6 | Style of music | 24 | Adjective |
| 7 | Style of music | 25 | Name of instrument |
| 8 | Body part | 26 | Name of popular musician |
| 9 | First name | 27 | Name of drug |
| 10 | Type of animal | 28 | Number between one and ten |
| 11 | Verb | 29 | Adjective |
| 12 | Repeat previous verb | 30 | Adjective |
| 13 | Plural noun | 31 | Name of band |
| 14 | Adjective | 32 | Plural noun |
| 15 | Brand name | 33 | Adjective |
| 16 | Verb | 34 | Repeat above adjective |
| 17 | Noun | 35 | Verb ending in -ing |
| 18 | Adjective | | |

# Fanzine Top Ten from the Musty Archives of Short Newz

## by Jim Short (a.k.a. Nancy Breslow)

Nancy Breslow was the brains behind *Short Newz*, which she published from 1979 to 1984. Now an attorney in New York City, she is currently dreaming up a new fanzine, which will be distributed via See Hear.

Beginning in October 1979, *Short Newz* (a.k.a. *NewsShorts*) was a free, one page, biweekly New York City fanzine, which reviewed gigs and recordings. The 'zine covered lots of hardcore bands, as well as other types of underground music. Occasionally, *Short Newz* appraised other 'zines, too. The following is what *Short Newz* had to say—way back when—about some of the other 'zines being published at the time:

"*Subterranean Pop* is one of the best fanzines we've ever got hold of. The magazine is made up entirely of local reports (local bands, records, and clubs) and an on-the-mark New Pop Manifesto. Complete addresses included and D.I.Y. record information. Made with care in the Midwest [*oops, actually published out of Olympia, Washington*] by Bruce Pavitt. He really cares a lot about new music, particularly local new music, and does his best to get information out to the 'starving' masses 'cross the U.S. wasteland..."

"L.A.'s *No Magazine* can be pretty gross, but it has good pictures of bands and interviews. A pervert's *Wet*. If you love John Waters, you can't mess with *No*..."

*"Jamming!*, a British fanzine based in London, just came out with its tenth is-sue. It's a big, forty-three page mag with a beautiful four-color cover and in-terviews with Delta 5, Au Pairs, a real piss-take interview with the Damned, plus others and D.I.Y. record discussion plus singles 'n' album reviews and Birmingham/S. London scene-pieces and other int'resting stuff. Straightfor-ward fanzine pulls with no punches..."

*"Bow to No Man* is put out by brain JFA [*Jodie Foster's Army, of Phoenix, Arizona*] and is, unsurprisingly, basically a skate 'n' thrash 'zine. Very local in its orientation, it's got pictures of the hometown crowd, interviews with and gossip about local luminaries, and other assorted in-news. Plus lots of skate pictures and skate stuff..."

*"I.T.* (In Touch for Men) is the bitchen-est gay guy magazine in the world by far. Issue #95 (the 'Back to School vs. Rock & Roll' issue) features an inter-view with Henry of Black Flag PLUS an absolutely stunning words 'n' pic-tures lowdown on 'The Sexiest Men in Rock (Part 2).' Included are 'members' of the Red Hot Chili Peppers ('young, dumb and full of cum'), Fear (Lee Ving), Mötley Crüe, Rank and File (without Alejandro and Slim Jim! Tsk tsk), Blood on the Saddle (Greg Davis), Social Distortion (Mike Ness), Tex and the Horseheads (Mike Martt) and of course Lux of the Cramps (anyone who's seen 'em knows he likes showin' 'it'). What, no Butthole Surfers?..."

"First issue of *Forced Exposure* is out now. They plan to concentrate mostly on the 'developing hc scene here in Boston,' and they did write about such MA bands as SS Decontrol, Gang Green, F.U.s, Groinoids, Jerry's Kids, C.O.s, Negative Fix, Proletariat and Decadence. Most of the issue was taken up by an interview with Ian MacKaye, an interview with Government Issue and some other D.C. stuff (D.C. invasion of Boston, they said, and more Boston stuff coming in issue two). Plus 'zine reviews, record reviews, write-ups of a couple of gigs, and a couple of other things..."

"Leading light of the Fanzine Column this week is Lindsay Hutton's unsur-passed *The Next Big Thing* ('Scotland's Ultimate Rock 'n Roll Maga-zine!!!!'). The title, you should know is from a Dictators song. And Lindsay also runs the official Cramps fan club, Legion of the Cramped. Latest issue (#13/14) features articles on Panther Burns, the Angry Samoans (!), the Chesterfield Kings, a short history entitled 'Bobby Fuller 4-Ever!!,' local news and a lot more. As you can see, this mag is dedicated to the pure r'n'r—the real thing—and as Lindsay says: 'What matters is that you enjoy yourself and you don't have to pretend that you're something you're not to do that.' "

"Send for a copy of L.A.'s famous fanzine *Flipside* and you won't be sorry. It's jammed full of loads of L.A. news. *Flipside* has the best local coverage we've seen in a fan mag in quite a while. Issue #17 has article/interviews on D.O.A., Red Cross [*later Redd Kross, of course*], Vidiots, a Halloween in L.A. report, a guide to L.A. clubs and hangouts, and a great singles [*review*] section. Get it!"

"*Punk Globe,* from San Francisco, is an insubstantial but charming fanzine with lots of local gossip, ads and calendar of events, photos, and even some record reviews and stories about bands. The February '80 issue has an interview with SF band No Alternative, stories on the Satellites and Pointed Sticks and—get this—a photo of our very own Nick Zodiak taken when he was out showing *They Eat Scum* on the West Coast. [NOTE: *the New York City underground filmmaker later changed his name to Nick Zedd.*]"

"And finally, a snippet of a larger 'zine listing, reprinted here sans addresses; all these 'zine reviews originally gave price and ordering info: *Creep,* Northern California's favorite hardcore coverage mag; *Damaged Goods,* New York City's favorite hardcore coverage mag; *Valium Addict* c/o R. Kern [*of later infamy as an underground filmmaker*], who says it's not art."

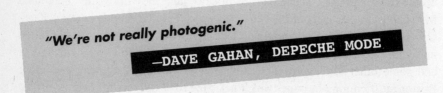

"We're not really photogenic."
—DAVE GAHAN, DEPECHE MODE

# See Hear's
# Top Ten Fanzines

by Ted Gottfried

See Hear is New York City's preeminent retail outlet for fanzines, music magazines, books, and related stuff. The following 'zines are the store's best-sellers according to See Hear proprietor Ted Gottfried.

**Answer Me.** Misanthropic 'zine that tracks down current trends and kills them where they breed. Between its admiration for serial killers and its pro-rape stance, a consistent favorite.

**Ben Is Dead.** Each issue has a different theme. Past themes have included the "Black Issue," examining all sort of dark and deathly things, and a pointed spoof of *Sassy*.

**Chickfactor.** Music 'zine with an emphasis on female artists and the female point of view. Very suave layout and interview style.

**Factsheet Five.** The ultimate 'zine about 'zines. A zillion and one reviews of mags about every subject you could think of and a few others too.

**Flipside.** Beginning with punk rock but hardly ending there. Interviews with the finest in alternative rock, with an emphasis on the "rock."

**Forced Exposure.** Long-running music 'zine that consistently anticipates tomorrow's hip. Amazing record review section.

**Maximum Rock 'n' Roll.** Newsprint punk monthly. The definitive word on the punk scene worldwide.

**Murder Can Be Fun.** Little 'zine with some of the best true-crime writing anywhere, ever.

**Teenage Gang Debs.** Focuses on TV culture and such, with a very humorous style.

**Your Flesh.** Minneapolis' finest in odd and indie music coverage. Opinions all over the place.

*See Hear is located at 59 E. 7 Street, New York, NY 10003. For a mail-order catalog, send $2 ($3 out of U.S.) to above address, or call (212) 505-9871.*

# The Top Ten Fat Greg Dulli Top Tens

by Veronica

Veronica started her fanzine *Fat Greg Dulli* as an outlet for her simultaneous love/hate for the Afghan Whigs and its lead singer Greg Dulli. We asked her to list her ten favorite Dulli-related Top Ten lists from the fanzine's pages.

1. Top Ten Facts Greg Dulli's Friends Told *Fat Greg Dulli*

2. Top Ten Other Embarrassing Names the Band Considered

3. Top Ten Sandwiches

4. Top Ten Women Who Will Never Date Greg Dulli Again

5. Top Ten Reasons Why the Whigs' Manager Broke Up with Their A&R Guy

6. Top Ten Uses for Cincinnati Chili

7. Top Ten Uses for Courtney Love

8. Top Ten Cities for Greg to Pick Up Chicks

9. Top Ten Professions Greg's Mom Wishes He'd Gone Into

10. Top Ten R&B Tunes Greg Croons as Part of Foreplay

# Four Years of Sassy's Cutest Bands

In February 1990 staff editor Christina Kelly experimented with a new entry in her "What's Now" column in the teen-oriented *Sassy* magazine. "Cute Band Alert" became hugely successful and was featured on a regular basis beginning with the January 1991 issue. Bands chosen were for the most part underground faves—some of whom went on to more widespread success after gracing the pages of *Sassy* (which ceased publication at the end of 1994).

Bullet Lavolta (February 1990)

Run Westy Run (January 1991)

Evan Dando/Lemonheads (February 1991)

Dharma Bums (April 1991)

Buffalo Tom (May 1991)

Trash Can Sinatras (June 1991)

Chapterhouse (July 1991)

Skunk (September 1991)

Beggar Weeds (November 1991)

Bratmobile (January 1992)

Miracle Legion (February 1992)

Bikini Kill (March 1992)

Ween (April 1992)

Unrest (May 1992)

Poison Idea (June 1992)

The Beautiful South (July 1992)

Daisy Chainsaw (August 1992)

Velocity Girl (September 1992)

Mary Lou Lord (October 1992)

Luscious Jackson (November 1992)

Bad Trip (January 1993)

Sloan (February 1993)

Shudder to Think (March 1993)

Bettie Serveert (April 1993)

Quicksand (May 1993)

Mystery Machine (June 1993)

Raymond Listen (July 1993)

The Devlins (August 1993)

Magnapop (September 1993)

That Dog (October 1993)

Barbara (November 1993)

Heavenly (January 1994)

Helium (February 1994)

Noise Addict (March 1994)

Roger Manning (April 1994)

Scarce (May 1994)

Blonde Redhead (June 1994)

Jale (July 1994)

Guided by Voices (August 1994)

Your Majesty (September 1994)

Jon Spencer Blues Explosion (October 1994)

Chavez (November 1994)

# Alt-Rock Acts on the Cover of ROLLING STONE

## (through mid-1995)

_____

The Bangles

The Beastie Boys

Belly

The B-52's

Blondie

David Bowie

The Cars

Charlatans UK

Neneh Cherry

The Clash's Mick Jones and Joe Strummer

Elvis Costello

Counting Crows

The Cranberries

De La Soul

Eurythmics' Annie Lennox

Fine Young Cannibals' Roland Gift

The Go-Go's

Hole

Ice-T

Living Colour

Nine Inch Nails' Trent Reznor

Nirvana

Sinéad O'Connor

Pearl Jam

Liz Phair

The Police

The Pretenders

R.E.M.

Red Hot Chili Peppers

Lou Reed

Johnny Rotten

Smashing Pumpkins

Patti Smith

Soul Asylum

Soundgarden

Talking Heads

10,000 Maniacs

U2

# "No, we don't review everything . . ."

by Scott Becker

Scott Becker is founder/publisher of *Option* magazine.

The following essay is entirely true.

In the fall of 1984, I began working on a music 'zine called *Option*. The idea was to document the wide world of music ignored by major publications: punk rock, industrial music, the avant garde, reggae, jazz, weird European art bands, dead blues singers, accordion orchestras, annoying psychopaths with home four-tracks, and so on. That's why we subtitled the magazine "Music Alternatives."

As if that weren't ambitious enough, *Option* also endeavored to consider formats beyond the LP, which ever since *Sgt. Pepper* had been the rock critic's Holy Grail (this was before you were born and before anyone took CDs seriously). Thus, we were deluged with seven-inches and ten-inches, imports and indie EPs, discs wrapped in roofing shingles and hand-painted sleeves, and hundreds and hundreds of cassettes. And somehow, somewhere along the line, the cassette had become the chosen medium of the mail-art scene (a story in itself). So we got cassettes encased in melted records, cassettes sealed in tin cans, cassettes in plastic bags full of trash, cassettes covered with sandpaper, cassettes with found snapshots, poetry and dried flowers, cassettes of white noise by the case. Some of these cassettes actually contained nice music. (I don't recall ever receiving any eight-track tapes, though these were popular before you were born and that's another story in itself.)

Eager to please, the busy beavers at *Option* wrote reviews of this stuff by the carload, printing it up in our ever-expanding magazine. Each review was accompanied by a contact address to encourage correspondence directly with the artistes. This two-way communication process, along with growing readership, led even more folks to send in their music.

And in it came: from Hungary, Poland, and Yugoslavia, even before the collapse of communism. It came from Iceland, Argentina, and Japan. It came from places I didn't think had electricity. And it came from every corner and crossroad in North America. This fringe movement was pretty widespread for something so alternative. In fact, somebody started calling it "alternative" music, as if that about covered it.

By this time, we were running up to 300 capsule reviews of the stuff per issue, and barely keeping up with the mail. At no point did we *ever* announce we'd review *everything,* but a doggedly persistent legend had cropped up. The myth was: "If you make a recording, send it to *Option.* They review everything they get." Everyone seemed to know this "fact" except us. Records arrived with the following notes:

"Let us know which issue the review will appear in."

"We sent this in already, but couldn't find the review. Here's another copy in case you lost the first."

"Let us know which issue the review will appear in so we can buy an ad."

"I heard you guys review everything, so here's my tape. Send me a copy of the review."

Getting little notes in the mail was one thing. But it got a little out of control when we began fielding angry phone calls: *"I just got your new issue. Where's my review, assholes?"*

It's not hard to see how people got the impression that we cover everything. Stuff from around the globe, on tiny, independent labels gets into the mag. Finnish folk fiddling, garage reissues, synthesized gamelan orchestras, cut-n-paste tape manipulation, Casio doodling, and loads more bad music made it into our pages. And some nut in Norway with too much time on his hands took it upon himself to *index* every issue. So with nearly 15,000 entries in the latest edition of his index, including ten for the Legendary Pink Dots, fifteen for Controlled Bleeding, and another twenty for Anthony Braxton, it's easy to see why some folks feel they're being left out. They just don't realize how many Anthony Braxton discs we've *passed* on.

A couple of things conspired to narrow the bandwidth of stuff we review. First, we spontaneously stopped covering singles over the course of one issue when the type just didn't fit (and we never looked back). Then we gradually eliminated cassettes from our pages and the cassette makers correspondingly stopped wasting their art on us. Later, even the do-it-yourselfers adopted the CD medium, our turntable broke, and we stopped writing about anything vinyl. Finally, the majors got into the "alternative" business bigtime, greatly increasing the pool of bad music. That still means we get about a hundred or so CDs in the mail every week. A hundred CDs a week. One issue every two months, with about 200 reviews. You do the math.

So no, we don't review everything. It just feels like it sometimes.

# Five Alt-Rock Biographies That Albert Goldman Is Writing in Hell

## by Jason Cohen and Michael Krugman

Jason Cohen and Michael Krugman are the authors of the book *Generation Ecch!* (Fireside) and are currently at work on a biography of artist/philosopher Jonathan Gordon.

When much reviled rock-biographer Albert Goldman died, he was hard at work on a book about Jim Morrison (get this—*he took drugs and hung out with witches!*). Given Goldman's tradition of writing exclusively about dead people, it's not surprising that partial manuscripts about dead Led Zeppelin drummer John Bonham, untalented but indisputedly dead Sid Vicious and still-kicking Boston leader Tom Scholz were also discovered in his ramshackle apartment, hidden amongst copious amount of jazz 78s, John Donne collections, and John Birch Society newsletters. With his bilious soul currently residing on the Upper West Side of Hades, Goldman can push his dictum of "you can't libel the dead" one step further—the dead can't libel the living, either. That's why Goldman is now turning his venomous pen toward contemporary subjects who (with one exception) still walk God's green earth. Some tomes to look forward to:

***Kurt: The Authorized Biography.*** A collaboration born of Goldman's unlikely postmortal coil friendship with the former Nirvana leader. Among the revelations: Kurt's loving nickname for his mother was "Sattnin"; the true story of Kurt's first meeting with his future wife (he was standing in the front row at a Hole show, looked up the skirt of Courtney's kinderwhore garb and saw the word "Yes"); and, of course, the truth about "little Kurt."

**The Young and the Useless: A Biography of the Beastie Boys.** Here Goldman makes the controversial contention that, with the help of a demented, oversized producer, these poor white Brooklyn Heights kids stole everything they knew about music from black people and everything they knew about fashion from an uncle in the *schmatte* business.

**"Nature Kid: Billy Corgan's Function."** A rarity for Goldman, who realized in the midst of his research that a full-length work wasn't warranted. Rather than tossing it into the circular file, he submitted it to *Vanity Fair* editor Everett True, who immediately commissioned a Helmut Newton cover portrait of a nude Corgan with his pregnant bride, Courtney Love, this time with her Marlboro Light untouched by airbrushing.

**The Lives and Loves of Paul Hewson.** In which Goldman makes it clear that, while Bono never actually *said* he was bigger than Jesus, in his heart that's what the U2 frontman's always believed.

**Ladies and Gentlemen, Adam Sandler!** No further comment necessary.

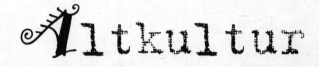

# Altkultur

**PART 13**

# Punks on Film: Notable Alt-Rock Documentaries

**Another State of Mind** (1983). California teen-punk combos Social Distortion and Youth Brigade on a tension-filled D.I.Y. tour. Also featuring an appearance by D.C. hardcore legends Minor Threat, whose Ian MacKaye (of subsequent Fugazi fame) is seen dispensing ice cream at his day job in a Washington, D.C., Haägen-Dazs shop.

**Athens, GA: Inside Out** (1986). A character-filled look at the now-famous college town/boho mecca's music scene, featuring the likes of R.E.M. (performing acoustic versions of "Swan Swan H" and "All I Have to Do Is Dream"), Pylon, the B-52's, Love Tractor, Flat Duo Jets and the B-B-Que Killers. Also included are visits to Peter Buck's bathroom Elvis shrine and the lair of eccentric folk artist Howard Finster.

**The Blank Generation** (1976). Not to be confused with the 1980 dramatic film of the same name starring Richard Hell, this collection of black-and-white performance footage (directed by underground vet Amos Poe and Patti Smith Group bassist Ivan Kral) from the heyday of CBGB features Patti Smith, Talking Heads, Television, the Ramones, Blondie, the Heartbreakers (with Hell and Johnny Thunders), a prerockabilly Robert Gordon as lead singer with the Tuff Darts, a pre-sex-change Wayne County, and the New York Dolls.

**D.O.A.** (1981). An appropriately ragged low-budget document of British punk's initial assault on the U.S.A. via the Sex Pistols' one and only American tour, which precipitated the band's messy breakup. Also featuring the Clash, Generation X (with a prestardom Billy Idol), Sham 69, X-Ray Spex, Iggy Pop, the Dead Boys, and ex-Pistol Glen Matlock's band, the Rich Kids, who perform the Pistols tune "Pretty Vacant."

**Dance Craze** (1980). A collection of filmed performances from most of the key bands in England's then-current ska revival, including the Specials, Madness, the (English) Beat, the Selecter, Bad Manners, and the Bodysnatchers.

**The Decline of Western Civilization** (1981). Future *Wayne's World* director Penelope Spheeris's influential memoir of the early L.A. punk scene features performance footage of X, the Circle Jerks, Fear, the Germs, and a pre-Henry Rollins Black Flag. Seven years later Spheeris took a similarly pointed look at the L.A. hard-rock rat race in *The Decline of Western Civilization Part II: The Metal Years*.

**The Great Rock 'n' Roll Swindle** (1980). The making of this muddled but perversely fascinating pseudo-doc of the Sex Pistols' rise and fall was almost as embattled as the group's career. What eventually emerged from the turmoil was manager/Svengali Malcolm McLaren's rather narcissistic tribute to his own string-pulling abilities, padded with staged post-breakup footage that Johnny Rotten/Lydon refused to participate in.

**Halber Mensch** (1986). A Japanese documentary on the pioneering German industrial ensemble Einstürzende Neubauten.

**Half Japanese: The Band That Would Be King** (1993). A loving tribute to brothers Jad and David Fair and their influential, long-running minimalist outfit Half Japanese, with testimonials from such acolytes as Moe Tucker and Penn Jillette (of Penn and Teller).

**Hated: G.G. Allin and the Murder Junkies** (1993). An appropriately ghoulish profile of über-punk exhibitionist Allin, whose infamous stage act got him arrested on numerous occasions. Though Allin had often threatened to off himself onstage, he actually died of an OD all alone in a friend's Manhattan apartment, shortly before *Hated* was released. Also appearing: Dee Dee Ramone, Geraldo Rivera.

**If It Ain't Stiff, It Ain't Worth A . . .** (1977). A peek inside the beloved Stiff label's first English package tour, featuring Elvis Costello and the Attractions, Nick Lowe with Rockpile (a.k.a. Last Chicken in the Shop), Ian Dury and the Blockheads, Wreckless Eric, and former Pink Fairy Larry Wallis.

**1991: The Year That Punk Broke** (1992). Shoestring auteur David Markey (of *Desperate Teenage Lovedolls* fame) directed this instructive account of Sonic Youth's 1991 European tour, but it is the soon-to-be-superstar support act, Nirvana, who steal the show. Also along for the ride are Babes in Toyland, Dinosaur Jr and Gumball, while long-serving elder statesmen the Ramones put in a guest appearance.

***The Punk Rock Movie*** (1978). Indie filmmaker (not to mention Clash road manager and future Big Audio Dynamite member) Don Letts shot this fly-on-the-wall document of the London punk scene in ultracheap Super 8, with performance footage of the Clash, Sex Pistols, Siouxsie and the Banshees, Generation X (with Billy Idol), the Heartbreakers (with Johnny Thunders), and the Slits. Future Pogues leader Shane McGowan can be seen pogoing beneath the opening credits.

***Reality 86ed*** (1986). As-yet-unreleased documentary of Black Flag's final tour, directed in Super 8 by David Markey, then the drummer of opening act Painted Willie.

***Rude Boy*** (1980). This ambitious combination of documentary footage and scripted dramatic scenes isn't a complete success, but it does include plenty of compelling up-close footage of the Clash. Main character Ray Gange briefly interrupts his hopeless existence (which mirrors the bleak reality described in numerous Clash tunes) for a disastrous stint as roadie with the band, who are seen onstage, in the studio, and in arguments with the protagonist.

***Stop Making Sense*** (1984). Honest-to-goodness Hollywood director Jonathan Demme brings his cinematic expertise to this generally riveting transposition of a Talking Heads concert to the cinematic medium, featuring the band's expanded instrumental lineup and David Byrne's famous Big Suit.

***The Unheard Music*** (1986). A thoughtful portrait of X, which began as the most compelling voice of Los Angeles's early-eighties punk scene but never quite achieved the breakthrough that their critical status as the Great Hope of American Rock suggested. Included are cameos by such scenesters as DJ Rodney Bingenheimer, ex–Dead Kennedys leader Jello Biafra, and former Doors member Ray Manzarek (who produced the band's first four albums).

***U2: Rattle and Hum*** (1988). Dublin's self-appointed Saviors of Rock continue to swallow their own hype in this lavishly mounted vanity project, which manages to make the band members look simultaneously pompous and naive. Despite the film's narcissistic humorlessness, the band achieves some transcendent musical moments.

***Velvet Redux*** (1993). The unspeakably seminal Velvet Underground caught live on the Paris stop of their brief 1993 European tour, proving that, whatever their personal differences, Reed, Cale, Morrison, and Tucker are still capable of the collective genius that made their short-lived reunion such an event.

# Movies with Alt-Rockers in Acting Roles

![black bar]

**_The Allnighter_** (1987). This dumb college sex comedy failed to ignite the acting career of Bangle Susanna Hoffs, who can't really complain about the pic's exploitive treatment of her bod, since the director was her mom.

**_Americathon_** (1979). This juvenile political satire marked the film debut of Elvis Costello, who performs "Crawling to the U.S.A."

**_The Blank Generation_** (1980). German director Ulli Lommel's combination of Euro-style romance and rock & roll star Richard Hell, who also performs several songs with his band the Voidoids (and whose best-known song provides the film's title).

**_Border Radio_** (1987). This rarely seen 16mm black-and-white project, directed by then–UCLA film student Allison Anders, stars L.A. scenesters Chris D. (Flesh Eaters), John Doe (X), Dave Alvin (Blasters), and Texacala Jones (Tex and the Horseheads), most of whom are also on the film's soundtrack album.

**_Born in Flames_** (1983). Lizzie Borden's futuristic feminist fantasy costars New York avant-chanteuse Adele Bertei.

**_Candy Goes to Hollywood_** (1978). This hardcore-porn showbiz spoof features Wendy O. Williams, prior to her fame with destructo-punk rockers the Plasmatics.

**_Car 54, Where Are You?_** (1994). Beloved New York Dolls frontman turned all-around entertainer David Johansen (who's also featured prominently in

*Scrooged, Let It Ride,* and the sci-fi fiasco *Freejack* with Mick Jagger, among other films) channels the spirit of Joe E. Ross to play garrulous cop Gunther Toody in this big-screen version of the beloved fifties sitcom. The Ramones also make a guest appearance, performing their 1989 tune "I Believe in Miracles" in a club scene (a reminder that the film had sat on the shelf for several years prior to release).

**The Chase** (1994). The dopey Charlie Sheen action comedy also features Henry Rollins as a cop and Red Hot Chili Pepper Flea and Anthony Kiedis as a pair of fame-hungry rednecks.

**Corrupt** (1983). Also known as *Order of Death* and *Cop Killers,* this creepy Italian (but shot in New York City) psychological thriller stars John Lydon (a.k.a. Johnny Rotten) as a disturbed young man held prisoner by crooked cop Harvey Keitel (a good decade before becoming *The Bad Lieutenant*).

**Cry-Baby** (1990). John Waters's juvenile-delinquent comedy features Iggy Pop in a character role.

**Desperately Seeking Susan** (1985). Director Susan Seidelman's hit, which featured Madonna in a timely co-starring role, also includes a cameo by New York City avant-jazzbo Arto Lindsay.

**Desperate Teenage Lovedolls** (1984) and **Lovedoll Superstar** (1986). Underground director David Markey shot these two ultra-cheap cult-classic spoofs in Super 8 with a cast comprised of members of such L.A. bands as Redd Kross, the Bangles, and Black Flag, and a script loaded with scene-oriented inside jokes.

**Dudes** (1987). The cast of this juvenile-delinquents-on-a-dude-ranch adventure includes Flea (also in *Back to the Future Part III* and *My Own Private Idaho,* among other films) and Lee Ving, frontman of the notorious L.A. punk combo Fear (who's also acted in *Flashdance, Get Crazy, Streets of Fire, Black Moon Rising, The Taking of Beverly Hills,* and others).

**Eat the Rich** (1987). Motörhead's Lemmy Kilmister appears (along with a host of music-related guest stars) in this violent comedy about a gang of social outcasts waging a class war against the London jet set.

**Faraway, So Close** (1994). Wim Wenders's sequel to *Wings of Desire* features Lou Reed as himself, both in a concert sequence and in some dramatic scenes, in one of which he offers a handout to a down-and-out ex angel.

**Gas Food Lodging** (1992). Alison Anders's critically acclaimed family drama features amusing cameos by Dinosaur Jr leader J Mascis (as a flaky desert-dwelling rock salesman) and Redd Kross's Jeff McDonald.

**Get Crazy** (1983). This dated, insipid rock "comedy" featured Lou Reed as reclusive Dylanesque rock star "Auden."

**Ghosts of the Civil Dead** (1988). Nick Cave is one of the stars of this bleak Australian prison drama.

**Hairspray** (1988). Camp-outrage auteur John Waters's surprisingly sensitive (for him) parable of rock & roll and racial tolerance in the pre-Beatles sixties features Debbie Harry and Ric Ocasek in supporting roles.

**Half-Cocked** (1995). The cast of this indie-rock-themed low-budgeter includes members of such indie bands as Rodan, Crain, Makeup, and the Grifters.

**The Hunger** (1983). This stylish but stupid vampire opus featuring David Bowie opens with Bauhaus performing "Bela Lugosi's Dead" in a nightclub, where Ann Magnuson (Pulsallama, Bongwater) gets picked up by the undead Thin White Duke.

**Johnny Mnemonic** (1995). Based on a William Gibson short story and directed by New York artist Robert Largo, this sci-fi thriller features Henry Rollins and Ice-T.

**Johnny Suede** (1991). Would-be rocker Brad Pitt is given pointers by punk-rock shyster Nick Cave.

**Jubilee** (1978). This early effort by cult director Derek Jarman featured transsexual punkette Jayne County and a then-unknown Adam Ant. Ant would soon achieve short-lived pop stardom before pursuing acting roles in *Nomads* (1986), *Slamdance* (1987), and *Trust Me* (1989), among others.

**La Bamba** (1987). The fictionalized, romanticized version of fifties rocker Ritchie Valens's life and death featured revivalist rockers Brian Setzer (Stray Cats) and Marshall Crenshaw typecast in the roles of their heroes Eddie Cochran and Buddy Holly, respectively. Meanwhile, Los Lobos, who performed the film's popular musical score, have a droll cameo as a band in a Mexican brothel.

**Ladies and Gentlemen, the Fabulous Stains** (1985). This comedy about an all-female teen punk combo features former Sex Pistols Paul Cook and Steve

Jones (who wrote the movie's songs) and former Clash member Paul Simonon as a members of a fictional band, along with Fee Waybill of the Tubes as a dissipated rock star, and an appearance by L.A.'s infamous Black Randy and the Metrosquad.

**The Man Who Fell to Earth** (1976). Director Nicolas Roeg's stylishly haunting sci-fi tale marked David Bowie's first starring role. Bowie subsequently appeared in *Just a Gigolo*; *The Hunger*; *Merry Christmas, Mr. Lawrence*; *Absolute Beginners*; *The Last Temptation of Christ;* and others.

**Mystery Train** (1989). Director (and onetime member of New York new-wavers the Del-Byzanteens) Jim Jarmusch's multi-story ode to the spirit of Memphis features a credible performance from ex-Clash man Joe Strummer and an amazing one by fifties proto-wildman Screamin' Jay Hawkins (plus a cameo by Elvis Presley's ghost).

**No Surrender** (1986). This British political satire features Elvis Costello as an inept magician.

**No Way Out** (1987). Though probably better known for the not-particularly titillating backseat sex scene featuring stars Kevin Costner and Sean Young, this convoluted mainstream thriller (a loose remake of the classic *The Big Clock*) features Flesh Eaters/Divine Horsemen leader Chris D. as one of the bad guys' evil henchmen.

**One Trick Pony** (1980). Lou Reed has a supporting role as a philistine record producer in Paul Simon's semi-autobiographical tale of a faded sixties singer/songwriter facing midlife crisis. The B-52's are also seen performing "Rock Lobster."

**Polyester** (1981). John Waters's Odorama classic features former Dead Boy (and future dead boy) Stiv Bators as Divine's daughter's boyfriend.

**Roadside Prophets** (1992). This tongue-in-cheek, cameo-filled road movie (directed by Alex Cox cohort Abbe Wool) stars John Doe (X) and Adam "Ad-Rock" Horovitz (Beastie Boys) as uneasy traveling companions.

**Rock 'n' Roll High School** (1979). This overrated but still enjoyable teen comedy features the Ramones (whose thespian abilities aren't likely to give John Gielgud any sleepless nights) as themselves. Beware of the abysmal straight-to-cable sequel, which replaced the Ramones with Corey Feldman and features an embarrassed-looking Mojo Nixon as "the Spirit of Rock & Roll."

**Salvation!** (1987). Former underground filmmaker Beth B's first mainstream feature is a comedy-drama about a corrupt TV evangelist, with X's Exene Cervenka in a leading role.

**Scandal** (1989). Fine Young Cannibals' Roland Gift plays the spurned lover in this portrayal of one of the British Parliament's biggest sex scandals. Gift also appeared in the provocative *Sammy and Rosie Get Laid* (1987).

**Sid and Nancy** (1986). Director Alex Cox's personalized view of the ill-fated Sid Vicious/Nancy Spungen romance features a premusical Courtney Love, as well as cameos by Iggy Pop and Eddie Tudor-Pole (of Tenpole Tudor fame—and reportedly Malcolm McLaren's one time choice as a replacement for Johnny Rotten in the Pistols).

**Singles** (1992). For this twentysomething comedy-drama's portrayal of the Seattle grunge scene, writer/director Cameron Crowe recruited such local color as Eddie Vedder, Jeff Ament, Chris Cornell, and Tad Doyle for supporting roles.

**Smithereens** (1982). The low-budget feature debut by future *Desperately Seeking Susan* director Susan Seidelman, set in the dregs of the downtown New York rock scene, features punk trendsetter Richard Hell as a narcissistic musician.

**The Spirit of '76** (1991). This jokey seventies tribute (liberally loaded with star cameos and pop-culture references) features Redd Kross leaders Jeff and Steve McDonald as a pair of Bill-and-Ted-type valley boys who lend a hand to a band of stranded time travelers led by former teen icon David Cassidy.

**Straight to Hell** (1987). Alex Cox's in-joke Western-noir features most of his musician friends, namely Joe Strummer, Elvis Costello, Grace Jones, Edward Tudor-Pole, and Courtney Love, plus the Pogues as a cretinous, coffee-addicted outlaw clan.

**Stranger Than Paradise** (1984). Jim Jarmusch's breakthrough low-budget road movie stars Lounge Lizards leader John Lurie and original Sonic Youth drummer Richard Edson as a sort of slacker Hope and Crosby.

**Union City** (1980). Deborah Harry made her "serious" film debut in this Jersey-lensed attempt at cult noir, in which she plays the long-suffering brunette wife of an unhinged accountant.

**What About Me?** (1993). New York City underground filmmaker Rachel Amodeo cast a slew of punk idols in her movie about the plight of an East Village homeless woman. Starring Richard Edson and Richard Hell, the film also features cameos by Dee Dee Ramone, Johnny Thunders, and Jerry Nolan. The latter two died before the film's completion.

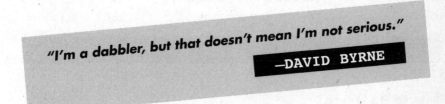

*"I'm a dabbler, but that doesn't mean I'm not serious."*
—DAVID BYRNE

# Alternative Artists Who Have Appeared on Wim Wenders's Soundtracks

---

Laurie Anderson

Simon Bonney

T Bone Burnett

Can

Nick Cave

Nick Cave and the Bad Seeds

Neneh Cherry

Elvis Costello

Crime and the City Solution

Julee Cruise

Depeche Mode

The House of Love

k.d. lang

Daniel Lanois

Lou Reed

R.E.M.

Jane Siberry

Patti Smith and Fred Smith

Talking Heads

U2

U2 with Johnny Cash

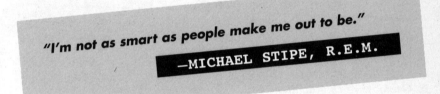

"I'm not as smart as people make me out to be."
—MICHAEL STIPE, R.E.M.

# The Cramps' Top Ten Sexploitation Movies

Lux Interior and Poison Ivy, the auteurs behind the Cramps, have been known to call upon their vast film library for inspiration.

**1.** *Nest of the Cuckoo Bird*

**2.** *Overdose of Degradation*

**3.** *Let Me Die a Woman*

**4.** *Another Day, Another Man*

**5.** *Wham-Bam, Thank You Spaceman*

**6.** *The Bellboy and the Playgirls* (directed by Francis Ford Coppola)

**7.** *Scare Their Pants Off*

**8.** *Blonde on a Bum Trip*

**9.** *Hallucinations of a Deranged Mind*

**10.** *Dr. Carstairs' Love-Root Elixir*

# Jim Reid's Ten Favorite Movies

Along with his guitarist brother William, singer Jim Reid has led the influential English noise-pop combo the Jesus and Mary Chain since 1984.

1. *If*

2. *O Lucky Man!*

3. *Performance*

4. *Billy Liar*

5. *Midnight Cowboy*

6. *Drugstore Cowboy*

7. *Withnail & I*

8. *The Servant*

9. *Taxi Driver*

10. *Broadway Danny Rose*

# Sixteen
# Literary Alt-Rockers

**Jim Carroll.** Like his pal Patti Smith, Carroll was already a respected writer and poet when he launched his recording career. A child prodigy who acquired and kicked a heroin habit early in life, Carroll published his first book of verse at age sixteen; his best known works are the autobiographical *Basketball Diaries* and the poetry collection *Living at the Movies*.

**Nick Cave.** The former Birthday Party goth-punk frontman turned Bad Seed Southern-gothic singer/songwriter has further indulged his taste for the morbid with his novel, *And the Ass Saw the Angel,* and a collection of song lyrics, plays, and prose pieces, *King Ink*.

**Exene Cervenka.** X's cofrontperson—who met her future husband and musical partner John Doe at a Venice, California, poetry workshop—coauthored a 1982 book of poetry, *Adulterers Anonymous,* with New York scum-rock goddess Lydia Lunch (see below), as well as produced a volume of her own writings, *Virtual Unreality*.

**Billy Childish.** The industrious (and dyslexic) leader of such stubbornly iconoclastic English combos as the Milkshakes and Thee Headcoats has been similarly prolific as a small-press tycoon, self-publishing more than thirty books of his own writings.

**Julian Cope.** Cope, perhaps the most colorful of English postpunk eccentrics, published *Head-On,* a humorously autobiographical account of his reckless youth as leader of the Teardrop Explodes.

**Marshall Crenshaw.** The power-pop tunesmith is also the author of *Hollywood Rock,* a guide to pop music in the movies.

**Roky Erickson.** The ex–13th Floor Elevators leader and psychedelic cult icon published a collection of mystical poetry, *Openers,* after a three-year stay in a Texas state mental hospital.

**Mick Farren.** Farren, a member of such weird-before-their-time English bands as the Deviants and the Pink Fairies, has also worked as a science-fiction novelist and music journalist.

**Sid Griffin.** Founding member of L.A. cowpunks the Long Ryders, Griffin — who now leads the London-based Coal Porters — penned a biography of his hero, Gram Parsons, originally published in 1985.

**Richard Hell.** The punk trendsetter has periodically dabbled in poetry and spoken-word performance. Using the collective pseudonym Teresa Stern, Hell and Tom Verlaine (with whom he'd later found Television) wrote a book of poems, *Wanna Go Out?* Hell recently completed a novel.

**Lydia Lunch.** The venerable New York punk priestess has extended her fascination with life's creepier back alleys into the printed word. Some of her writings are collected in the best-of *Incriminating Evidence*.

**Lou Reed.** The undisputed pioneer of punk's drive toward literary pretension, Reed studied poetry with Delmore Schwartz at Syracuse University in the early sixties. Since then, he's had his work published in various magazines, in the 1991 book *Between Thought and Expression,* and even had the lyrics to his song "Hold On" published on the Op-Ed page of *The New York Times*.

**Henry Rollins.** The current king of alt-rock lit, the ex-Black Flag frontman has created a punk cottage industry, publishing over a dozen books of his autobiographical musings through his own 2.13.61 imprint.

**Patti Smith.** The punk godmother coauthored the 1971 play *Cowboy Mouth* with poet/musician (and future movie star and director) Sam Shepard, three years prior to her recording debut. The Patti Smith Group subsequently grew out of Smith's use of guitarist (and rock critic) Lenny Kaye to accompany her early poetry readings. She's continued to write and publish poetry, to no small acclaim, between album projects.

**Bruce Thomas.** During a period of estrangement from his perennial employer Elvis Costello, Attractions bassist Thomas wrote the novel *The Big Wheel,* a thinly veiled account of his experiences in Costello's band.

**Alan Vega.** The vocalist of the influential electro-punk duo Suicide also published a book of his poetry, *Cripple Nation*.

# David Gedge Picks His Favorite Comic Books

Since 1985 David Gedge—singer, songwriter and comics enthusiast—has led England's the Wedding Present through a variety of upheavals, musical and otherwise.

*Ed the Happy Clown.* Concerns a talking penis and a man whose anus forms the entry to another world, and so says a great deal to me about my life.

*Bizarro.* Cubic other world where everything is fatally flawed (e.g., Bizarro balls don't bounce), and therefore an obvious Wedding Present LP title.

*Tin Tin.* Stories evolved as Herge grew older; "Tin Tin au Tibet," for instance, is oddly philosophical.

*The Watchmen.* The first modern superhero story. Suddenly, blokes wearing their underpants over their trousers became strangely acceptable.

*Steven.* Features an alcoholic cactus and a "badly drawn Snoopy." I enjoyed the bit where all the characters go on strike but the comic continues!

*Brassneck.* Schoolboy robot friend from a British comic. I always wanted a magic pal who could do cool tricks, so I named a song after him.

*Spiderman.* He was brainy, he was bullied, his school friend died! Yet he had a secret identity. I wanted to be Peter Parker. . . . But how does he cram so much webbing into those tiny wristband containers?

*Hate.* While recording in Seattle, we met author Peter Bagge, but I think the pleasure was all ours because he's never been too flattering about "alternative music."

**2000 A.D.** Rejuvenated the medium in Britain. Everything *didn't* live happily ever after, and now it's the U.K.'s biggest-selling comic.

**Batman.** Used to be a goody-goody but has recently been reinvented as a baddy-goody. Julie Newmar was the best Catwoman.

# My Favorite Rock & Roll Novel

by Dean Wareham

When he's not reading, singer/guitarist/songwriter Dean Wareham leads the New York-based quartet Luna, whose second album, *Bewitched,* includes a song entitled "Great Jones Street."

"Perhaps the only natural law attaching to true fame is that the famous man is compelled, eventually, to commit suicide. (Is it clear I was a hero of rock & roll?)"

Certain people are a constant source of inspiration to me. Jonathan Richman. Lee Hazlewood. Woody Allen. And Don DeLillo, who wrote the best novel ever about rock & roll, 1973's *Great Jones Street*.

Did you hate the Doors movie as much as I did? It seems that just about every novel or movie or TV show that deals with rock & roll is overblown romanticized crap, filled with sillyisms. Actors generally can't play rock & rollers, because that's a *different* kind of narcissistic preening. Matt Dillon was good in *Drugstore Cowboy,* but not so hot in *Singles*. And Ethan Hawke was pretty ludicrous onstage with his band in *Reality Bites*. At the same time, rock performers tend to be better at playing musicians than real people. Mick Jagger, for instance was pretty good playing a rock star in *Performance,* but he was pretty bad playing a nonrock star in *Freejack*. But I'm getting off the subject here.

*Great Jones Street* is firstly about fame. A famous rock star, a sort of Jagger/Barrett/Morrison/Cobain figure named Bucky Wunderlick, quits his band after a riot at a Houston Astrodome gig, and holes up in a Manhattan apartment across from the fire station on Great Jones Street. The apartment is empty save for a bathtub, a radio that picks up only AM, and an unplugged refrigerator filled with records and magazines. (Incidentally, the fire station is still there, but the neighborhood has changed today—no Time Cafe back in 1973, no CBGB's even.)

Bucky is attempting to "test the depths of silence." His telephone is disconnected. Meanwhile, in the outside world, there are many rumors concerning Bucky's condition. He's been murdered, or maimed, he's been in an accident, he's hiding in Morocco, he's in Philadelphia, he's doing a concert in England. "There's rumor, there's counter-rumor, there's manipulation, and there's, you know, this ultramorbid promotional activity. What's it all mean?"

As we know, death can be a tremendous boon to sales if exploited properly. So Bucky's manager Globke (of Transparanoia Inc.) tracks him down to find out what his intentions are (there's a lot of money at stake—tour plans, studio commitments etc.). "I have no intentions," says Bucky. Globke wants to get his hands on the lost "mountain tapes," recorded at Bucky's private mountain retreat studio.

Along with the rock & roll angle, *Great Jones Street* also contains various elements of mystery and sci-fi. A government laboratory on Long Island has developed a mind-numbing new superdrug, a "colossal downer." The drug has been stolen by the "Happy Valley Farm Commune" (resettled in the East Village), who want to entrust Bucky with its safekeeping until it can be tested by "Dr. Pepper." The Commune's members admire Bucky, and are convinced that he is "returning the idea of privacy to American life." I guess that when you're famous, people impart a special meaning to everything you do and say. Retroactively. You've made the right decisions. If you like something, then it's good.

Well, that's the setup. *Great Jones Street* is a great book about New York City, drugs, fame, rock lyrics as poetry, rock music as religion, rock music as commodity, rock musician as commodity, the ostensible underground (hippies, anarchists, sectarians), and another, more powerful underground (government agents of various stripes). DeLillo deals with the idea of the underground more fully in his subsequent *Running Dog*. (Who is more "underground," Steve Albini or Oliver North?)

Anyhow, *Great Jones Street* is a hugely funny and prescient book. When you're done with it, you might want to try DeLillo's *White Noise,* which again deals such things as a mysterious drug that alleviates the fear of death; the modern phenomenon of the "daily toxic spill"; a professor of Hitler Studies who lives in fear of his colleagues' discovery that he cannot read German; and his professor pal who wishes to establish a department of Elvis Studies.

"Wrestling is the only thing I have to shut the world out; I'm a really big fan. I follow it like somebody who really likes baseball would follow that. I'm privy to a lot of insider stuff, and I know a lot of the power brokers in the business. I probably know more than I want to know about it."

—BOB MOULD

# Gerard Langley Lists His Ten Biggest Literary/Lyrical Influences

**Vocalist/lyricist Gerard Langley has led the Bristol, England-based Blue Aeroplanes, one of Britain's most literate, tuneful, and personnel-change-prone bands, since the mid-1980s.**

**W. H. Auden.** Spokesman for his generation—and the one after and the one after *that*. Quit England for the States in 1939 after having spent the Spanish Civil War in a tank wearing carpet slippers. Thereafter the Brits booed his gigs and the Yanks hung on his every word. I side with the Yanks. Introduced airmen, borders, suburban surrealism, and sheer pissed-offness to the culture. Sentiment with desperation.

**Louis MacNeice.** Top dude. Due for a revival. The only straight in a predominantly gay scene, 30s-a-go-go, most natural axeman. Words for him were almost like talking, know what I mean? Commissioned Dylan Thomas to write *Under Milk Wood* in the local pub sitting next to Francis Bacon. Made poetry sound like breathing.

**e.e. cummings.** Like Status Quo, you can't defend him. A guilty pleasure, a marketing exercise, the kind of thing that gets you into writing rather than reading. Dig the lowercase name, dig the concepts, dig the sweetness. If he was born fifty years later he'd be making a fortune in adverts and movies.

**Jim Morrison.** Influences are influences. Later you can come to think they're a horse's ass, you can spend your whole life trying not to write "Ode to Me Cock"; they're still an influence. As the first person to read bad poetry seductively (in leather trousers) to an audience prepared to connect hips and brain, he influenced everyone.

**Bob Dylan.** The only rocker to be a real heavyweight in the lit world. Like the Righteous Brothers playing the Apollo, it's a shock to realize *that* stuff can be done by *this* person. Not a considered artist but a natural, like Stevie Smith. Would have been significant just as a writer, which—given his guitar-playing, singing and chutzpah—makes him the biggest all-rounder since Byron.

**Sandy Denny.** Bob Dylan is often quoted as saying that Smokey Robinson is/was America's greatest poet, but he was actually talking about his *voice*. (Check it out.) Sandy Denny is/was England's greatest voice. Drunk, sexy, pure, sensitive, raucous, rock & roll, fucked-up, in control. I bought her first album when I was seventeen, and I tried to write like she sounded. She died when she was thirty-seven and I miss her more than any other artist.

**Punk.** Punk, for me, wasn't any one band, not even the Pistols, it was seventy or eighty people in a room with a band playing. Twenty minutes earlier, the band had been just four or five of those people. I was into punk, poetry, British folk-rock, and Bob Dylan. I joined a band and everyone said it was copying the Velvets. Well, there you go.

**Jacques Tati.** I saw *Monsieur Hulot's Holiday* when I was at school. I saw it five times in a week at a cinema that's now a Mothercare Shop. Later, two French people gave me a handmade T-shirt saying "Jacques Tati loves the Blue Aeroplanes." I don't know why he should be an influence except: Humanism? Awkwardness? A love of the personal? Sympathy? Tolerance?

**Kenneth Patchen.** Kenneth Patchen was a beat poet in the thirties, twenty years before Ginsberg or Kerouac. He painted his poems into a corner and suffocated because of it. I covered one of his poems, "Do the Dead Know What Time It Is?," after I borrowed an LP of him performing it with a jazz band. I wish I could find the LP now. He taught me that poems and paintings are the same.

**Ray Davies.** Ray Davies is not so much an influence as an inspiration. I don't understand how one person could write so many brilliant tunes in such a short space of time. I don't write music very often, but I know enough about it to realize that "Days," "Celluloid Heroes," and "There's a New World Opening for Me" replicate emotion as directly as anyone could wish. If Shakespeare had hung out with Ray, we would never have had to invent pop music.

# Paul K's Ten Favorite Crime Novels

On his seven albums, much-traveled singer/songwriter Paul K has demonstrated a special affinity for gangster folklore and wrong-side-of-life scenarios. His lyrics have been compared by some to the work of Raymond Chandler and James Ellroy, from each of whom he's nicked an album title—*The Killer in the Rain* and *The Big Nowhere*, respectively.

**1.** *The Long Goodbye,* by Raymond Chandler. Perhaps not as original as Hammett (see below), but it's plotted with genius and has a stunningly beautiful sadness. A gift for his dying wife.

**2.** *Red Harvest,* by Dashiell Hammett. An absolute epiphany of glorious nihilism. A textbook of plotting and dialogue, which established a lineage that's given us folks like Quentin Tarantino and Madison Smartt Bell.

**3.** *The Big Nowhere,* by James Ellroy. The most intricately plotted and original crime novel in decades. From a man who is worshipped by rock musicians (including Nick Cave, Sonic Youth, and the Flesh Eaters' Chris D.), but eschews rock & roll in favor of big-band jazz.

**4.** *True Confessions,* by John Gregory Dunne. A wondrously believable Black Dahlia scenario, with just the right balance of noir atmosphere and modern realism.

**5.** *The Friends of Eddie Coyle,* by George V. Higgins. The best dialogue in a tragedy since Shakespeare.

**6.** *The Getaway,* by Jim Thompson. Or practically anything by Thompson; this one strikes me as the leanest and most efficient.

**7.** *Get Shorty,* by Elmore Leonard. Maybe the funniest crime novel I've ever read. And Leonard's from Detroit, so he's automatically in the top percentile of cool.

**8.** *Waiting for the End of the World,* by Madison Smartt Bell. Perfectly paced, topical, and masterfully executed. The title is borrowed from the Elvis Costello song.

**9.** *Perfume,* by Patrick Susskind. An exquisitely detailed map of the mind of a psychopath. Later inspired the Nirvana song "Scentless Apprentice."

**10.** *Money Men,* by Gerald Petievich. A brilliantly concise and funny plot involving counterfeiting, brought to you by a genuine ex-Treasury agent.

# Talking

PART 14

# Heads

# Curt Kirkwood's Greatest Hits

## Compiled by Derrick Bostrom

Fans of Arizona's Meat Puppets have always derived inspiration from the elliptical wordplay of Curt Kirkwood, the band's guitarist, vocalist, and main songwriter. But some of Curt's most quixotic ideas can't be found on any of the band's albums; they appear hidden within the hundreds of interviews he's given since the trio began recording in the early 1980s. Here are some examples of Kirkwood's wit and wisdom, collected by his band mate, Derrick Bostrom:

**1.** "When I go to the grocery store, I'm on an artistic mission."—*New Times* weekly (Phoenix, Arizona), February 15, 1994

**2.** "The two things that playing the guitar has always reminded me of the most is riding motorcycles and shooting guns, my two other favorite things to do."—*Breakfast Without Meat,* issue #8

**3.** "I want a real fucking explanation of why we're so different from White Lion. We both shit purple, although I probably use a little less mousse." —*Alternative Press,* March 1990

**4.** "The more simple we are, especially as complex people, the more grandeur we can achieve."—*Request,* September 1991

**5.** "I'm trying to deflate the idea that somebody like Bruce Springsteen isn't incredibly avant-garde. I may not listen to his music very much, but it sure is weird to me."—*Tempe Daily News Tribune* (Tempe, Arizona), September 5, 1985

**6.** "I wasn't put on this earth to make friends with myself."—*Shephard Express* (Milwaukee, Wisconsin), December 13, 1987

**7.** "The first step is to make sure your perception is accurate. I tend to open up my perception as wide as I can. Then I arrange the results of what has become stuck in my mind in whatever way I think is the most beautiful. That's where my ego comes in. I'll change a perception if it's not delicious enough—and that becomes almost as real to me as the original perception. I trust myself."—publication title unknown, 1985

**8.** "The concept of life itself is a prostitution."—*Notes from Underground,* Summer 1983

**9.** "Music is the last refuge of the nihilist."—*Solid,* 1986

**10.** "I'm into baffling people. It leaves me with a sense of having gained something."—*Morning Call* (Allentown, Pennsylvania), Spring 1983

# Is Nick Cave Really Such a Gloomy Guy?

From his early days in Australian avant-goth punks the Boys Next Door, to his subsequent work with the combustible Birthday Party, to his current incarnation as leader of the Bad Seeds, Nick Cave has consistently explored the soul's darker back alleys. Is this tendency a subconscious fulfillment of his surname? Perhaps the answer lurks beneath the surface of Cave's own thoughts on the subject.

"I don't see my work as being 'dark.' I fucking hate this word, and it's constantly used in reference to my music. I certainly don't deliberately make things depressing, nor am I dissatisfied with a song if it's kind of light and happy. I just tend to write in, for want of a better word, 'negative' kind of moods. [When] I'm happy and content and relaxed, the last thing on my mind is to sit down and put myself through what is a reasonably painful process of actually sitting down and writing."

"To tell the truth, nothing I've accomplished has brought me a great deal of pleasure."

"I'm not the happiest person in the world, but I'm not desperately miserable, either. . . . I have a rich life and I don't think I'm any less happy than most people. I'm not leaping out of bed throwing open the blinds and whooping with joy, but who is?"

"I just don't feel that I have to round things off with a happy ending. . . . I always prefer my nightmares to my dreams; there's something more exciting about nightmares."

"As a public figure, I have a license to behave in any way I like, and it will be accepted to a certain degree. I can be a complete asshole, socially inept, or an alcoholic, and people accept that because I'm a musician, a rock star. But I can't be that way with a three-year-old kid. I can't expect my child to look to an utterly irresponsible father and nod his head and say, 'Oh, that's okay, my dad's a rock star.' "

"I have an incredibly romantic view of life. I see a lot of beauty in it. But I see a lot of sadness in it too. And the two things can't be separated."

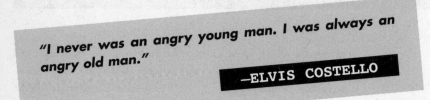

"I never was an angry young man. I was always an angry old man."

—ELVIS COSTELLO

# The Discreet Charm of Morrissey

As pop idol and role model to millions of impressionable young people all over the world, Morrissey is one of music's most quotable figures, his every word eagerly devoured by his fanatical legions of followers. Fortunately, pop's answer to Oscar Wilde always exercises the utmost care in keeping his public statements as moderate and responsible as possible, lest his more impressionable fans miss the sweet ironies inherent in his colorful public persona. Here are a few of his carefully thought-out policy statements, from his days as leader of the Smiths to his present-day solo gig.

"I wish there were other songwriters I could claim kinship with, but there is no one. I consider myself to be a genius."

"I really do expect the highest critical praise for the album. I think it's a complete signal post in the history of popular music."

"The synthesizer should be symbolically burned."

"To be quite honest, (the Smiths) are very angry. I mean, in very simple terms, we are very, very angry. We're angry about the music industry; we're very angry about pop music."

"There's no point being incredibly enlightened and incredibly aware if nobody can actually hear you. You do have to break through—and I think the Smiths are the first group in musical history to do that."

"Everything we produce is wonderful."

"I've always believed that whatever I wear is fashionable and whatever somebody else wears is unfashionable."

"A drunken goat could direct a Duran Duran video."

"We'll never make a video as long as we live."

(On the Band Aid single) "It's one thing to want to save lives in Ethiopia, but it's another thing to inflict so much torture on the British public. It's quite easy to sit here and agree and feel very passionate about the cause—everybody does—but what about the record? Nobody's actually mentioned that foul, disgusting thing!"

"I don't try and inflict the way I feel upon other people, because that's quite boring."

"To me, the Smiths are great by definition. Once they stop being great, they'll cease to exist."

"Age shouldn't affect you. It's just like the size of your shoes—they don't determine how you live your life. You're either marvelous or you're boring, regardless of your age . . . and I'm sure you know what we are."

"When the day arrives when I can't write, when I'm drained, I'll just step down—I won't go on. There's nothing worse than the writer, the singer, who's outlived his usefulness, who's drained his diary, as it were. When I've drained the resources, I will step down—much to the relief, I'm sure, of the British public."

"The Smiths provoke . . . absolute adoration or absolute murderous hatred. There are people out there who would like to disembowel me, just as there are people who would smother me with kisses."

"I am not even vaguely interested in the idea of being a pop star or a rock star or wearing leather trousers and telling everyone that I am the most wonderful person on Earth. I'd like to think that in some way, I'm helping move pop music away from those notions."

"It's only the very simple things and the very simple artists who just breeze straight through and find life very easy. If you're agreeable to anything that's put before you, if you're desperate to do anything in order to be famous, which I most certainly am not, then life is relatively easy."

"I think pop music is basically finished."

"Rap . . . continues in the same old way, which has never, ever, ever, ever changed. I mean, there is only one rap song in the entire universe, which is frightening when you consider how many rap records have been made."

"Rave is the refuge of the mentally deficient. It's made by dull people for dull people."

"It does hurt me that the absurd issue called my sex life has been so pathetic. I do feel like the strangest living oddity, or whatever those circus folk in the twenties were called. I've never, ever had what one might lazily call a sex life. . . . I've always felt that I was cursed, that I was never meant to have a sex life. And that is as true today as it was when I was seventeen and wondering why."

"I'm just not a sexual creature. I don't wake up each morning and say 'I must remember I'm celibate, I must remember I'm celibate.' There simply is no sex in my life."

"As far as I can tell, any fool can have a hit record in America—except me."

"Any pop journalist who wants to do a savage critique of anything I've done is wasting their time, because I get there before they do."

"I have always been overlooked. I think that the audience is perfectly aware of this and they feel that I have been enormously shortchanged [by] the entire music industry and all of their relatives."

"I don't get a sense of any degree of support [in the United States] from the media. Therefore, my success, what I've achieved, is completely pure. There's no hype involved anywhere."

"I think I embarrass the music industry. . . . I feel like I'm embarrassing to a lot of people, but I never feel embarrassed at all."

"I don't understand this notion that I'm some kind of cross-legged folk artist who's lying in a bed of daffodils singing about some twee matters. The opposite is true. . . . I feel that there's more passion and more anger in my performance than there is in most people's performances."

"I'm no rock star. I'm here by complete default."

"I don't play down to people and I don't belittle them. I don't use the word 'fans,' and I don't use the word 'kids,' and I think people appreciate that."

"I feel like a complete imposter, a trespasser. I'm trespassing here tonight. I expect to be escorted off the premises."

# Kurt on Kurt: Cobain Speaks

**Before he became the Lollapalooza Generation's Most Popular Dead Rock Star, Kurt Cobain gave lots of interviews. Not that any of his quotes ever gave any indication that he might be in trouble . . .**

"If there was a Rock Star 101 course, I would have liked to take it. It might have helped me."

"Everyone thinks of me as this emotional wreck, this total negative black star—*all the time*. They're always asking 'What's the matter?' And there's nothing wrong with me at all. I'm not feeling blue at all."

"I never wanted to sing. I just wanted to play rhythm guitar—hide in the back and just play. But during those high-school years when I was playing guitar in my bedroom, I at least had the intuition that I had to write my own songs."

"I have an M-16, which is fun to shoot. It's the only sport I have ever liked. It's not something I'm obsessed with or even condone. . . . Sometimes it's fun to go out and shoot. At targets. I want to make that clear."

"I just like to sleep. I find myself falling asleep at times when I'm fed up with people or bored. . . . I would prefer to be in a coma and just be woken up and wheeled out onto the stage and play and then put back in my own little world. . . . I'd rather just be asleep."

"My body wouldn't allow me to take drugs if I wanted to, because I'm so weak. All drugs are a waste of time. They destroy your memory and your self-respect and everything that goes along with your self-esteem. They're no good at all. But I'm not going to go around preaching against it. It's your choice, but in my experience, I've found they're a waste of time."

"It's my problem and they shouldn't be so concerned with it. I could point fingers at everybody else and tell them that they're drunks. They've bought the same drug hysteria propaganda that has been going on in the United States since the Reagan years. They don't understand it, they've never done it, and so they're afraid."

"No matter what we do or how clean we live our lives, we're not going to survive this because there are too many enemies and we threaten too many people. Everyone wants to see us die. We might just keep going just to spite those fuckheads."

"I really haven't had that exciting of a life. There are a lot of things I wish I would have done, instead of just sitting around and complaining about having a boring life."

"It's impossible for me to look into the future and say I'm going to be able to play Nirvana songs in ten years. There's no way."

# What the Heck Is Trent Reznor Thinking?

Nine Inch Nails is Trent Reznor, but what is Trent Reznor? If the bilious misanthropy of his albums doesn't provide enough clues, perhaps the following statements will.

"I want to give the impression that it is a band. 'Cause I like to hide behind that. . . . I need the control, I have to get the thing out the way I want it to be. . . . I'm the closest one to Nine Inch Nails."

"I'm not very well-rounded, and I can't maintain a personal life very actively *and* try to make a record that takes every waking minute of my consciousness. I've just been trying to figure out what I really want to do and coming to terms with realizing that I can't be well-rounded for several years."

"I guess I have a real affinity for working with machines in certain ways. It's like they're my friends."

"I got everything I wanted in my life . . . except I don't really have a life now. I don't have any real friends, any relationships that mean anything to me, and I've turned myself into this music-creation-performance machine."

"I probably rely too much on sexual imagery as a metaphor for control, but I'm totally intrigued by it. I think Nine Inch Nails are big enough and mainstream enough to gently lead people into the back room a little bit, maybe show them some things it might have taken them a little longer to stumble into on their own. . . . I think that back room could represent anything that an individual might consider taboo yet intriguing, anything we're conditioned to abhor. Why do you look at an accident when you drive past, secretly hoping that you see some gore? I shamefully admit it—I do."

402

"I'm not as afraid to question my own sexual orientation as I might have been ten years ago. I'm not afraid to think about certain things you aren't supposed to think about. I mean, I do wonder what it would be like to kill somebody, though I'm not going to do it. I don't want to do it. But I know why people idolize serial killers."

"I can make something loud, but how can I make it the loudest, noisiest, most abrasive thing I've ever heard? Can I go ten steps past the goriest horror film you've ever seen in a way that's more disturbing than cheesy? I know I can; I've done it."

"I don't know why I want to do these things, other than my desire to escape from Small Town, U.S.A., to dismiss the boundaries, to explore. It isn't a bad place where I grew up, but there was nothing going on but the cornfields. My life experience came from watching movies, watching TV and reading books and looking at magazines. And when your fucking culture comes from watching TV every day, you're bombarded with images of things that seem cool, places that seem interesting, people who have jobs and careers and opportunities. None of that happened where I was. You're almost taught to realize it's not for you."

"I got dragged into a strip club a few months ago. . . . To my absolute horror, I realized the DJ was playing 'Hurt,' the last track on *Downward Spiral* and a song based on the most personal sentiments, the deepest emotions I have ever had. . . . We were crying when we made it, it was so intense. I didn't know if I even wanted to put it on the album. But there we were, and there it was, and girls were taking their clothes off to it."

# Eddie Vedder:
# Portrait of
# the Artist as a
# Young Malcontent

Lord knows, being a superstar is no picnic. Just ask Eddie Vedder. Too often a glimpse into the pain of genius, we have collected some of his most piquant interview quotes.

"The fact that so many people relate to [our] songs is kind of depressing."

"I wish we weren't on MTV, man. I just feel silly talking about our band all the time."

"The whole success thing, I feel like everybody else in the band is a lot happier with it than me. Happy-go-lucky. They kind of roll with it. They enjoy it, even. I can't seem to do that. It's not that I think I'm better than it. I don't know. I'm just not that happy a person."

"Any kinda quick success of the kind we had is inevitably bound to provoke some degree of contempt. I end up having a lot of difficulty with it myself. I'm being honest when I say that sometimes when I see a picture of the band or a picture of my face taking up a whole page of a magazine, I hate that guy."

"I have a problem with the *good* things people write about us. I have a problem with everything. I don't know, there are so many people out there talking about music who don't listen to music. They know it all, they know everything about music. Why? Because they read about it. They aren't listening. So that's what upsets me. It's all just talk, it's all just words."

"I don't want to understand [Pearl Jam's success], because as soon as I understand it, I get real upset about it, and either want to shoot myself, or go through the thirty-day process and get my machine gun—'cause I'll still be angry about it in thirty days—and then go in and take care of some of my problems."

"A lot of the problems seem tied to the music—and that's why it turns your world upside down. You feel like you want to protect the music and yourself, and there's a lot of things that are attacking both."

*"Pain is my girlfriend, that's how I see it. I feel pain every day of my life. When you see me perform, it's that pain you're seeing, coming out. I put all my emotions, all my feelings, and my body on the line. People hurt me, I hurt myself—mentally, physically."*

**—HENRY ROLLINS**

# Smashing It Up
# with Billy Corgan

As leader of the much-loved, sometimes-reviled Smashing Pumpkins, Billy Corgan has always shown a flair for the dramatic. Here are a few of our favorite Corgan quotes.

"To me, the newest generation of bands is not a reaction against something, but a reaction because there is nothing. It's like there's so much apathy and people are frustrated and we don't even know why."

"I wonder what it is about America that makes kids wanna be in bands. The European kids, it's no big deal to them. What is it that we're so desperately trying to get away from?"

"I've never had a stable life. I lived in five different places before I was five. I saw divorces, messy breakups, boyfriends, girlfriends, drugs. I don't trust stability. I understand chaos. I muck things up because it forces you to react."

"When I wrote the lyrics for [*Siamese Dream*], I would just sit down at the typewriter and just type pages and pages, and then when I came to a line that made me cringe with embarrassment, that's the one I would use."

"We've become extremely jaded as a band. And I think that's really sad. I don't think there's anything cool about it. We've lost perspective about how lucky we are and how wonderful a position we're in."

"If I had been accepted [as a child], I never would have been as independent as I am. I wish from Day One, people would have looked at me and said, 'You're all right, come on, join the team,' but it's never been that way with me. I don't know why. Maybe I'm a dick, maybe it shows."

"I'm surrounded by these people who I care about very much, yet they continue to keep failing me. I say, 'I need this, I need that,' and they don't do the job, and what it does in me is it makes me feel the same abandonment I felt as a child. And then what it says to me is, 'You're not worth the trouble.' You take it to a level where it's very personal. If you really think about it, of course, someone doesn't do the job because they're lazy, or they don't think it's important. But I [take] it as, 'You're not worth going home and working on the song.' "

"My reputation as a tyrant, Svengali, asshole, there's truth in that. Where the discrepancies come in is *why*. I took a drummer who didn't even know what alternative music was and took two people who could barely play their instruments and made a band. That's not to say they didn't do anything, but I created something beyond the sum of its parts. Maybe I pushed people, maybe I was a dick, maybe I said, 'Let me play this part,' but it worked. If I hadn't done that, it wouldn't even be a point of contention, because there would be no Smashing Pumpkins."

"When I was twenty years old, the idea of being in a band that was popular and played huge places seemed really exciting. But the road to travel to get here was not much fun. And it's made me evaluate why I even bother, why my heart is still in music. If the Pumpkins ever blew apart. . . . I don't think I'd ever go down the same road again. I think I'd do music that I knew would be nowhere near as commercial."

"Long ago I found out that I couldn't be fashionable if I tried. You begin to revel in your own lack of ability to be cool."

"That's the whole sickness of alternative music, independent music. They're no different from the Paula Abduls of the world; they sit in their little castles and say, 'Well, you're not cool enough' and 'You're not *this* enough. . . .' It's never based on 'Is your band good or bad?' It's 'Are you politically correct?' and 'Who do you hang out with?' It's so easy to get caught up in the small, bitchy, bickering world of the music industry, and everybody's little allegiances and rat packs and football teams, and lose sight of the fact that it's still about: you make a record and people like it, or they don't like it; they put it on and it makes them feel good, and it makes them love their boyfriend or girlfriend more, or whatever. I don't have to please the Thurston Moores of the world and get their approval."

"All these alternative bands today are so high up on their punk-rock horse that they're in denial about being huge and playing big shows. Not only do we respect the clichés, we see the truth in them. So we simultaneously make fun of them and embrace them."

"People just think in terms of arguments and drug abuse and mental breakdown and therapy. The last thing they look at is the songs. We play beautiful music together every day. If that's the way we apologize to each other, then that's the way we do it."

# Surfin' the Net
# with Courtney Love
## (w/all original typos)

████████████████████████████████████████

The advent of the information superhighway as a forum
for public discussion has already had a pronounced effect on the way American music fans relate to their
favorite music and musicians. This is particularly
true within the word-of-mouth—driven alt-rock community, for which the gossip potential of the on-line
world would seem to be a made-to-order vehicle.

Leave it to Courtney Love to demonstrate the Internet's potential for multimedia outrage. The leader of
Hole and widow of Kurt Cobain swiftly became the first
alt-rocker to extend her stardom into cyberspace
when, within weeks of her husband's April 5, 1994, suicide, she posted the first in a lengthy series of bitterly accusatory messages on the America Online
information service. Despite the best spin-control efforts of her label, Geffen, and management, Gold Mountain, the singer's stream-of-consciousness rants—rife
with misspellings, bizarre syntactical gyrations and
sheer undiluted bile—solidified Love's image as an
acid-tongued loose cannon.

"I'm on fire, you fuckers, and all of you that ever denigrate or blaspheme
Kurt, have ever violated him, be afraid, be very fucking afraid," she wrote in
an early posting, adding, "a note to all you biographers out there; YOU ARE
ALL WRITING ME THE SAME LETTER AND AT THIS POINT YOU
ARE ALL MALE i wish i could show you all the form letters you are sending, the vaguelt threatening tone, the 'This book WILL be written' platitude
and im the guy to do it blanket statement, as if you think somewhere between

striking the right chord and provoking me into the wrong you can gleefully rush into the alleged publishers office with 'IVE GOT HER' written all over tr face, gee as a buch of writers with no actual publishing deals yet you should get some tips from biodad, there is nothing you can do to me to ellicit a response . . . im not as stupid as the dozen of you think, ive been through this, if i smack you upside yr head, well them im giving you all the fiery tabloid fodder you need to set up yr marketing campaigns, and if i open my home and heart to you, ill get screwed, no duh, yes boys this book WILL GET WRITTEN COURTNEY And so will 300yhty ones and i chris and dave dont care, we've gone through this so much we dont care I DONT CaaaaaaaaaaaaaaaaaaaaaaaaaaaaaaaaaaaaaaaaaaaaRRRRRRRRRREEEEEEE OK? theres nothing left of me."

The aforementioned "BioDad" refers to Courtney's estranged father, writer, and onetime Grateful Dead crony Hank Harrison, who himself had been posting messages on AOL under that name, and was reportedly attempting to contact Love while trying to find a publisher for a proposed Cobain biography. Other targets for Courtney's wrath included such alt-rock figures as riot-grrrl icons Bikini Kill and Lois Maffeo (the latter once led a band called Courtney Love), the proprietors of the indie labels K and Kill Rock Stars, and journalist Lynn Hirschberg (who wrote the now-infamous *Vanity Fair* piece on Love that launched an avalanche of controversy over her and Cobain's heroin use).

She also aimed her wrath at her Gold Mountain management stablemates the Beastie Boys, whom she derides as "lotsa testoterone running rampant . . . a band w/no choruses! a band i especially loathe because my husbands success was used in very unethical ways to get that band on track, Kurt was utterly traded for that band by certain people involved in his life . . . and the biggest reason he didnt want to do Lollapalooza was that band . . . he knew FULL WELL what went on with his ass getting traded re; Beastie Boys. How would you like it if you knew that you were purchasing real estate, swimming pools, merchandise franchises etc. for people who did not believe in you and who you couldn't stand . . . whose careers you made possible is enough to make anyone sick!!!!"

One of the more vicious postings—which Courtney later denied writing— addresses the (false) rumor that Nirvana drummer Dave Grohl was about to join much-despised (by Cobain) Seattle rivals Pearl Jam: "uhhh . . . grohl has JOINED PEARL JAM. this will undouebtly be pubished but i dont fucking care, fyi, Kurt was not on speaking terms w/Dave Iscariot anyway 4 over a year, fuck him yeah fuck you dave, ill be yr fuckin Yoko nightmare you fucking traitor . . . Thanks for not even calling after Rome, thanks for being a fuck you have now made lifes rich shit list; the company of albini, mike D (Silva), Hershberg and the lovely Tina Brown get those Jeremy royalties dave, fuck you, why didn't you just join the fucking cult . . . God you are LOW and KC would juest shrug, im sure he wouldnt be surprised anyeway . . . i like doing this on the void, better thanever speaking to you again . . . im going w/Stipe to the aewards, lets maake those rumors finally cum true, uck you dave, shoot some hoop w/jeffy ok?fucker."

Later, Courtney posted, "ummm.i did not post the Dave Grohl piece on Internet, lately postings aooearing asmine have been coming out . . . I really love Dave and I don't even know that this is true . . . albeit id be peeved-PJ-i mean, its his life and he has a right to go on with it . . ."

She later added, "2 people i respect—one whom i really love and value have accused me of being a liar—you know that feeling—when you didn't do something. Well i didn't post to you about Dave Grohl Joiing Pearl Jam . . . to be honest i would not really care—its his life . . . I loved Dave. I love Krist. Now they are madat me they think I did this thing—and they think im lying, im not . . . by the way Dave was very supportive after Rome . . ."

A response from Pearl Jam frontman Eddie Vedder—confirmed by the band's management as genuine—read, "Hey, C Love Doll, Relax, okay . . . Just stop for a second. Stop . . . nobody has talked to Grohl . . . Calm down. What are you so upset about anything having to do with us for? Other than me as a person, which is how I talked to you before. A person that cares for you and has told you so. Look Courtney, I am just trying to keep my chin up and my focus on the positive . . .

"I just can't have all this negative shit in my life. Why should there be a place for it? Get rid of it. I don't wish it upon anyone and I don't want it from anyone . . . Quit dealing out the shit, OK? . . . ok. Have fun at the awards. Say hello to Michael. I'm going camping. Love, Eddie."

Elsewhere in her postings, Courtney blames a Los Angeles hotel where she was staying for contributing to Kurt's suicide. "he didn't have a habit per se when he died . . . i want them busted because i lived with him, accesability is 9 tenths of the law for someone without a habit and trying to stay clean. he was so spiritual, so honest, he prayed nearly every night, he taught our daughter the words 'god' and 'buddah' he addressed his note to "Boddah", a combo of a real belief and an imagined friend, on april 2 at 8;54 am the phone bill states he called the Beverly Penninsula Hotel, that vile place we recall were i was arrested—then exonerated 50,000 dollars later—for calling the concierge for Benadryl—i had a blok on my phone "unless my husband calls" i cannot express the importance i placed on that last statement—i checked every shift—every few hours—so at 8;54 he called from our phone—for over 6 minutes he tried to get through my block—if you knew him trust me it is hard to imagine Kurt arguing w/anyone for six minutes, but he did, and he failed, all i can think is that he thought my block was for him—that i blocked HIM . . . i imagine him sitting on our bed, just thinking, shes not even taking my calls, ok, thats it. Im gonna do it, and he did. i hate that Hotel, its nothing but fleiss ewhores entwined w/Spelling llookalikes—they just used my photo in an LA Times piece to emphasize they're "glamorous" image—its sick_ok theres a thousand reasons—but i know him and thats the big one. 854am . . . 854am . . . 854am . . . as for the other i couldnt have sex if i wanted too, unless your in the mood to be called Kurt the whole time, 854am . . . those pigs . . ."

Elsewhere, Love pointed an accusing finger at the female drug dealer who allegedly supplied Kurt and Hole bassist Kristen Pfaff (who died of a heroin overdose two months after Cobain): "IVE GOT A DEAD HUSBAND IVE GOT A DEAD BASS PLAYER THE SAME EVIL COW SOLD THEM DRUGS . . ." In another posting, she wrote, ". . . she only sells speedballs and only to people in bands—she preys on the bi-polar depressives AND the highly motivated, talented, pretty, and genius alike. i would love the cops to pop her."

Courtney also urged fans to "Pray for (Kurt) and kristen. . . . they hear it i know. . . . turn off yr little macs and PRAY or better chant NAM MYOHO RENGE KYO as kurt & kristen both did this practise of buddhism . . , erratically . . . but w/some faith . . . please pray, i dont know to who but it will help them, i know it."

She also complained that the tragedy was overshadowing the then-current Hole album *Live Through This,* claiming that MTV was neglecting her band in favor of old Nirvana videos. "at kurts passing they pulled our video—put teen spirit on heavy—and out of good taste—wich i agreed w/ pulled us, months later theygave us an inch again—'active' rotation—thats called a crumb but oh well—w/Kristen, they again out of good taste pulled us immediatly—fine."

One of the messages' recurrent themes is Love luxuriating in the role of martyr. For example, "oh, i know, im supposed to DIE. im sorry it slipped my mind while i was FEEDING MY CHILD! that in yr cartoon world where i am not ACTAULLY A HUMAN BEING the nice ending to Hamlet is when Ophelia drowned, well thanks to [name of aforementioned alleged drug dealer] youve got both yr victims now and next time, ill remind myself, hmmmm, i dont do dope so thats out although obviously some of you know how to get it, i gave the fire arms to Mothers against violence—maybe i should ask for them back? i cant tie a noose . . . there are valiums in the house, mostly so my mother in law can survive the loss of her only son, breast cancer, and a divorce after her husband tried to make off w/the money her son left her, i think it'd be plain selfish to down her supply—I KNOW! ONE OF YOU CAN KILL ME!" That missive was signed "Blood, guts, vomit and shit your friend Courtney".

The messages contain several references to Michael Stipe, with whom Kurt had been communicating prior to his death and who was spotted escorting Love to the 1994 MTV Video Music Awards. One Stipe-related message refers to REM's then-in-the-works album *Monster*. "we laughed at how no one accused him of the scratches, i mean the 'scratches' on my back . . . cos hes such a big homo . . . ha . . . not, both ways if you must know . . . i love him.the orig. lp title was; 'Exploding Head', Thurston sings on a song called 'Crush With Eyeliner' i was there . . . sample lyric . . . 'Shes three miles of bad road' thank you, uncle mike'she's a sad tomato' and a song re; Kurt that had us bboth bawling like babies . . . i was screaming 'the snare dammit' and got to fake mix one w/Litt Kurt stylee—marshalls ways up and fucking snare snare snare—au naturale—berry walked in on my . . . uh 'mix' and sed wheres the damn ORGAN—oh well i tried—it IS really rock and raw and my fave for a long long time—kinda punk even . . . he is truly well adjusted, parents/family all great . . . i wish hed love me . . . but boy does he ever have a bbullshit detector . . . he sees right through my bullshit—i cant pull ANY-THING over on him."

At the end of an unrelated posting, Courtney addressed fellow AOL subscriber Stipe directly: "PS STIPE—i just got back tonite are you at the seasons du 4?pls call me in the next few days—i must tell you my funfunfun ADVENTURE—my mother in law and kurts sister (8) brianne are up and shes a dyin to meet you . . . Luvvv cccc"

Love also defends Smashing Pumpkins leader Billy Corgan, with whom she'd previously been romantically linked, and with whose band she made her first public performances following Kurt's death: "William Patrcik and me, id die b4 id ask him a professional favor—but that man is HONOR-ABLE—YES i love him i also love Stipe . . . ase foer affaires if you ewant to bee called Kurt the whole time and are Brad Pitt and weear Ks pjs—well maybe—that gut and Kurt love/hated one another . . . left handeed Pisces with virgo risings . . . same year same hour . . . i don't think it was jealousy on kurts part not until rome . . . when he came out of it he asked for me not to call Billy—wich was rare occasion anyway . . . Do you know that after V<F, Billy (just like Kurt) ignored it and was intensly loyal—on top of wich if he hadnt come to Tucson after K Bjelland left, i would certainly have died . . . for nearly 2 months i did dope in the bathroom—say what you will—but God/budddah put poppies here for intense pain—Billy and Janet (one of his best friends who signed him to Caroline/Virgin on thee basis of a demo-essentionaly because she has geeenius eears) conttinueed tolerant support, but Billy essentially said be a pig or be wht i know you can be . . . and hee saved me . . . he and Danny Goldberg saved me—hee forced me to do music 2hours a day—and i hope i can get him out of his agnostic 90s rut and heelp him to learn to offer true prayer—in all honesty—he loved Kurt . . . people like to portray him as an asshole hes not, hes sterling, if noone out there understands

the idea of a friend of thee opposite sex then your dorks . . . his wife—who i understand is extremely vulnerable and sweet—does not deserve the humiliation of these rumors and postings . . . you deserve to know the facts and to treat me, Billy and his wife with some sort of respect and grace sincerely Courtney L Cobain."

By way of explaining her postings, she wrote, "The reason I post so intimately in here is because I won't give direct interviews and this seems to be a small, anon, cross-section of issues and opinions affecting my life. contrary to EW's claim that I'm "losing it" . . . I am really quite all here. OK?"

After a while, though, she seemed to lose interest in her high-tech hobby, urging fans to "start a Juliana (Hatfield) folder-i know her life is ten times more exciting than mine . . ."

Love finally commented more definitively on her postings, in a November 1994 interview with *Rolling Stone* editor David Fricke. "It was the only person I talked to for months," she said of her computer. "I just got caught up in it. It was the void that you talk to. And since I didn't speak to anybody else, I had to get in trouble some way. I thought it was normal. I know that Michael Stipe posts, and Perry Farrell posts. I know that Trent (Reznor) and his drummer were kicked off Prodigy because no one believed them."

In April 1995, AOL officially banished the Hole forum because of violations of its customer regulations. But as of this writing six months later, Love continues her AOL postings, under an ever-changing assortment of account names, seemingly one step ahead of the on-line authorities. In the meantime, commenting on the criticism directed at her grammar and typing skills, Love stated, "The smack-addled vs. Joycean argument about my typing skills is hysterical. I didn't study to be a clerk. My keyboard is sticky. There's a cigarette burn on it. There's some baby applesauce on it. It's literally a sticky, fucked-up keyboard. My y doesn't work."

Well, uh, that explains everything, I guess . . .

# The

## PART 15

# Critical
# List

# The Lester Bangs Discography: The Records in His Life

## Compiled by Robot A. Hull (under duress)

No one knows for sure what record albums Lester Bangs truly believed to be essential, perhaps not even his ghost, who stalks used record stores and cutout bins dreaming of a more innocent age. But there's no doubt that his collection was a mess, judging from the photograph on the back of his published anthology, *Psychotic Reactions and Carburetor Dung*, his albums strewn about and piled up against cheap metal shelving. What we have here, then, is a wild guess, compiled from Bangs's own reports, reviews and remarks, and from those few artifacts that were kept and treasured by his closest friends. For almost a decade, I worked with Bangs as my editor, and I was always compelled by the strength of his opinions, no matter how seemingly outlandish. Often his tastes were downright perverse. As a gift to his growing legions of fans, here's a list of what Bangs felt were mighty fine recordings. You should, however, purchase these at your own risk.

*Alphabet Rock* (TeeVee)

The Animals: *Animal Tracks* (MGM)

Ross Bagdasarian: *The Crazy, Mixed-Up World of* (Liberty)

The Beach Boys: *All Summer Long* (Capitol)

The Beatles: *VI* (Capitol)

*Chuck Berry Is on Top* (Chess)

Big Youth: *Natts Cultural Dread* (Trojan)

Blue Cheer: *Oh! Pleasant Hope* (Philips)

Brave Combo: *Music for Squares* (Four Dots)

James Brown: *Live and Lowdown at the Apollo* (Solid Smoke)

Lenny Bruce: *American* (Fantasy)

Lord Buckley: *Bad Rapping of the Marquis De Sade* (World Pacific)

Lord Buckley: *Blowing His Mind (and Yours Too)* (World Pacific)

Lord Buckley: *A Most Immaculately Hip Aristocrat* (Bizarre)

Burning Spear: *Harder Than the Best* (Mango)

The Byrds: *The Notorious Byrd Brothers* (Columbia)

Captain Beefheart and the Magic Band: *Trout Mask Replica* (Bizarre/Reprise)

Joe "King" Carrasco and El Molino: *Tex-Mex Rock-Roll* (Lisa)

Jimmy Castor: *Hey Leroy* (Smash)

Ray Charles: *The Genius Sings the Blues* (Atlantic)

*The Clash* (CBS import)

George Coleman: *Bongo Joe* (Arhoolie)

*The Collected Broadcasts of Idi Amin* (Transatlantic)

The Count Five: *Psychotic Reaction* (Double Shot)

*Rockin' with Jimmy Crain* (White Label)

*The Best of Creedence Clearwater Revival* (K-Tel)

*Darby and Tarlton* (Old Timey)

Miles Davis: *On the Corner* (Columbia)

Miles Davis: *Get Up with It* (Columbia)

The Dictators: *Go Girl Crazy* (Epic)

Bo Diddley: *The Originator* (Checker)

*Doo Wop* (Specialty)

*Dust* (Kama Sutra)

Bob Dylan: *Pat Garrett and Billy the Kid* (Columbia)

Joe Ely: *Honky Tonk Masquerade* (MCA)

Brian Eno: *Taking Tiger Mountain (by Strategy)* (Island)

The Everly Brothers: *Gone Gone Gone* (Warner Bros.)

The Faces: *Ooh La La* (Warner Bros.)

Marianne Faithfull: *Broken English* (Island)

*Fifteen Original Big Hits, Volume One* (Stax)

The Five Americans: *I See the Light* (Hanna-Barbera)

Frank Fontaine: *Songs I Sing on the Jackie Gleason Show* (ABC-Paramount)

The Fugs: *Fugs 4: Rounder Score* (ESP)

Marvin Gaye: *What's Going On* (Tamla)

The Godz: *Contact High with the Godz* (ESP)

The Godz: *Godz 2* (ESP)

*Godzilla, King of the Monsters* (Wonderland)

*The Gospel Sound. Volumes 1 and 2* (Columbia)

Andy Griffith: *This Here Andy Griffith* (Capitol)

Jody Harris/Robert Quine: *Escape* (Infidelity)

Richard Hell and the Voidoids: *Blank Generation* (Sire)

*Bernard Hermann Conducts Psycho and Other Film Scores* (London)

The Hombres: *Let It Out* (Verve/Forecast)

John Lee Hooker: *The Blues* (United)

Iggy and the Stooges: *Raw Power* (Columbia)

*Incense and Oldies* (Kama Sutra)

The Incredible String Band: *The 5000 Spirits or the Layers of the Onion* (Elektra)

*Instrumental Golden Goodies, Volume Thirteen* (Roulette)

Blind Willie Johnson: *Praise God I'm Satisfied* (Yazoo)

The Kinks: *Kinks Kontroversy* (Reprise)

Kiss: *Alive* (Casablanca)

Kraftwerk: *Ralf and Florian* (Vertigo import)

John Lennon and Yoko Ono: *Unfinished Music No. 2 Life with the Lions* (Zapple)

*The Best of Gary Lewis and the Playboys* (United Artists)

Jerry Lee Lewis: *The Greatest Live Show on Earth* (Smash)

*Mad "Twists" Rock 'n' Roll* (Big Top)

*Make Way for Dionne Warwick* (Scepter)

Henry Mancini: *Hatari!* (RCA)

The Mar-Keys: *The Great Memphis Sound* (Stax)

Curtis Mayfield: *Superfly* (Curtom)

MC5: *Back in the USA* (Atlantic)

*The Mekons Story* (CNT)

The Memphis Goons: *Bold Beatniks* (unreleased garbage)

*Michigan Rocks* (Seeds and Stems)

*Moby Grape* (Columbia)

Van Morrison: *Astral Weeks* (Warner Bros.)

Van Morrison: *Common One* (Warner Bros.)

Van Morrison: *Into the Music* (Warner Bros.)

Van Morrison: *Veedon Fleece* (Warner Bros.)

Billy Mure's Supersonic Guitars: *Supersonics in Flight* (RCA)

*Music of Bulgaria* (Nonesuch)

Nico: *The Marble Index* (Elektra)

*No New York* (Antilles)

*Pee Wee Crayton* (Crown)

Public Image Ltd.: *Metal Box* (Virgin import)

The Ramones: *Rocket to Russia* (Sire)

Red Crayola with the Familiar Ugly: *The Parable of Arable Land* (International Artists)

Jimmy Reed: *The Legend, The Man* (Vee-Jay)

Lou Reed: *Metal Machine Music* (RCA)

Paul Revere and the Raiders: *Midnight Ride* (Columbia)

The Rolling Stones: *England's Newest Hitmakers* (London)

Otis Rush: *Groaning the Blues* (Flyright import)

*The Best of Sam the Sham and the Pharaohs* (MGM)

The Seeds: *Web of Sound* (GNP Crescendo)

The Sex Pistols: *The Great Rock 'n' Roll Swindle* (Virgin)

The Shaggs: *Philosophy of the World* (Third World/Rounder)

*Sick Dick and the Volkswagons* (unreleased tape)

Sly and the Family Stone: *There's a Riot Goin' On* (Epic)

Soloists, Chorus, and Orchestra of the Ensemble of the Bulgarian Republic: *Sounds of Insects* (Scholastic)

*The Sounds of the Junk Yard* (Folkways)

*Southern Folk Heritage* Series (Atlantic)

Alexander "Skip" Spence: *Oar* (Columbia)

Spencer Davis Group: *Gimme Some Lovin'* (United Artists)

Rod Stewart: *Every Picture Tells a Story* (Mercury)

Street and Gangland Rhythms: *Beats and Improvisations by Six Boys in Trouble* (Folkways)

The Supremes: *Floy Joy* (Motown)

Swamp Dogg: *Total Destruction to Your Mind* (Canyon)

*The Swan Silvertones* (Vee-Jay)

Howard Tate: *Get It While You Can* (Verve)

*Them Featuring Van Morrison* (Parrot)

*Meet Sue Thompson* (Hickory)

Peter Tosh: *Equal Rights* (Columbia)

*Union Avenue Breakdown* (Charly import)

*The Velvet Underground and Nico* (Verve)

Velvet Underground: *White Light/White Heat* (Verve)

Junior Wells: *Comin' at You* (Vanguard)

Bukka White: *Parchman Farm* (Columbia)

Wild Man Fischer: *An Evening with Wild Man Fischer* (Bizarre)

*The Lonesome Sound of Hank Williams* (MGM)

Iannis Xenakis: *Electro Acoustic Music* (Nonesuch)

The Yardbirds: *For Your Love* (Epic)

# Fifteen Essential Obscurities

## by Ira Robbins

Founder of the now-legendary *Trouser Press* and former pop-music critic for *New York Newsday*, Ira Robbins is the editor of *The Trouser Press Record Guide*.

**1. The Avengers,** *Avengers* (CD Presents, 1983). Quite unlike the self-consciously arty or outrageous punk bands of Los Angeles, San Francisco spawned a more thoughtful, creatively ambitious crop of shorthairs in the seventies. With a defiant political consciousness, strong musical backbone, and articulate singer Penelope Houston, the Avengers were the city's hardcore best, and this belated compilation of the quartet's work is still a resume worth hearing. Energetic, angry, melodic and focused, songs like "The Amerikan in Me" and "I Believe in Me" are timely manifestos for an alienated generation looking for answers in all the wrong places.

**2. John Cooper Clarke,** *Snap, Crackle (&) Bop* (Epic U.K., 1980). With his rail-thin body, matching rat's nest, and shades straight from *Blonde on Blonde*–era Dylan and an adenoidal Mancunian accent thick enough to pierce with a safety pin, John Cooper Clarke was England's first punk poet, swordsman of the sharp tongue, and fearless baiter of surly audiences. This sardonic proto-rapper brought a fine sense of rhythm to his daffy social criticism, laid on a musical bed provided by such northern lights as producer Martin Hannett and moonlighting Buzzcock Pete Shelley. Having nearly talked his way onto the British charts in 1978 with "(I Married a) Monster from Outer Space," Cooper Clarke reached the peak of his creative ambition on this, his third album, a Dylanesque hallucinogenic haze of bizarre experience and epic recapitulation.

**3. The Dictators,** *The Dictators Go Girl Crazy!* (Epic, 1975). Before new-wavers glorified and trivialized stupidity as a social ideal, the Dictators came out of the Bronx with a wealth of junk culture (and junk food) references, a working knowledge of radical undergrounders from the Stooges and MC5 to the Velvet Underground and the New York Dolls, and a corrosive, wasted-youth sense of humor that left no turn unstoned. Despite lead guitarist Ross the Boss's ferocious skills, this, the first of the Dictators' three studio albums, is amateurish and ridiculous in the best possible sense, a springtime-for-punk-rock spectacle of cracked songs and cracked voices that achieves a profound musical victory by failing to sound anything like a band on a major label was expected to sound.

**4. The Elvis Brothers,** *Adventure Time* (Portrait, 1985). Equally true to the giddy Anglophilia of power pop and the pure Americana of rockabilly, the Illinois trio's second album—produced with hands-off care by Adrian Belew—mills sterling tunes through nothing more intricate than guitar, bass, and drums played with exacting simplicity. While each instrument comes across with individual valor, winning vocals shape the blend into an affecting puree with the aura of significance while definitely skirting hollow main-stream pandering. "Akiko Shinoda," a fan letter to a fan, is a sublime achievement of three-chord beauty.

**5. Fingerprintz,** *Distinguishing Marks* (Virgin, 1980). Through the velocity gap that separated the Bay City Rollers from the Undertones, Scottish pop auteur Jimme O'Neill slid a flawless song suite that makes up the breathtaking first side of his foursome's second album. Hardboiled pulp may have inspired the fancifully anxious lyrics of "Houdini Love," "Criminal Mind," and "Bul-letproof Heart," but the music is an immaculate distillation of every bond be-tween catchy melodies and crisp electric guitar rock. Skinny-tie new wave at its finest, with not a note wasted nor a beat misplaced.

**6. Vic Godard and the Subway Sect,** *Songs for Sale* (London U.K., 1982). Poppish punk eccentrics in 1976 Britain, the Subway Sect would have been contenders had the group released an album in time to prove its potential or catch the commercial (new) wave. With nothing to lose, singer Vic Godard crooned this shockingly dapper tribute to the nightclub sound of an earlier era (and, specifically, Cole Porter), a snappy, unself-conscious dose of fin-ger-popping romance that prefigured the lounge-music revival by a cool decade.

**7. Green,** *Elaine MacKenzie* (Pravda, 1988). Barely beyond amateurish and recorded crudely enough to reveal it, Green's second album has enough great qualities to render the shortcomings in its execution irrelevant. Praying to dual musical deities of sixties Kinks and eighties Prince, Chicago-based singer/songwriter/guitarist Jeff Lescher sings simple, unabashedly nostalgic Anglo-pop tunes in a strong voice, which passion frequently takes to an effectively controlled shriek as hair-raising as any in rock. The flaming emotionalism of the falsettofied "My Love's on Fire" isn't limited to the lyrics; Lescher takes a while before heading for the upper registers in the pretty, wistful "She Was My Girl," but when he finally goes for it, the release splatters raw emotionalism all over the disappointed lyrics. The real thing, with no use for slick studio reduction.

**8. A. More,** *Flying Doesn't Help* (Quango U.K., 1979). Between the inestimable credibility of membership in the prog-garde trio Slapp Happy and the degradation of writing lyrics (and *bad* ones at that) for the post–Roger Waters Pink Floyd, the enigmatic Anthony More (né Moore) produced a couple of spectacular solo albums, spinning the dry European musicality of John Cale and the raucous recriminations of Lou Reed through a Robyn Hitchcock–like pop cycle, an Eno-esque brain scan and a Talking Headsy tempo shifter. Think of it as a telescoped view of the Velvet Underground and its effects. A rococo puzzle as opaque as its non sequitur title, damaged photograph cover, and lack of credits, *Flying Doesn't Help* layers guitar, piano, drums, noise generators, and other instruments in compellingly complex rhythmic waves, presenting arcane thoughts ("Judy Get Down," "Girl Its Yr Time," "Caught Being in Love") in wickedly memorable melodies. Utterly without context or connection to time or place, but perfect unto itself.

**9. The Pink Fairies,** *Kings of Oblivion* (Polydor, 1973). Exactly *what* were these guys on about? The third LP (and first to be released in America) by this bunch of Britain's Deviants/Hawkwind/Motörhead family tree slaps Larry Wallis's surging, inventive guitar power onto brisk, oddly tuneful numbers like "I Wish I Was a Girl," "When's the Fun Begin?" and "City Kids," digging a neat sonic ditch somewhere between Bowie at his glitter-best, tougher prog-rockers like Nektar and the amphetamine overdrive of Lemmy's thundering horde. Beneath the credits lies an epigram by Jean Cocteau. Balancing the expansiveness of pomp-rock with the angry thrust of metal, each of the trio's songs is memorable and dramatic, the work of hippies on speed playing for the finish line. Although it doesn't include the epochal "Do It," this is rare rock from a unique corner of the electric universe.

**10. The Rich Kids,** *Ghosts of Princes in Towers* (EMI U.K., 1978). With ex-Pistol Glen Matlock on bass and vocals and future Ultravox leader Midge Ure on guitar and vocals, the Rich Kids were the Blind Faith of new wave: a supergroup with a distinct sound, enormous promise and no future. Despite a maddening soft-focus mix by producer Mick Ronson, the quartet's lone album managed an intriguing update of the Small Faces' chartable rock ethos;

strange, strong anthems like the title track, "Rich Kids" and "Marching Men" distilled the pop instincts from punk dogma for true late-seventies originality.

**11. Frank Sidebottom,** *Timperley EP* (In Tape U.K., 1987). Timperley, the Northern English hamlet to which Frank Sidebottom pays frequent and tuneful homage, is far more real than the inexplicably lovable character incarnated by ex-punk Chris Sievey: a whiny, pompous homebody who's into soccer and Kylie Minogue, Frank wears a spherical papier-mâché cartoon head and deploys a gratingly nasal voice to sing rinky-dink parodies of rock songs as if he were channeling Rudy Vallee. Frank's full-length releases are rambling radio plays with song breaks; this brief twelve-inch includes a contentious dialogue with junior partner Little Frank but concentrates on such geocentric adaptations as "Next Train to Timperley," "Timperley Sunset," "Born in Timperley," and the fuzzed-up "J'Taime (sic) Wild Thing in Timperley."

**12. Sparks,** *A Woofer in Tweeter's Clothing* (Bearsville, 1972). Before hitting paydirt as colorful characters in glam-rock England, Sparks were a group of inventively uncommercial Californians indulging a bizarre sense of absurdity via a farfetched record deal. With Russell Mael singing twisted lyrics suitable for psychoanalysis in a helium falsetto atop brittle, claustrophobically contained spare guitar rock no less catchy for its weirdness, this sophomore album is a self-deluded exercise in art-rock as bizarre and brilliant as early Roxy Music, made all the more subversive by the confident sense of mission in the face of certain failure.

**13. The Suburbs,** *Credit in Heaven* (Twin/Tone, 1981). One of the first heretical rethinks in new wave was the embrace of that old devil, dance rhythms. The circle from disco to danceable underground rock to the electronic fabrications of the New Romantics ultimately brought it all back home to disco, but the pioneers with the courage to throw the backbeat out with the backwater had to find imaginative uses for their decisive rhythms. Minneapolis's Suburbs mastered the skittish, high-pressure groove and used it as a vehicle for Blaine John Chaney's edgy, Bryan Ferry-meets-David Byrne vocals and the smart, (self-) critical lyrics of tunes like "Pipsqueak Millionaire," "Ghoul of Goodwill," and "Tired of My Plans." For its second album, this well-dressed quintet reared back and fired off this ambitious double, seventeen songs with the nerve-wracking ambience of a late-night coffee jag in an emergency room.

**14. Holly Beth Vincent,** *Holly and the Italians* (Virgin/Epic, 1982). Best known for "Tell That Girl to Shut Up," a small U.K. hit for her previous group Holly and the Italians (and later a sizable one for Transvision Vamp), American singer/guitarist Vincent was going it solo when she cut this mistitled masterpiece. With producer Mike Thorne crafting an atmospheric cavern of laconically intense, hauntingly beautiful rock with prominent violin, Vincent sings her intriguingly open-toed songs of dissipation and devotion with majestic grace, cocky aplomb dripping from lines like "She hangs around, this girl I found, she's just like me" and "Let's not get too serious, I came as just a toy." Bonus historical rabbit punch: Vincent's handsomely rearranged rendition of Stephen Stills's "For What It's Worth."

**15. World Domination Enterprises,** *Let's Play Domination* (Product Inc., 1988). The Beastie Boys and Killing Joke notwithstanding, before Lollapalooza popularized thrash-punk, rock's white noise terrorists simply didn't have the nerve to take on incongruous genres like rap, disco or sixties Britbeat. But on its one proper studio album, this intense mid-eighties London band had the initiative and confidence to dive headlong into Lipps Inc.'s "Funkytown" and L. L. Cool J's "I Can't Live Without My Radio." The trio also hammers home a Yardbird-like original, "Message for You People," with six-inch nails, peels some skronk-guitar paint and generally mixes up a rumbling, scathing, abrasive roar held together by limber songwriting.

# The Lo-Fi Top Ten

by Mark Kemp

As editor of *Option* magazine, Mark Kemp has heard more lo-fi recordings than you can shake a stick at.

**1. Hasil Adkins:** The original DIY artist. Back in the fifties, long before lo-fi became a self-conscious Artistic Statement, this wild man from West Virginia was making raw, disjointed homemade rockabilly for tiny independent labels. (Adkins's "She Said" was later recorded by the Cramps.)

**2. The Velvet Underground:** *This* is the band that made lo-fi a self-conscious Artistic Statement. (In fact, this is the band that made *everything* a self-conscious Artistic Statement.) VU's first two records, the Andy Warhol-produced "banana album" and *White Light/White Heat,* introduced at least two generations of post-punk artistes to fizz, fuzz, and tinnitus-inducing distortion.

**3. Half Japanese:** Half Jap's Jad Fair once told me that he had originally thought the band's homemade debut release of 1977—the loud, nerve-racking, nine-song seven-inch EP, *Calling All Girls*—"sounded very accessible . . . very normal, very rock & roll straightforward." Sure, and Hasil Adkins's singles sound like Elvis.

**4. Billy Childish:** By the mid-eighties, this U.K. artist, poet, musician, and all-around Renaissance man was churning out albums of stripped-down, first-take punkabilly faster than Warhol could say "silk screen." Opting for quantity over accuracy, Childish believed that selling 1,000 copies of fifty crudely produced albums was vastly superior to the corporate-rock conventional wisdom of selling 50,000 copies of one slickly produced bore.

**5. Beat Happening:** If it weren't for the raw, minimalistic, lo-fi righteousness of Olympia, Washington's Beat Happening, there would be no K Records. (B.H.'s Calvin Johnson started the label.) If there had been no K Records, young Beat Happening fan Kurt Cobain might not have had so much conviction. If young Mr. Cobain hadn't had so much conviction, *you* wouldn't be reading this book.

**6. Royal Trux:** By the late eighties, the lo-fi aesthetic had been overrun by geeks who wore Coke-bottle glasses and spent their nonsocial lives in the basement experimenting with tape loops on their four-tracks. The Royal Trux exploded that view. The duo, which grew out of New York deconstructionist art project Pussy Galore, is equal parts indie pure and rock & roll decadent. They blend tape loops and synthesizers with normal R&R staples like heroin and Keith Richards-inspired riffage.

**6. Sebadoh:** When Lou Barlow left Dinosaur Jr in a bitter feud with guitarist J Mascis, he marched into his bedroom and spewed his hurt feelings into a four-track. In private, Barlow could vent all he wished without being bothered by some second-guessing producer. What eventually came out was Sebadoh's "The Freed Pig," a diatribe so personal it makes you wince. Today Barlow's raw, ultra-personal songs—recorded solo, with Sebadoh, and with his acoustic side-project Sentridoh—still make you wince.

**7. Liz Phair:** The lo-fi underground's first bona-fide superstar, Phair is one of the few D.I.Y. geeks with a Y chromosome. Before the albums *Exile in Guyville* and *Whip-Smart* landed Phair on the cover of ROLLING STONE, she distributed her homemade recordings as a cassette series entitled "The Girly Tapes." In late 1994 Phair announced in *Option:* "I like that four-track sound, man. I'm going back, I'm fucking going back!" *Hmmm.*

**8. Guided by Voices:** Critical darlings of the lo-fi underground, this Dayton, Ohio, group had been making lo-fi home recordings for about a decade when the Breeders helped introduce the band to the mainstream music press. Soon thereafter, in 1994, GBV got a four-star rave in ROLLING STONE for the album, *Bee Thousand,* released on the tiny Scat label. Where were the mainstream folks when GBV was putting out homemade gems like *Devil Between My Toes* and *Self-Inflicted Aerial Nostalgia*? Oh yeah, that was when it was still okay to like Guns n' Roses.

**9. Daniel Johnston:** This practitioner of the lo-fi aesthetic has little choice but to work alone. A diagnosed schizophrenic, Johnston began writing songs out of his love for The Beatles, and became an underground cult item when he began distributing his homemade cassettes on the streets of Austin. In 1994, fourteen years after Johnston put out his first tape, *Songs of Pain,* Atlantic signed him and released the critically lauded *Fun*. Now Johnston finds himself in the company of Led Zeppelin and Aretha Franklin.

**10. Beck:** The first to get a genuine lo-fi recording into the Top Ten, Beck— like Liz Phair—has taken the lo-fi theory into the mainstream. His runaway hit, "Loser," was recorded in six hours at a friend's house in Los Angeles. The quintessential eccentric lo-fi artist, Beck uses everything but the kitchen sink in his warbly, highly experimental, yet seductively melodic mix of folk, hip-hop, and grungy avant-rock.

**10. Pavement:** Like Liz Phair and Beck, this band of flannel-flying indie purists has also given lo-fi a hi-profile. Although Pavement's music is not actually recorded on four-track, their early singles and EPs were marked by a Velvety use of fuzz and distortion. By the time of their first two full-length albums—*Slanted and Enchanted* and *Crooked Rain, Crooked Rain*—the group's sound had become slightly more polished, though not much.

# Shonen Knife's Favorite Japanese Bands

## by Naoko Yamano

Naoko Yamano sings and plays guitar with Osaka, Japan's, favorite musical export, Shonen Knife, whose unaffectedly exuberant pop tunes have been endearing themselves to Western ears since the early 1980s.

Actually, we don't have many favorite Japanese bands. The music style of mainstream bands are very different from western pop or rock music. Most artist in Japanese mainstream are solo singers or unit who sing along with computer background sounds. They are artificial and controlled by record companies. Only songs which are suitable for karaoke become big hit in Japan now. We like rock music and rock spirits.

**Vampire!** Three piece band. They are influenced by XTC. They use irregular rhythm for their songs. We often used to have shows with them. Members are our good friends. They recently released an album, *Vampire!*, from Japanese independent record label, Gator Wobble Records.

**Mops.** There was a "Group Sounds" movement in sixties in Japan. Many Japanese young boys bands imitated Beatles, Animals, Beach Boys, and other western sixties bands. They wore the same suits like early Beatles. Some of these bands were very popular to Japanese girls. Most of their songs were close to Japanese style pop song called "Kaya-kyoku," and made the good matching of western pop music and Japanese pop music. The Mops appeared almost the end of Group Sounds movement. Their fashion were hippie style. Sound was western-Japanese mixture rock.

**Blue Hearts.** They released album from Japanese major record company. Their lyrics (Japanese language) are nice. They are very honest lyrics.

**Happy End.** I don't know very much of this band but I like their guitar play. I think that they played seventies.

**Boredoms.** Maybe you know them. They are noise band from Osaka. They are friends and neighbors of Shonen Knife. Their show is very fun.

Also, here are Shonen Knife's ten American bands who we want to play with or we want to meet.

1. Redd Kross

2. Ramones

3. Jonathan Richman

4. Green Day

5. Dinosaur Jr

6. Posies

7. Cheap Trick

8. Blue Cheer

9. Meat Puppets

10. Meices

And I also want to meet Kiss, Joan Jett, Doors (if Jim Morrison is alive), too. P.S. Michie want to meet Ween.

# $teve Wynn's System for Rating Classic Records

As leader of Los Angeles's Dream Syndicate, Steve Wynn was a prime mover in that city's "Paisley Underground" in the early eighties. He has since performed and recorded as a solo artist and with the semi-supergroup Gutterball.

*M*aybe it was my early training as a sportswriter, but I've always felt the temptation to break my musical tastes down into statistical categories. With this obsession in mind, my friend and then-bandmate Kendra Smith and I got into a late-night discussion many years ago and realized that all of our favorite records shared four basic qualities in common. A record with each of these components couldn't *help* but be amazing and eternally wonderful. Here's the checklist, so you can play along at home.

A great record must be:

**1. Funny.** Now, we're not celebrating the disposability of novelty records here: Weird Al Yankovic need not apply. In this case, "funny" refers to music that has a sense of humor about itself. A sly nod, a wink and the refusal to take oneself too seriously qualifies a disc to pass this part of the checklist.

**2. Scary.** We're not talking about the hollow gothic horror of, say, Bauhaus, or even the vastly overrated Jim Morrison (who might better qualify in the "funny" category). No, in this case "scary" means a raw, unsettling glimpse into the more disturbing aspects of the human psyche—the three A.M. glance when the defenses are down and the bars are closed.

**3. Sexy.** Forget the puerile, gratuitous soft-porn delivered by 2 Live Crew or, at his worst, Prince ("funny" again). Instead, this qualification reflects the steamy sultry swagger that seduces and devastates, pulling you into a nether-world groove only to leave you in a helpless puddle at the end. This is the quality that gave rock & roll its name.

**4. The potential of falling apart at any moment.** *This* is the most important factor. The sound of too much rehearsal, production, forethought or (God forbid), cleverness can ruin the whole thing. Each song has to sound as if it's the only time the band has ever or would ever play it in its life. The best songs teeter, wobble and threaten to fall off the tightrope, but never fully plummet from those heights.

Now, let's give it a shot. This system was conceived around 1981, and at the time we applied it to some of the "classics." Sure enough, our favorite records passed all four tests. Some of the records that scored high in all four categories were: the Rolling Stones' *Exile on Main Street,* the New York Dolls' *Too Much Too Soon,* the Stooges' *Fun House,* Bob Dylan's *Blonde on Blonde,* the Clash's *London Calling,* Sly and the Family Stone's *There's a Riot Goin' On,* the Velvet Underground's *White Light/White Heat,* anything by Howlin' Wolf. In the time since this system was first devised, surely the best work of Sonic Youth, the Replacements, Nick Cave, the Pixies, and Pavement would make the grade.

Many worthy records could handily score in three of the above categories but fall fatally short in a fourth, often humor (i.e., Television's *Marquee Moon* or anything by Hüsker Dü). Others are just plain sexless (Neil Young's *Tonight's the Night* and Big Star's *Third/Sister Lovers*). The otherwise unas-sailable Kinks couldn't be scary even if they wore large paper bags with a gi-ant BOO printed across the front. And even at their most earnest and knowing, singer/songwriters like Elvis Costello and Randy Newman were *too* know-ing—no room to fall apart, no moment of accidental vulnerability.

So there you go. It's an old game, so I'll leave you to update the rules your-self. And as for me? The selections from my own personal output that, for me, meet these four standards are the Dream Syndicate's *The Days of Wine and Roses* and both albums by Gutterball. Three albums in a career isn't a bad showing, but then again I didn't make the rules.

# Mark Eitzel's Desert Island Discs

## (in alphabetical order)

As singer/songwriter of American Music Club and as a solo artist, Mark Eitzel has on occasion been known to betray the following influences.

1. The Blue Nile, *Hats*

2. David Bowie, *Heroes*

3. Nick Drake, *Pink Moon*

4. Joy Division, *Closer*

5. Nico, *Desertshore*

6. Iggy Pop, *Lust for Life*

7. The Replacements, *Let It Be*

8. Jonathan Richman and the Modern Lovers, *Back in Your Life*

9. The Sex Pistols, *Never Mind the Bollocks, Here's the Sex Pistols*

10. Neil Young, *Harvest*

# Joan Jett's Favorite New Bands

## (as of 1995)

As a result of her work with the all-female teen combo the Runaways and leader of the Blackhearts, Joan Jett has been acknowledged as an influential figure by a generation of female rockers.

**Fugazi.** The ultimate in integrity. No posing. No posturing. Totally loyal to their own ethic.

**Lungfish.** Dischord band from Baltimore. Toured with us for about a month. Excellent straight-up guitar band with driving rhythm section and heartfelt vocals.

**L7.** Great sense of humor, but very serious about what they do. Great musicians and people. Not Riot Grrrls.

**Bikini Kill.** Love the songs, energy, and the in-your-face attitude. Not to mention the 'zine thing for women/grrrls as a free-for-all forum. Riot Grrrls.

**Babes in Toyland.** Energy, songwriting, and unpredictability. Not Riot Grrrls.

**Stone Fox.** San Francisco band. Played with us for about two weeks, and I thought they were excellent. Driving songs, powerful playing, with attitude. They were excited about everything, and that's refreshing.

**Mazzy Star.** Change of pace for me. Their songs are beautiful, as are Hope Sandoval's vocals. When I hear this music, I can feel good or cry, depending on my mood.

**Liz Phair.** Love her song structures. Interesting chordal progressions that work well. Fantastic songs and an unbelievable voice.

**7 Year Bitch.** I love their energy live; their album *Viva Zapata!* shows how good they've become. Gotta see them live again.

**Bratmobile.** Unpretentious, wonderful people, fun. Riot Grrrls.

**MUDWIMIN.** Pronounced "Mudwomen." Outrageous-sounding, gut-wrenching vocals, explosive music.

**Favorite Compilation Album:** *Stars Kill Rock,* on Kill Rock Stars label, with Tiger Trap, Jack Acid, Tribe 8, Versus, Slant 6, Karp, Mary Lou Lord, Calamity Jane, C.W.A., Bumblescrump, Cheesecake, Pansy Division, and more.

# Nick Lowe Names the Five Recordings He's Proudest to Have Been Involved with, as an Artist, Songwriter, Producer, or Sideman

In his quarter-century or so in the music biz, beloved Englishman Nick Lowe has had a hand in these records and countless others.

**Elvis Costello, "Watching the Detectives"** (from *My Aim Is True,* 1977)
I think this was the last track I produced for Elvis where he was still listening to me. I love the way this sounds; we really got lucky that day.

**John Lee Hooker, "This Is Hip"** (from *Mr. Lucky,* 1991)
I played a sort of skiffle bass on this, with Ry Cooder, Jim Keltner, and Johnnie Johnson. It was a great session, and I wouldn't change a note.

**The Pretenders, "Stop Your Sobbing"** (from *Pretenders,* 1980)
They recorded this before they had Martin Chambers on drums—they had a rather surly Irish guy who didn't really get it—but I really like the way it came out. They asked me to produce their first album and I turned them down, because I thought they were never gonna make it.

**Johnny Cash, "The Beast in Me"** (from *American Recordings,* 1994)
I originally wrote this in 1980 with Johnny in mind; I just had the title and a few lines and filled the rest of it up with a load of nonsense. I sang it to him, and he saw through it straight away. Through the years, every time I'd see him he'd always say "Hey Nick, how's 'The Beast in Me' coming along?" In 1993 I finally realized that the song wasn't about Johnny Cash, it was about *me*—and also about Johnny Cash and lots of other people. And suddenly the rest of it came to me in a rush. Johnny ended up recording a lovely version of it, so I'm glad I stuck with it.

**Nick Lowe, "Shting-Shtang"** (from *Party of One,* 1990)
I'd imagine that people who know and like my stuff probably don't think of
this as a major track, but to me, this is about as good as I get. Everything on
this turned out right.

# The Garage Band Revival Top Ten

by Greg Shaw

Greg Shaw began writing about music in 1965, later becoming editor/publisher of *BOMP* magazine. In the mid-seventies *BOMP* also became a record company, a pioneer in the punk/new-wave movement, and since then Shaw has devoted himself to making what he likes to think are "underground" records in the sixties tradition. He has also compiled reissues for various labels, written several books of arcane lore, and is best known to many for the more than 100 albums of obscure sixties garage music assembled and annotated under the title *Pebbles*. Currently, he is exploring grassroots music-community electronic interaction on the World Wide Web.

**1. The Cramps.** Perhaps too well known to qualify as a true garage band, these long-serving true believers have lost none of their raw rootsiness, transcending mere revivalism by adding a unique personal vision to the prehistoric sounds that originally inspired them. Within the genre, the Cramps are indisputably visionaries.

**2. Spacemen 3.** The same applies here, except that these influential Brits used their garage roots as a jumping-off point to an entirely original style, creating a trippier, more intense approach that holds traditional appeal while remaining consistently challenging.

**3. The Miracle Workers.** Of all the garage-revivalist bands of the eighties, Portland, Oregon's Miracle Workers were the most multi-talented. With three strong singer/writers (each possessing a distinctive style) and solid musicianship, the band's first album offered the raw power of Sonics-style grunge alongside Byrdsily textured tunes, with each song sounding like a hit. Later on the group integrated Stooges influences with similar success.

**4. The Pandoras.** While their musicianship was never more than average and their originality nearly zilch, L.A.'s Pandoras oozed authenticity from every orifice. The late Paula Pierce's vision of a raunchy, aggressive, all-female orgy of sound 'n' sleaze was ahead of its time, as attested by a number of recent examples; she deserves more credit.

**5. The Barracudas.** This venerable London combo forged an idiosyncratic blend of garage fuzz, folk rock, surf, and punk, filtered through singer Jeremy Gluck's distinct brand of cynical sarcasm but never losing its heartfelt spirit of loving homage. After more than a dozen years in business, the Barracudas have inspired garage scenes throughout Europe, exerting an influence far beyond their modest commercial success.

**6. The Chesterfield Kings.** Frontman Greg Prevost was among the first to join the sixties fuzz cult, and his durable outfit has taken its quest for authenticity to devotional extremes that rival bands could only envy. The upstate New York combo looked perfect and played great, bringing the authentic garage experience to a wide audience before anyone else.

**7. The Crawdaddys.** During the band's existence, it only released one low-budget album and a couple of singles, all in 1979, but this San Diego outfit nonetheless exercised an enormous influence throughout the 1980s, with former members going on to launch such bands as the Tell-Tale Hearts, the Hoods, and the Beat Farmers. More importantly, the Crawdaddys were gods to the West Coast mod scene that's served as the core audience for countless cool bands over the years.

**8. DMZ/The Lyres.** When Boston's DMZ came along in '77, it was lumped in with the punk scene, but the band was closer in spirit to classic sixties frat-rock. Out of DMZ's ashes rose singer/organist Jeff "Mono Man" Conolly's equally obsessive Lyres, who continue brilliantly in the same sweat-drenched spirit regardless of innumerable personnel changes.

**9. The Tell-Tale Hearts.** Like the Chesterfield Kings, the San Diego-based Tell-Tale Hearts brought class and style to an already classic style while adding their own colorful quirks, including a fondness for obscure Dutch beat groups. Add a phenomenal vocalist in Ray Brandes (vocals generally being a weak spot in garage bands) and memorable original compositions, and you've got a taste treat for true connoisseurs.

**10. The Cynics.** Invariably compared to the Chesterfield Kings, this ambitious Pittsburgh group rivals them at every step in the authenticity sweepstakes. They're no strangers to hard work, turning out an album every year or so, and guitarist/leader Gregg Kostelich is a hero to the hundreds of bands for whom his Get Hip label (for which the Cynics record) is the sole distribution outlet.

# Jack Endino's Twelve Most Memorable Recording Experiences

Jack Endino, former guitarist for the Seattle band Skin Yard, has produced, played on or engineered more than a hundred albums in eight different countries.

**1. First Nirvana demos, January 1988.** Yeah, right. Eight-track, ten songs recorded and mixed in six hours. The band, though still nameless and unknown, amazed me, and I begged them to let me keep a copy of the tape, which I later passed around to various friends. Half these songs eventually ended up on *Incesticide* in their original form; I still wish they'd have let me do a proper remix on 'em, 'cause they would have sounded at least as good as *Bleach*. 'Twas not to be, alas.

**2. Thrown-Ups, "Eat My Dump" single (Amphetamine Reptile), Valentine's Day 1988.** Seattle's most hilarious band at their most inspired. This was their "romantic" phase, with classics like "Flubbermate" and the coy "The Ladies Love Me." A companion piece to their earlier, equally classic *Felch* EP.

**3. Mudhoney, "Touch Me I'm Sick" single (Sub Pop), early 1988.** Witnessing the birth of a sound, I probably said something like "Are you guys sure you want the guitars to sound THAT distorted?" I remember driving back to my house to get a glass guitar slide for Mark Arm.

**4. Mark Lanegan, *The Winding Sheet* (Sub Pop), December 1989.** One of the all-time classic Seattle albums. A magical time in the studio for everyone involved, and you can hear it on the record.

**5. Blue Cheer, *Highlights and Low Lives* (Nibelung), 1990.** When the crazed German manager of the reformed band—Dickie Peterson, Paul Whaley, and new guitarist Andrew "Duck" McDonald—offered to fly me to Europe to record them, I didn't realize that I would be walking into a *Spinal Tap*-ish alternate reality. I soon found myself marooned with the band—for a month—at a very, *very* rustic studio in rural Wales with no car, very little food, and nothing but sheep for miles in every direction. The studio alone would qualify as a memorable recording experience, but fortunately everything was made to function, and the band could still play—although in an ill-advised heavy-metal sort of style. Of course, Dickie and Paul were founts of history, full of great stories. So was Dave Anderson, an early Hawkwind bassist. Too bad the album we made was DESTROYED in the mastering process without my input, and the best cuts were inexplicably left off. In fact, the whole experience was pretty inexplicable.

**6. The Accused, *Grinning Like an Undertaker* (Nastymix), 1990.** I finally had a chance to do a speed-thrash record. Working with these guys was like mainlining gallons of espresso. I got so amped I couldn't sleep for a week afterwards. Practically everyone I know hates this record. Splatter rock, indeed. . . . Great version of "Boris the Spider."

**7. Rein Sanction, *Mariposa* (Sub Pop), 1992.** Musically, this power trio seemed to be from some alien parallel universe. Noisy, distorted and chaotic on the surface, but with a strange underlying beauty that I found haunting. Over people's heads, this band.

**8. Titas, *Titanomaquia* (Warner Brazil), 1993.** Got to spend two months in Brazil recording the country's Portuguese-language rock band. Never had so much fun in my life, and the people were the coolest. Great food, and how about that nifty 1 percent-a-day inflation rate!

**9. Helios Creed, *The Last Laugh* (Amphetamine Reptile), 1989.** Crazed guitar genius from outer space. We tried a lot of nutty stuff in the studio, and Helios's playing made my jaw drop. A good time was had by all.

**10. Guillotina, *Guillotina* (Warner Mexico), 1994.** Spent a month in Mexico City for this one. Pretty big city but not as bad as L.A. Now I know that our Mexican food in the U.S. is crap. The band was incredible, I got to brush up on my high school Spanish, and on our day off they took me to the pyramids at Teotihuacan, just a few miles outside the city. Standing on top of a pyramid, huffing and puffing with extertion and thin air, I found myself marveling at how punk rock has taken me to the damnedest places. Great band, great album.

**11. Kerbdog, *Kerbdog* (Mercury), 1994.** Back to remote Wales again, but this time to the legendary Rockfield studio, the one place I have always wanted to work because so many cool records have been made there since it opened in the late sixties. Longtime owner Kingsley Ward is another fascinating fount-of-history type, and the band were a delightful bunch of Irish boys who were eager to work, and definitely *not* rock stars (give 'em time). From the backyard of the studio you could walk literally for miles through the woods, and I did, many times.

**12. Skin Yard/Jack Endino, any of five albums, 1986 to 1992.** What could be more memorable than recording your own band, especially if you're the guitarist? I got to try every wacko guitar sound I could think of, and tried stuff in the studio I would never use anyone else as a guinea pig for! I learned much.

# Some Eighties Bands That Would Have a Million Dollars if They Hadn't Broken Up Before the Alt-Rock Revolution

## by Jason Cohen

Jason Cohen has written about music for numerous publications, including ROLLING STONE, *Option,* and *Details.*
He has been researching the history of American indie-
rock labels for years and may even be writing a book
about it by now.

**Big Black.** Longstanding musician/producer/journalist gadfly Steve Albini's
talismanic trio broke up specifically to avoid the possibility of hugeness, the-
orizing that once their gigs began drawing more than a thousand heads, it automatically meant that the majority of their fans were stupid people.

**Breaking Circus.** In a world where Helmet can sell half a million records,
this Minneapolis band's steely noise-pop should have been instant precious
metal.

**Mission of Burma.** This propulsive, oft-covered Boston combo has been
namechecked as a major influence by everyone from R.E.M. to Sonic Youth;
some semi-clever A&R guy was bound to sign them for that alone.

**Naked Raygun.** These hardcore progenitors turned kings of Chicago punk-
pop played to thousands in their hometown, blending brute force with catch-
iness every bit as well as Nirvana or Green Day. But peaking artistically by
1991, the band broke up just in time to watch much younger groups break out.
Raygun guitarist John Haggerty and bassist Pierre Kezdy still play together in
Pegboy.

**Die Kreuzen.** Milwaukee punk-metalheads who, it's rumored, actually had
an offer to re-form and sign with a major some two years after they broke up.

# . . . And Some That Sort of Would Have

**Black Flag/The Necros.** One of the key guys from each of these bands found a new life as an indie-label mogul (Greg Ginn with SST and Corey Rusk with Touch and Go, respectively). Meanwhile, their frontmen have moved on, the Flag's Henry Rollins to the business of being Henry Rollins (surely a fulltime job) and Necros singer Barry Henssler to Big Chief, last spotted pursuing the brass ring as Capitol recording artists.

**Green River.** Granted, the half of this band currently in Pearl Jam *have* more than a million dollars, but the other guys—members of Mudhoney for nearly a decade—don't, at least not as this book went to press.

**Killing Joke.** Their best work has been ridiculously influential (hell, they practically wrote Nirvana's "Come As You Are"). Unfortunately, they still exist, albeit in a mutated—and utterly worthless—form.

**The Misfits.** This influential horror-rock combo is long defunct, but Glenn Danzig is finally getting his with the band that bears his name.

**Scratch Acid/Minor Threat.** As with Danzig, the two current bands whose roots go back to these seminal groups (the Jesus Lizard and Fugazi, respectively) probably could have the major-label cash if they wanted it. But they don't, content to sell hundreds of thousands of records on indie labels (at least they still were at the time of this writing).

# Damien Lovelock's Eleven Favorite Australian Records

Damien Lovelock has been the lead singer and songwriter of the Celibate Rifles since 1982. More recently, he's released several singles and albums via his solo guise, Wigworld, as well as publishing a cookbook and a collection of short stories and working as a sports reporter on Australian TV and radio.

**1. "20 Miles," Ray Brown and the Whispers (1965).** Great piece of early Australian pop. I suppose he was like an Australian Bobby Vee, but funkier. Great teeth, great voice, great songs.

**2. "Velvet Water," Tony Worsley (1965).** If Ray Brown was Bobby Vee, then Tony Worsley was P. J. Proby. Wild man in the true spirit of the times. Played great harmonica.

**3. "Women," the Easybeats (1965).** The real McCoy. Pop stars. Screaming girls. International success. They were irresistible. Pure energy and excitement. I could pick half a dozen favorite songs, but this one will do.

**4. "Sea of Joy," Tully (1970).** Part of a soundtrack to a surfing movie of the same name. One of the original Australian "underground" bands; jazz and classical players doing anything and everything.

**5. "I'm Stranded," the Saints (1976).** Couldn't believe it when I heard it. As near to a perfect distillation of the times as I'm ever likely to hear. Outstanding!

**6. *Radios Appear* (original version), Radio Birdman (1976).** Same as previous entry. An absolute revelation.

**7. "Run by Night," Midnight Oil (1979).** Great blend of power and swing. Just wish I'd seen them do it live.

**8. "My Confession," the End (1980).** Died Pretty before they were. Brisbane band, Brisbane sound. Still one of my favorite singles. The only thing they left us.

**9. "Nick the Stripper," the Birthday Party (1981).** A friend thought this was the most evil song she'd ever heard—but, hey, she liked Hall and Oates.

**10. "Hindu Gods of Love," Lipstick Killers (1981).** Fantastic single. Worth owning for the cover alone. Just buying it made you feel hip. Classic three-chord rock.

**11. *Born Out of Time*, the New Christs (1983).** The king of swing. Also features some of the best playing by some of the best players. A great dissertation on the notion of feel.

# Chris Mars's
# Ten Favorite
# Drummer Jokes

**Q:** What's the last thing a drummer ever says to his band?
**A:** "Hey guys . . . how 'bout we try one of my songs?"

**Q:** What you call a drummer who just broke up with his girlfriend?
**A:** Homeless.

**Q:** How many drummers does it take to screw in a lightbulb?
**A:** Just one, so long as a roadie gets the ladder, sets it up and puts the bulb in the socket for him.

**Q:** How many drummers does it take to screw in a lightbulb?
**A:** None, there's a machine that does that now.

**Q:** Hear the one about the drummer who graduated from high school?
**A:** Me either.

**Q:** What do you call a guy who hangs out with musicians?
**A:** A drummer.

**Q:** What does the average drummer get on an IQ test?
**A:** Drool.

**Q:** How can you tell when a stage riser is level?
**A:** The drool comes out of both sides of the drummer's mouth.

Johnny says to his mom, "I want to be a drummer when I grow up."
Mom says, "But Johnny, you can't do both."

Did you hear the one about the guitarist who locked his keys in the car on the way to a gig? It took him two hours to get the drummer out.

# No
PART 16
# Alternative!

# Don't Call It Alternative!

## by Mark Kemp and Scott Becker

1. Lollapalooza

2. Seattle

3. Bud Dry

4. Kennedy

5. Getting a tattoo

6. Stone Temple Pilots

7. Prodigy, Compuserve, AOL

8. X-Girl

9. Coffeehouses

10. Smoking pot

11. Goatees on boys; nose rings on girls

12. Being gay

13. *Option*

# Ten Things That Make a Band Quintessentially Generation Ecch!

by Jason Cohen and Michael Krugman

If you're truly a masochist and wish to find out even more about Generation Ecch! and how to change your life to join its membership, then run out and buy Jason Cohen and Michael Krugman's authoritative tome entitled (you guessed it!) *Generation Ecch!* (Fireside Books, 1994).

Rock bands define and reflect the mood and mores of their era and their audience. The current alternative-rock "revolution" is intextricably linked with that pesky group of 48 million known as Generation Ecch! As in high school—the defining moment of any generation—you have to fit in. For all the claims of rebellion and idiosyncracy, there are certain qualities that mark a band as quintessentially *Ecch!*

**1. Flannel.** Simply because lots of important *Ecch*-rock pioneers come from cold places like Minnesota (Replacements, Soul Asylum, Hüsker Dü) and Seattle (Nirvana, Pearl Jam, Mudhoney), lots of skinny, white, college-age kids look like they're majoring in Lumberjacking 101. Guess the holes in their jeans are from that pop quiz on tree-climbing. Best worn over a *Family Ties* T-shirt, just like Sebadoh's Lou Barlow.

**2. Piercings.** Sure, musicians in the seventies were famous for their perforated noses, but those guys' holes were *inside*. *Ecch* rock gods like Billie Joe out of Green Day wear little rings in their nostrils, while others, like Perry

Farrell or those really scary guys in Biohazard, adorn their nipples and eyebrows (Jane Child, come back, all is forgiven!). Prince Albert in the can, anyone?

**3. Dreadlocks.** Duritz? What? This is a name for a rock star? Y'know, had his hero Robert Zimmerman gone by his given name, perhaps Dave Van Ronk might have gotten the respect he deserved. But we digress . . . Point is, a nice Jewish boy should never, ever have a hairstyle that requires him not to wash. On the other hand, rock & roll has *always* looked to black culture for a sense of downtrodden alienation (for a historical reference, see the MC5's famous three-foot Jewish afros).

**4. Restless ennui and dysfunctional self-pity.** Major leitmotifs: Rock critics use the word "slacker" whenever they write about you; you confess that you were a victim of sexual abuse as a youth; or, failing that, you were psychologically scarred by your stepbrother's half-sister. Also, kvetching and whining about how difficult it is to be a rock star. Important note: It's one thing to write a song called "I Hate Myself and I Want to Die," but actually sucking the Winchester is overdoing it a tad.

**5. Obscure influences.** In the never-ending race for arcane referencing, *Ecch* artists attempt to convince the world that they spent their teens listening to Skip James, Skip Spence, and Skip Battin, when we all know they were really grooving on Black Sabbath, the Beatles' Red and Blue albums, and the Knack. Does anyone really give a shit what Evan Dando's favorite Kiss solo record was? (He probably liked Paul's.)

**6. Vinyl.** Continuing the *Ecch* obsession with things past, bands now force their corporate masters to crank up the cobwebbed record presses to spew out a couple hundred of those black plastic things with, like, the lines in them that the music comes out of. They even put their bonus tracks on the wax as a sop to the seven or eight record geeks who still insist that music sounds best with just a little static (which it might, but we wouldn't know, since we haven't spun a platter in years). Also, it's really hard to clean your weed on a jewel box.

**7. Heroin.** See 4.

**8. Chick bass player.** PC is nice, and feminism is good, but most *Ecch* rock women hit the glass ceiling with the fourth string. Following in the tradition of Sonic Youth's Kim Gordon, the godmamma of girl bassists everywhere and the most alternative of Baby Boomers, there's Laura out of Superchunk, D'Arcy out of Smashing Pumpkins, and of course Michael out of the Bangles.

**9. Punk rock image, classic rock sound.** Pearl Jam may think that by suing Ticketmaster and not making videos, they are upholding the lofty values of Fugazi. Alas, no punk-rock band ever, ever, *ever* sounded like a cross between Led Zeppelin and Gordon Lightfoot.

**10. Volume! Volume! Volume!**

"Any more slamdancing and this band walks. This isn't some grunge alternative thing. We're playing music up here. Am I Courtney Love? Do I have fake tits? Come on, I'm forty-three years old—and I'm too old for this shit."

—CHRISSIE HYNDE ONSTAGE AT THE HOLLYWOOD PALLADIUM

# And Now . . .
# Welcome to
# Rock Talk . . .

## by Caroline Azar

Caroline Azar sings with Toronto's Fifth Column, North America's favorite lesbian punk-pop band.

his is the rock of these ages. Rock ravages time. The good thing is that it will one day be ridiculous to define it. Everybody will just have to shut up and listen for themselves. One can only wish . . . wish . . . wishing, wishest.

Aren't you glad that so many outsiders looking in keep destroying the Status . . . I'm glad when I'm out of touch with trends by even a week . . . Anthropologists one hundred years from today will be embroiled with headaches and ridiculous work loads.

This happens cause new "ROCKS" have to suit their own mean of existence. In the end it provokes the "SUITS" to rock by a *new* mean of existence . . . hahahahahahahahahahahahahahaha.

When I was a preteen in them thar seventies, my favorite instrument to tamper with was the turntable. The first singles I ever bought were Sammy Davis Jr.'s "The Candy Man" and Helen Reddy's "I Am Woman," which as I recall many years later, I mocked voraciously . . . I'm sorry, Helen, I'm back to my senses . . . TRUTH . . . REALLY SORRY HELEN!

I liked the Men rockers but I was kinda jealous of them. But I didn't want to be one, nosiree. There was no need for anymore of that. The factory line was pretty crowded. No oxygen, just the smell of Hai Karate and amyl nitrate. P.U.!

I liked the boy stars who were femmie, cause they were too spindly to rip your underwear off your person and throw it around the room, larf hysterically and call you a cow. Oh god, I once had a nightmare like that . . . The Place: Maple Leaf Gardens in Toronto . . . The Perpetrator: Frank Zappa.

Like millions of others, I was chemically ensconced by David Cassidy, Mark Lester, and Bowie, 'cause they looked frightened by us Female monsters, even though they kidnapped our Estrogenial style. I liked that, I thought it was funny, ironic.

For a while I thought I was Jim Morrison, 'cause I really dug my Mom and made up stupid songs for her on the spot. I thought that if she got rid of her man . . . we could have us some real fun.

Just like you . . . I practiced tribadism with my Brigitte Bardot pillow.

"A lot of bands we play with are just bad, especially those alternative-rock bands. I see the audience applauding while they're playing, and I wonder if it's just because they're fans of the band and don't care, or out of spite. Because it certainly isn't because they sound good."

—FORMER TONIGHT SHOW BANDLEADER, BRANFORD MARSALIS

# Picks

# and

# Pans

# 7 × 4:
# Seven Year Bitch's
# Top Sevens

Though they are female and from Seattle, 7 Year Bitch
wish it to be known that they are neither grunge nor
riot grrrls.

## Valerie Agnew's Seven Biggest Bitches

1. Wimpy pop/college bands
2. Piss-water beer
3. Guys who fuck with socks on
4. Being accused of being a riot grrrl
5. Women who benefit from feminism but won't give it props
6. Flying
7. Prolife fanatical assholes

## Elizabeth Davis' Seven Stupidest Interview Questions

1. "What do you wear onstage?"
2. "Why did Kurt Cobain commit suicide?"
3. "How does it feel to be a woman in rock?"
4. "Why are so many more girls playing music these days?"

**5.** "Would you rather rock & roll all night or party every day?"

**6.** "Why are you girls so angry?"

**7.** "Are there any questions I didn't ask that you want to address?"

### Roisin Dunne's Seven Favorite Things

**1.** The Clash, *London Calling*

**2.** David Bowie, "Queen Bitch"

**3.** Neil Young's guitar solo on "Down by the River"

**4.** XTC, "Snowman"

**5.** Bob Dylan, "Positively 4th Street"

**6.** John Cale's piano on the Stooges' "I Wanna Be Your Dog"

**7.** Everything the Damned has ever done

### Selene Vigil's Seven Favorite Clubs to Play in the U.S.

**1.** Emo's, Austin

**2.** O.K. Hotel (old style, '89–'92), Seattle

**3.** Lounge Ax, Chicago

**4.** The Rat, Boston

**5.** Emo's, Houston

**6.** The Crocodile, Seattle

**7.** The Fillmore, San Francisco

# The Top Ten Likes and Hates of the Muffs' Kim Shattuck

Kim Shattuck sings and plays guitar in L.A.'s Muffs, whose two albums combine punk spunk and pop chops.

## Likes:

**1.** Attention

**2.** Quisp

**3.** The lead in "Biff Bang Pow" by the Creation

**4.** Ray and Dave Davies

**5.** Feeling no pain

**6.** Mood lipstick

**7.** Jack Webb

**8.** Guys who wear glasses

**9.** Writing songs

**10.** Loud guitar

## Hates:

**1.** German prison

**2.** Pantyhose

**3.** Neck warmer hairdos

**4.** Trendiness

**5.** Liars

**6.** Menstrual cramps

**7.** Most music

**8.** Aging

**9.** Mediocrity

**10.** Perfume

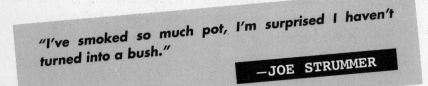

"I've smoked so much pot, I'm surprised I haven't turned into a bush."

—JOE STRUMMER

# $onic $oom's
# Top Six Toys

Sonic Boom's work as founding member of England's
Spacemen 3 has been acknowledged as a crucial influence by countless drone, rave, and hypno-whatever
bands. He continues to ply his trade with his current
outfit, Spectrum.

**1.** Mattel farting Ren doll

**2.** Hawk "Hodad making the scene" model

**3.** Hot Wheels Beatnik Bandit

**4.** Presents Ignatz mouse doll

**5.** Arloy Motley figure

**6.** Vivid Imaginations Mysteron Light Gun

# Collapalooza
# Main Stage Acts,
# 1991–1995

## 1991
Butthole Surfers

Ice-T

Jane's Addiction

Living Colour

Nine Inch Nails

Henry Rollins

Siouxsie and the Banshees

## 1992
Ice Cube

The Jesus and Mary Chain

Lush

Ministry

Pearl Jam

Red Hot Chili Peppers

Soundgarden

## 1993
Alice in Chains

Arrested Development

Babes in Toyland

Dinosaur Jr

Fishbone

Front 242

Primus

Rage Against the Machine

Tool


**1994**

The Beastie Boys

The Boredoms

The Breeders

George Clinton and the P-Funk All Stars

Green Day

L7

Nick Cave and the Bad Seeds

Smashing Pumpkins

A Tribe Called Quest


**1995**

Beck

Cypress Hill

Elastica

Hole

The Jesus Lizard

The Mighty Mighty Bosstones

Sinéad O'Connor

Pavement

Sonic Youth

"Remember those paint-wheel things they used to have at carnivals and you squish out the paint? It spins, stops, and there's your painting. That's what I want to do with entertainment."

**—PERRY FARRELL**

# Yuletide Top Twenty

"All I Want for Christmas," Timbuk 3

"Baby Jesus," Matthew Sweet

"Christmas Day," Squeeze

"Christmas Everyday (Maybe It'll Help)," Giant Sand

"Christmas Is for Mugs" Graham Parker

"Christmas Time," Chris Stamey

"The Christmas Twist," Syd Straw

"Christmas Wish," NRBQ

"Christmas Wrapping," the Waitresses

"Fairytale of New York," the Pogues

"Good King Wenceslas," R.E.M.

"Home for the Holidays," the dB's

"Jesus Christ," Big Star

"Little Drummer Boy," Hoodoo Gurus

"O Little Town of Bethlehem," Young Fresh Fellows

"Rudolph the Red-Nosed Reindeer," Los Lobos

"Space Christmas," Shonen Knife

"Thanks for Christmas," Three Wise Men, a.k.a. XTC

"There Ain't No Sanity Clause," the Damned

"O Tannenbaum Now," Das Furlines

# Top Ten
# Danzig Tribute Songs

1. "Danzig with Myself"
2. "You Make Me Feel Like Danzig"
3. "You Should Be Danzig"
4. "John, I'm Only Danzig"
5. "Danzig in the Dark"
6. "Danzig Fool"
7. "Danzig the Night Away"
8. "Danzig in the Streets"
9. "Danzig Queen"
10. "Danzig on the Ceiling"

# Kramer's Top Ten List of Projected Top Ten List Subjects for the Next Edition of This Book

In addition to having recorded as a solo artist and member of Shockabilly, B.A.L.L., Bongwater, and Captain Howdy, Kramer runs the Shimmy-Disc and KokoPop labels and has produced records for such acts as King Missile, the Butthole Surfers, Luna, Ween, Half Japanese, Daniel Johnston, Unrest, White Zombie, Royal Trux, Nova Mob, and the Fugs.

**10.** Top Ten Excuses Used by Former Alternative Music Critics for Ever Liking Liz Phair

**9.** Top Ten G. G. Allin Sightings

**8.** Top Ten Jewish Record Producers Currently Urging Philip Glass to Compose an Opera Based Upon Salman Rushdie's *Satanic Verses*

**7.** Top Ten Drug Overdoses or Suicides Resulting in Increased Creative Output or Increased Record Sales

**6.** Top Ten Reasons to Hate Kramer Passionately

**5.** Top Ten Kurt Cobain Sightings

**4.** Top Ten Ex-members of Funkadelic or Parliament Currently in Solitary Confinement

**3.** Top Ten Former Soviet States Currently Attempting to Introduce Legislation to Change Their National Anthem to "Achy Breaky Heart"

**2.** Top Ten Attorneys Retained by Ann Magnuson

(tie for #1)
**1a.** Top Ten Excuses Uttered by Major-Label Executives for Ever Having Invested in Alternative Music in the First Place

**1b.** Top Ten New Names for Alternative Music

# Index

# Index